21$19.95

OLOGY

ARCHAEOLOGY

ARCHAEOLOGY

William L. Rathje

University of Arizona

Michael B. Schiffer

University of Arizona

Harcourt Brace Jovanovich, Inc.

*New York / San Diego / Chicago / San Francisco / Atlanta
London / Sydney / Toronto*

ISBN: 0-15-502950-9

Library of Congress Catalog Card Number: 81-86321

Printed in the United States of America

For our parents

PREFACE

In the two-million-year evolution of human societies, each change in behavior and artifacts—from the crude pebble tools of Olduvai Gorge to high-speed computers that can simulate the rise and fall of our own civilization—has left its mark. We aim to tell the reader how archaeologists read the stories of change from those marks—from whatever material evidence they can find.

We have organized the book around the broadest possible definition of archaeology: The study of artifacts in relation to human behavior at any time and place. With this as a starting point we have tried to present the traditional aspects of the subject within a unified, coherent, and highly readable framework while pointing up the relevance of the discipline to contemporary concerns. The basic plan of the book is an orderly presentation of the concepts and principles that make archaeology work today. Each chapter builds upon those it follows. Chapters 1 to 4 introduce the special world view of the archaeologist and the resultant perspective from which come the research questions archaeologists take to the field. Chapters 5 to 8 discuss fieldwork, with Chapters 5 and 6 giving uniquely comprehensive coverage of the way sites are formed. Chapters 7 and 8 describe the techniques of excavation of artifacts and their analysis. Inference and explanation concerning human behavior are the subjects of Chapters 9 and 10. In the former, our approach has been to identify the basic ideas regarding explanation while avoiding the polemics so often generated by the subject. Chapter 11 deals with trends in human societal change derived from the record of human change, and Chapter 12 offers a look at archaeology's role in modern society. Throughout, the basic theme is identification of the causes of variability in artifacts and behaviors from different times and places.

We owe several large debts of gratitude. Phil Ressner, our editor, has contributed enough to this book to be virtually a co-author. We thank Peter Dougherty, Acquisition Editor, for his unflagging support through all the vicissitudes experienced in the making of a book. We thank also all those others at Harcourt Brace Jovanovich whose labors have culminated in the production of this book: Lisa Haugaard, Jean T. Davis, Marilyn Marcus, Marian Griffith, and Nina A. Indig.

Heartfelt thanks also go to Natalie Harding and Doris Sample, who typed several drafts of this manuscript by decoding the cryptic scribblings of the authors, and to all those colleagues, students, friends, and relatives who have helped by providing comments on the manuscript: Robert L. Bettinger, Eileen Brady, Linda S. Cordell, T. Patrick Culbert, James Hewitt, Rochelle Lurie, Randall H. McGuire, Jane Heald Rathje, Jeremy A. Sabloff, Jerome Schaefer, Frances-Fera Schiffer, William Turnbaugh, Bernard Wailes, H. Martin Wobst, and Jennifer Woodcock and William E. Woodcock. And, to our wives and children, for their patience and support, kisses.

William L. Rathje
Michael B. Schiffer

CONTENTS

3 BASIC CONCEPTS OF HUMAN BEHAVIOR 43

4 ARTIFACTS AND BEHAVIOR 63

5

CULTURAL FORMATION PROCESSES 105

6

ENVIRONMENTAL FORMATION PROCESSES 127

7 RECOVERY 155

8 ANALYSIS 205

9 INFERENCE 249

10 EXPLANATION 297

11 THE COURSE OF CULTURE 329

12 ARCHAEOLOGY AND SOCIETY 359

ARCHAEOLOGY

Howard Carter (1873–1939)   Howard Carter discovered Tutankhamen's tomb; the surprising thing is that he was looking for it. But this dramatic find did not come easy. In 1922, after seven years of fruitless searching, Carter returned again to the Valley of the Kings in southern Egypt. What kept him coming back was his belief in the methodical research that had first brought him to this burial ground of Egypt's Middle Kingdom Pharaohs.   □   By the early 1900s, the prevailing opinion was that no Pharaoh's tomb remained unlooted in the Valley of the Kings. Howard Carter wanted to be certain. In 1881 the remains of forty Pharaohs were discovered at the bottom of a 35-foot shaft near the valley. These mummies had been collected from looted tombs and reburied in ancient times by Egyptian priests. Carter compared the list of mummies to the list of Middle Kingdom Pharaohs recorded in hieroglyphic texts. The mummy of one Eighteenth Dynasty king—Tutankhamen—was missing.   □   Next, Carter sifted through the relics modern explorers had taken from the valley. In one collection he found a glass cup bearing the seal of Tutankhamen. Carter identified the cup as part of the standard paraphernalia used in the mummification process. Recalling from hieroglyphic texts that embalming ceremonies took place near tombs, Carter reasoned that somewhere in the Valley of the Kings lay Tutankhamen's unlooted burial chamber. After eliminating areas that had been previously explored, Carter began his systematic search for the tomb.   □   In November of 1922, as a result of his insight and perseverance, Carter had uncovered a flight of steps that led down to a sealed door. On the twenty-fourth he broke the seal and peered in: "At first I could see nothing. . . . But presently, as my eyes grew accustomed to the light, details of the room emerged slowly from the mist, strange animals, statues, and gold—everywhere the glint of gold."   □   Gold indeed! Three gold coffins lying one inside the other, rosewood and gold shrines, furniture inlaid with gold (and silver and semiprecious stones), and over a thousand other artifacts (FIGURE 12-2). The real treasure, however, was not the individual objects, but that they were found intact, together, as they had been left by Egyptian mortuary priests more than 3,000 years before. When Howard Carter crossed the threshold, he entered ancient Egypt.   □   Then there was the curse. Lord Carnarvon, Carter's patron, died less than a year after the tomb was opened. At the hour of his death the lights of Cairo mysteriously failed, and, in England, his dog howled and fell over dead. This commotion seems to have sapped the strength of the curse, even though Lord Carnarvon was already sickly; all the others directly involved in opening the tomb, including Carter, died at ripe old ages.   □   All archaeologists dream of making a spectacular discovery. Howard Carter lived out his dream. He was not especially lucky; he was especially methodical and determined.

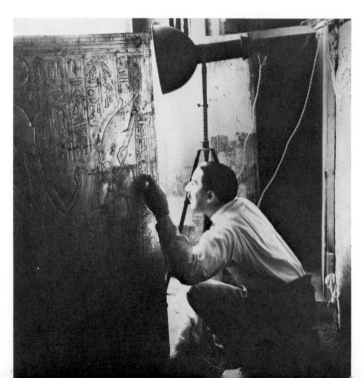

Howard Carter opening the door of the second gilded shrine in the burial chamber of Tutankhamen. He found four shrines, which encased a stone sarcophagus that weighed 2,500 pounds and took 84 days of painstaking work to dismantle. Beneath the lid, which required an ingenious contrivance of ropes and pulleys to raise, were three ritual coffins and, finally, the mummy of the boy-king.

1

INTRODUCTION

Following the discovery of King Tutankhamen's tomb, the media view of the archaeologist came to be cast more or less in Howard Carter's image. It goes something like this: first of all, you are male (highest rank for women is "archaeologist's assistant") and upper-middle class. At Cambridge or Harvard you become the world's foremost authority on some very obscure facts. At thirty you accompany a famed old professor into the field. The old professor, or "Dr. Kirby," as you will call him, has spent his life in dusty libraries in hot pursuit of trivia. However, by a quirk of fate he will have latched onto the "key" to some treasure that is "lost," "hidden," "buried," or worse. (In a more recent version—the film "Raiders of the Lost Ark"—the dashing archaeologist finds a "key" that leads to no less than the ark of the covenant—and a confrontation with divine powers.) All his colleagues call him a crackpot and his schemes harebrained, but not you. The professor wants the treasure for science; he is too far gone to be sincerely greedy. So are you; all you want is his shapely daughter, but this is not to be. If you are not crushed by a crumbling city, boiled in lava, or dispatched by a mummy looking for tanna leaves, your one moment of glory awaits. Having passed middle age and any danger of brilliance, you mysteriously turn into a full archaeologist and find *your* "key." Now you can have your own expedition. Somewhere you have acquired a daughter, a thirty-year-old assistant, and a great white beard. With these well in hand you set off into the wilds. In the end you die happy, crushed by either your

FIGURE **1-1**   The discovery of King Tut's tomb and subsequent mummy movies of the 1930s helped to shape the popular image of archaeologists. Here an archaeologist is about to be mishandled by what should be his data.

hidden city or your mummy, knowing that your theory has been vindicated (FIGURE 1-1).

Real archaeologists lead a different sort of life. While it may have had some reality forty years ago, today the media image is wrong in almost every respect. Forty years ago, there *were* few women archaeologists. The rigors of the field were considered too harsh. Today, a quarter of all archaeologists in the United States are women and the percentage of women training to be archaeologists is considerably higher. Forty years ago, lone archaeologists faced the challenge of excavating and interpreting a site largely unaided. Today, it takes many archaeologists and other scientists working together in multidisciplinary teams to produce results. Forty years ago, archaeology was a rich man's game played to satisfy intellectual curiosity. Today, in addition to satisfying our curiosity about the past, the results of archaeological research are finding applications in the modern world.

In its Greek roots *archaeology* means the study of the ancient world, and it was in the study (in the eighteenth century) of the world of ancient Greece and Rome that archaeology began to emerge as a discipline.

In their search for tangible remains that would give proof to the past, archaeologists found that *artifacts* —any objects affected by human behavior—opened a new doorway to antiquity. Once across the threshold into the classical world, archaeologists used their shovels to discover worlds unknown to the writers of ancient histories. By the nineteenth century, European archaeologists had entered the tombs and shrines of the barbarian ancestors of Greece and Rome. In North America, archaeologists exhumed the temple mounds and ball-courts of Indians who were age-old residents when Columbus arrived. In Africa and Asia archaeologists intruded on the remains of even more ancient peoples. By the early twentieth century, archaeology had taken shape as the study of all dead societies through the artifacts they left behind. In the past few decades, as archaeologists have become more confident in their methods, they have applied their skills to the study of living societies as well.

BASIC DEFINITIONS

Archaeology is a specialized field of study within anthropology, which itself is a behavioral science that studies human societies and the culture, language, and biology of their people. Languages are studied by linguists and human biology by physical anthropologists. Culture—a society's distinctive behaviors, artifacts, and beliefs—is the province of both cultural anthropologists and archaeologists. Cultural anthropologists investigate living societies and focus on belief and behavior. Archaeologists study both modern and ancient societies, emphasizing the relationship between artifacts and human behavior in all times and places.

Other disciplines, such as sociology and chemical engineering, primarily study either social behavior or artifacts. What distinguishes archaeology's perspective is its emphasis on artifacts and human behavior taken together. Artifacts can be gold cups, jade beads, pyramids, brick walls, broken pots, dinner leftovers, diesel locomotives, plowed fields, lawns (and the random paths that crisscross them), polluted streams; in short, anything that is influenced by human activity. Because artifacts are tangible, they can usually be subjected to standardized tests and measures. Unlike people's ideas and attitudes, jade beads and food scraps can be weighed, pyramids measured, broken pots counted, plowed fields photographed, and gold cups analyzed chemically. In the process archaeologists often rely on other sciences for technical assistance. With the help of mineralogists, for example, jade beads (sliced into thin sections and examined microscopically) can be identified as to the place where the jade was mined. Architects and engineers have helped archaeologists determine how massive stones were cut, transported, and assembled into such monuments as the Great Pyramids of Egypt (FIGURE 1-2). Tests developed by civil engineers for measuring the strength of brittle solids can help archaeologists identify differences in the strength and utility of everyday pottery. Soil scientists analyze the chemical composition of soils to help archaeologists project crop yields into the distant past by estimating current soil fertility. Gold cups can be assayed by metallurgists to determine manufacturing techniques. However, although mineralogists, metallurgists, and engineers provide valuable technical assistance, they

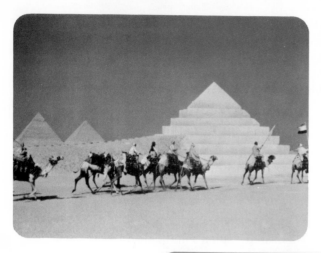

FIGURE **1-2**

Replica of an Egyptian pyramid constructed at one-third scale to investigate ways in which the Great Pyramids may have been built.

are not archaeologists: they do not emphasize the relation between artifacts and human behavior.

Human behavior is everything people do—from chipping stone arrowheads to cooking a meal or smoking a cigar, attending a religious service, going on a picnic, raising children. Though many behavioral scientists, such as sociologists and psychologists, study human behavior, their methods are of limited use to archaeologists because most do not usually study "real world" behavior, but rather people's actions in artificial situations and laboratories or what people *say* about their behavior. Nevertheless, when studying behavior, many archaeologists find themselves borrowing concepts from their colleagues—particularly those in cultural anthropology, cultural geography, and economics—though they borrow only those that can be related to their study of artifacts.

From an archaeologist's perspective, human behavior occurs in an environment of artifacts. The behaviors of chipping stone, preparing food, and smoking all clearly involve material elements; the artifacts of other activities, though less obvious, may be more numerous and complex. Religious services, for example, usually take place in specialized structures, such as churches, synagogues, and mosques, which are adorned with many complex material symbols, such as crucifixes, Stars of David, and minarets. Attendance often requires special dress, such as "Sunday best," prayer shawls, or bare feet. Particular ceremonies may make use of unique paraphernalia, such as incense burners, Torahs, and Korans. As another example, the arrival of a child brings with it more than the patter of little feet; it summons a veritable din of artifacts. Even before the birth, parents in our society begin to buy the incredible variety of baby paraphernalia we deem appropriate for infant care, such as bassinets, cribs, diapers and other articles of clothing, nursing bottles, vaporizers, safety pins, baby medicines, and rectal thermometers.

The archaeologist's focus on human behavior and artifacts is easily explained. We know now of at least 2 million years of human history, during which time societies have undergone countless changes. The majority of the societies that inhabited the earth are now defunct and cannot be directly observed. They are, however, survived by artifacts in the form of ruined structures, garbage dumps, and treasures intentionally buried in graves and caches. Today, artifacts are a part of almost everything people do. In fact, it is difficult to imagine any type of human activity, even the most personal, that does not involve artifacts. To some extent this has always been true. Thus artifacts are a link between our society and all past societies. We need not remain ignorant of our past; 2 million years of artifact debris can be studied to learn about the past behaviors that left this litter.

Although it seems feasible to learn about past societies from their material remains, it is not easy. Pieces of stone or pottery or metal, by themselves, tell us nothing about the past. In fact, many seventeenth- and eighteenth-century naturalists did not recognize that Stone Age tools were of human manufacture, and attributed those oddly shaped pieces of flint to congealed lightning or other curious forces. In order to infer human behavior from artifacts, archaeologists must be able to read behavior from the characteristics, or *attributes,* of artifacts—to reconstruct toolmaking activities from flint chips, hunting and butchering techniques from animal bones, trading patterns from exotic goods, and differences in social standing among individuals from the offerings placed in graves. The methods of inferring behavior from artifacts are extremely complex and time-consuming, requiring familiarity with a wide range of modern societies and how they use artifacts, an understanding of how artifacts get into the ground and how they are affected by decades or millennia of burial, a knowledge of how to find, record, and remove them, and many specialized techniques of analysis. From this base, archaeologists can seek those principles that give our past meaning and can give us a sense of direction in the present as we rush into the future.

THE ARCHAEOLOGICAL APPROACH: EXAMPLES

We begin our examination of archaeology with a familiar artifact of our own society and, though archaeologists work mainly with stone tools and broken pottery, we look first at yellow arches.

McDonald's Restaurants

Because you can always get a Big Mac or a Quarter Pounder at any McDonald's restaurant, most Americans see little difference between one and another. An archaeologist, aware of the similarities, would see many differences as well. Some McDonald's have playgrounds, some do not. Some have large Golden Arches as part of the restaurant building, some have Golden Arches only as part of their signs. Almost all differ in some way in their interior decoration. Because archaeologists are trained to study artifacts, they are particularly aware of the differences among the man-made things that surround us. They notice too that people use different artifacts in different ways, and so look at variability in artifacts to learn about variability in human behavior.

An archaeologist studying McDonald's restaurants in the same way he or she would study the ruins of Pompeii or prehistoric villages in the American Southwest might begin by listing the many ways in which McDonald's restaurants differ: in building materials, such as brick, ceramic tile, and plastics; in type of sign and design of the Golden Arches emblem; in the presence or absence of inside seating; and in location, such as downtown or suburban. The first questions one is likely to ask are: When was each restaurant constructed? How much of the observed variability is explained by the date of construction? A glance at FIGURE 1-3 shows that many of the differences among restaurants are related to the date of construction. In general, McDonald's have changed from simple, compact drive-ins to larger restaurants with interior seating and sometimes elaborate decoration.

Once the restaurants are ordered in time—put in an *archaeological sequence*—questions can be asked about the causes of change. For example, what changes are due to style? *Style* is defined by a society's tastes and standards, which vary—hemlines rise and fall, neckties widen and narrow, and the popularity of roller-skating comes and goes. The best example of stylistic change in McDonald's restaurants is the alteration of the Golden Arches. Once standing proudly more than fifteen feet in the air, they have been slowly reduced to a more modest two-dimensional symbol. This conversion reflects the shift in taste from the garishness of 1950s drive-ins to the more subtle "plastic" look of the 1980s.

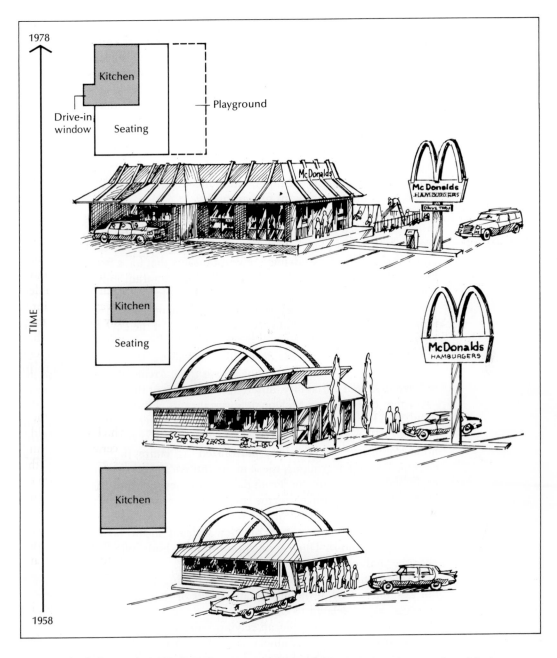

FIGURE **1-3**   An archaeological sequence of McDonald's restaurants: bottom, the original McDonald's drive-in of the late 1950s and early 1960s; middle, a transitional restaurant of the late 1960s and early 1970s; and top, the most recent form, introduced in the late 1970s. Interior seating and the addition of playgrounds testify to the trend toward family orientation. The decrease in the garishness of their signs follows trends in other fashions.

Some stylistic changes also serve a more practical purpose. The reduction of the Golden Arches to a simple symbol allows McDonald's to open restaurants in urban places—on the ground floor of office buildings in downtown Manhattan, for example—where large free-standing signs are impractical. This brings up the next question: What changes are *utilitarian?* That is, what variability in artifacts is due to changes in the way McDonald's serves its customers? In the 1950s a McDonald's was a drive-in that catered to teenagers. These teenagers have grown up and now have children of their own. McDonald's accommodation of this change from drive-in to family restaurant was signaled by the appearance of inside seating areas. Other indicators of this accommodation include the addition of public restrooms and, most recently, of playgrounds.

We could define the specific stages through which McDonald's restaurants have passed by comparing a large number of existing buildings, since it is likely that a few will have survived from each stage. We could also learn about these stages by studying a few restaurants that have been in use for a long time, for, in order to keep functioning, a restaurant must change with styles and with the nature of its clientele. These changes are reflected in the alterations made in existing restaurants. By dismantling such remodeled restaurants, archaeologists could reconstruct stages in the development of the McDonald's chain.

The archaeological procedures discussed above are concerned with explaining *temporal* variability, changes over time. Archaeologists are also interested in *spatial* variability, differences that exist at the same point in time — in this case, among McDonald's restaurants. From a utilitarian viewpoint, the clientele of a restaurant will obviously affect its artifacts, and that clientele will vary depending on the location and surrounding neighborhood. Suburban McDonald's, patronized by entire families, are being equipped with playgrounds; those in downtown areas, used more by workers on meal breaks, are not. From the stylistic viewpoint, exteriors are being kept relatively uniform across the country for easy identification by customers, while interiors vary according to local styles—for example, a McDonald's (one of our favorites) near the New Orleans airport boasts tables done in an airplane motif. Thus, at one point in time, both style and utility influence the characteristics of artifacts.

To explain variability one begins by looking at it in a broad context. For example, many of the utilitarian aspects of change in McDonald's restaurants can be related to other changes in today's economy and society. During the 1970s people began relying more heavily on fast-food service and ate an ever increasing number of meals in fast-food restaurants. This, in turn, was partially related to the downturn in the national economy and, more specifically, to the increasing percentage of women who worked outside the home. The developmental sequence of McDonald's restaurants can be understood as a response to the growth of a demand for fast foods, and as adaptations to the needs and preferences of local customers.

Our McDonald's archaeologist, then, like all others, tried to make sense of the material world people create and their behavior in it: first, by recording changes in artifacts through time and space; second, by using this information to infer human behavior; third, by explaining variability and change in human behavior. Thus, archaeologists approach unknown areas by trying to understand the variability in artifacts in the same way we approached McDonald's restaurants. The following is a more conventional example from the American Southwest.

Pithouse and Pueblo

In the American Southwest at the close of the nineteenth century, explorers had discovered and described a variety of prehistoric Indian structures found at archaeological *sites,* the places where material remains were left by human activities. At first, only pithouses and pueblo structures were distinguished (FIGURE 1-4). Pithouses are exactly that, pits dug as the foundations for roundish structures made of logs and dirt. These structures usually occurred in loose clusters called pithouse villages. Pueblos are rectangular rooms of sandstone blocks roofed with logs. Large pueblos often had two or three stories and were forerunners of the modern apartment building.

In approaching the material evidence, the first question asked was: Were these different structures built at different times? Alfred Kidder and Samuel Guernsey led an expedition to northern Arizona to tackle this question. Their excavations, including sites designated Firestick House and Waterfall Ruin, unearthed the remains of pithouses below pueblo rooms. Clearly these pithouses were built before the pueblos above them. This information, in hand by 1920, provided hard evidence for one of the first archaeological sequences worked out in the Southwest.

Archaeological sequences, constructed from dated sites and artifacts, consist of named segments called *phases* or *periods,* the number and duration of which depend on how fast changes occurred and especially on how finely archaeologists can estimate time; the better their control, the shorter the phases or periods that they can identify.

As techniques for assigning dates to archaeological finds (tree-ring analysis, radiocarbon dating, and others) became more sophisticated, it was possible to fill in the Southwest sequence with a variety of intermediate phases and relate them all to the modern calendar. The archaeological sequence for southeastern Utah and southwestern Colorado provides an example (FIGURE 1-4). Beginning around the time of Christ, small pithouse villages were being built. By A.D. 600, people in some pithouse villages were adding rows of connected rectangular rooms made of *wattle and daub* (mud plastered over a framework of cut branches). Within a hundred years, wattle-and-daub structures were replaced by the masonry architecture of pueblos. Pithouses and pueblo rooms were then built side by side. Shortly thereafter, traditional pithouses disappeared in many villages. At the same time, large pueblos began incorporating a few round masonry rooms. The

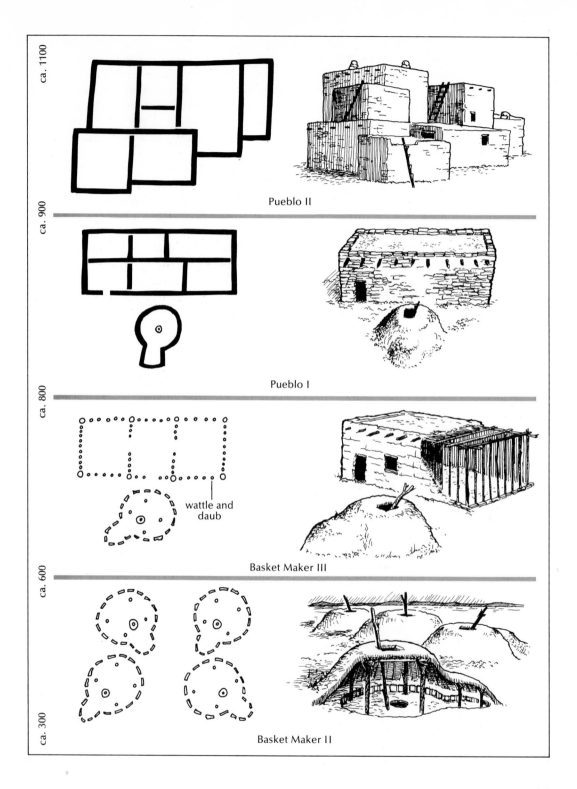

ca. 1100

Pueblo II

ca. 900

Pueblo I

ca. 800

wattle and daub

Basket Maker III

ca. 600

ca. 300

Basket Maker II

shift from pithouse architecture was complete. In fact, many Southwestern Indians still live in pueblo towns today.

Once this sequence of building practices was established, it became possible to ask how the changes related to the development of Southwestern society. The first explanation attributed these differences to changes in style. In fact, for some time it was even thought that a group that preferred pueblos had migrated into this area and simply replaced an earlier group that had chosen to live in pithouses. The discovery in the same villages of wattle-and-daub structures, pueblo rooms, and pithouses—all used at the same time—quickly raised new questions that the migration explanation did not answer. More recent interpretations have shifted toward utilitarian explanations seeking to identify changes in the economy and society that may have been responsible for the changes in architecture.

It is now commonly believed that the shift from pithouse to pueblo architecture is closely related to a fundamental change in the way people made a living—the *economic strategy*—in these communities. Careful study of other remains, such as animal bones, plants, milling stones, and cooking, serving, and storage pots, has shown that pithouse villagers were casual farmers who obtained most of their food from wild plants and animals. On the other hand, remains in pueblo communities indicate a greatly increased reliance on farming and, often, large populations. From this perspective, the early wattle-and-daub structures are seen as storage rooms for increased amounts of corn and other farm products. The rapid shift to masonry walls may reflect their better ability to protect stores of corn and beans against rodents and moisture. However, while this may explain why masonry storehouses were built, it does not explain why, in effect, people began living in them.

The building of masonry homes seems to relate to changes in the length of time villages were occupied. Hunting and the gathering of wild plants require considerable *residential mobility,* or frequent movement from place to place as the hunters and gatherers follow migrating animals and harvest the wild plants, which ripen in various places at different seasons. Increased reliance on farming also implies more *sedentary,* or permanent, residence as farmers must tend their fields for part of the year and their storehouses for the rest. Masonry houses were sturdier, lasted longer, and probably were more difficult to build. Stones had to be quarried and shaped and sometimes

FIGURE **1-4**   (Facing page) An archaeological sequence of prehistoric dwellings in the American Southwest showing the transition from pithouse to pueblo architecture. In the Basketmaker II phase, small villages consist of a few scattered pithouses; in Basketmaker III, surface rooms made of wattle and daub appear, usually accompanied by a single pithouse; in Pueblo I, a small masonry pueblo used for habitation develops, with a pithouse nearby that has probably taken on ceremonial functions as a *kiva.* In Pueblo II, villages have attained the full-scale pueblo form and consist of contiguous masonry rooms. Kivas may be contained within the pueblo.

FIGURE **1-5**   Pueblo Bonito, in Chaco Canyon, New Mexico. One of the largest prehistoric pueblos in the American Southwest, it had a height of 5 stories in places and contained over 800 rooms, including 37 kivas. It was occupied during the tenth through the twelfth centuries A.D.

carried a considerable distance. Such investments of time and effort on housing could be seen as worthwhile, as single farming settlements were occupied for longer periods of time. In some areas, however, pithouses remained in use, suggesting that this explanation is incomplete. After all, a pithouse is a serviceable dwelling.

As in the McDonald's example, changes in the pithouse and pueblo communities were probably often the result of a mixture of style and utility. While typical rectangular pueblo rooms are interpreted in terms of practical uses, the round subterranean rooms of late pueblos are a likely example of stylistic effects. Archaeologists propose that the concept of a pithouse was retained in the round pueblo rooms. Such stylistic conservatism is often found in religious structures, such as churches. It is particularly interesting, then, that artifacts found on the floor of these round masonry rooms indicate ritual activities similar to those that take place in *kivas*, the ceremonial rooms of modern Pueblo Indians.

Pueblo architecture has been in use for about a thousand years in the American Southwest. Among abandoned pueblo villages archaeologists can find many differences that existed at the same time. For example, at about A.D. 1100, there were villages of only four or five pueblo rooms and others of fifty or seventy-five. A few villages resembled small towns, such as Pueblo Bonito, with eight hundred rooms (FIGURE 1-5). Variability in pueblo size seems to have had utilitarian causes. In some places with good land and adequate rainfall, where farming could be readily practiced by just a few families, small pueblo homesteads dotted the landscape. Larger settlements, on the other hand, may have developed in those places where farming could be carried out only by larger groups able to build and maintain irrigation canals.

Pueblos also display variability in techniques of construction. For example, some have carefully shaped sandstone blocks that were fitted together in intricate patterns that differ from pueblo to pueblo (FIGURE 1-6). These differences may be stylistic, based on the preferences of different Pueblo Indian groups. They have not been explained in relation to other trends in the Southwest.

While not complete, the two examples just described show the kinds of questions archaeologists ask about variability in human behavior and artifacts. Archaeologists want to know how and why human societies made the change from stone tools to McDonald's restaurants and what changes have occurred in human behavior and artifacts along the way. They also want to know why there are so many different kinds of societies at any one time. In the process of answering these questions, archaeologists establish sequences and determine the influence of style and utility on artifacts in order to explain temporal change and spatial variability.

The sequences that archaeologists have studied show that many of the changes societies go through are not unique. For example, at the close of the last Ice Age, some 10,000 years ago, hunters and gatherers in at least a dozen places around the world began to practice agriculture. Over the last 5,000 years, hundreds of civilizations have followed similar patterns in their beginnings, expansions, and collapses. These and other similarities, which stretch across vast expanses of time and space, indicate that there are some underlying principles of change. It is a widespread belief that discovering these principles will give order to the diversity of human societies and our current existence; thus, many archaeologists begin their studies with research questions that focus on determining trends—over decades, centuries, and even millennia—in the way societies change and on discovering the basic principles behind these changes.

Archaeologists ask questions about where people choose to live, their diets and the way they obtain food, their use and abuse of the environment,

FIGURE **1-6**   Several styles of pueblo masonry construction. These examples are from Southwestern sites dating from A.D. 900 to 1400.

the products they make, their social and religious activities, and the growth and decline of their villages, cities, and empires. They ask their questions for the entire sweep of human existence—from the first crude pebble tools used by our ancestors foraging for food 2 million years ago, to the specialized hamburger stands that are just a small part of the complex world of industrial societies today. Of course, no archaeologist—not even the one created by the media in Howard Carter's image—studies this whole spectrum of human activities. In the following chapter, we will discuss some of the specific types of studies that individual archaeologists undertake to contribute to anthropology's broadest goal—understanding human societies.

Patty Jo Watson (b. 1932)   Patty Jo Watson has many talents and a wide range of archaeological interests. In 1956, while at the University of Chicago, she and fellow graduate student Maxine Kleindienst published an article called "Action Archaeology," which was the first statement of the goals of ethnoarchaeology—the archaeological study of living societies. The article encouraged archaeologists to spend extended periods observing behavior and artifacts in living communities. In 1979, having followed her own advice, she published *Archaeological Ethnography in Western Iran*.   □   In addition to its focus on pioneering ethnoarchaeology, Watson's work has dealt with many important research problems and methods in archaeology, and, in 1971, she coauthored the innovative text *Explanation in Archaeology*. One longstanding interest—the origins of agriculture in both the Old and New Worlds—has led to innovations in the recovery and analysis of plant remains. While working on large, deep sites, she studied methods of using surface debris to determine a site's contents. These and other technical contributions have been complemented by research aimed at disclosing the prehistory of specific peoples. She has investigated, for example, the Zuñi's hundreds of years of existence before the first written reports of their pueblos. In following her many interests, Watson has excavated in caves and shell mounds in Kentucky, large pueblos in New Mexico, and some of the earliest farming villages and towns in Iraq and Turkey. Her students are always given opportunities for field training wherever she has digs.

Patty Jo Watson recovering plant remains with a flotation machine she helped to perfect.

2

TRADITIONAL AND APPLIED ARCHAEOLOGY

The research archaeologists carry out can be divided into two categories—*traditional* and *applied*. The goal of traditional archaeology is to learn about the past; that of applied archaeology is to learn about contemporary society and where it is heading. We present three examples of traditional archaeology: MacNeish's tracing of the process of corn domestication; Jewell and Dimbleby's Overton Down experiment, aimed at improving interpretation of ancient earthworks; and Yellen's ethnoarchaeology of modern Bushman camps to help interpret remains of prehistoric campsites of hunter-gatherer societies. Applied archaeology is also represented by three examples: O'Connell's study of and advice concerning housing for Australian aborigines; the Garbage Project's food-waste study; and the Village Creek Project's study and recommendations regarding certain archaeological resources. We will also discuss archaeological synthesis —summarizing the findings of archaeology—which, when done well, incorporates the best of traditional and applied research.

TRADITIONAL ARCHAEOLOGY: EXAMPLES

The Beginnings of Maize Agriculture

Modern corn, or *maize,* is an artifact of human behavior; it is a domesticated plant, one whose survival depends upon farmers preserving and planting its seeds. Although modern agronomists are given credit for developing the varieties of corn that feed a large portion of the world, the most striking changes in the development of corn took place in Mexico more than 7,000

19

years ago. Uncovering the early history of the process by which corn was domesticated is one of the success stories of archaeology.

Each such story begins with an archaeologist's research question. Richard S. MacNeish's major research interest was, literally, the roots of civilization. Speculating that agriculture and permanent settlements were the basis for the first civilizations, MacNeish set out to dig up information on when and how plant domestication occurred in the Americas. He chose Mexico, heartland of the Aztec and other civilizations, as his study area, and corn, the staple food crop of New World civilizations, as his focus.

MacNeish began his search in Tamaulipas, Mexico (FIGURE 2-1), for two reasons. First, many grasses that botanists considered similar to early corn grew in the hills of Tamaulipas. Second, the Tamaulipas mountains were dotted with dry caves, likely camping spots, where ancient plant remains would probably be preserved. MacNeish examined 160 caves and carefully excavated 2. From remains of tools and plants, he constructed an archaeological sequence for Tamaulipas that ran from 7000 to 2000 B.C. The sequence documented changes in methods of food procurement—how people gather, grow, or otherwise obtain food. Remarkably, the earliest occupants of the Tamaulipas caves were already experimenting with plant cultivation. Botanists collaborating with MacNeish concluded that bottle gourds (used as containers), chili peppers, and pumpkins found in the caves were different from their wild ancestors and on the way to their fully domesticated forms.

From this start the sequence followed two clear trends: plants showing obvious signs of domestication made up an ever larger proportion of the diet through time, and many new plants were added to the inventory of cultivated foods. Within this latter group, corn was a relative latecomer, appearing around 3000 B.C. and already bearing the marks of human meddling. Despite the great leap in information provided by the Tamaulipas discoveries, the earliest stages of corn domestication had to be sought elsewhere.

MacNeish turned to the south and Chiapas. His excavation at Santa Marta Rock Shelter unearthed corn, but it was fully domesticated and appeared late in the sequence, 1,500 years after the corn found in Tamaulipas. These seeming failures to find early domesticated varieties of corn provided a clue to tracking down the original centers of corn domestication: since both the areas MacNeish had studied received corn after 3000 B.C., it was likely that the source lay somewhere between Tamaulipas and Chiapas.

MacNeish next chose to investigate in the semiarid Tehuacán Valley (FIGURE 2-1), located in the Mexican highlands midway between his two previous study areas. There, he organized a large multidisciplinary team that included botanists, zooarchaeologists, geographers, geologists, a cultural anthropologist, a fecal analyst, and skilled excavators. He selected seven cave sites and noncave or *open sites* for excavation. In one of the excavated caves (Coxcatlán, FIGURE 2-2), under twenty-eight layers of occupa-

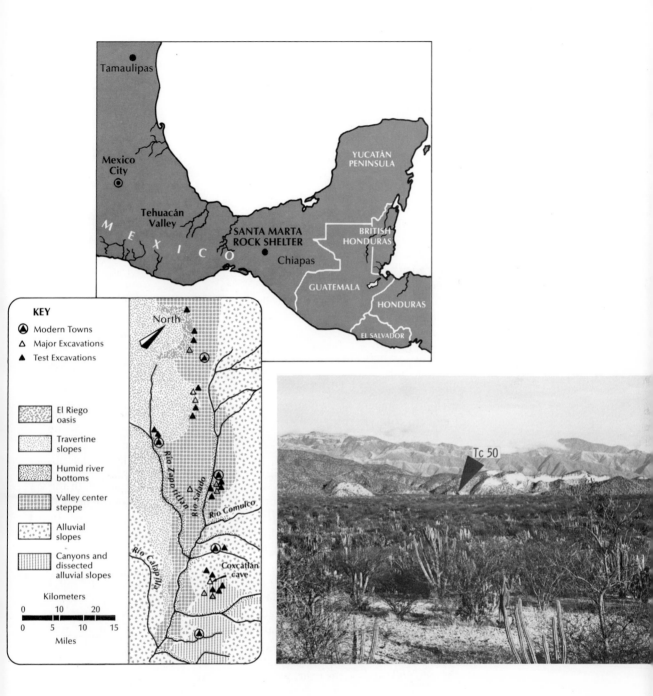

KEY

- ⊕ Modern Towns
- △ Major Excavations
- ▲ Test Excavations

- El Riego oasis
- Travertine slopes
- Humid river bottoms
- Valley center steppe
- Alluvial slopes
- Canyons and dissected alluvial slopes

Kilometers
0 10 20

0 5 10 15
Miles

FIGURE **2-1**   The Tehuacán Valley project. Map, lower left, shows major environmental zones in the Tehuacán Valley as well as important sites. At lower right is view of general environment of the Tehuacán Valley. Inset map at top indicates location of valley.

FIGURE **2-2**

Excavations in progress
at Coxcatlán Cave,
Tehuacán Valley project
(FIGURE 2-1).

tion debris, where they had lain undisturbed for several thousand years, were remnants of small and very primitive cobs of *Zea mays* (early corn, whose exact ancestry is still in question, but which many botanists believe developed from teosinte, a wild grass). These are the earliest direct ancestors of modern corn yet recovered.

The selection of dry cave sites and careful screening of dirt produced 24,186 corncobs from the Tehuacán Valley. From these and tons of other plant and artifact remains, MacNeish built the Tehuacán sequence familiar to nearly every archaeologist. The sequence begins at 10,000 B.C. with the Ajuereado phase (FIGURE 2-3), identified in the bottom levels of the deepest caves. Stone spearpoints, scraping tools, net bags, and large numbers of bones of jack rabbits and other small animals—all that remain of the artifacts of the earliest occupants—suggest that food was procured by hunting animals and gathering wild plants.

By 7000 B.C. and the El Riego phase, the people had shifted toward a more intensive collection of wild plant foods, although deer and small game were still hunted and trapped. Many new tools, including stone grinding tools useful for collecting and preparing plant foods, were added to the artifact inventory. As shown by plant remains, wild fruits, which ripened at different seasons, were collected from the hilly thorn and pine forest areas, and mesquite pods and cactus fruits were harvested on the valley floor. Although located all over the valley, sites were divisible into two types according to size and (on the basis of the evidence provided by plant remains) season of occupation. During the dry season (October to May) small groups of people —MacNeish guesses six to eight—lived in camps in the hill country and collected maguey (century plant) and a number of other desert plants. Dur-

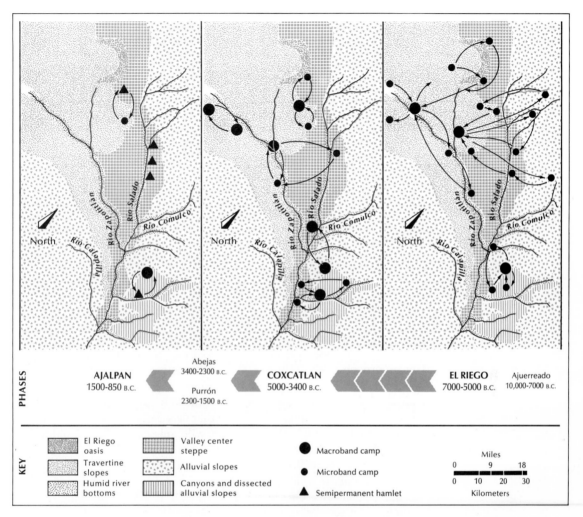

	El Riego oasis		Valley center steppe		Macroband camp		
	Travertine slopes		Alluvial slopes		Microband camp		
	Humid river bottoms		Canyons and dissected alluvial slopes		Semipermanent hamlet		

PHASES

| AJALPAN 1500–850 B.C. | Abejas 3400–2300 B.C. | COXCATLAN 5000–3400 B.C. | EL RIEGO 7000–5000 B.C. | Ajuerreado 10,000–7000 B.C. |
| | Purrón 2300–1500 B.C. | | | |

Miles
0   9   18
0 10 20 30
Kilometers

FIGURE **2-3**   The Tehuacán Valley sequence, showing MacNeish's reconstructions of band size and movement patterns for three periods.

ing the rainy season (June to September), larger groups assembled at caves near streams to collect mesquite and other seeds available in large quantities in the fall. Even at this early time, the increased size of pits shows that avocados were receiving artificial care.

The Coxcatlán phase, at 5000 B.C., ushered in several changes. Many more plants showed signs of intentional cultivation, including maize, chili peppers, gourds, tepary beans, several varieties of squash, jack beans, pinto beans, and white and black zapotes. The finding of zapotes, pearlike fruits, is significant because they are not native to the Tehuacán Valley, and so must have been brought in from wetter regions and carefully watered. The presence of corn, beans, and squash is especially important because they are nutritionally complementary, together filling human carbohydrate, fat, and protein needs. These three crops are still the mainstay of the rural populations in all of Middle America. With the increase in the variety of cultivated plants, larger sites were occupied for longer periods. Nevertheless, population remained small, estimated at fewer than 300 people in the 1,400 square miles of the valley.

The Abejas phase, at 3500 B.C., was characterized by another change. In addition to seasonal settlements in upland areas, small pithouse villages appeared on the valley floor near rivers, where plants like corn could be easily cultivated. Storage pits and stone bowls were added to the artifact inventory in this phase. The supposition that these changes resulted from an increasing reliance on cultivated food is supported by the continuing development of the plants themselves. It is also supported by fecal analyses, which show that 30 percent of the remains identified are parts of domesticated plants. This represents a significant increase of 20 percent over the proportion found in the Coxcatlán phase. During the eight hundred years of the Purrón phase, which followed the Abejas, dependence on agricultural products became all but total, completing the current picture of Middle American village farming.

Once the basic sequences, as described above, have been established, archaeologists can speculate on the causes of the changes that occurred. A look at a corncob from 3000 B.C. shows that it was not much of a meal (FIGURE 2-4). One archaeologist, Kent Flannery, suggests that the shift to a dependence on domestic crops was due to the way labor was allocated to ensure a reliable food supply. He believes that very early attempts at domestication occurred in humid canyons, where wild grasses like foxtail and teosinte grew. Such wild plants were a part of the native diet. Because the amount available for collecting can vary greatly from year to year depending on rainfall, it seems possible that cultivation began in canyons to try to improve harvests. One factor that resulted in more time being spent cultivating was a series of genetic mutations that made plants like teosinte potentially more productive as well as easier to harvest and prepare. (In fact, it is by the presence of these mutations that botanists identify corn or bean plants as domesticated.) Some of these changes would have been disadvantageous for plants in the wild. For example, in a wild stand of corn there were probably always some genetic mutants that had firmly attached kernels and large husks. Such plants could not disperse their seed by themselves and, under normal conditions, would have died out without human intervention. It is just these plants, however, that would have remained available longest for harvesting by humans. In addition, plants with larger ears would have been the ones most likely to be picked and eaten or used for seeds. Thus, over time, plants with those characteristics most suited to human needs would have most often ended as seed and would, thereby, have become more and more prevalent in cultivated fields.

FIGURE **2-4**   The evolution of domesticated corn as disclosed by the Tehuacán Valley project. On the far left is the most primitive variety of domesticated corn, retaining many characteristics of its wild ancestors, such as small pod-size and few kernels. Over the millennia, the modern form of corn (far right) evolved through selective cultivation.

Domestication is, then, a process of genetic change under the influence of human behavior. Eventually, the harvests of domesticated plants became great enough that people reduced their dependence on the wild plants. In fact, as maize yields increased, farmers cleared mesquite groves that lay next to rivers and planted corn in their place. Thus, changes in plants made reliance on them increasingly attractive. This growing reliance on domesticated plants, documented by MacNeish in Tamaulipas and Tehuacán, would seem to be inevitable—but we still do not really understand how the process begins.

Research into domestication is one of the most active areas of interest today. All over the world archaeologists are studying the beginnings of plant and animal domestication and the trend toward increasing dependence on artificially produced foods. These studies all indicate that domestication was not a single invention that spread, but a gradual process linked to other changes in behavior that occurred in dozens of places throughout the world beginning more than 10,000 years ago (Chapter 11). The details of, and the explanations for, these processes are being worked out by multidisciplinary teams modeled after the pioneering investigations of MacNeish and others. Such research projects are designed to learn about the past by recovering and interpreting ancient artifacts.

Experimental Archaeology and Overton Down

In order to reconstruct past behavior from archaeological remains, MacNeish needed more than highly technical analyses of plants and feces. To estimate population size and to infer season of occupation, MacNeish drew upon knowledge about behavior in present-day societies. It is in these living societies that the relation between artifacts and behavior can be readily observed. These observations provide the specific ideas and general principles needed to infer the behavior responsible for archaeological remains. One source of such observations is experimentation.

MacNeish found his caves littered with quids, balls of inedible maguey stems that remained after the edible pulp had been chewed out. Few people in the Tehuacán Valley today eat maguey, which is used as a food source only in the face of starvation. In order to find out how much food was represented (by the quids) in the archaeological record, MacNeish boiled a given amount of maguey stems and set his crew to chewing for a full day. From the spent and dried quids they produced, MacNeish derived a ratio of maguey quid to pulp that allowed him to estimate (from the quids found in the caves) the quantity of pulp chewed in the past.

Other experimental studies, while often more complicated and time-consuming, follow the same basic approach. The Overton Down Earthwork, an ambitious, long-term project designed to study the changes occurring in an artificial mound and in the artifacts buried in it, was undertaken to help archaeologists distinguish material patterns due to behavior from those caused by the natural environment.

In 1960 two British investigators, P. A. Jewell and G. W. Dimbleby, built a mound or bank 5 feet high and 20 feet across and an adjacent ditch 5 feet deep and 8 feet across (FIGURE 2-5). (Such *earthworks,* many built by Roman troops or the Britons who fought them, are common features in the British Isles.) Samples of various artifacts—fragments of pottery, wood, textiles, and leather—were placed at recorded locations in the mound. The research plan called for observations and limited excavations after 2, 4, 8, 16, 32, 64, and 128 years. The goal of the experiment is to record the physical changes in the mound, the ditch, and their contents and to specify the natural forces that produced the changes. The patterns of deterioration and disturbance that are recorded will help archaeologists interpret the remains of ancient earthworks.

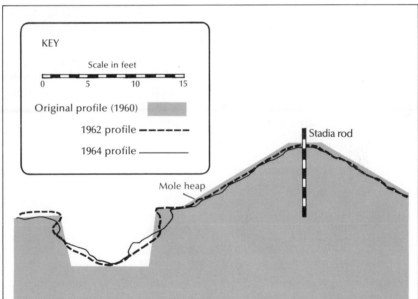

KEY

Scale in feet

0   5   10   15

Original profile (1960)

1962 profile - - - - - -

1964 profile ——————

Stadia rod

Mole heap

FIGURE **2-5**   Overton Down experimental earthwork, Wiltshire, England. Note progressive erosion of soil from the side of the earthwork and its accumulation in the bottom of the adjacent trench.

By 1964, at the end of the second observation period, interesting results had already been produced. To even the casual observer the most obvious change was the rapid erosion and collapse of the sides of the ditch and the resulting accumulation of a sloping deposit on the bottom (FIGURE 2-5). One of the major problems in archaeology is pinpointing the time of construction of earthworks. This early finding from the Overton Down experiment furnishes a useful guide. Because of the rapid rate at which the ditch edges erode and collapse, objects found at the corners of the ditch will be closer in time to the original construction than the materials in the center.

Although the expected erosion of the exterior of the mound (apart from the edges) seemed slow, the inside was a hotbed of biological turmoil. Descriptions of the resulting disturbances alert the archaeologist that the distribution of artifacts at any site cannot be taken at face value. The Overton Down Earthwork experiment has defined two major agents of disturbance —earthworms and moles—and shown how their effects could, if not taken into account, warp archaeological interpretations. Tiny fungal spores, used as ingenious tracers for recording movement of very small objects within the mound, had been displaced considerably both upward and downward by earthworms. This finding suggests that in soils where worm action is prevalent, care is needed in interpreting the distribution of pollen, seeds, and other small items. The burrowing activities of moles created similar disturbances, but on a larger scale.

The Overton Down experiment has already produced other intriguing findings and more will follow. But perhaps the most interesting results await the archaeologists who make the final observations of the experiment at the end of the twenty-first century.

This example shows how archaeologists use experiments, in which they can control many conditions, to reproduce or simulate processes that are important in learning about the past. The success of these experiments often requires the assistance of collaborators from other disciplines, such as botany, geology, and engineering.

The !Kung Bushmen

Archaeologists can often find the behaviors they wish to investigate occurring among living societies. The study of behavior and artifacts in present-day societies, called ethnoarchaeology, is a research specialty attracting more and more archaeologists. MacNeish, for example, depended heavily on studies of modern hunters and gatherers in his reconstruction of the seasonal collection of plants in the Tehuacán Valley.

One example of ethnoarchaeology is furnished by John Yellen's work among the !Kung (pronounced with a loud clicking noise before the *k*) Bushmen of Africa. Yellen's main goal was to show how observations of modern hunter-gatherer societies could be used for interpreting the remains of ancient hunter-gatherer societies. The Dobe !Kung, whom Yellen studied, occupy the northern fringe of the Kalahari Desert in Namibia. In this inhospitable environment, small groups of Dobe subsist by collecting nuts and

FIGURE **2-6**

FIGURE **2-6**

A !Kung Bushman camp in Namibia, Africa. Note the position of huts, artifacts, and people in relation to model shown in FIGURE 2-7.

other plant foods and hunting large and small game. They construct simple brush shelters or huts as temporary living quarters (FIGURE 2-6), and their stay at any one place is rarely more than a few weeks, depending on how much water and food is available nearby. Although Bushman behavior does show some effects of Western civilization, little beyond tin cans and steel knives is directly useful or relevant to their traditional nomadic way of life.

In the late 1960s and early 1970s, Yellen spent more than two and one-half years among the Dobe, recording their artifacts and behavior and collecting information needed for examining a few common assumptions made by archaeologists in interpreting the remains of prehistoric hunter-gatherers.

Archaeologists frequently try to estimate the number of people that inhabited a site. One way they do this is by assuming that the more people, the larger the area covered by the debris they left behind. Thus, two hundred people should create a larger site than one hundred people. In the 1960s, MacNeish used such an assumption as part of his method for calculating Tehuacán Valley populations. Yellen decided to evaluate the basic assumption that as the number of people increases so does the area covered by debris in their campsites. He observed fifteen Bushman camps, both during and after occupation, and found that reality in the Kalahari was more complex.

Yellen first noted that camps were not haphazard scatters of huts and debris. In fact, there were patterns in the distribution of brush huts and the debris of camp activities. Huts, used primarily for shade and sleeping, were

FIGURE **2-7**

John Yellen's ring model for the layout of activity areas in !Kung Bushman camps. Typical specialized activities (outer ring) include butchering and untidy cooking. (After Yellen.)

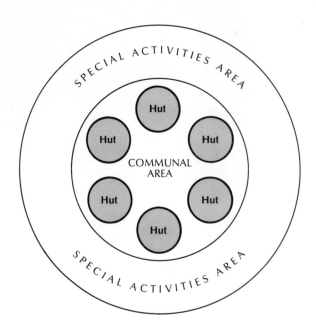

placed in a generally circular arrangement. Associated with each hut was a hearth that served as the focal point of a work area for the family using the hut. In these work areas, families prepared and cooked food, manufactured poison arrows, and cut beads from ostrich shells. In the center of the ring of shelters was a communal area where dancing occurred and where meat from hunts was distributed among families. Activities that were messy, such as butchering and the cooking of animal heads, were located outside the hut circle.

Bushman camps can be conceived as two concentric rings (FIGURE 2-7), the inner ring including the hut circle, the outer the activity area beyond. Yellen's basic conclusion was that the size of the inner ring was directly related to the number of resident families; the size of the outer ring, however, was determined by how long the camp had been occupied. The difference that length of occupation can make in terms of the scatter of debris is shown in FIGURE 2-8, which compares two camps occupied by the same number of families, but for different periods of time. Thus, the size of the hut ring is directly related to camp population; the total area over which camp debris is spread is *not*.

FIGURE **2-8**   (facing page) Debris from two !Kung Bushman camps shows how length of occupation affects the spread of artifacts in the outer ring. Camp 5 was occupied by 2 families (5 adults, 7 children) for 3 days. Camp 2, also occupied by 2 families (4 adults, 7 children), was inhabited for 9 days. The greater duration of occupation of the latter is reflected in the greater spread of artifacts in the outer ring. (After Yellen.)

CAMP 2
9 Days
2 Families
4 Adults
7 Young

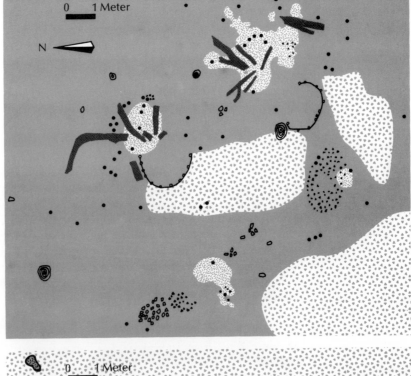

KEY

 Bone

 Mongongo nuts or shells

 Tsin bean pods

 Cracked boab shells

 Tree

 Log

 Hut

Charcoal

Depressed hearth

Bushes

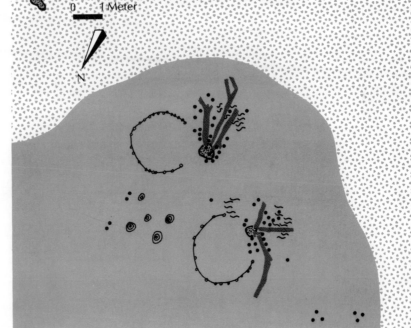

CAMP 5
3 Days
2 Families
5 Adults
7 Young

At first, Yellen's conclusions seem to provide archaeologists with an easy formula for camp population estimates. In actual archaeological situations, and even in recently abandoned !Kung camps, the remains of huts are often no longer visible and it is hard to draw a dividing line between inner and outer rings. Nevertheless, assuming that Yellen's findings can be generalized to other hunter-gatherer societies, the archaeologist interested in estimating population sizes should strive to identify huts or hearths or other indications of family work areas. In like manner, other ethnoarchaeologists study human behavior and artifacts in living societies to help interpret the past.

APPLIED ARCHAEOLOGY: EXAMPLES

Alyawara Housing

It is ironic that, as more archaeologists become interested in studying primitive, living societies, these same societies are rapidly being overrun and transformed by modern nation-states. In fact, most nomadic hunter-gatherer strategies are being replaced by a sedentary "welfare" strategy, where more-or-less permanent camps are made in the vicinity of government services and general stores. However, ethnoarchaeological study of mobile hunter-gatherers may be useful not only in solving archaeological problems of the past, but also in solving those of government planners and the native peoples themselves.

FIGURE 2-9

An Alyawara camp in central Australia shows use of both traditional and modern building materials. Although camps are now relatively permanent and located near government stations and stores, individual dwellings are often moved.

James O'Connell has been studying the traditional economic strategies and social organization of the Alyawara of central Australia for much the same reason that Yellen studied the !Kung. The Alyawara, hunter-gatherers like the !Kung, are undergoing a transition to permanent settlements around government stations (FIGURE 2-9). Government agencies have been concerned that housing supplied by their contractors has often been either badly treated or abandoned completely by the Alyawara. Australian officials explained this behavior by citing the "primitiveness of the people involved," concluding that, given time and education, the Alyawara "will eventually achieve the level of sophistication and social responsibility necessary to live in a modern house." O'Connell's familiarity with traditional Alyawara behavior and artifacts provided him with insights into the problem that were useful in correcting this impression.

The amount of household movement within Alyawara camps is truly astonishing. O'Connell found that over an eleven-month period the nineteen core households of one settlement moved their shelters eighty-five times. All the while, other households were moving in and out of camp. This constant movement, O'Connell found, could be for any of the following reasons: the death of a household member, conflicts in obligations to family and friends, domestic quarrels, a desire to make use of newly available building materials, weather, deterioration of structures, and the build-up of refuse. For the Alyawara, household mobility is a solution to a number of recurrent problems. Given these mobility patterns, the Alyawara shelter, which may be no more than a windbreak of corrugated iron, is well suited; European-type housing is not. Such permanent dwellings prohibit traditional solutions to many community problems without providing any new alternatives.

O'Connell identified garbage as one of the problems. The aborigine solution to the accumulation of garbage is to move away from it. With permanent housing, the refuse rather than the people must be moved. Such an adjustment is difficult for people used to casually discarding refuse rather than carefully storing it for later removal to a distant dump or landfill. This was especially true because housing planners provided no facilities to store or transport garbage.

O'Connell raises an even more fundamental question. He suggests that the real issue is how groups like the Alyawara will survive economically if they become permanently settled. Present government policies assume that there will be a stable economic base, yet, beyond welfare, there are few realistic possibilities. For O'Connell, questions of permanent aboriginal housing are premature. Improvements can be made in portable dwellings, but until there is a stable economic base, it is not feasible to contemplate permanent housing for the Alyawara. O'Connell's study illustrates the interesting possibility that by studying behavior and artifacts in any society, archaeologists can add to an understanding of a wide variety of matters, including some that apply to our own industrial civilization.

The Garbage Project

In the past few years, a number of investigators have done studies of swap meets, drive-in theaters, vacant lots, and other aspects of modern life in industrial society from an archaeological perspective. The longest-running investigation of this kind is the Garbage Project.

Since the favorite research tools of behavioral scientists who study our modern civilization are questionnaires and interviews, most of what we know about our own mass behavior is based on what we *say* about it. Garbage analysis offers an alternative source of data. Items in garbage, which can be identified, counted, and weighed, are the remains of what people actually did (FIGURE 2-10). In 1973, William Rathje began the Garbage Project to analyze modern household garbage. Rathje reasoned that at one time or another all archaeologists study garbage; the Garbage Project's raw data would be just a little fresher than most. From 1973 to the present a multidisciplinary team of student volunteers has sorted and recorded garbage from more than 7,000 households in Tucson, in Milwaukee, and in Marin County, California.

Comparisons of interview and garbage data from the same neighborhoods demonstrated that there are differences in the information collected at the "front door" (interviews) and that collected at the "back door." Far more beer containers and cigarette packages, for example, were found in garbage than would have been expected on the basis of interviews. Other garbage studies have begun to produce useful insights into modern America.

With food supply becoming an ever more important problem, even in the United States, Americans have traditionally reacted to the need for more

FIGURE **2-10**

In the Garbage Project at the University of Arizona, student participants sort and record modern household garbage from Tucson. Shown on facing page is a portion of the recording form used to tabulate data.

NAME OF RECORDER: *Kelly Allen*
DATE OF ANALYSIS: *Oct. 30*

PACK NUMBERS TO RIGHT OF COLUMN, LETTERS TO LEFT (49-68)
WRITE NUMBERS CLEARLY AND USE CAPITAL LETTERS ONLY.

(FOR OFFICE USE ONLY)

MATERIAL COMPOSITION CODES

CODE (LIST MOST PREVALENT MATERIAL FIRST)

CODE		
A PAPER	H RETURNABLE GLASS	R COPPER AND BRASS
B FERROUS (STEEL/TIN)	J AEROSOL CANS	S BIODEGRADABLE PLASTIC
C ALUMINUM	K WOOD	T TEXTILES
D PLASTIC (CELLOPHANE)	M CERAMICS	V CORRUGATED CARDBOARD
E NON-RETURN GLASS	P LEATHER	X OTHER(SPECIFY ON BACK)
	Q RUBBER	

	CENSUS TRACT 16 17 18	COLLECTION MO. 19 20	DAY 21 22	ITEM CODE 23 24 25	NO. OF ITEMS 26 27 28	FLUID OUNCES 29 30 31 32 33	SOLID OUNCES 34 35 36 37 38	COST 39 40 41 42 43 44	WASTE (GRAMS) 45 46 47 48	SPOILAGE INDICATOR (SEE VEG. LIST) 49	BRAND 50 51 52 53 54 55 56 57	TYPE 58 59 60 61 62 63 64 65	MATERIAL COMPOSITION CODE 66 67 68
1	019	10	30	041	001		16.0		70		MARSHBUR	CARROT	D
2	019	10	30	086	003	36.1		.87			SCHLITZ	MALT	C
3	019	10	30	079	002	24.0					SEVENUP		BC
4	019	10	30	027	001		16.0	.65	282	X	NORTHRID	HONEYEGG	D
5	019	10	30	011	001	32.0		.43			CIRCLEK	WHOLE	A
6	019	10	30	086	002	24.0					LITE		C
7	019	10	30	051	001		32.0	1.19	40		WELCHS	JELLY	E
8	019	10	30	041	001				55	X		LETTUCE	
9	019	10	30	010	001				45	X	LONGHORN	CHEDDAR	D
10	019	10	30	048	003				260			BANANA	
11	019	10	30	181	001			.15				CITIZEN	A
12	019	10	30	044	001				95				
13	019	10	30	084	001	25.6					ROYALOCC	VODKA	ED
14	019	10	30	027	001			.65	105		HARVESTD	BUNS	D
15	019	10	30	096	001		10.7	.23			CAMPBELL	TURKEYNO	B
16	019	10	30	018	001		16.0	.40			WESTERN	HARDMARG	A
17	019	10	30	124	001						MARLBORO	FILTER	A
18	019	10	30	069	001				372				
19	019	10	30	002	001		12.0	1.73			FOODGIAN	PORKCHOP	D
20	019	10	30	095	001						HARDEES	FRENCHFR	A
21	019	10	30	055	001		1.2	.15			REESES	CHOCOLAT	
22	019	10	30	102	001						BAYER		E
23	019	10	30	034	001		9.0				CRISPIES	PRETZELS	A
24	019	10	30	001	001		20.0				FOODGIAN	GROUND	D
25	019	10	30	001	001		18.0		85	X	FOODGIAN	SIRLOIN	D

food with technological solutions—more fertilizer, bigger tractors, and new processing, storage, and delivery systems—all of which consume ever greater amounts of energy. It may be time to look for solutions that depend on changes in behavior rather than changes in technology. To find these solutions we must understand food-waste behavior. With few people willing to admit they are wasteful, the Garbage Project offered an objective method of estimating the quantity of food discarded. The amount of food purchased by a household was learned from package labels, and *food waste* was defined as any discarded once-edible food item, with certain exclusions. Adjustments were made for households using garbage-disposal devices.

The average household in the study discarded between 7 and 14 percent, by weight, of its purchased food, estimated by the U.S. General Accounting Office to come to about $11 billion a year nationally. This represents enough food to feed the entire population of Canada for one year.

The Garbage Project has also identified many specific patterns of food waste. One, unexpected on the basis of questionnaire studies, occurred during the beef shortage of 1973. Surprisingly, the project showed that the rate of waste of beef *during* the shortage was three times that of the following years. (The explanation may be that, as a hedge against rising prices and real or perceived shortages, people engaged in "crisis buying"—of more beef than they could store properly, and of cuts with whose preparation they were unfamiliar.) The method developed in the Garbage Project is now being used to identify the behaviors involved in food discard in order to decrease waste. Archaeology has documented the successes and failures of many past societies in coping with problems of diminishing resources. Archaeologists are now interested in applying their special knowledge of human behavior and artifacts to studying our own ways of solving this pressing problem.

The Village Creek Project

A more common concern of archaeologists today than the conservation of food is the conservation of archaeological resources—sites and other artifacts that survive from past societies. As a result of federal, state, and local legislation, archaeologists are increasingly playing an advisory role in the planning of land use as a means of minimizing damage to sites from dams, roads, and other construction activities. In these sorts of applied studies (Chapter 12), the *conservation archaeologist* must answer questions posed by planners and land managers in addition to typical research questions. The Village Creek Archaeological Project was one such study.

In 1974, the U.S. Army Corps of Engineers, planning to enlarge and realign 57 miles of Village Creek in northeastern Arkansas, contracted for a study of the archaeological resources in the 250-square-mile Village Creek basin. The Corps wanted to know (1) the type, extent, and importance of the archaeological resources; (2) the impact that the planned project would have on those resources; and (3) measures it could take to mitigate adverse impacts. Specifically, the Corps asked the archaeologists to tell them exactly how to align the channel to minimize damage to archaeological sites.

The problem of designing an archaeological project to supply this kind of information is one faced almost daily by conservation archaeologists. Projects of this kind often have no prior work to build on, and, in fact, Village Creek was almost an archaeological blank; only twenty-eight sites had been reported, and none of these had been excavated. A large-scale *archaeological survey,* first-hand inspection of the area, was needed.

Because there was neither time nor money to locate all sites that might be damaged by the construction, archaeologist Jacqueline Fehon devised a *sampling strategy* in which blocks of land, a third of a square mile each, were chosen randomly for study (FIGURE 2-11). Systematic examination on foot of each of these units produced eighty-five sites. Fehon, grouping the sites according to type of terrain—flood plain, first river terrace, or second river terrace—found that sites occurred four and one-half times more frequently on first terraces than on the flood plain. (Those on first terraces also showed greater variety.) Because of this finding, Fehon recommended that channelization be confined to the flood plain, immediately adjacent to the creek.

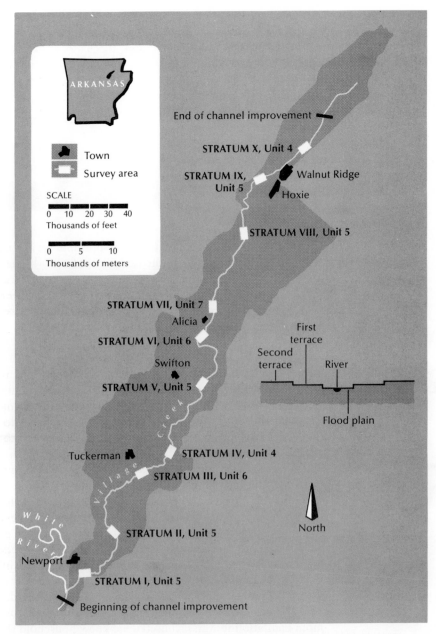

FIGURE **2-11** The Village Creek basin in northeastern Arkansas. Lozenge-shaped units along creek show locations of transects used in sample survey. Cross-section of basin (lower right) illustrates relation of creek to flood plain, first terrace, and second terrace.

FIGURE **2-12**

Changes in ceramic discard rates at Plimoth Plantation, Plymouth, Massachusetts. Ceramic sherds shown are those excavated from *A*, the Edward Wilson site, occupied 1635–50; *B*, the Joseph Howland site, occupied 1675–1725; and *C*, one trash pit used by a single family, 1830–35.

A

Conservation archaeologists are responsible for the entire range of archaeological resources, from the campsites of early humans to historic villages and even to modern cities. The broadness of this range requires that archaeologists—with their goal of preserving our past for the future—have a long-term perspective in both management recommendations and basic research questions.

SYNTHESIS AND LONG-TERM CHANGE

Perhaps the most demanding of archaeological activities is the synthesizing of the larger pictures of human history from research findings from different areas and times. Through a century of work archaeologists have clearly identified the broad outlines of prehistory and have described the great changes in human behavior and artifacts that have occurred over many millennia (Chapter 11).

We are always in the process of creating the past. In fact, we can often catch ourselves in the act of continuing the trends that archaeologists describe in their studies of change in ancient societies. Identifying the extremely long-term trends that tie us to our remotest ancestors is an increasingly important contribution of archaeology. These studies, which compare our life styles to those of our predecessors, give us a new perspective on our own society. They can even be useful in anticipating the direction of change.

One example of a long-term trend is the directional change obvious in the number and variety of items that households discard. In the 1960s and 1970s James Deetz excavated a number of colonial household sites at Plimoth Plantation in Massachusetts. He knew household sizes and the length of time specific household dumps were used from historic records. In his analyses, Deetz noticed an increase with time in the quantity and variety of items discarded by households of similar size, beginning in the 1600s and running through the 1700s and 1800s (FIGURE 2-12). This pattern, isolated by Deetz, is only one segment of a trend that runs from 2,000,000 B.P. (Before Present) to today.

B   C

The earliest trash of humanlike creatures consists of broken rocks, little modified from their natural state. At the other extreme is the garbage of modern America, full of more than 57 varieties of Heinz products alone and untold quantities of packaging and household commodities. It is estimated that each year the average sample household of the above-mentioned Garbage Project discards 800 steel cans, 500 aluminum cans, 500 glass bottles (10 returnable), 1,300 plastic items, and 18,000 items of cardboard and paper. This increase in garbage reflects an astounding increase in the number and variety of items that are part of a household's artifact inventory. It also reflects an unprecedented increase in the use and discard by households of *nonrenewable resources,* those whose supply in the world is sharply limited and that are replenished slowly or not at all—oil, bauxite, uranium, and many others. The typical discards of ancient societies—chippable rocks for stone tools, clay for pots, and sand for glass—were available in virtually inexhaustible quantities. Today, in contrast, oil (in the form of plastics) and bauxite (in the form of aluminum products like foil and beer cans) are systematically discarded in modern household garbage and deposited in landfills.

By comparing past and present societies in this fashion, and by discerning trends and discovering principles of change, archaeologists hope to anticipate, and perhaps even influence, the future of society.

■ Each of the studies we have just described was done by a different archaeologist, in a different place, using different methods to answer different questions. In spite of this obvious diversity, each study contributes to a better understanding of artifacts and, thereby, of human behavior. These descriptions of archaeologists at work are examples, then, of the building blocks that together form the discipline of archaeology. These building blocks are held together by the concepts and principles about artifacts and behavior that archaeologists share, which will be described in the next two chapters.

The Scientific Method in Archaeology

In the examples of research given in this chapter and throughout the text, the underlying approach has its basis in the *scientific method,* which is described below in terms of eight research stages. In day-to-day practice, these stages are not slavishly followed. Not all research begins with a hypothesis, and chance discoveries have always played an important part in scientific progress.

1 Conceptual Scheme

The major assumptions or underpinnings of a discipline form its *conceptual scheme.* Conceptual schemes define certain areas as worthy of attention and also structure the way that questions are asked about these areas. One of archaeology's most important assumptions is that, in all societies, artifacts and human behavior are systematically related. This assumption is a cornerstone of modern archaeology's conceptual scheme (see Chapter 3).

2 Specific Research Questions

Drawing on previous work, a researcher frames specific research problems or questions. (Recall Yellen's question: What determines the area of artifact scatter in hunter-gatherer campsites? Is it population size, or something else?)

3 Hypotheses

Tentative answers to questions are known as *hypotheses.* Such "educated guesses" may come from any source—previous work, information from other fields, even a dream. Ideally, several competing hypotheses are proposed. This is the method of *multiple working hypotheses,* which is useful because it forces a researcher to consider all likely alternative explanations. John Yellen sought to examine the hypothesis that the number of people living in a hunter-gatherer camp determines the area over which artifacts are scattered. He also suspected that the size of artifact scatters might be the result of the length of time the camp was occupied. These two possible factors that were thought to determine site areas—number of people and length of stay—were Yellen's multiple working hypotheses.

4 Test Implications

If a hypothesis is true, it should have a number of expectable consequences. *Test implications* state these expectations and clearly specify the *relevant data*—those specific observations that are crucial for hypothesis testing—that need to be collected. For example, Yellen proposed that comparison of different Dobe Bushmen campsites of known population size and period of occupation should disclose artifact scatters of different sizes. Relevant data included ethnoarchaeological observations on the length of time the camps were occupied, the number of people in the camps, and the areas of artifact scatter.

5 Data Recovery

Relevant data in the form of observations and artifacts are collected in the field. This information may come from experiments, ethnoarchaeology, archaeological survey, excavation, or examination of historic documents. Yellen took up residence among the Bushmen, recording activities at campsites as well as population size and duration of occupation of the camps. He made detailed maps of each camp after abandonment, showing the distribution of huts, artifacts, and even vegetation. In this and other cases, one usually gathers a great deal more than just the relevant data, and much of this often becomes relevant in subsequent stages of research.

6 Data Analysis

In the analysis stage, data are quantitatively and qualitatively manipulated, sometimes with the aid of computers, in order to learn how well the data match the test implications. In doing this Yellen was able to see immediately that site area was not determined by just one factor and had to be studied as the product of a number of complex behaviors. He developed the idea of the inside and outside rings and quantitatively compared their areas with known factors—number of people and length of stay.

7 Synthesis of Analysis

Analysis results are synthesized and assessed as to whether the new evidence supports or refutes the hypotheses. Yellen found that the first hypothesis was not supported in its initial form; population was related not to total camp area, but only to the area of the inner ring. The second hypothesis was supported; length of occupation was related to total area of artifact scatter.

8 Results and Rethinking

Hypotheses may be rejected or retained. Scientists relate their findings to their initial questions and try to evaluate the overall contributions of their research. Good research usually leads to many new questions. Yellen's ethnoarchaeological findings cast doubt on many traditional methods for estimating population from site area. His study emphasized the importance of looking at a camp as a number of different activity areas rather than as an indivisible unit. Further research is needed in other ethnoarchaeological settings in order to find out if Yellen's discoveries are typical of all hunter-gatherers. Thus, as one research project draws to a close, it generates others, which begin again at Research Stage 2.

Leslie A. White (1900–1975)   Leslie White is an ironic figure. In his theory of cultural evolution, he argued that individuals are swept along with the flow of change, and that "great men," by themselves, could not change the course of history. For Leslie White, great men were successful only when history was ready for them. White was fond of saying that in another time or place, Jesus would have remained a simple carpenter. The irony is that White himself was the major force behind a revival of evolutionary thinking in cultural anthropology. For more than twenty years he seemed single-handedly to carry the banner of cultural evolution amidst colleagues hostile to the idea. While other anthropologists recorded the exotic details of simpler societies and claimed that they did not know enough yet to construct theories, White proved himself to be a master builder. White's belief, simply put, was that culture evolves as inventions and other technological advances make possible the use of greater amounts of energy. From his perspective, fire, sailing ships, the plow, and the steam engine were among the more important cultural developments that helped societies evolve.   □   During most of his lifetime, White and his ideas were controversial. A group of anthropologists in the University of Chicago's Sociology Department formed their own anthropology department as a result of a dispute over his doctoral dissertation. Ironically, the sociologists claimed that the dissertation was not theoretical enough. White was never again similarly accused; in fact, in Ann Arbor, where White taught for four decades at the University of Michigan, a major church campaigned vigorously to have him fired on the grounds that his theories, which denied the existence of free will, would corrupt young minds. The university resisted such pressures, but for many years protected its freshmen from exposure to White's anthropology.   □   Leslie White had a profound effect on both writers of this text as undergraduates. One of us considers White's *The Science of Culture*, diligently studied as a junior, to be the most important anthropology book he read in college; the other, as a senior, was unable to identify Leslie White in an interview for a fellowship and is properly mortified.

Leslie A. White
at the University
of Michigan.

3

BASIC CONCEPTS OF HUMAN BEHAVIOR

lthough Leslie White was concerned with the evolution of human societies, he never believed that artifacts could evolve by themselves.
Some archaeologists give a different impression. They talk about
pottery types joining to produce new "daughter" types. Such words might
evoke a fantastic vision of the past: an ancient landscape inhabited by artifacts with lives of their own—mom and dad pots raising little baby pots to
grow up to be new ceramic styles or stone tool types breeding new chips off
old blocks.

For most of the societies that archaeologists want to study, artifacts are
all that remain. Surrounded in their laboratories by crates and boxes of ancient objects (FIGURE 3-1), archaeologists must constantly remind themselves that these artifacts had no lives of their own, but were made, used,
and discarded by people. While it is tempting to write prehistory as a history
of artifacts, prehistory is really the story of human societies. Instead of family trees of pots, it is the kinship, political, and social behaviors of people
that archaeologists are trying to reconstruct.

We know that our behavior is different from that of the ancient native
Americans of the Tehuacán Valley, and archaeologists want to know why
behaviors have changed over time. The !Kung Bushmen, although our contemporaries, also do things differently from us. Again, archaeologists want
to know why. Change through time and variability at any one time are
characteristics of human behavior and make up the focus of archaeological
studies.

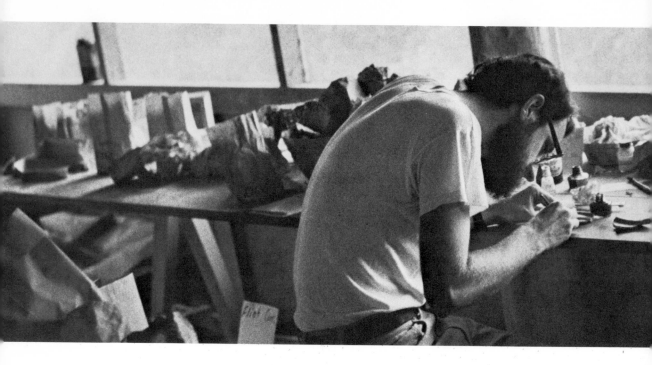

Living societies are an interlinked mix of behaviors and artifacts; dead societies are just artifacts. For archaeologists, therefore, whole societies consist of two halves, one usually invisible—behavior, one usually visible—artifacts. Taken by themselves, artifacts are like a jumble of letters without meaning, so that archaeologists studying a dead society are like someone learning to read a new language. It is only when linked to common human behaviors of manufacture, use, and discard, that patterns in artifacts begin to make sense. Therefore, we need to be familiar with important concepts that describe the behaviors that, when combined with artifacts, allow archaeologists to read the invisible or "living" half of human societies from their "dead" remains.

Because our primary evidence is variability and patterning in artifacts, individuals from the past remain anonymous to archaeologists. Individual behavior, however, fits into larger patterns of behavior, called social organization, which vary from society to society and change over time. We discuss below the concepts for describing and investigating behavior and social organization.

ARCHAEOLOGICAL ELEMENTS OF HUMAN BEHAVIOR

Human behavior patterns occur along a continuum of complexity—from an individual blinking, to several people building a house, to the rise and fall of whole civilizations. Archaeologists subdivide this continuum in several ways: a guitar-player attaching a capo and tuning up is performing a simple

FIGURE **3-1**

An archaeologist sorts artifacts in the laboratory.

act, a recurrent behavior involving particular artifacts. A set of related acts is an *activity,* such as all the behaviors involved in practicing and playing the guitar.

Most activities involve artifacts and activity areas. An *activity area* is the place an activity occurs, whether it is repeated many times or takes place once. Most activities are repeated, and certain activities tend to take place in the same area time after time. (Recall Yellen's ring model in Chapter 2. The location of activities in Bushman camps is clearly patterned in relation to the hut circle.) Generally, the more frequently an activity is carried out, the more predictable will be its location. Many activities come to take place in highly specialized locations and structures. It is even hard to find behaviors that do not have specialized activity areas. Hikers usually follow well-worn trails, hunters hunt in prescribed areas, and teenagers make out in parked cars.

Archaeologists approach activity areas from two standpoints: given an activity, the question is, Where did it occur? Given an activity area, the question is, What activities went on there?

Activities are carried out by machines, animals, people, and other dynamic objects. A *social unit* is a group of people organized to carry out particular activities. Members of social units can be defined in several ways—people who are related to each other by kinship, people who work together and frequently interact, and people who live together in a community. Most social units are organized to perform similar activities again and again. In-

Archaeological Elements of Human Behavior □ **45**

deed, it is such frequently occurring activities that give rise to society's basic social units, such as the family.

Within social units, the activities of members form patterns. These patterns can be thought of as social roles within social units, such as *father* within a household, *pledge* within a fraternity, *teller* within a bank, or *mayor* of a community. Individuals perform several roles in all of the social units to which they belong. When all of these roles are considered together for one person, they form that person's social standing. This varies along a continuum based on control over resources and power—from high (such as a corporation president who participates in many community activities) to low (such as a derelict who drifts from town to town).

By relating individuals and social units to activities, activity areas, and artifacts, archaeologists define the *behavioral components* of social organization. Several behavioral components are important to archaeological research because they make, use, and discard artifacts in patterned ways.

Behavioral Components

The basic behavioral component is the *household,* the group whose members regularly eat and sleep together. The household's social unit is generally a family, small or large, perhaps incorporating grandparents, uncles, nieces, and sundry relatives. It may also consist of unrelated and unmarried individuals, and it may even be one person living alone. Many household activities are involved in maintenance of the social unit—activities such as obtaining and preparing food, caring for children, storing clothing and tools, and providing for entertainment and creature comforts. Households occupy a dwelling, which may be a house, apartment, mobile home, hut, or cave, and each of these dwellings is filled with the artifacts of everyday life. Our definition of household is exceedingly general, a necessity since archaeologists study many diverse societies. By this definition, fraternities/sororities, dormitories, and prisons are all *special-purpose households*. A little reflection will show that they do have some things in common.

Groups of households form *communities.* The activities of a community are mainly those needed to maintain its households. Such activities involve leadership, religion, commerce, and law and order. The activity area of a community is a *settlement* or *settlement system,* which includes the dwellings, markets, temples, palaces, roads, and other activity areas used by the members of the community. The social unit of a community is composed of those people who occupy a settlement or settlement system and are regularly served by, and participate in, community organizations, such as markets, churches, and political organizations. All the settlements occupied by people, such as the Bushmen, who move around during the year form a settlement system and are part of a single community. More often today, communities occupy just one major settlement, such as the city of London and its several million people.

Communities related to each other by trade, political alliances, and *social interaction* (face-to-face contact and other forms of interpersonal communication) form *regional systems*. Regional systems are usually bounded by natural features, such as mountain ranges and rivers, and have many similar artifacts in common. Thus, farming and other special-purpose settlements outside of London are part of the London regional system and share British-style artifacts. Moreover, on a slightly larger scale, the farming, mining, and manufacturing communities in the whole of Britain that have regular contacts with the city of London can be viewed as part of the London regional system.

A mega-center such as London in the 1800s, which traded around the globe, was the hub of an *empire*. Such empires control far-flung trade and political and military activities that involve a number of regional systems. These ties can often be traced by "artifacts of empire"—special building styles and trade goods. Thus, the influences of many modern nation-states, such as the United States, which are at the hub of empires, can be traced through such artifacts as Coke bottles, Holiday Inns, and sophisticated weapons. Today, empires overlap and encompass almost every society on earth.

All the bigger behavioral components—communities, regional systems, and empires—are composed of ever larger groupings of households. *Task groups,* however, are behavioral components built of groupings of individuals, not households. They are formed to carry out activities. All individuals belong to a variety of task groups. The social unit of the task group is those people, who may be drawn from different households, communities, and even regions, who assemble to perform tasks. This could be an army on a battlefield or archaeologists at a convention. Task groups carry out the bulk of a society's activities. Such groups include churches and clubs, factories, legislatures, councils of chiefs, Scotland Yard. Task groups often carry out activities in specialized structures, such as a temple or a factory, a corporate headquarters, or meeting places that have additional functions, such as restaurants used for Rotary Club luncheons or a house used by a group of males gathered to make tools for a hunt. Some of the artifacts of task groups—for example, tools—relate to their tasks; others—such as insignia—identify the group.

One type of large-scale task group that deserves special mention is the *institution*, a large, formal task group with a portion of its members organized into hierarchies of bureaucrats. The U.S. Postal Service is an institution, as are General Motors and the Catholic church.

Some behavioral components are loosely integrated and very difficult to define. *Ethnic groups*, whose social units are based largely on common ancestry and self-identification, are the best example. Mexican-Americans in the Southwest, Irish Catholics in Boston, and Puerto Ricans in New York are ethnic groups. The boundaries of these groups are extremely vague because individuals may or may not claim membership. Although some groups have clear neighborhoods, many members live in mixed ethnic areas. Few, if any, distinctive artifacts are shared by *all* the members of an ethnic

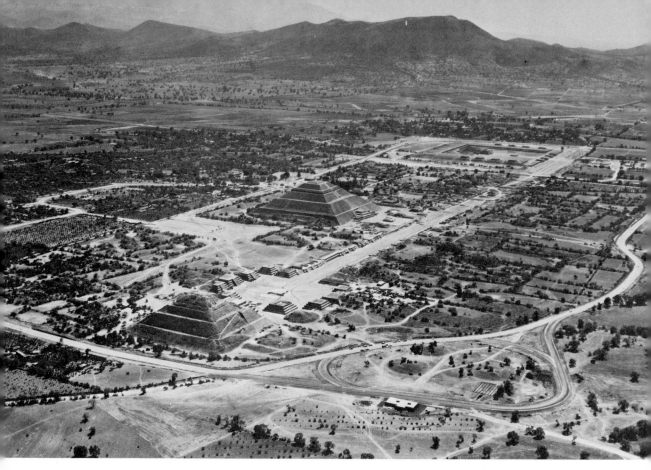

FIGURE **3-2** The site of Teotihuacán, Mexico. Note the generally arid highland landscape. The Pyramid of the Sun is at the center, the Pyramid of the Moon, lower left. (These names are largely arbitrary.)

group. In addition, the members of ethnic groups do not necessarily share activities: Irish Catholics from Boston are cabdrivers, priests, senators. It is difficult to define boundaries of ethnic groups, especially those in multiethnic communities. For example, at the site of Teotihuacán (FIGURE 3-2), near Mexico City, home to more than two hundred thousand people around A.D. 500, archaeologists identified (because of the presence of large quantities of Oaxaca-style pottery) what they believe to be a *barrio*, or neighborhood, of residents from Oaxaca, a valley 300 kilometers away. On the other hand, although archaeologists at the site of Kültepe in Turkey (dating around 1850 B.C.) found documents indicating that it had been an enclave of Assyrian merchants, there were few other special artifacts to identify the Assyrian presence; the merchants seem to have lived in local-style houses and used local pottery. Without the texts that describe their activities, the colony probably would not have been noticed.

Basic Concepts of Human Behavior □ **48**

Archaeologists ask a number of questions about behavioral components. What activities were carried on by households? How did the different settlements used by a community fit into a settlement system? What were the economic, political, and social ties between communities in regional systems and empires? How did the boundaries of communities, regional systems, and empires change through time? How do task groups and ethnic groups fit into these other behavioral components?

CONCEPTUAL SCHEMES

In answering these research questions, archaeologists have shown that human behavior has varied considerably throughout the past and is varied today. In seeking the causes of this variability, archaeologists draw upon a number of interrelated *conceptual schemes*, the basic assumptions about human behavior that are used to organize archaeological research.

A basic part of most archaeologists' conceptual schemes is the idea of *adaptation*. Human societies organize behavior and artifacts into systems (which we have called behavioral components) that are adapted to, or fit in with, their environments. The basic function of a human *adaptive system* is to extract resources from its environment and convert them into the energy and products that supply people's needs. For example, prehistoric hunters and gatherers in the Tehuacán Valley, using mobility and a kit of simple but effective tools, formed an adaptive system to contend with seasonal changes in the location of food resources. At the other extreme, modern Americans have highly complex adaptations—intricate technologies and many different behavioral components that make it possible to obtain rubber in Brazil that is made into tires in Detroit for a camper sold to a farmer in California whose tomatoes end up in a New York taxi-driver's salad. Regardless of complexity, the success of an adaptation is judged by how well it provides for the needs of a human population.

Although they exist at different levels of complexity, all adaptive systems change: they change as they grow and decline; they change as the world around them changes. To simplify the study of change in adaptive systems, archaeologists often describe them in terms of three dimensions: technology, social organization, and ideology. *Technology* is society's way of procuring resources and producing energy from its environment to manufacture and maintain its artifacts and ultimately its people. To operate technologies, adaptive systems need *social organization,* which consists of social units and their patterns of interaction. *Ideology* is a society's beliefs, attitudes, values, knowledge, and information, much of which helps to structure and maintain social organization and technology.

The environment in which all human adaptive systems exist can be divided into natural and social elements. The *natural environment* consists of local climate, terrain, geological resources, and *flora* (plants) and *fauna* (animals). The *social environment* is other surrounding human adaptive systems—other households, communities, regional systems, or empires. The natural and social environments of any adaptive system are always changing. In order for groups to persist, their adaptations must change too. Repeated crop failures due to drought may cause village farmers to depend more heavily on hunting and gathering; excess population may lead to the development of more complex and costly technology for extracting energy; an oil embargo may cause industrial nations to attempt to reduce oil consumption and experiment with alternative energy sources.

Adaptations are not always successful in the long run. In fact, if one lesson is clear from the archaeological record, it is that most adaptive systems ultimately fail. The reason seems to be that adaptations that provide short-term solutions often create long-term problems, which accumulate until no solutions can be found. For example, farmers facing economic problems may reduce the time their fields lie fallow. In the short run, their production is increased; in the long run, though, they have sown the seeds of poor harvests ahead. Slowly the fertility of their fields declines and, eventually, production falls rapidly to an uneconomic level. Indeed, most changes in adaptation may be the result of trying to adjust to the unanticipated consequences of seemingly rational decisions. For example, the invention and mass production of the car solved many transportation problems in the United States. It also solved the pollution problem of urban horse droppings. We now realize, however, that the car has created unforeseen problems, including increased injuries and deaths, traffic jams, a more serious kind of pollution, and dependence on oil imports (FIGURE 3-3).

FIGURE **3-3**

The ideal and the real: here, a rosy 1932 vision of an automobile-enhanced future; on facing page, one 1980 reality—a camp ground choked with cars.

As archaeologists begin to approach specific problems, they develop more specialized versions of the basic conceptual scheme. One version is *cultural ecology,* which focuses on the specific manner in which a society adapts to its environment, examining the effects of environment and technology on social organization and ideology. It also studies how social organization and ideology influence the way adaptive systems work. *Cultural evolution,* another version of the archaeologist's conceptual scheme, examines how and why adaptive systems have changed over the last two million years. Cultural evolutionists use the concept of *complexity* to compare all human societies. The more complex a society is, the larger the number and kinds of behavioral components it will have, and the more varied the relationships among components will be. This is best illustrated by the extreme cases of modern America and the !Kung Bushmen. Cultural evolutionists group societies according to complexity, each group taken as a basic *stage,* or step, in the evolution of human adaptive systems. The main question is how groups evolve from one stage to the next.

The Stage Model of Societies

From the work of cultural anthropologists who are "cultural evolutionists," archaeologists have borrowed the *stage model,* whose intellectual roots go back to the 1800s. The most recent form, derived from the work of cultural anthropologist Elman Service, has five stages: bands, tribes, chiefdoms, agrarian states, industrial states. These stages are defined on the basis of a number of characteristics, including population size, subsistence activities and economics, social roles, and ideology. It is useful to think of the stages as general forms of adaptation. The differences between consecutive stages can be viewed as the addition of new kinds of behavior.

In *band* societies, such as the Australian aborigines, subsistence activities are hunting and gathering. Bands are composed of small groups of households that occupy a number of settlements, usually in a yearly cycle or *seasonal round* in response to the changing availability of plants, animals, and water. Individual communities vary in size, but usually average twenty-five people. The criteria for membership in task groups, such as hunting parties, are based primarily on age and sex. Thus, adult males hunt together while adult females and children collect plant foods. Beyond such divisions, there are very few social roles. One exception is the role of *shaman,* a specialist in magic and curing. Ideologies stress communal ownership and sharing of resources. Households seem to have an even share of what material goods there are, but there aren't many. Because bands move often, they do not spend much time on building dwellings and they carry few possessions with them.

Band communities tend to be economically self-sufficient. Communities are *integrated* into regional systems by trade and by *exogamy,* the practice of marrying outside the community. (In the Australian aborigine case young women usually marry outside the local band.) Regional systems may contain as many as five hundred people. The !Kung Bushmen are organized at the band level, as are some groups of Eskimos, and Shoshone and Paiute (FIGURE 3-4).

Tribes, such as the Pueblo societies described by early Spanish priests and explorers, rely on farming and/or herding. Full-time herders still move their settlements in a yearly cycle related to the grazing needs of their animals, but plants don't move around, and farmers usually reside in permanent villages. Such communities may hold several hundred people. Tribes are composed of regional systems of villages or pastoral communities, and an entire society may reach a population of several thousand persons.

FIGURE **3-4**   Shoshone hunters and gatherers in the Great Basin of Nevada. That the photograph was taken in the late 1800s demonstrates the long-term stability of such a life style—until it clashes with modern Western civilization.

Tribes may include the social role of *part-time specialist,* such as potters who produce cooking wares for households other than their own. Gifts and exchanges of goods take place largely on a household-to-household basis, and acquisitions and losses usually balance out in the long run. Although trade and intermarriage occur between tribes, farming communities are largely self-sufficient, and even households tend to be self-contained production-and-consumption units. Pastoral tribes are sometimes linked economically to agricultural communities, such as historic-period Navajo sheepherders and Hopi farmers, but their social units remain distinct. Recruitment for task groups is again mainly based on age and sex. Dance groups, which perform at important ceremonies (FIGURE 3-5), and men's clubs recruit people from many different families, and this serves to integrate the community. Leadership roles often depend upon personal achievement (such as the case of a village elder who has lived long enough to become one) and are not usually inherited by relatives.

Because tribes tend to be sedentary, the number of material possessions grows and much more durable dwellings and facilities are constructed. In tribal societies we see the beginnings of *social inequality.* Kin groups may control differing quantities and qualities of such critical resources as agricultural lands and animals. There are also important and relatively permanent leadership roles within kin groups. This inequality in critical resources and power results in variability in the dwellings and material possessions of households. Nevertheless, though noticeable, social inequality is still not very great.

Ideologies become more formal, with greater emphasis on following strict schedules in the performance of community rituals, such as those for the "first planting" and the "first harvest". Tribal societies are likely even to develop calendars and astronomy for the precise timing of rituals and important subsistence activities. In addition to the Pueblo Indians of the American Southwest, the sweet-potato farmers of highland New Guinea and many pastoral groups in Asia are tribal societies.

Chiefdoms, such as the Polynesian societies Captain Cook found in Hawaii and Tahiti, represent a marked departure from bands and tribes. Chiefdoms are regional systems composed of a variety of communities that contribute different products to the economy. As the head of a regional system, a chief has more than a simple leadership role. He is the center of the first institution, the institution of chief. It is composed of the chief, attendants, and close kinsmen and serves as an economic, political, and religious focal point. A new important economic activity, found in chiefdoms, is *redistribution.* In this activity, the chief makes use of numerous ceremonies to collect and redistribute as gifts a variety of different products within and between communities. On a single formal occasion, a Hawaiian chief would receive as many as 20,000 gourds of poi and 40,000 pigs (FIGURE 3-6). In the process of redistribution, the chief takes a sizable commission for his services. The regional systems that chiefs control may embrace 100,000 people.

FIGURE **3-5** In early twentieth-century Arizona, Kachina dancers, representing spirits, perform in a Hopi tribal ceremonial.

Specialized task groups other than the institution of chief are important. Most directly support the chief's household and the rituals that legitimize the authority of the chief. Particularly important are the craftsmen, often *full-time specialists*, who produce the showy objects needed to symbolize the chief's unique social role. The most obvious artifacts of this type are forms of *monumental architecture*, such as big houses, ceremonial structures and carvings, and ostentatious burial sites. The temples of the paramount chiefs in ancient Polynesia were massive structures of wood and stone that could accommodate hundreds of people. In chiefdoms, inequality between social units can be easily recognized. Individual kin groups are ranked by their family background relative to the chief's. These differences in social standing are accompanied by differences in dwellings and household artifacts.

` FIGURE **3-6**   Captain Cook pays his respects to a Polynesian chieftain amidst the pomp and
ceremony that are the focus of most community activities in chiefdoms.

Ideologies and rituals center on the chief and his life crises—birth, marriage, coronation, and death—and serve to legitimize his powerful role in
the economic and social life of the community. Archaeologists infer that the
societies that carved the stone heads on Easter Island were chiefdoms, as
were those of the architects of Stonehenge in England and the mound builders of the eastern United States.

Agrarian states, such as ancient Athens or Sparta, integrate sizable
numbers of large communities into regional systems with mixed agricultural
economies. Integration is accomplished mainly through specialized political
institutions, the most typical being the institution of king and palace. When
supported by large armies, size may reach 5 million people, one of the estimates for the Roman Empire. Specialized households, task groups, and even
communities create a complex network of interdependent social units.
Agrarian states are characterized by large ritual, administrative, mercantile,
military, and judicial institutions, and by others that tie these units together.

Rural farming communities are the backbone of agrarian states, supporting their many specialized institutions with taxes or tribute. Those who
man the specialized institutions form the core of a new form of settlement—
densely populated cities. Huge monumental structures such as the Agora

and Acropolis of Athens usually dominate the center of cities, serving as visual symbols of the power and glory of the state. Ancient cities would be familiar to all of us, with their noise and garbage, thieves and beggars, prostitutes and sailors, fishmongers and judges.

For some groups of specialists recruitment is based on kinship, as in the cases of craft guilds and of hereditary leadership in the institution of king and palace. Nevertheless, relative to the case of tribes and chiefdoms, the role of kinship in assigning occupations is greatly diminished. People of similar social standing form *social classes* that can be ranked from high to low, such as from nobles to merchants to peasants to slaves. The result is an extreme form of social inequality, with marked differences in the basic resources, wealth, and political power of households. The increase in *social differentiation,* more social roles, classes, and behavioral components, is symbolized by a greatly expanded array of artifacts. Ornate craft items are produced by a large cadre of artisans; an increased quantity of more basic commodities, such as simply decorated pots or clothing, are produced by rudimentary forms of mass production. Trading groups, large workshops, and markets make all these goods available.

Agrarian states tend to grow at the expense of their neighbors—chiefdoms, tribes, bands, and even other agrarian states. Empires are created through military conquest, extended trade, and political ties. The colonial empires formed by ancient agrarian states were often extensive and relatively long-lasting. The Roman Empire stretched from Britain to Mesopotamia and persisted nearly five hundred years (FIGURE 3-7). This expansionist

FIGURE **3-7**   Elaborate ceremony in ancient Rome (as recreated by Hollywood) testifies to the wide range of large institutions—such as the military—and to the expansionism that characterize the agrarian state.

FIGURE **3-8**   An oil storage facility, apt symbol of a complex society based on exploitation of nonrenewable energy resources.

form of organization was replaced only after the Industrial Revolution created an adaptive system that grew even more rapidly.

We live in an *industrial state*. The adaptation of the industrial state is based on work performed by machines whose operation in turn depends upon a continuous supply of raw materials and fuels—usually nonrenewable resources. The specialization in jobs and institutions, the production of great quantities of material goods, and increasing social inequality are trends begun in agrarian states that are continued and intensified in industrial states. One of the more dramatic differences is the development of faster means of transportation and communication which, among other things, has led to an increased ability to market products. Thus, despite social inequality, most households become superconsumers of artifacts, well beyond the basic needs of life. Another difference is the growth of institutions that store and process information, such as libraries, schools, and government bureaucracies. One effect of such institutions as schools has been an increased ability in some industrial states of individuals to become *socially mobile,* to change their social class by means of their individual accomplishments. This is a clear contrast with agrarian states, where changes in social class are much more difficult. Another contrast is in the increased number of city dwellers and the vastly greater size of communities—Tokyo, for example, has a population of about 9 million—made possible by elaborate transportation and communication systems and by the use of machines in agriculture—all of which consume huge amounts of petroleum products (FIGURE 3-8).

The industrial state, like the agrarian state, is predatory, but in a somewhat different sense. Not only does it engulf other societies, but it consumes an ever greater share of the world's energy. Although future steps in the stage model are uncertain, what is clear is that the days of the insatiable industrial state as we know it are numbered by the dwindling of the world's nonrenewable energy sources.

Although this stage model seems clearcut and is able to separate Australian aborigines from modern Americans, it seems deficient in that it would lump into a single stage adaptive systems that differ considerably—such as those of the Soviet Union, South Africa, and the United States. In addition, it places in different stages, simply on the basis of one or two criteria, societies that are quite similar. For example, many African societies look for all the world like tribes, except that they have kings and standing armies. As a result, they are classified as agrarian states, even though they have no cities and little specialization in jobs beyond soldiering.

Despite its flaws, the stage model calls attention to variability in adaptive systems and challenges us to explain that variability. In particular, archaeologists are beginning to realize that in some sense specialization, social inequality, and other properties identified by the cultural evolutionists are fundamental for the study of behavioral variability and change. Even if the model is incorrect in detail, it is still useful in describing gross differences between societies. Archaeologists often use these stages for convenience in their discussions of change in past societies, and we will also—in Chapters 10 and 11.

The Accumulation Model

The basic problem with the stage model is that it assumes that the groups of behaviors that distinguish stages always appear together. This cannot be expected, given that many societies are in flux and that societies must adapt to many different environments. Recent work by cultural evolutionists has shifted away from stage models and toward models of the way certain properties interact in the evolution of adaptive systems. For example, Robert

FIGURE **3-9**

Accumulation of 50 culture traits as an expression of degree of cultural evolution of societies. The simplest, such as band societies, fall at the top of the chart; tribal and chiefdom societies—of intermediate complexity—fall at the middle; and agrarian states are at the bottom.

Society	
TASMANIANS	
BAMBUTI	
AMAHUACA	
NASKAPI	(1)
WASHO	(1)
LENGUA	(1)
SEMANG	(1)
COPPER ESKIMO	(2)
YAHGAN	(2)
BUSHMEN	(2)
KURNAI	(2)
MURNGIN	(2)
WALBIRI	(2)
KASKA	(2)
SIRIONO	(2)
ANDAMANESE	(2)
AMMASSALIK	(3)
VEDDA	(3)
YARURO	(3)
BAHAMA	(3)
KORYAK	(3)
JIVARO	(3)
NORTHERN MAIDU	(4)
CHIPPEWA	(4)
GROS VENTRES	(4)
MUNDURUCU	(4)
CAMPA	(4)
CUBEO	(5)
YUKASHIR	(5)
TEHUELCHE	(5)
COMANCHE	(6)
YUPA	(6)
TUKUNA	(6)
TANAINA	(7)
BLACKFOOT	(7)
HAVASUPAI	(7)
KUIKURU	(7)
KAMAR	(7)
LAPPS	(7)
TENINO	(7)
XARAO	(8)
CANELA	(8)
KLALLAM	(8)
NUER	(8)
GUARANI	(8)
GURURUMBA	(8)
CHEYENNE	(8)
KAREN	(8)
KWAKIUTL	(8)
TUPINAMBA	(9)
KIWAI	(9)
AO NAGA	(9)
MANDAN	(9)
MANOBO	(9)
MOLIMA	(9)
OMAHA	(9)
MALA	(9)
IFALUK	(10)
SIUAI	(10)
CHIGA	(10)
MENOMINI	(10)
NAMA	(10)
TODA	(10)
FLATHEAD	(10)
DONTOC	(10)
KAYAN	(11)
LANGO	(11)
ELGEYO	(11)
ACOMA	(11)
POKOT	(12)
IROQUOIS	(12)
MAORI	(12)
BOLOKI	(12)
KOFYAR	(12)
CREEK	(13)
TUAREG	(15)
FUTUNA	(17)
BATAK	(18)
RWALA	(18)
THONGA	(19)
TANALA	(19)
MARQUESANS	(21)
FIJI	(22)
MANO	(23)
SUKU	(23)
BAVENDA	(25)
BEMBA	(25)
TAHITI	(27)
HAWAII	(30)
VIKINGS	(33)
BACANDA	(36)
DAHOMEY	(37)
ASHANTI	(37)
LEON	(43)
INCAS	(47)
AZTECS	(49)
CHINA (HAN)	(49)
ROMAN EMPIRE	(50)
ASSYRIA	(50)
EGYPT (NEW KINGDOM)	(50)

Traits (columns, with frequencies):

(93) SPECIAL RELIGIOUS PRACTITIONERS
(82) TRADE BETWEEN COMMUNITIES
(81) FORMAL POLITICAL LEADERSHIP
(75) SOCIAL SEGMENTS ABOVE FAMILY
(69) PEACE-KEEPING MACHINERY
(62) COMMUNITIES OF 100 OR MORE
(62) SOCIAL STRATIFICATION
(60) SEXUAL SPECIALIZATION
(60) DOMESTICATED FOOD SOURCES PREDOMINANT
(53) JUDICIAL PROCESS
(47) CRAFT PRODUCTION FOR EXCHANGE
(32) FULL-TIME POLITICAL LEADERS
(27) DEATH PENALTY
(26) SUPRA-PROVINCIAL ORGANIZATION
(24) FULL-TIME RETAINERS FOR POLITICAL LEADERS
(24) RULER GRANTS AUDIENCES
(23) FULL-TIME CRAFT SPECIALISTS
(23) ADMINISTRATIVE HIERARCHY
(22) SPECIAL DEFERENCE TO POLITICAL LEADER
(21) POLITICAL LEADER APPOINTS OFFICIALS
(21) RULER BESTOWS LAND, SLAVES, OR RANK
(20) CORVÉE
(19) TAXATION IN KIND
(15) TOWNS OF 2,000 OR MORE
(15) MILITARY CONSCRIPTION
(15) STATE CHURCH EMPLOYS ARTISANS
(15) MARKETS
(11) ROYAL COURT
(11) ROYAL TREASURY
(11) SUMPTUARY LAWS
(9) MONARCHY
(9) STATE INSPECTORS
(8) STATE REGULATION OF COMMERCE
(8) CENSUS TAKEN
(8) CALENDRICAL SYSTEM
(8) CODE OF LAWS
(8) MONUMENTAL STONE ARCHITECTURE
(8) THREE OR MORE LEVELS OF TERRITORIAL ADMINISTRATION
(8) FULL-TIME PAINTERS OR SCULPTORS
(8) FULL-TIME ARCHITECTS OR ENGINEERS
(7) CITY OF 10,000 OR MORE
(7) ARCH USED IN CONSTRUCTION
(6) PAPERMAKING
(6) SEDENTARY MERCHANTS
(6) CITY OF 100,000 OR MORE
(6) TOWNS OF 100 OR MORE
(6) EMPIRE
(6) TWO OR MORE CITIES
(3) TEMPLE EXACTS TITHES

Carneiro is concerned with a large-scale view of the evolution of societies; but rather than classify societies into stages such as bands, tribes, chiefdoms, and states, he orders them in terms of population size. When various kinds of behaviors are tallied for each society, the result seems to be, rather than a set of separate stages, a steady accumulation of traits with increase in population (FIGURE 3-9).

Both the stage model and Carneiro's *accumulation model* claim to describe the evolution of human adaptive systems. These models, however, are based on the behaviors of living or recently extinct societies. A developmental sequence has not been demonstrated conclusively. Instead, both models provide hypotheses to be tested against the record of past human societies. Only archaeologists have access to the evidence of what actually occurred.

In Summary   Archaeology studies all the societies that have inhabited this planet. It particularly concentrates on the long sequences, such as that recorded for the Tehuacán Valley, that show change at work from earliest prehistoric times to the present.

In order to use these sequences for testing models of change, archaeologists need to reconstruct the behaviors of extinct societies. To reconstruct stages, behavioral components, and even the smallest activities, archaeologists must, like Sherlock Holmes, draw inferences from mute artifacts. But how can population size be estimated from floor space? Or social inequality from garbage? Or specialized jobs from manufacturing debris? These are the mysteries with which archaeologists grapple. Solving them depends in large part on understanding how behavior is related to artifacts, the topic of Chapter 4.

James Deetz (b. 1930)   In the late 1950s, long before most archaeologists had even heard of computers, Jim Deetz had seen their possibilities for use in archaeology. There were very few computers at that time and access to them was difficult, which accounts for the many tales still abroad of Deetz's ingenuity in gaining entrance to the MIT computer center.   □   Deetz employed the computer to examine stylistic changes through time in pottery from Arikara Indian villages in South Dakota. In a study that earned him a Harvard Ph.D., Deetz used stylistic changes to document some ways in which the introduction of the horse to the Arikara area in the mid-1700s created new subsistence opportunities, marriage patterns, and living arrangements.   □   His next major project, an excavation at La Purísima Mission in southern California, also focused on the impact of Europeans on Native Americans. An analysis of everyday artifacts showed that, under the domination of the mission system, traditional men's activities were changed far more than those of women.   □   In the mid-1960s, Deetz and his colleague Edwin Dethlefsen began cataloguing headstones in historic graveyards in the vicinity of Boston. The goal of their study was to evaluate several archaeological hypotheses about patterns in stylistic change. The headstones were perfect for their purpose because designs were commonly associated with a date (FIGURE 4-19). Designs and inscriptions—some quite poetic—were also studied to identify changes in popular attitudes toward religion and death.   □   These projects established Deetz as one of the foremost historical archaeologists in America. During the 1970s he spent most of his time studying the American Colonial period at Plimoth Plantation, a partially restored settlement. He dug and he engaged volunteers in experiments in colonial living. Today, he is back in California and working on a project to capture the way of life in a historic coal-mining town.   □   Deetz is best known for his two popular books, *Invitation to Archaeology* and *In Small Things Forgotten,* both of which clearly show the way Deetz, perhaps more than anyone in archaeology, has added a human touch to the study of artifacts. Among archaeologists, Deetz is also renowned for his lecturing style, his banjo picking, and his nine children.

James Deetz, archaeologist
and banjo picker.

4

ARTIFACTS AND BEHAVIOR

In the long sweep of cultural evolution, human adaptations have been characterized by an uncompromising reliance on artifacts. The first crude pebble tools, which differ hardly at all from the tools used by chimpanzees and sea otters, were used to butcher animals. From this unpretentious start, the functions of artifacts have expanded relentlessly. In addition to the basic uses of providing food, clothing, and shelter, artifacts have come to allow us to communicate over long distances, travel to other planets, and even replace our body parts. Beyond these technological functions, artifacts form a vast network of symbols that tell us about social standing and sexual availability, give cues to accepted behavior in places such as churches and supermarkets, and embody individual and group self-images—the way we see ourselves and our society. Today, life without artifacts is inconceivable.

The most obvious source of information about all societies, past and present, is written records; however, only a few societies have left behind such documents. Even when written evidence is available, it does not tell us everything we want to know. Most available documents tend to record only a limited range of political, economic, and military events and deal mainly with leaders and an upper class—with the distortions of the facts that this often entails.

Luckily for the archaeologist, written documents are only one kind of artifact. Every society has left a material record of its existence that is a product of the activities of the majority of people, as well as of their leaders. Like documents, this material record is also biased, but toward what people actually did rather than what a few said or thought. Thus, every archaeologist studies artifacts and, while some collections of artifacts include documents, most do not.

Archaeologists study artifacts for evidence from which to make inferences about behavior. For archaeologists, evidence is observable *traces,* which are all the characteristics of artifacts that can be described. When a bicycle crosses a dirt field, the track it leaves is a trace of its passage. The gouged surface of a cutting board holds the traces of innumerable cutting and chopping acts. The arrangement of chairs in a classroom is a trace of the activities that go on there.

Artifacts and inference are tied together by general principles that identify specific traces and the types of behavior that created them. This chapter discusses some of the principles that describe the effects of behavior on artifacts in adaptive systems. It defines the major kinds of variability in artifacts and the way the functions of artifacts affect that variability. Next, the influence of social organization and of ideology on artifacts is described. The last section discusses behavior and material items in relation to the developmental cycles of individuals, of social units, and of artifacts themselves. As a whole, this chapter summarizes the role of artifacts in societies so that, with this knowledge, we can use artifacts to understand human behavior better.

DIMENSIONS OF ARTIFACT VARIABILITY

Archaeologists recognize four dimensions of variability in artifacts. The first dimension is *form,* the physical properties of artifacts. In describing formal characteristics, archaeologists measure *attributes,* such as size, shape, weight, color, texture and other surface treatments (including painted designs), plasticity and elasticity, composition, and arrangement of parts. Within the *formal dimension,* artifacts are distinguished by differences and similarities among these attributes. In this process, items are grouped on the basis of shared formal attributes to create *artifact types* (Chapter 8)—for example, kitchen sinks, bathroom sinks, and wet bar sinks.

The second dimension of variability is *spatial*—the exact location of artifacts. It is convenient to discuss location in terms of the position of objects within activity areas (such as where sinks are positioned in a dwelling), activity areas within settlements, settlements within regions, and the proximity of settlements to environmental features, such as rivers and arable land.

Once an object's formal properties have been defined and it has been located in space, the *frequency dimension,* or the number of occurrences of a particular kind of object, such as sinks in a dwelling, is described.

The fourth, and in some ways the most important, dimension is *relational*—descriptions of *associated* artifacts. Thus, some sinks are associated with hand soap, toilets, and towels; some with dishwashing detergent, dish towels, and steel-wool soap pads; and others with hard liquor, ice buckets, and cocktail mixers. Associations in archaeological sites can be caused by many factors, including the use of different artifacts together in activities; Chapters 5 and 6 describe other causes for association.

Archaeologists have neither the time nor the need to study every trace on every artifact within the four dimensions of variability. Choice of specific attributes depends on the specific questions asked about human behavior. If we were interested in the mass production of sinks, we would select a particular community (spatial dimension) and describe artifacts in terms of material composition, the arrangement of parts, and any mold or casting marks on the surface (formal dimension). If we were interested in differences in the social standing of families, we would look at attributes such as the material out of which the sink is made (formal dimension) and the number of sinks within houses (frequency dimension). We would also want to know how sinks were used, and an examination of the plumbing would give a general idea that sinks are used to control the flow of two fluids. As other artifacts associated with sinks—such as detergents, towels, and toothbrushes (relational dimension)—were examined, more specific inferences would be made.

But how does one decide what attributes to examine? This is one of the most fundamental questions in archaeology. To answer it, archaeologists must know what kinds of behaviors create what kinds of material traces. In our sink example, when we wanted to know about social standing, we assumed—from our knowledge of existing societies—that the quality of the materials making up the sink (and even the number of sinks in a dwelling) could be a good index of the owner's social standing. Knowing the basic principles of variability in artifacts makes archaeological inferences about behavior possible.

EFFECTS OF FUNCTION

The functions that artifacts are designed to perform affect all of their dimensions of variability. Objects may carry out one or more functions in a society's technology (*techno-function*), a society's social organization (*socio-function*), and a society's ideology (*ideo-function*).

Techno-functions include extracting, processing, and storing resources, maintaining technology, and fulfilling the biological needs of people. A scythe, a hammer, a blast furnace, slacks, and a dormitory all have techno-functions. Artifacts with socio-functions symbolically influence social interactions: uniforms and insignia identify special roles, jewelry communicates social standing, and walls and partitions divide up social space. Artifacts with ideo-functions symbolize ideology: sacred paraphernalia represent religious beliefs, bumper stickers express opinions, and novels, paintings, and films present widely shared views of reality.

Most artifacts perform more than one function, and each function influences at least some of their attributes. The techno-function of chairs is to support the bottom and back of a seated person. To carry out this job, most chairs have four legs, a seat, and a back. Some chairs and chair-like objects have additional techno-functions: dentist's chairs, wheelchairs, and toilets have certain forms because of the specialized activities they help carry out. Chairs also have socio-functions. In some cases, they can express social standing. Today we can buy anything from low-cost, molded plastic chairs

FIGURE **4-1**   Chairs that express a broad range of techno-, socio-, and ideo-functions: plastic and metal dinette chair, chrome and leather Barcelona chair, old rocking chair, modern Naugahyde lazy-boy chair, Chippendale chair, and throne.

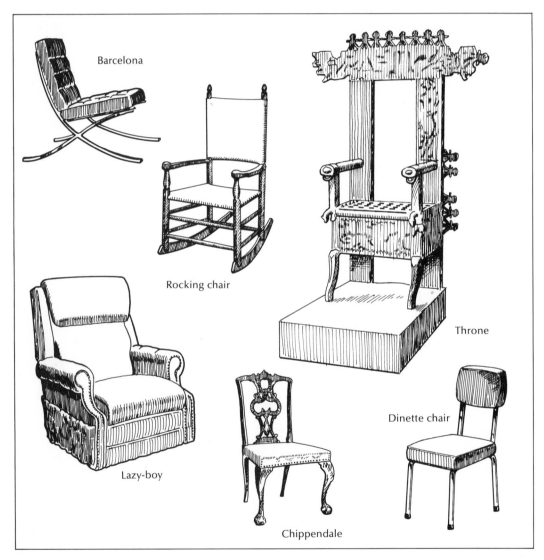

and folding metal chairs to valuable Chippendale and Barcelona chairs (FIGURE 4-1). This variety can express the range of social classes in our society. Chairs may have ideo-functions as well: the chair that the Pope sits on during ceremonies at St. Peter's in Rome does more than hold up the Pope; it is a symbol of the Pope's position relative to God and the entire hierarchy of the Catholic church.

The techno-functions of objects can influence more than the formal dimension of variability. For example, the distribution of chairs in a house—their spatial dimension—is determined by the activities performed in different rooms. The number of chairs in a room, reflecting the size of the social unit, involves the frequency dimension. The items associated with chairs, also determined by the activities performed, affect the relational dimension. Socio-function and ideo-function also influence these dimensions; for example, the chair at the head of a dining-room table (spatial and relational dimensions) denotes the social role of head of household.

Because it is often difficult to distinguish between socio-function and ideo-function, both are frequently lumped under the heading *stylistic* variability. Style is then one of two categories, with *utility* (techno-function) the other. Thus, archaeologists are apt to ask, given a set of material objects: What attributes are utilitarian and what attributes are stylistic?

The causes of variability are not always clear-cut; even the most eminent archaeologists can disagree. One closely watched debate was between Lewis Binford and François Bordes. At the center of the maelstrom were Mousterian tools, the chipped stones made by Neanderthal populations from about 100,000 to 40,000 B.P., and found throughout Europe and western Asia (FIGURE 4-2). On the basis of form, Bordes had defined some sixty types of Mousterian stone tools. Curiously, however, individual sites, and even levels within sites, often contain different combinations and frequencies of these tools. Binford argued that this variability is the result of techno-function, a product of different activities. He proposed, for example, that a Neanderthal would use one *tool kit* (a set of tools used together) to butcher a horse, and a different tool kit to scrape hides. Thus, the variability in tools would be due to differences in activities at different sites.

Bordes countered that activities were probably much the same from site to site and that the variability in stone tools was caused by socio-function, different types identifying different Mousterian tribes. Thus, two distinct Mousterian tribes might well have used different tool kits to butcher a horse, while within a tribe the same tool kit might be used to both butcher horses and scrape hides. In such a case, stylistic preference rather than the nature of specific activities would be said to determine which tools made up a kit.

At our present level of understanding, we cannot say that either Binford or Bordes is right. In fact, the authors of this book do not agree on an answer. Much remains to be learned through experimentation, ethnoarchaeology, and careful excavations, before this controversy is resolved.

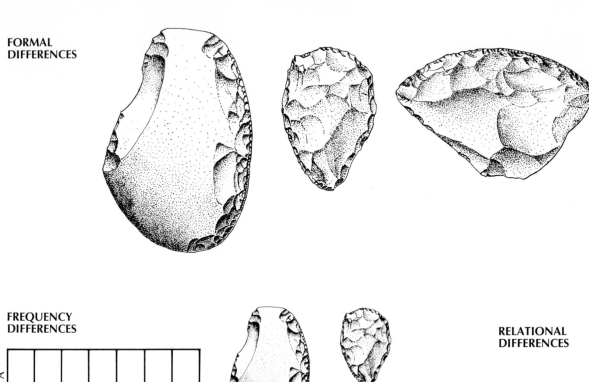

**FORMAL
DIFFERENCES**

**FREQUENCY
DIFFERENCES**

**RELATIONAL
DIFFERENCES**

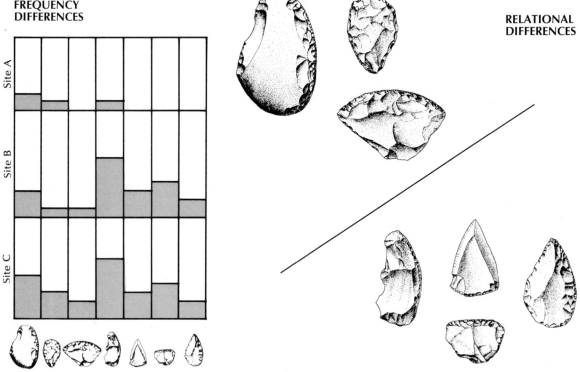

FIGURE **4-2**   Dimensions of artifact variability illustrated by Mousterian tool types. Formal differences are represented by variations in shape and size, relational differences by the dissimilarity of artifact types found together, and frequency differences by the distribution of the tool types (bar graphs) among three sites.

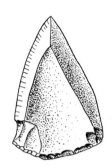

Stylistic Elements

Presented with a painted prehistoric pot of American origin, an archaeologist of the Southwest will be able to supply it with a name, say "Pinedale Black-on-white," the time of manufacture and use, "A.D. 1250–1350," and where it is found, "in the mountainous country of east-central Arizona" (FIGURE 4-3). Presented with a pot made by a modern Pueblo Indian, the same archaeologist could probably tell in which village it was made, and might even be able to name the potter. If you could assemble a sample of archaeologists familiar with the artifacts of the world, most items, especially those having socio-functions and ideo-functions, could be similarly identified. All such identifications are possible because styles vary from place to place and through time. In the following section, we will explore the general characteristics of stylistic variability, which are the basis of our ability to make these identifications.

FIGURE **4-3**

Example of a Southwestern pottery type—"Pinedale Black-on-white" (A.D. 1250–1350)—which was most common in east-central Arizona.

Individual Style

The most basic source of stylistic variability in artifacts is the individual style of a craftsman. Art experts have long been able to identify the works of great masters by studying brush strokes and other aspects of *individual style.* Similarly, archaeologists who study classical Greece and Rome can attribute sculptures to specific masters. Graphologists are able to identify individuals by distinctive features of their handwriting. It is possible to generalize the idea that underlies all of these examples: designs executed by individual artisans will, to some degree, be distinctive because of differences in their motor skills and personal preferences. For archaeologists the important issue is how this principle of individual style applies to such mundane artifacts as chipped stone and pottery.

Archaeologist James Hill conducted an experiment to confront this issue. He had five local potters in Tijuana, Mexico, copy as closely as they could the same painted design, composed of a number of *design elements* such as flowers and wavy lines. He broke the seventy-five resulting pots into *potsherds* and then recorded the design elements of each potsherd, describing minute stylistic attributes such as the width of a line. Next, a computer analysis was used to compare the potsherds in terms of these attributes. The results clearly segregated the work of specific individuals (FIGURE 4-4).

Similar kinds of studies that have been done on basketry, intricate chipped-stone artifacts, and other types of pottery provide additional support for the uniqueness of individual creations. Direct archaeological applications, however, are still at preliminary stages. Wesley Jernigan, for example, believes he can identify several pots from the Grasshopper Ruin in Arizona as having been painted by the same artist. The attributes Jernigan uses include the shape of the pot, the base color, the layout of the design, and the details of painting. As more archaeologists attempt such studies, anonymous individuals will begin to leave their mark on history through their artifacts.

Styles can also be used to identify groups. Three basic principles explain stylistic variability above the level of the individual. Similarities in style are usually produced when artisans are trained in a particular tradition that is passed on by personal contact from generation to generation, from mother to daughter, or from master to apprentice. This observation leads to the first principle of style: stylistic similarity varies directly with the amount of social interaction and communication among craftsmen. Thus, artisans in the same shop produce designs that are more similar than artisans in different shops. Cultural geographers have formulated a second principle relevant to the study of style—the *gravity model,* which attempts to describe the amount of social interaction between two settlements. According to this model, social interaction increases with increases in population of one or both settlements and decreases with the distance between them. This principle, modeled after Newton's law of gravity, adequately describes major patterns of social interaction at a regional scale, but tends to oversimplify reality; in order to make accurate predictions about social interaction, variations in transport and communication technology—as well as environ-

FIGURE **4-4**

Pots painted by different
artists in Tijuana, Mexico,
as part of James Hill's
experimental study.
Though both artists
copied the same design,
differences in execution
can readily be seen.

mental features such as oceans, deserts, and mountain ranges—must be taken into account. As a result of all of these factors, for example, social interaction may be greater between New York City and Los Angeles—thousands of miles apart—than between New York City and, say, Binghamton, New York.

Effects of Function ◻ **71**

According to a third principle, for any given type of behavioral component, there is more social interaction within units than between them. For example, the members of a work group interact more frequently with each other than they do with workers not part of their group. The same is usually true for the members of a community. As with the gravity model, there are many exceptions to this pattern. Nevertheless, both models describe general tendencies of social interaction.

When these three principles involving stylistic variability, social interaction, distance, and behavioral components are taken together, we obtain a number of expectations for the spatial distribution of stylistic variability and its relation to behavioral components. These expectations constitute a *sociological model of style.* Underlying the model is the idea that stylistic similarities should be high within behavioral components where social interaction is frequent, and should decrease with distance between behavioral components as social interaction falls off (FIGURE 4-5).

Parts of the sociological model of style are now being tested by ethnoarchaeologists, such as William Longacre. Longacre spent a year in a Kalinga village in the remote, rice-farming highlands of Northern Luzon in the Philippines. During this time he photographed and described 1,000 pots made by the female potters in Dangtalan and neighboring villages. Longacre reasoned that the pots of people who have the same *learning frameworks* and who work together would resemble one another in style. Thus, he believed that if art experts can talk about the Flemish School of painters, he would be able to discern "schools" of Kalinga potters in Dangtalan, perhaps at the level of households or task groups.

On the basis of their research, Longacre and his colleague Michael Graves described a hierarchical structure of style. First, they discovered that Kalinga themselves could tell who made a particular pot. Next, using statistical analyses of minute stylistic attributes they determined that the pots made by women who were close kin showed stylistic similarities. In addition, Longacre found that even without statistical analysis, he was able to distinguish Dangtalan pottery from that made in other Kalinga communities. At a more general level, the Kalinga, as an ethnic group, produce a distinct pottery that differs from the pottery of other ethnic groups in the Phil-

FIGURE **4-5** Southwestern pueblo pots illustrate the sociological model of style, in which stylistic differences become greater as social interaction between potters decreases from family/individuals through regional systems. Here pots made by three generations of the Nampeyo family of the Hopi exhibit individual styles and many shared features. Pots made by other Hopi work groups exhibit greater variability but, with the Nampeyo pots, are recognizably Hopi. Vessels made in different pueblos are clearly distinguishable as shown by the illustrated pots from Acoma, Zuni, and Laguna—other Southwestern Pueblos, which also have their own pottery traditions. At the level of regional systems, variability is more evident, and few similarities are to be found among pueblo pots (Western Pueblo), Tarascan pots (Mexico), and those of modern Anglo-American potters.

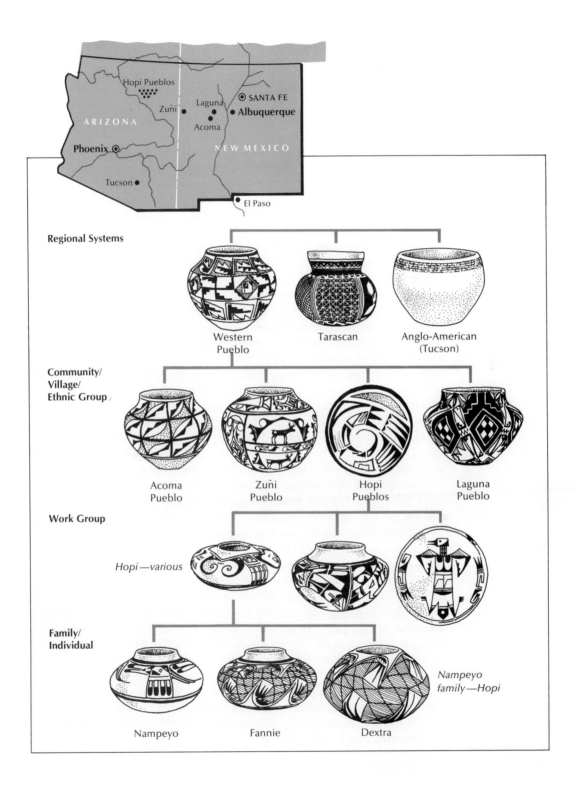

Regional Systems

Western Pueblo

Tarascan

Anglo-American (Tucson)

Community/ Village/ Ethnic Group

Acoma Pueblo

Zuñi Pueblo

Hopi Pueblos

Laguna Pueblo

Work Group

Hopi—various

Family/ Individual

Nampeyo family—Hopi

Nampeyo

Fannie

Dextra

ippines. Similar ethnoarchaeological studies of stylistic variability within and between communities are occurring throughout the world and also support the sociological model of style.

Stylistic boundaries often parallel the boundaries of social units above the community level—such as tribes, chiefdoms, ethnic groups within states, and states themselves. Thus, it should come as no surprise that archaeologists can distinguish the pottery of Filipino tribes from that of Southwestern Pueblo Indians or East Africans.

Disturbance
Patterns

A neat hierarchical pattern of style is not always found. Indeed, the reader has probably thought of exceptions to these patterns already, factors that may disturb the spatial distributions of styles. In order for this model to apply, it must deal with the production of items made largely by hand and for domestic use. Migration, trade, and mass production alter the simple picture of variability that the sociological model furnishes.

MOVEMENT OF PEOPLE   The most common types of disturbance of distribution involve the movement of people and the movement of goods. People move by way of a variety of factors, among the most prevalent being exogamy (marrying out of the group) and migration. High levels of exogamy will create larger-than-expected *style zones,* areas of stylistic similarity, by continually shuffling artisans among the communities of a region. The main cause of exogamy is community size: the smaller the community, the more often people marry out. Thus, small and highly mobile bands are usually characterized by extensive style zones, with little tendency toward differences (in artifacts) that are related to community or ethnicity. Very small farming villages are also exogamous and participate in widespread style zones. During the earliest period when pottery was adopted in the Southwest, major design similarities were shared by small communities spread over a large area. In contrast, large, self-sufficient farming settlements offer more possibilities for *endogamy* (marrying within a community) and, consequently, for the emergence of highly distinctive community styles.

Migration is another form of population movement that affects the spatial character of style. Immigrants bring with them material possessions and patterns of behavior from their former communities. Many factors influence whether or not and how long immigrant enclaves remain distinctive in their artifacts. One factor is the nature of the migration and conditions of life. English colonists who settled on the eastern seaboard brought large quantities of European goods, which intruded upon Native American style zones; in contrast, black African slaves, lucky to arrive with their lives, were forced to use mainly colonial American artifacts.

Other factors in the perseverance of immigrant styles are the attitudes and beliefs of the newcomers. At one extreme are recent European immigrants to the United States, who often consciously embrace the American style of life and its material elaborations. At the other extreme are Shaker communities, which actively resist change and integration into the larger society to the point that they make their own distinctive artifacts. Between these extremes one finds immigrant groups that maintain some behavior patterns while losing others. A further factor in maintaining ethnic distinctiveness is whether immigrants continue contact with their home areas. The introduction of new immigrants as wives and husbands and the continual flow of nonlocal commodities obtained through traders and merchants are further sources of stylistic differences. Some disruption to style zones will be caused by any migration; for example, historical archaeologist Leland Ferguson has discovered similarities between pottery made on slave plantations and ceramics from West Africa.

Archaeologists are now studying how population movements affect style zones. In Arizona, the Tucson Urban Renewal Project, under historical archaeologist James Ayres, has identified the archaeological remains of large numbers of Chinese who arrived in Tucson in the late 1800s to work on the railroad. Two kinds of artifacts set the Chinese apart from other contemporary Tucsonans. The most obvious kind consisted of such items as Chinese coins, opium-smoking paraphernalia, Chinese porcelain, and other household goods manufactured in China. Some of these items were rapidly replaced by American materials, the most interesting substitution being in opium paraphernalia, where Coca-Cola bottles and parts of kerosene lamps replaced traditional pipes.

The second type of material marker of ethnicity, much more subtle and long-lasting, includes the artifacts of traditional Chinese behaviors that persisted in mundane household activities such as meal preparation. John Clonts studied the bone remains in household garbage to identify types of animals consumed for food and styles of butchering. To test the hypothesis that the variability he found might be related to ethnicity, Clonts studied traditional Chinese food preparation activities and historic maps and census data that identified owners of houses at specific points in time. All the evidence pointed to the existence of a Chinese immigrant group that lived in an ethnic enclave, consumed primarily pork, and followed traditional Chinese butchering practices. Today, although Tucson's Chinese ethnic group no longer lives in an enclave and shares little in the way of activities, it can still be identified in terms of artifacts. While some of the distinctive food preparation behaviors have been replaced, many still persist and are reflected in stores that sell only specialized oriental foods and in household garbage. This example suggests an intriguing hypothesis: that when most other trappings of ethnicity have disappeared, food preferences usually remain.

MOVEMENT OF GOODS   Other disturbances are caused by trade, which moves goods produced in one style zone into other style zones. Different types of trade create different disturbance patterns. Archaeologists are now mapping distributions of goods in order to identify specific types of trade. One study contrasts trade between individuals with trade largely in the hands of specialist merchants.

In the case of trade between individuals, distribution frequencies of

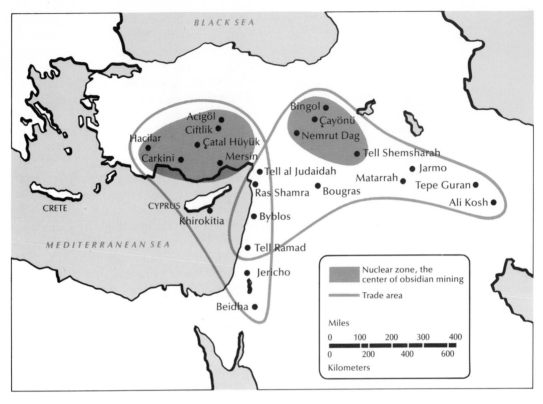

FIGURE **4-6**   Obsidian distribution patterns in the Near East. Within each of the designated distribution areas the quantity of obsidian at sites decreases as their distance from the source increases.

items would tend to decrease with distance from manufacturing locations. Colin Renfrew has documented this *gradient,* or gradual fall-off pattern, for the trade of obsidian among early farming villages in the Near East (FIGURE 4-6). In the case of specialized merchant and trade organizations, the gradient pattern is broken. Archaeologists are now examining the hypothesis that the quantities in which some goods are distributed vary with the size of the markets and the boundaries of regional systems, not with the distance over which goods must be moved by individuals. This can be illustrated with the trade goods from three large Mesoamerican sites that reached peak populations at about the same time, between A.D. 600 and 750. The Maya site of Tikal, in Guatemala, is more than 1,000 kilometers from the central Mexican site of Teotihuacán; nevertheless, the tombs of the lords of Tikal contain large quantities of Teotihuacán pottery, though little is found in the intervening areas. The Mexican site of Monte Alban is in this pathway, only 400 kilometers from Teotihuacán, and at its height had a population greater than Tikal. Yet few Teotihuacán pots have been found at Monte Alban

(FIGURE 4-7), illustrating the erratic effects of merchant trade. Similar leap-frog patterns are readily illustrated by the distribution of American, Russian, and Chinese arms among third-world countries.

MEANS OF PRODUCTION   Mass production also greatly affects style distributions. Artifacts are manufactured in two ways, by *unit production* and by *mass production*. In unit production, a craftsman sees the artifact through from start to finish; in mass production, individuals specialize in specific activities in the production process. Unit production results in considerable variability from item to item; stained-glass windows are examples.

One of the principal objectives of mass production is to decrease manufacturing costs. This is generally accomplished by strict division of labor, standardization of parts, and simplification of activities. As a result, variety within kinds of objects is minimized and variability within batches of items is considerably reduced. Whether in the place of manufacture or in areas where products are traded, mass production has the effect of decreasing local variability in style.

Mass production can, however, also be designed to express local stylistic preferences. For example, most of the Postclassic Maya *incensarios*, or incense burners, were assembled from components made in molds. Although a mold is a mass-production device, even a modest variety of components made it possible to create a wide range of finished incense burners to suit many tastes. Thus, this form of mass production creates variability

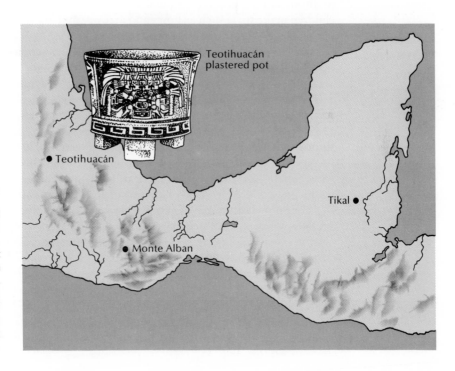

FIGURE **4-7**

Teotihuacán pottery and mercantile trade in ancient Mesoamerica. Trade items made at Teotihuacán are found in quantity at distant sites, such as Tikal, suggesting the existence of specialized traders who could leap-frog intermediate areas.

in style and counteracts the tendency of other forms of mass production to produce widespread uniformity.

EFFECT OF DEVELOPMENTAL CYCLES

All forms of matter—ourselves, our artifacts, even our universe—have definable stages of existence. Individuals grow through childhood, adolescence, adulthood, and old age; artifacts are made, used, and discarded; civilizations rise and fall; and the universe, in the prevalent view, passes through phases of expansion and contraction. As a result, adaptive systems, seen as combinations of entities—individuals, behavioral components and artifacts—can also be regarded as passing through developmental cycles. Thus, to the utilitarian and stylistic causes of variability in the material remains of adaptive systems we can add the influence of developmental change.

Role of Individuals

At the individual level, the main origins of variability in artifacts are sex, growth, and changes in roles and social standing. Age, a major source of variability, can be divided into two components: biological development and social-role development. Most societies have special paraphernalia for the newborn; in simpler societies cradle boards are common, while in our own the list of items, from pacifiers to cribs, is endless. A large number of the artifacts used by infants and adolescents, especially models and toys, are a part of the process of *enculturation*, the learning of basic skills needed to perform adult roles. Even within the most materially impoverished societies, children make toys, such as bows and arrows, that are scaled-down versions of adult tools, used to mimic productive activities.

At the other end of the scale, most of the artifacts for older people in our society—such as false teeth, pacemakers, and canes—compensate for deteriorating bodily functions. While middle age is typified by the acquisition of artifacts, the rates decrease as those growing older participate in fewer activities.

Between the extremes of childhood and old age, adults usually pass through a series of social roles. Variability in artifacts is influenced by both the specific physical tasks or techno-functions and the social standing or socio-functions of these roles. Obviously, the more social roles in a society, the greater the proliferation of utilitarian and stylistic variability in artifacts.

An important source of variability in social roles and related artifacts is sex. Many artifact differences, such as in clothing and the use of cosmetics, are for visual displays in social situations. Others are associated with specific forms of work and relaxation. Although sex-role differences in work and play are becoming somewhat blurred in our society, in most other societies sex differences are still rigidly maintained in artifacts and recognized throughout the life cycle.

Every society recognizes certain mileposts that combine both growth and social roles, and some of these—birth, puberty, marriage, death—

assume near universality. These mileposts are marked by ceremonial occasions called *rites of passage* and usually involve a set of prescribed ritual objects. Beyond the most basic rites of passage, the nature and number of these mileposts in a society is dependent on the variety of social units in which individuals participate.

Artifacts figure prominently in rite-of-passage ceremonies in four ways. First, there are the specific symbols of the ceremony, most of which are primarily ideo-functional, such as the cap and gown at graduations. Second, many ceremonies include items the individual will use in his or her new role. Among Jews, for example, a male first wears the prayer shawl (*tallit*) at his bar-mitzvah and continues to wear it on ritual occasions thereafter. Third, many ceremonies include the giving of gifts or other transfers of artifacts between social units. In our society, for example, wedding gifts are given to a couple by friends and relatives. In some societies, large quantities of goods will be exchanged between the social units of the marrying couple. For example, among African pastoralists a *bride price* is paid in cattle by the groom's family to the bride's. Fourth, the area where the ceremony takes place may consist of specialized facilities and artifacts used extensively or exclusively for that purpose.

The rite of passage of most interest to archaeologists is the disposal of the dead, in which artifacts are often left in association with human remains, including the specialized items used in preparing the corpse for disposal. Societies also use a number of ways to dispose of a dead person's possessions. These objects may be divided among the heirs, apportioned to the state, buried with the body, or even destroyed in public view. (For a fuller discussion of burial practices see Chapters 5 and 8.)

Role of Behavioral Components

Behavioral components—households, task groups, communities, and even regional systems—also go through developmental cycles. The artifacts of a behavioral component are determined by five factors. First is the behavioral component's stage in its developmental cycle, which is a product of the component's activities and the age and sex of the members of the social unit. Second is the rate of growth of the behavioral component; some are stable relative to others, which expand or collapse rapidly. The last three factors are: the wealth of the component, the social standing of the social unit, and how often the behavioral component moves its location. American households provide an example in which these factors all have a role.

Households go through developmental cycles which relate to stages of families. The first stage is one of setting up housekeeping and acquiring basic necessities, usually including a dwelling. Many of the setting-up artifacts are wedding gifts, dowries, and hand-me-downs. The second stage, child raising, is ushered in by the arrival of children and child-care paraphernalia. By this time the household may occupy a larger dwelling to accommodate its greater number of activities and artifacts. The third stage, maturity, occurs when the children become adolescents. During maturity, the household often achieves its peak income and wealth, as the productive members of the household achieve their greatest social standing. The acquisition of artifacts continues, with a strong emphasis on socio-functions. The final stage, old age, is often signaled by the formation of independent households by the grown children. This produces a contraction in the activities of the parents and a corresponding decrease in their need for artifacts. Households in this stage may occupy mobile homes or condominiums. Although the techno-functional requirements decrease, the socio- and ideo-functional reasons for artifacts, especially in the form of mementos, may not.

Differences in the emphasis on artifacts in this developmental cycle are created in a variety of ways. Variations in social standing produce enormous differences in the artifacts among households. These differences are clearest in the socio-functional artifacts during all stages. Upper-class households will, even in the setting-up phase, possess more items altogether and more items with important socio-functions. Another factor creating variability is how frequently the household moves. The more often a household changes its place of residence, the fewer its possessions. Thus, among hunters and gatherers who are constantly moving and who have few artifacts to begin with, the changes from one stage to another may be almost imperceptible. In contrast, in industrial states, there is a wide range of products designed especially for particular stages.

For various reasons, there are households in every society that do not raise children. These households go through stages that involve changes in social standing, income, and activities, but the stages are much less distinct. Small task groups and special-purpose households—such as dormitories, nursing homes, and communes—are different from family households because their activities do not change; in such behavioral components, the artifacts change less over time.

Archaeologists have observed a number of patterns in the way communities develop. Rick Ahlstrom and Jeff Dean believe that as communities age there is an increase in the scavenging and reuse of building materials. This hypothesis is based on a careful study of dated roof beams from the Hopi pueblo of Walpi. The community of Walpi was founded in its present location about A.D. 1680. During its existence, the pueblo inhabitants reused more and more roof beams from abandoned rooms in their new construction.

Complex societies do not stand still; they grow or decline. According to Jane Jacobs' economic model, communities grow as long as they consistently develop local task groups that manufacture products that replace imports and even become new exports. Thus, over the long term, the economic health of a community can be measured by changes in the ratio of imports to exports. The original thirteen colonies of the United States are an example. Such colonies are special-purpose communities. They begin by extracting local raw materials, exporting them to a "mother country," and purchasing the resulting manufactured commodities. As colonies grow, they

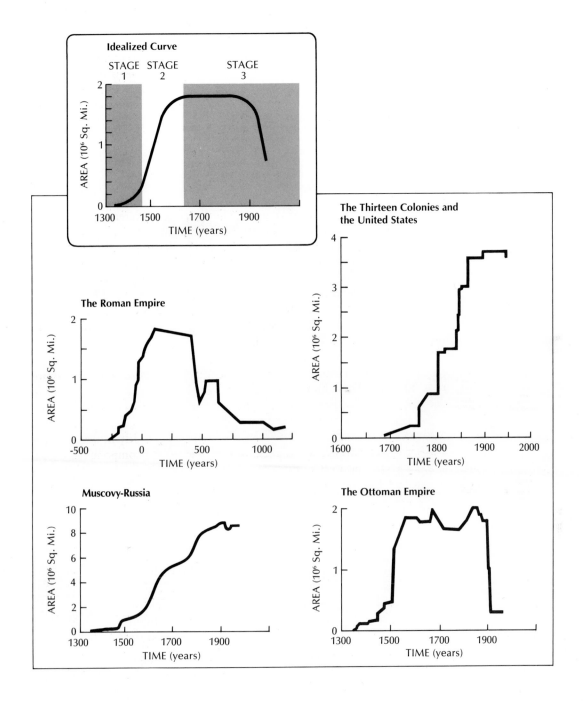

FIGURE **4-8**   The growth curves of various empires show a strong similarity—with a rapid increase in the amount of territory controlled, stabilization for a short period, and then collapse.

FIGURE **4-9**   Artifacts of empire: a British tea service imported to the United States during the
Colonial period. Through time, fewer silver pieces were imported as local
silversmiths, like Paul Revere, competed in Colonial markets.

develop their own local manufacturing capabilities. The finished products of
the colonies are sold in local markets and in other markets in competition
with the finished products of the mother country. Thus, the economic health
of the thirteen colonies improved as they replaced imports and added exports. The economic health of Great Britain declined as she sold fewer products to the colonies and imported more of their manufactures.

As this example illustrates, the import/export developmental pattern is
visible in regional systems and empires. Rein Taagapera has described the
basic form of the growth of empires (measured by the area of land controlled) as a logistic curve. This type of curve has three subdivisions: rapid
expansion followed by some period of *maintenance* or stability and then
rapid *collapse* (FIGURE 4-8). This pattern is clearly reflected in artifacts. The

growth stage of empires is marked by the spread of their artifacts (FIGURE 4-9). The manufactured goods of the British East India Company; the coins, bricks, mosaics, and architectural styles of the Romans; and the majolica pottery and church architecture of the Spanish conquistadores are obvious examples. During the maintenance period, local commodities and styles emerge as distinctive from "empire" styles. By the time of collapse, local

FIGURE **4-10**   The rank-size rule is illustrated here by Roman-British walled towns in southern England. Note the larger number of walled towns (small filled circles) and cantonal capitals (large circles) relative to the number of sizable administrative centers (dot and circle). White arcs indicate regularity of placement of smaller towns around cantonal capitals.

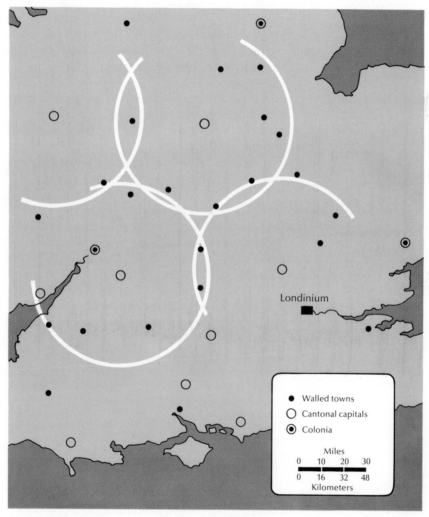

styles have almost completely replaced empire styles. This pattern, like other artifact patterns, is not simply a reflection of the history of an empire. As Jacobs' model suggests, the changing economic conditions of manufacture and trade are at the heart of the developmental cycles of empires.

Empires also have capitals, which are special-purpose settlements full of ideo-functional artifacts symbolizing power and glory. Rome, London, Teotihuacán, Cuzco, and Moscow are examples. Such capitals are at the pinnacle of a hierarchy of settlements based on size and function—cities, towns, agrarian communities, colonies, and others. Cultural geographers are interested in the characteristics of these hierarchies in regional systems and empires and how they change through time. One of their principles, the *rank-size rule,* holds that the larger the settlements, the fewer there are (FIGURE 4-10). Further, a change in the number of settlements of one size will result in a change in the number of settlements of other sizes. Thus, during the growth stage, when small settlements proliferate through colonization, larger settlements and the capital itself will expand. During decline, this trend reverses as the total number of settlements decreases and the number of levels in the settlement hierarchy is reduced.

Roles of Artifacts Themselves

One of the most important sources of variability in material items is the development cycle of artifacts themselves. Artifacts go through a life cycle that is composed of distinct stages. They start as raw materials, which are fashioned into commodities—foods, fuels, tools, symbols. These are consumed, used or even reused, and ultimately lost, discarded, or abandoned. Each stage (FIGURE 4-11) is made up of specific activities.

Procurement

The artifact life cycle begins with *procurement.* Procurement takes place at specialized activity areas known as *extraction loci.* Obsidian quarries, clay pits, coal mines, areas where hunters and gatherers collect plant foods, and the places where game are killed (*kill sites*) are examples. Extraction activities often leave large amounts of debris, usually resulting from some type of preliminary processing or manufacture. Prehistoric hunters often did some butchering at kill sites, leaving behind the unneeded parts of the carcass.

FIGURE **4-11**   The life cycle of a paleo-Indian biface: *A*, chippable stone is obtained at a quarry and flakes are removed with a cobble hammerstone (hard-hammer percussion), leaving useless flakes and worn or broken cobbles; *B*, suitable flakes brought from the quarry to a camp are chipped with an antler hammer (soft-hammer percussion), producing many smaller flakes and debris; *C*, the completed biface is set in a wooden handle or haft, and the resulting knife is used for butchering a bison. (Butchering produces use-wear, *E*, in the form of minute flakes removed from the working edges of the biface.) Next, the dull biface is resharpened by the process (*D*) of retouching, in which an antler flaker is delicately positioned on the edge of the biface and tiny pressure flakes pushed off. In the final stage of its uselife (*E*) the biface, perhaps broken, but more likely worn out from many resharpenings, is discarded.

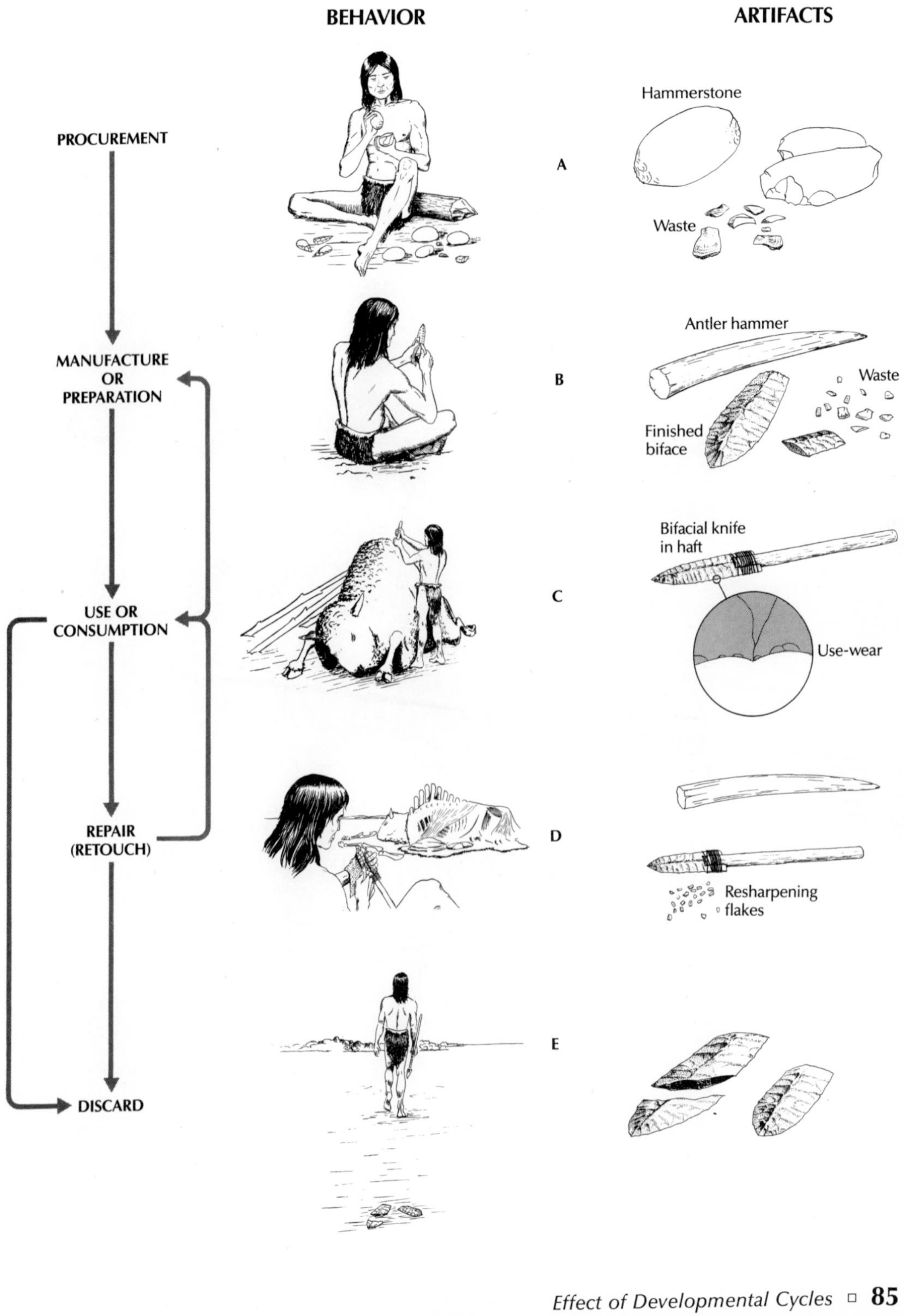

BEHAVIOR ARTIFACTS

PROCUREMENT

MANUFACTURE
OR
PREPARATION

USE OR
CONSUMPTION

REPAIR
(RETOUCH)

DISCARD

A

Hammerstone

Waste

B

Antler hammer

Finished
biface

Waste

C

Bifacial knife
in haft

Use-wear

D

Resharpening
flakes

E

FIGURE **4-12**   The remains of over 100 bison uncovered by archaeologist Joe Ben Wheat at the Olsen-Chubbock kill site. Seven thousand years ago, hunters of the high plains in Colorado stampeded these bison into a ditch from which they could not escape.

Sometimes the quantities of bone are considerable, as at the Olsen-Chubbuck site in Colorado (FIGURE 4-12), where, 7,000 years ago, some one hundred bison were killed and butchered. Generally, the bulkier and less costly the material, the more likely it is that some preliminary manufacturing activities will occur at the extraction locus to reduce the mass to be transported. Of course, transport capabilities can affect this activity. Stone quarries often consist of large mounds of chipping debris, including rejected raw materials and items broken in the earliest stages of manufacture. Modern open-pit mines for copper and coal create large holes, several hundred feet deep, that extend for many acres; they are usually flanked by artificial, flat-top mountains of waste material (FIGURE 4-13). Extraction loci for nonrenewable resources have a limited life expectancy. They are established rapidly and can be just as rapidly abandoned. The mining "ghost towns" that dot the western United States are familiar examples.

Very often tools used in procurement and preliminary processing are left behind at extraction loci and furnish evidence about the nature of these activities. For example, remains of hunting equipment and camps—ancient and modern—can be found throughout the world in prime deer habitats. At stone quarries, hammerstones can be found that were used for testing raw materials and for the first stages of manufacture. Ore-crushing machines are frequently found near abandoned gold mines in California. At prehistoric turquoise mines in the American Southwest, charcoal and discolored rocks suggest that rapid heating and cooling was used to break up the turquoise matrix into manageable pieces for transport.

In studying procurement, one of the first questions is: Where did the raw material originate? Archaeologists usually begin by looking for the places where the raw materials occur naturally. Plants and animals can usually be matched to a particular area. For minerals, chemical and other types of analyses can be used to identify their source. For example, *neutron activation* of obsidian, volcanic glass, can be used to assign individual artifacts to specific volcanic flows.

Manufacture

Manufacture or *preparation* is the next stage in the life cycle of artifacts. Like procurement, it takes place in specialized activity areas, usually in larger settlements. Manufacture changes the physical and/or chemical properties of raw materials. It is during manufacture that stylistic and utilitarian factors are combined into the attributes of finished products. Inferences about manufacture are based on several lines of evidence, including tools and facilities used in manufacturing activities, unused raw materials, waste products, defective items, by-products, and the products themselves.

Manufacturing tool kits are sometimes found intact or in association with raw materials. For example, at many Southwestern pueblo ruins, the items used to make pottery are found on room floors: lumps of clay, pieces of ochre or hematite used as paint, yucca fiber brushes, scrapers cut from gourds or sherds, and pebbles for polishing the surface of a pot.

FIGURE **4-13**   On facing page, at top, a trench excavated through the flint mining and manufacturing site of Colha, Belize, occupied by the Maya until the end of the Classic period; bottom, an open-pit copper mine operating currently in Butte, Montana. The drag-line bucket and truck indicate the enormous scale of the mining.

For many products, waste occurs in abundance and furnishes evidence of manufacture. Workshops that produced stone tools are usually littered with hundreds of thousands of chips, called *debitage*. The formal properties and relative frequencies of debitage indicate specific stages of tool manufacture. *Rejects*, broken or otherwise unsuitable items, like debitage, furnish useful information about the stages of manufacture.

Finished products are also found, although seldom at manufacturing locations. Specific production stages often leave identifiable traces on finished products. For example, certain heating and cooling techniques used in the manufacture of metal objects result in a particular crystalline structure that can be identified by microscopic examination. Various attributes of pots indicate the specific shaping techniques used, such as wheel-made or hand modeled. Sometimes by-products of manufacture furnish clues to activities that may leave no other evidence. For example, a tool made of animal bone is evidence that an animal was butchered. At a village site, that bone tool may be the only trace that remains of the butchering activity.

A great deal of experimental work has produced some principles for inferring specific manufacturing activities. Such experiments aim to simulate the sequence of acts that go into manufacture or preparation. The resulting waste products, defective items, tools used, and finished products are carefully documented and provide a basis for formulating principles that link manufacture activities to traces on artifacts. One experimenter, François Bordes, became an accomplished flint-knapper and learned to replicate ancient chipped-stone tools. The most famous American knapper was Don Crabtree, an ex-postman from Lubbock, Texas, who began chipping stones as a hobby more than forty years ago. He succeeded in re-creating a vast array of tools—from "Aztec" sacrificial knives to "Paleo-Indian" spearpoints. One of Crabtree's most spectacular successes was replication of the long, thin obsidian flakes, known as blades, found at Aztec sites in Mexico. For decades the manufacturing process was the subject of debate. It was clear that the blades were removed from long cylindrical stone *cores,* but how this was done was unknown. There are basically two techniques for removing flakes from cores—*percussion,* in which chips are removed by striking a core with a hammer made of rock or a piece of antler, and *pressure flaking,* in which chips are, in effect, pushed off a core by pressure applied through a tool resting on the core. Percussion flaking could not replicate the long, thin blades, and no one seemed able to exert enough pressure to remove blades as long as the ancient Aztec examples. Drawing inspiration from historical accounts of Aztec knappers, Crabtree made a "chest crutch" and developed a technique that produced blades that rivaled those of the Aztecs (FIGURE 4-14).

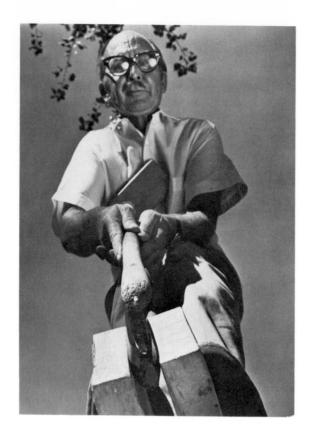

FIGURE **4-14**

Don Crabtree using the "chest crutch" for extra force to produce long blades by pressure-flaking.

Similar kinds of experiments are now taking place on a variety of materials and manufacturing processes, such as the lost-wax technique of casting metal and the crude wine press. Slowly the principles are being developed experimentally to allow the reinvention of long forgotten technologies.

Use:
Techno-Function

Inferences about an artifact's use or techno-function (p. 65) depend on a number of lines of evidence. From ethnoarchaeology and experiments such as those described above, archaeologists have established relationships between form and function. These relationships, however, are usually useful only in establishing very general categories. For example, we may infer from its form that a ceramic jar was used as a container, but we do not necessarily know what it contained.

As in the stages of procurement and manufacture, the formal properties of items are modified during use, but, unlike the case with the previous stages, the modifications are largely unintentional. There are several kinds of use modifications. The most obvious is breakage, which if unrepaired usually signals the end of an item's *uselife,* at least if it is to be employed for the same job. In contrast to the abrupt event of breakage, *use-wear* is the

Artifacts and Behavior □ **90**

Artifacts and Behavior □ **90**

gradual attrition or accumulation of materials that occurs on an artifact during use. For example, foot traffic on carpets wears down the material at the same time that it deposits residues in the form of stains and debris. When information on use-wear and the formal properties of artifacts are combined, strong inferences about techno-function can be made. For example, soot on the outside of a jar and food residue on its interior clearly indicate a role in cooking.

The experimental use of artifacts and analysis of the use-wear patterns that result is one of the most active areas of research in archaeology. There is a growing arsenal of machines that tirelessly scrape hides and cut bones with stone tools. There is also a second arsenal of machines—including scanning electron microscopes—used to detect the resultant wear patterns.

Objects that are associated with its use can provide clues to an artifact's techno-function. For example, even after form and wear patterns had been considered, the purpose of numerous "bent-nails" found at ancient Near Eastern sites still remained puzzling. These strange items were made of fired clay and shaped like dome-headed nails with bent shafts. An examination of their distribution patterns revealed that they were often associated with stone mortars. With this as a clue, experiments were then conducted that showed that, grasped by the shaft, the "bent nails" could be used as pestles for grinding.

Many objects, particularly the most common household objects, have more than one techno-function. This is known as multiple use. For example, when asked what they used screwdrivers for, most of a group of Tucsonans said they used them for turning screws. Examination of their household screwdrivers for use-wear, however, often showed battered handles, paint stains, and chipped blades. Obviously, regardless of what we conceive the use of screwdrivers to be, they are a multiple-use tool. Multiple-use tools present problems for archaeological inference because of their highly variable patterns of wear and associations.

When activities are carried out by specialists, especially in workshops, tool kits become larger from the addition of many specialized single-purpose tools. Compare, for example, the auto repair tools owned by most households with those of service stations. In modern workshops this differentiation has increased to the point that most industrial tool kits contain artifacts whose use cannot even be identified by other members of the community. (See boxed unit, "Identifying Techno-functions, on p. 92.)

Use: Socio-Function and Ideo-Function

Archaeologists have tried to separate utilitarian from stylistic characteristics and so identify the specific socio-functional and ideo-functional uses of artifacts. The principle that guides these use studies is that once the utilitarian attributes have been identified, the remaining attributes are stylistic. Recall the chair example from the beginning of this chapter. An archaeologist studying style in chairs begins by identifying their techno-functions. A chair's techno-functions usually place only a small number of limits on form

Identifying Techno-functions

Identifying techno-functions can be challenging. The objects shown below are products of contemporary American industry; they are identified below.

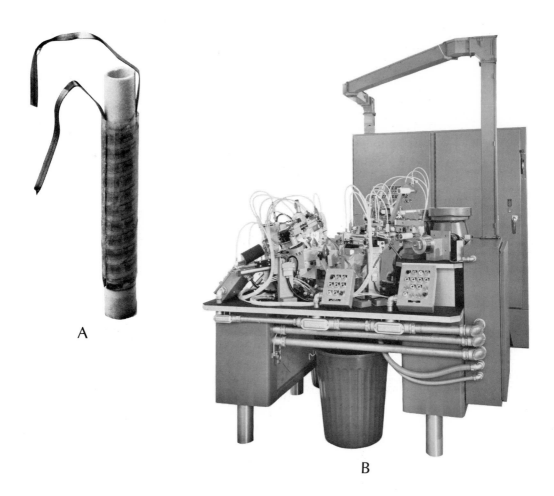

A

B

B. The automated machine that assembles the coil (A). It was manufactured in 1971 by Solatron Enterprises. Note the waste basket that serves as receptacle for the finished product.

A. An electrical coil (about one inch high) from the antenna assembly of an FM automobile radio.

and require of materials only that they be sturdy enough to hold up a seated person. Thus, in chairs, most specific differences in form and material are stylistic. On the basis of the remaining stylistic attributes, hypotheses would be formulated about the particular socio-functions and ideo-functions of chairs, and tests would be conducted using information on the other dimensions of variability—frequency, spatial, and relational. For example, if a chair is hypothesized to be a throne, its socio-function might be visible in several ways: first, by its relative scarcity, with one or only a very few examples found; second, by its location in a large settlement that seems to be the capital of a regional system or empire; and third, by its being found with other artifacts that denote the role of king.

In trying to identify differences in social standing within a society, archaeologists usually examine differences in the socio-functional characteristics of dwellings and personal possessions. It is generally assumed that the presence of persons with high social standing is marked by extravagant housing, such as palaces, and ornate objects—sometimes made of exotic materials—such as jade necklaces and gold wine cups. As a general rule, the material markers of an upper class are rare objects that require for their manufacture great quantities of labor and materials that are difficult to obtain. The patterns archaeologists see in the socio-functional characteristics of dwellings and the offerings in burials furnish a basis for inferring the degree of social inequality in a society. The way these inferences are made will be discussed in Chapters 5, 8, and 9.

A number of archaeologists have tried to use stylistic variability to indicate—beyond general patterns of social inequality—the nature of household and community social organization. One example is William Longacre's classic study of the pottery excavated at Carter Ranch, a small twelfth-century pueblo in the Southwest. Longacre proposed that the frequency with which various design elements were used on pots reflected marriage patterns and the way people learned ceramic art. On the basis of cultural anthropologists' descriptions of lifeways in recent pueblos, Longacre assumed that in prehistoric times mothers taught daughters to make pots. Thus, it would be likely that such mothers and daughters would produce similar styles. He also assumed that marriage was *matrilocal*—that newlyweds established residence in the vicinity of the wife's parents. Using the sociological model of style, he further reasoned that closely related women would favor the same design elements in decorating pots. Longacre expected to find different *micro-traditions* of style (distinctive sets of design elements) on pottery from different parts of the pueblo.

Longacre began his analysis of Carter Ranch pottery by distinguishing (with the aid of an artist) almost two hundred design elements. Statistical analysis showed that distinct sets of design elements were found in different sections of the pueblo (FIGURE 4-15). Using these results, Longacre claimed that the inhabitants of Carter Ranch Pueblo practiced matrilocal residence.

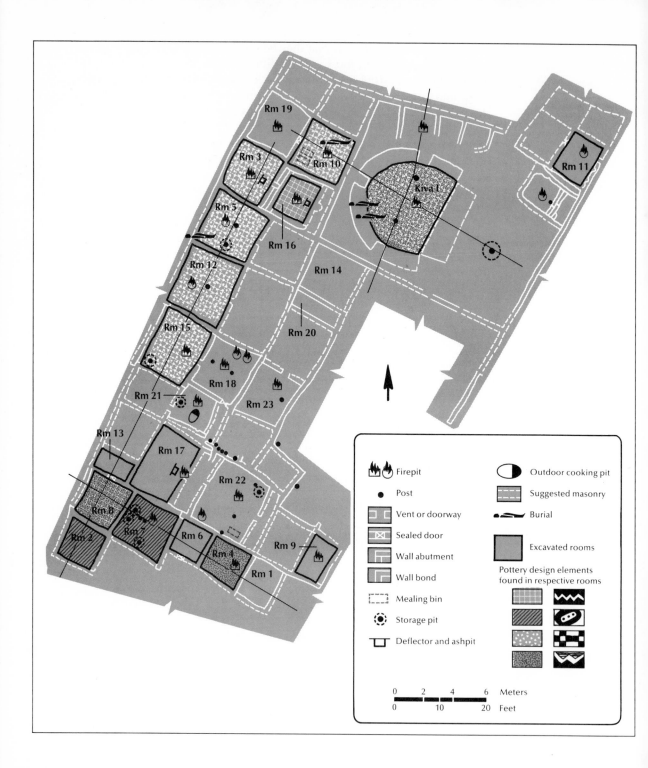

Rm 19

Rm 3

Rm 5

Rm 16

Rm 10

Kiva 1

Rm 11

Rm 12

Rm 14

Rm 15

Rm 20

Rm 18

Rm 21

Rm 23

Rm 13

Rm 17

Rm 22

Rm 8

Rm 2

Rm 7

Rm 6

Rm 4

Rm 9

Rm 1

🔥🔥 Firepit

● Post

Vent or doorway

Sealed door

Wall abutment

Wall bond

Mealing bin

Storage pit

Deflector and ashpit

Outdoor cooking pit

Suggested masonry

Burial

Excavated rooms

Pottery design elements
found in respective rooms

0   2   4   6   Meters
0   10   20   Feet

This claim was criticized on several bases. First, Longacre failed to consider a number of potential sources of variability, which we will take up in the next chapter, such as how and why pottery was deposited in pueblo rooms. More important, he did not rule out other possible causes of stylistic variability: that different design elements were popular and different parts of the pueblo were occupied at different times; that the products of specialized potters were distributed to different parts of the pueblo; that the design elements could be traces of work groups whose members came from different families; or, that the pottery could have been painted by men. We do not know which if any of these alternatives are correct. The need for principles to differentiate between different causes of stylistic variability is obvious. It is no accident that Longacre has recently been investigating stylistic variability among women potters in Kalinga villages in the Philippines (see FIGURE 7-20).

Although the specific beliefs represented in ideo-functional artifacts are usually beyond the archaeologist's grasp, the ritual use involved can sometimes be inferred. For example, in many rich Maya tombs of the Classic period (A.D. 250–850), stingray spines are found lying between the skeleton's legs just below the pelvis, sometimes in association with a bowl. Ethnohistoric reports by Catholic priests in Yucatán, written more than eight hundred years later, describe how the Maya elite pushed sharp objects through the fleshy parts of their bodies to draw blood into bowls for ritual use. The inference that stingray spines were used as part of religious ceremonies during the Classic period is made possible by ethnohistoric clues and the archaeological patterns of association.

Certain beliefs also seem to be indicated by the macabre skulls (covered with plaster and molded into human features) found at the 9000-year-old farming village site of Jericho. The care with which the modeling was done suggests an attempt to portray specific individuals (FIGURE 4-16). Some archaeologists have seen these special skulls as part of an ancestor cult, a belief system that emphasizes the influence of dead relatives in everyday life. Although similar treatment of human remains, documented by cultural anthropologists, has been correlated in some societies with ancestor worship, the inference is suggestive but weak for Jericho.

Many developments in style seem to parallel developments in the social and political evolution of societies. When early villagers first made ceramics, their pots tended to have no decoration, not even a wash or *slip* of wet clay to change the color or smooth the surface. As villages became larger and social roles and social units became more numerous, pottery decoration appeared. In some areas this involved only a one-color slip or two-colored

FIGURE **4-15**   The distribution of four pottery designs in excavated rooms at Carter Ranch Pueblo. Such patterns (involving 175 designs) were used by Longacre to infer family living arrangements at the pueblo.

FIGURE **4-16**

Skulls found at Jericho, in Jordan, with features molded in plaster and eyes of imported cowrie shells. The skulls may have had a role in an ancestor cult.

painted designs (FIGURE 4-17). In still larger communities, stylistic development continued in the form of elaborate polychrome, or multicolor, designs. Archaeologists have not yet worked out precisely what these stylistic changes mean in terms of specific socio-functions and ideo-functions, but they do see a link between more complex social units and roles and more elaborate styles, which reflect them.

Transport and Storage

Between one life-cycle stage of an artifact and another a number of other activities may occur, mainly involved in the transport and storage of items and, in more complex societies, their marketing and distribution. Obviously, if procurement, manufacture, and use occur in different places, there has to be transport. A parallel principle is that if these stages occur at different times, there must be storage; if a crop is harvested once a year, but consumed year-round, there will be storage facilities for the crop.

Although transport and storage seldom affect the form of items, these activities leave material remains. The most obvious result of transport is the distribution of commodities in areas distant from their zone of procurement or production. In addition, if the traffic between two settlements is heavy,

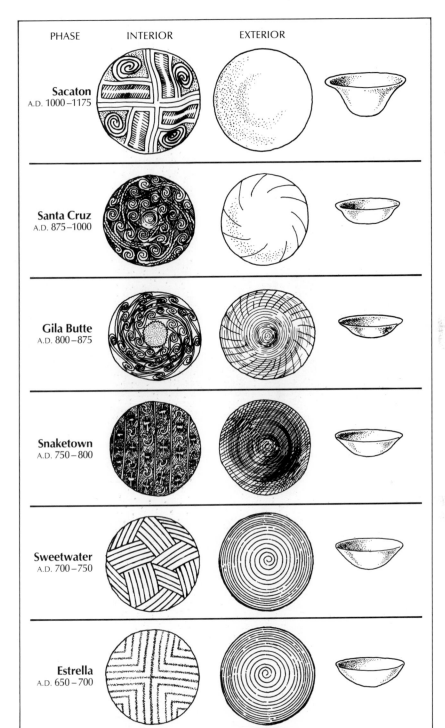

PHASE	INTERIOR	EXTERIOR	

Sacaton
A.D. 1000–1175

Santa Cruz
A.D. 875–1000

Gila Butte
A.D. 800–875

Snaketown
A.D. 750–800

Sweetwater
A.D. 700–750

Estrella
A.D. 650–700

FIGURE **4-17**

Examples of stylistic change—in this case, in Hohokam pottery bowls of southern Arizona. Gradual changes in painted decoration and vessel shape took place over a 500-year period.

Effect of Developmental Cycles □ **97**

 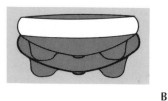 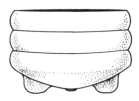

A   B

FIGURE **4-18**   Pots made to be traded over a wide area are often designed so that they can be nested inside one another. Shown in *A* are bowls from a Classic Maya burial at Seibal, Guatemala; and, in *B*, a way bowls from Postclassic Seibal—which were imported—could have been nested for transport. At top is shown a modern pottery seller with nested wares at a market in Chichicastenango, Guatemala.

paths, trails and, in complex societies, roads will develop. Transport often requires specialized artifacts, such as boats, way stations, trucks, and packs designed for animals or men. Sometimes the product itself may even be modified for transport or storage. For example, ceramics designed for transport will have standardized shapes and sizes that allow nesting or stacking (FIGURE 4-18).

For storage, products may be modified by drying, smoking, salting, or freezing. With increasing dependence on stored grains, there is a corresponding development of processing equipment, such as grinding stones and containers for soaking and softening the dried grain or meal, and of storage facilities, such as large containers, special-purpose rooms and buildings, or pits. It is no coincidence that pottery often first appears in regional sequences at about the same time as dependence on agriculture or other stored resources. Storage structures occur in consumption centers, in procurement areas, at manufacture sites, and at critical points along transportation routes. These processes can occur anywhere in the life cycle of commodities.

The next two phases of an object's life cycle, reuse and deposition, are central to the understanding of the formation of sites. These principles are the subject of the next chapter.

Developmental Cycles of Artifact Types

It is not only individual items that have life cycles, but also whole categories of artifacts. Investigation of such artifact types has produced several important principles, one of the most fundamental of which is the *frequency law*. This law applies to types of objects, such as snowmobiles, skateboards, and video-cassette recorders. Such types are usually defined by combinations of utilitarian and stylistic characteristics. According to the law, types of objects: (1) come into existence at a point in time, (2) gradually increase in popularity to a peak, (3) then gradually decline until they are no longer produced. The designs on historic grave markers, recorded by James Deetz around Boston, provide a good example (FIGURE 4-19). Because "popularity" curves plotting such typical life cycles look roughly like battleships (in plan), archaeologists call them *battleship curves*.

There often seem to be exceptions to this law. Dresses were made in the 1970s that are copies of 1940s styles. Skateboards were popular in the early 1960s in California, all but died out, and then rode to national popularity in 1978. The law, however, is not violated; when styles are revived they are not perfect copies. The 1970 copies of 1940 dresses are distinct new types because they are made with new technologies and new synthetic materials. The utilitarian attributes of 1960s skateboards have been changed to accommodate feats unheard of a decade earlier. For example, the boards are made of more resilient materials and the wheels are farther apart. The 1970s skateboards are also made in new styles by new manufacturers. Thus, each type of artifact—1940 dresses, 1970 dresses, 1960 skateboards, 1970 skateboards—follows its own battleship curve.

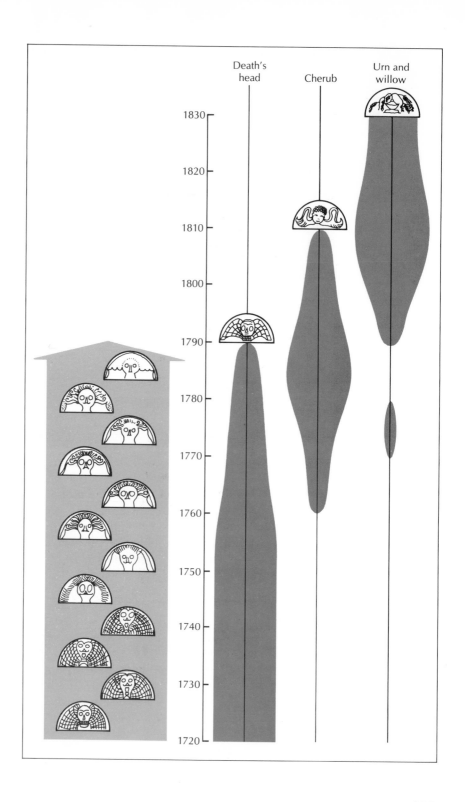

FIGURE **4-19** A graph of changes in the relative popularity of three gravestone styles in New England from A.D. 1720 to 1829 shows the "battleship curve" typical of such seriations (Chapter 8). The death's head motif, very popular in the earlier years, begins to decline as the cherub motif starts to compete with it in the 1760–69 period. In just three decades the cherub style becomes the most popular, and death's heads are no longer made. The urn-and-willow style sees a brief introduction in the 1770–79 period, does not really begin to take hold until after 1790, and, by 1820, is clearly dominant. As frequencies change, so do styles, as the sequence of renderings of death's heads shows.

A related principle, the *age-area hypothesis*, states that as time passes, artifacts will follow patterns of social interaction and will be distributed farther and farther from their source of manufacture. Thus, the geographic spread of a type of item should be directly related to the time elapsed since it was first manufactured. Unfortunately, rates of spread differ from item to item, which limits the usefulness of the age-area hypothesis. For example, radios, which were first sold in the 1920s, are more widespread than phonographs, which were available decades earlier. In some situations, archaeologists have found it convenient to assume that the rates of spread for all types of objects are similar. In many cases this works; for example, the early style DC-3 propeller-driven airplanes, which were first manufactured in 1937, are found in airports worldwide, while more recent jet aircraft are not yet as widespread. There are, of course, exceptions. The most obvious is a kind of artifact distribution called a *horizon style* or *marker*. Horizon markers are types of objects that spread rapidly and widely and cease to be produced just as quickly, thereby constituting a "marker" for a sharply delineated period. The "punch-top" on Coors beer cans is an excellent example of a horizon marker (FIGURE 4-20). Large numbers of these "easy-opening" cans were

FIGURE **4-20**

Because of its short life, the Coors punch-top can —manufactured between 1974 and 1977—is a very effective horizon marker. Levels in modern landfills that contain this type could be precisely dated.

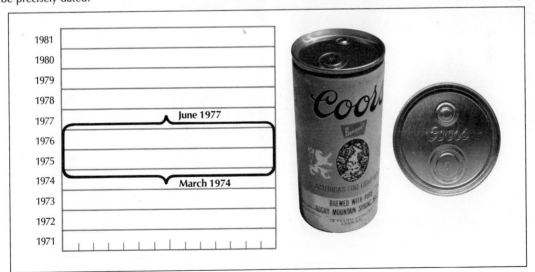

FIGURE **4-21**

The Chavín art style, from Peru, here represented by a pot and a stone relief of the feline god, was a longer-lived horizon (900–200 B.C.) than that constituted by the Coors can of FIGURE 4-20.

manufactured and widely distributed only between 1974 and 1977. The punch-top was discontinued because it tended to cut users' fingers. In the future when archaeologists find punch-top Coors cans in landfill strata, they will be able to date associated artifacts to the mid-1970s. The horizon markers of the past were often manufactured for a hundred years or more. One such horizon style, the Chavín art style in Peru, spread throughout the highlands within the seven hundred years from 900 to 200 B.C., greatly influenced coastal lowland styles, and then died out (FIGURE 4-21). Although seven hundred years is a long horizon style, it is still relatively short compared to other artifact changes.

At the opposite extreme of a horizon style is the concept of a *tradition,* which refers to a basic stability in the artifacts of a specific regional system. A long tradition presupposes gradual changes in behavior and substantial continuity in the population of an area. It would be reflected in elongated and overlapping battleship curves. One example is China; although it has changed dramatically in the last few decades, there was a clear Chinese tradition from 2500 B.C. to Sun Yat-sen and the modern communist revolution.

In Summary   This chapter has discussed the principles that link behavior and artifacts in adaptive systems. It began by defining the major kinds of variability in artifacts and the way the functions of artifacts affect that variability. Next, the effects on artifacts of social organization and ideology were described. Finally, the last section showed how artifacts are influenced by the life cycles of individuals and social units and by their own life cycles.

The artifacts archaeologists most often study come not from living societies, but dead ones. In these cases, our artifacts are a part of the archaeological record. Unfortunately, most archaeological sites are not societies frozen in time, like Pompeii, ready to give up their secrets about the past. Usually, the archaeological record is produced by much more complex and devious processes. These introduce considerable variability by altering the formal, spatial, frequency, and relational properties of artifacts. The processes that create the archaeological record are of two types, cultural and environmental. *Cultural formation processes,* the human factors that affect the deposition of artifacts, are the subject of Chapter 5. *Environmental formation processes,* the effects of environmental factors on deposited artifacts, are treated in Chapter 6. It is only by understanding cultural and environmental formation processes that archaeologists can identify the causes of variability in the archaeological record and infer human behavior.

Alfred Vincent Kidder (1885–1963)   A. V. Kidder was a pioneer archaeologist. He was twenty-one years old when he embarked on his first fieldwork with little ceremony and less training. According to his diary, the first day of work began with Kidder and two other novices standing on top of a high mesa in Colorado with the seasoned archaeologist Edgar Lee Hewitt. Hewitt nonchalantly waved his arm "taking in, it seemed, about half the world [and said] I want you boys to make an archaeological survey of this country. I'll be back in three weeks." Kidder obviously survived this endurance test. In 1914 he received his doctorate from Harvard, and the next year launched what was to become one of the most important projects in the Southwest. Kidder spent ten subsequent summers digging at Pecos, a large pueblo in northern New Mexico.   □   The excavation problems at Pecos Pueblo were complex. The first residents had set up house in the thirteenth century A.D., and the last moved out in 1838, leaving behind deposits of trash and building debris that were 20 feet deep in some places. To solve the problems, Kidder became one of the first archaeologists to engage a team of specialists to help in the analysis of artifacts and human remains. Of course, Kidder himself made contributions; in the process of building a developmental sequence for Pecos Pueblo, he added several refinements to existing excavation techniques.   □   Even before he finished digging at Pecos, he wrote *An Introduction to Southwestern Archaeology,* the first textbook to summarize the region's development sequences. Three years later, in 1927, he invited virtually every archaeologist in the Southwest to a meeting at Pecos Pueblo to swap data and stories. Now called the "Pecos Conference," though seldom held at Pecos, these meetings draw several hundred archaeologists every August.   □   The second half of Kidder's archaeological career was spent in southern Mexico and Guatemala. Kidder directed excavations at several Maya ruins, but as in the Southwest, he never stopped looking for the larger significance of archaeological finds. Archaeologists will always consider him a pioneer of modern archaeology. This is especially true of Southwestern and Maya archaeologists, many of whom view Kidder with no less than awe. We share this feeling, perhaps heightened by the fact that Kidder took time to examine our modern society with a trench he dug through the garbage dump at Andover, Massachusetts.

Alfred V. Kidder
in the field.

5

CULTURAL FORMATION PROCESSES

A little over 100 miles from the Andover Dump which Kidder dug is another site important to archaeologists. It is Ebbets Field, where the Brooklyn Dodgers played their home baseball games and where, on May 21, 1952, they set a major league record by scoring fifteen runs in the first inning against the Cincinnati Reds. As Americans who were kids during the Brooklyn Dodgers era, we think of Ebbets Field (FIGURE 5-1) as a holy shrine in the history of sport; as archaeologists, we would define it as an activity area for a specialized task group.

In 1952 Joseph Greenberg added Ebbets Field to archaeological folklore. In a humorous essay Greenberg fantasized what archaeologists would find in A.D. 2026 when they uncovered the ruins of Ebbets Field in "Tel-el-New York III." According to Greenberg's scenario, the most useful data would be tattered newspapers from the early 1950s. Archaeologists would reconstruct the religious ceremonies conducted in Ebbets Field on the basis of newspaper reports that the catcher, who was already known to wear a mask and other ritual regalia, "sacrificed a fly to the infield."

While it is fun to play the game of How will future archaeologists interpret our society?, that game is not as easy to play as it might seem. The newspapers that Greenberg thought archaeologists would find were most likely swept up by maintenance personnel each day after a game and are now rotting somewhere in the great dump on Ward's Island. The stadium

105

itself was torn down (with some hoopla) in March 1964. The destruction
was thorough. Even the foundations were bulldozed. Some seats were sold
to memorabilia buffs and are now widely scattered throughout the United
States. Plumbing and electrical fixtures and other reusable items were sold
and may still be found as parts of other buildings. The rest of Ebbets Field
lies in bits and pieces deep in the layers of garbage on Ward's Island. Today,
an apartment complex stands on the site where Duke Snider swung his
mighty bat and where Roy Campanella caught the sliders from the left arm
of Sandy Koufax (FIGURE 5-1).

Archaeologists study artifacts in two states: *systemic context*, where
the artifacts are a part of activities within an adaptive system, and *archaeological context*, where artifacts have been deposited and are no longer involved in activities. During the years that fans stood on their seats to cheer
or boo the Dodgers, all of Ebbets Field was in systemic context. The newspapers and the stadium rubble in New York dumps are now in archaeological context. The way in which materials are moved between systemic and
archaeological context affects the nature of archaeological evidence, or the
archaeological record. The processes that govern these movements are
known as the *cultural formation processes* of the archaeological record.

Cultural formation processes alter the formal, spatial, frequency, and
relational characteristics of artifacts, often drastically. The shape of Ebbets
Field (formal) was altered by demolition. Practically no artifacts of Ebbets
Field remain at their original place of use (spatial). There were 40,000 seats
in Ebbets Field; today there are 3 seats in St. Louis, 10 in San Francisco, 6 in
. . . (frequency). All the artifacts of Ebbets Field have new associations (relational). Obviously the archaeologist in the year A.D. 2026 would have to
be aware of these processes and their effects on artifacts to reconstruct

EBBETS FIELD

Ebbets Field in its 1952 systemic context. In fact, it is by knowing cultural formation processes that archaeologists can, to some extent, predict the future archaeological context of our American artifacts. But more importantly, these principles help the archaeologist to design fieldwork aimed at inferring behavior from archaeological remains.

Each of the four basic categories of cultural formation processes—(1) *reuse*, (2) *deposition*, (3) *reclamation*, and (4) *disturbance*—is comprised of a group of related processes that are important in forming the archaeological record, and each is associated with a number of principles. These four processes are aspects of the *principle of dissociation*, according to which items found associated in the archaeological record were not necessarily used in the same activity or activity area, and items that *were* used together are not necessarily found together in archaeological context. Perhaps the simplest example is a soda can and its pull-tab. When O'Connell studied Alyawara camps, he found many small pull-tabs lying in activity areas near shelters; he found soda cans in refuse associated with bulkier garbage. Archaeologists diligently record the associations of the artifacts they find. At the same time, they are careful to keep in mind the principle of dissociation.

THE REUSE PROCESSES

The first major set of cultural formation processes is reuse, which occurs whenever there is a change in the user or in the use of an object. Reuse operates entirely within systemic context. In fact, it consists of activities that prolong the use of an object in systemic context when normally the object would be discarded.

One well-known reuse process is *recycling,* in which an item is remade into a new product. In our society we are familiar with recycling old aluminum cans into new aluminum products, glass bottles into cullet for new glass bottles, and old newspapers into wallboard and cardboard. In prehistoric societies broken pottery was often ground up and mixed with clay for making new pots.

Generally, the amount of recycling is a function of the cost of recycling relative to the costs of obtaining virgin materials. The computation of costs is often quite tricky; for example, in the United States today, the costs for recycling are held artificially high by tax allowances given the producers and transporters of virgin materials.

Secondary use is a change in use that requires no modification of the original object. Familiar archaeological examples include the use of a *metate*—a flat stone for grinding—as a building stone, the use of a core (p. 89) as a hammerstone, and the use of a storage pit for refuse. A specialized form of secondary use occurs when the preservation of objects is intentional. These *conservatory processes* counteract the normal tendency of objects to enter the archaeological record. For example, government agencies and historical societies preserve old buildings; libraries and archives acquire and store manuscripts and books; museums accumulate all sorts of artifacts; and individuals and institutions collect everything from toy trains to beer cans. (Much of what we know of ancient Near Eastern societies has come from the study of records and books written on clay tablets and excavated from archives, such as those of the temple-estate of Lagash—from about 2400 B.C.—in Iraq.) Objects preserved in this way, regardless of their original purpose, become mainly socio-functional and ideo-functional artifacts (p. 65).

As a general rule, the most common items are the least likely to be conserved. For example, although many people collect antique rocking chairs, few have collections of old bobby pins. The surprising result of this phenomenon is that there are more surviving examples of genuine Tiffany lamps than of the once ubiquitous toothbrushes used at the same time. One can see this principle at work by leafing through a Sears-Roebuck catalogue from the early 1900s (FIGURE 5-2). How many of the most common household items advertised there—made at the turn of the century—have you seen?

Recycling, secondary use, and conservatory processes may or may not involve a change in the user. When there is a change only in the user of an object, *lateral cycling* has occurred. Lateral cycling includes the many activities by which used objects circulate within a society and remain in use. Lat-

$3.15 No. 18K1079 This Beautiful Ladies' Hand Bag must be seen to be appreciated. We cannot show the quality in the illustration, and the quality of this article is its leading feature. Made of the finest grade walrus grain leather, lined throughout with calfskin. Large stitched inner pocket containing handsomely finished coin purse. Has flexible leather handle fastened to a 10-inch leather covered frame. This is an excellent $4.50 value and should wear for years. Size, 10¾x6 inches. Color, black only. **$3.15**
Our price.
If by mail, postage extra, 21 cents.

Ladies' Skates, 70 Cents.

No. 6K5990 Ladies' Strap Skate. Runner is made of cold rolled steel, is highly polished with finely ground cutting edge. The foot and heel plates are made from the best grade of cold rolled open hearth homogeneous steel. The heel and toe straps are of the best oak tanned russet grain leather, tongue buckles and nickel plated heel bands. Sizes, 8 to 11½ inches. Price, per pair.............................**70c**
If by mail, postage extra, 32 to 40 cents.
When ordering skates give length of shoe in inches.

HEIGHT, 2 INCHES
SIZES 14 TO 18 IN.

No. 33K8076 A Popular Collar for any occasion. Medium height and comfortable. Sizes, 14 to 18.
Price, each......**7c**

42c BIGGEST VALUE 42c
WE EVER QUOTED
IN MEN'S BALBRIGGAN UNDERWEAR

IMPROVED QUALITY

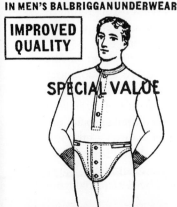

SPECIAL VALUE

Balbriggan Underwear for men that we can absolutely guarantee to give positive wear and satisfaction. We make use of several hundred cases of this number in a year; the purchase of this great quantity places us in a position to say how it should be made and what it should be made of and we can assure our customers that we have secured a garment that is made from the very best cotton yarns, perfectly and thoroughly sewed together. The drawers are adjustable in the back with buttoned straps and have a large double seat which gives it thorough reinforcement. The buttons are sewed on to stay. Every piece of underwear in our stock is examined before it is sent out, and we can guarantee this garment to give positive satisfaction. Color, ecru (cream color.)
No. 16K5032 Undershirts. Sizes, 34, 36, 38, 40, 42, 44, 46, 48, 50 and 52 inches breast measure.
Price, each.......................**42c**
No. 16K5033 Drawers to match above shirts. Sizes, 30, 32, 34, 36, 38, 40, 42, 44, 46, 48, 50 and 52 inches waist measure.
Price, each.......................**42c**
We must have size or we cannot fill your order.
If by mail, postage extra, each, 10 cents.

Basket Ball Goals.

No. 6K7098 Basket Ball Goals, regulation style, made of iron frame with cotton netting. Weight, per pair, 12 lbs. Price, per pair..**$2.74**

Bed Bug Exterminator

This product is entirely different from most other products, in being more effective and absolutely non-inflammable. Do you want the best? This preparation is in liquid form and furnished in a patent can with large spout, which makes its application easy and sure to reach the smallest opening. Bed Bug Exterminator will not only exterminate every bed bug and roach, but rid a room or building of these little pests entirely. Full directions with each can. Unmailable.

No. 8K894	Price, ½-pint can **$0.17**
No. 8K895	Price, one pint......**.27**
No. 8K896	Price, one gallon....**1.85**

No. 18K625 Our Leading Value Steel Studded Elastic Belt. 1½ inches wide, ribbed elastic, studded on back and sides with fifty-seven cut steel studs. The black harness buckle is ornamented with five cut riveted steel studs. Black only. Sizes, 22 to 36 inches. Be **25c** sure to state size. Price.............
If by mail, postage extra, 5 cents.

The Canned Vegetables on our shelves are always up to a general high standard of excellence. When you buy of us we sell you what you pay for, and that isn't an attractive can, only two-thirds full of inferior goods. Full measure and big value is the rule in this department. Buy and you will buy again. It pays to make up a hundred pound order by adding such canned goods as you need. Freight is very little when compared with what we save you.

	(2 dozen in case.)	Doz.	Can.
G 990	Marrowfat Peas, standards.............	$1 05	$0 09
G 991	Early June Peas, standards.............	1 20	11
G 992	Pumpkin, 3-lb cans, best quality....	95	09
G 993	Succotash, very best.............	95	09
G 994	White Wax Beans, extras.............	1 00	09
G 995	White Wax Beans, very finest quality..	1 50	14
G 996	Marrowfat Peas, best quality........	1 35	12
G 997	Extra Sifted Peas	1 40	13
G 998	String Beans, standards.............	70	07
G 999	Sweet Potatoes, best goods.........	1 40	13
G 1000	Squash, extra quality.............	1 00	09
G 1001	Lima Beans, extra quality	1 10	11
G 1002	Lima Beans, standard.............	75	08
G 1003	Gallon Pumpkin...................	2 25	23

		Doz.	Can.
G 1004	Elgin Corn......	$0 95	$0 09
G 1005	Corn, Paris, 2-lb cans. B. & M....	1 00	10
G 1006	Corn, standard...	70	06
G 1007	Corn, Illinois, standard, good......	50	05
G 1008	Corn, Loomis, Portland, Maine, very fancy and sweet...............	1 00	09
G 1009	Beans, Boston Baked, 3-lb cans....	1 00	09

G 2105 Parlor Matches, put up in boxes containing 100 matches; 144 boxes in a case, making 14,400 matches. Every match is perfect and full count warranted. Price per case....................$1 15
In lots of 5 cases, crated 5 50
G 2106 Telegraph Matches, sulphur, 200 matches in each box, 24 boxes in a wood caddy, making 4,800 matches. Price per caddy $0 35

FIGURE **5-2** Common artifacts of the early 1900s as depicted in a Sears-Roebuck mail-order catalogue. Most of these items are unfamiliar today. Ironically, these once-abundant objects are the least likely to be preserved in systemic context by reuse processes.

eral cycling and other forms of reuse are made possible by a number of specialized activities and behavioral components, including inheritance, gift exchanges, yard sales, swap meets, auctions, resale shops, and other dealers in artifacts. Theft is also an ever-popular form of lateral cycling.

While lateral cycling may not change an object's techno-function, it can change its symbolic meaning. In complex societies, when symbols go out of style as markers of high social standing, they are often obtained by lower-class users. In our own society a new Oldsmobile is a symbol of success for many middle-income Americans; a few years later, that same Oldsmobile has a different symbolic value as a used car.

At various points in the life cycles of individuals, households, and institutions, opportunities are created for lateral cycling. Whenever an individual or behavioral component passes to a new stage (p. 79), items from the previous stage may be laterally cycled. For example, when a family no longer has small children, it may sell or hand down baby paraphernalia. When people die, their belongings are often laterally cycled through inheritance. When people switch activity areas or move from a dwelling, some artifacts may be laterally cycled to people they leave behind.

In small communities where everyone knows everyone else (and may be related as well), lateral cycling occurs through social ties. As communities grow, more formal types of lateral cycling, such as markets and second-hand shops, are needed to act as middlemen between those disposing of, and others acquiring, artifacts. Even in the present-day United States, social ties still account for a great deal of lateral cycling. Michael Schiffer's ethnoarchaeological study in Tucson showed that in at least one-third of the households surveyed more than half of the furniture and major appliances had been obtained used; of this, more than forty percent had been acquired from a friend or relative.

The study of reused objects can furnish information about the past. They are the *historical record*, which is composed of manuscripts, museum collections, "antiques," and records of all sorts. Though these documents and objects usually retain their form, their other dimensions of variability are modified by reuse (recall the seats from Ebbets Field sold to collectors). Historical archaeologists, therefore, and all others that employ the historical record, need to understand the principles of cultural formation processes such as reuse in order to find and interpret relevant evidence. (See Chapter 7 for a specific discussion of historical research.)

DEPOSITIONAL PROCESSES

Depositional processes result in the movement of artifacts from systemic context to archaeological context. The most general principle of deposition is the *law of superposition*, which states that later deposits overlie earlier ones. During excavation, archaeologists strive to identify individual strata. Using the law of superposition, they work out a *depositional history*, the order in which strata were deposited (FIGURE 5-3). This activity is called

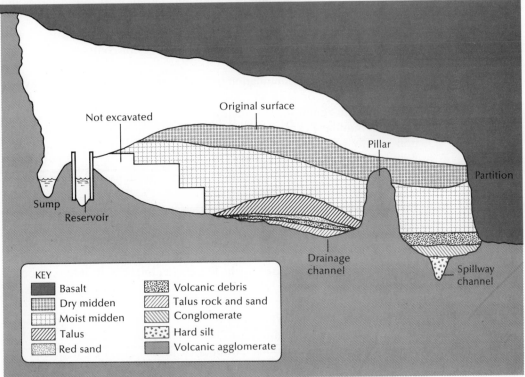

KEY

Basalt	Volcanic debris
Dry midden	Talus rock and sand
Moist midden	Conglomerate
Talus	Hard silt
Red sand	Volcanic agglomerate

FIGURE **5-3**   The Ventana Cave (top) and a stratification diagram (bottom) of the upper cave, the entrance of which is the dark area near left center of photograph. Much of the cave was excavated. The layers spanned 12,000 years of occupation, beginning with Paleoindian artifacts in the "volcanic agglomerate" layer. The "red sand" layer contained artifacts that may have been left 8,000 to 10,000 years ago. The "moist midden" held Hohokam materials and recent debris from Papago Indian camps.

stratigraphy. The next several chapters (especially the discussion of stratigraphy in Chapter 7) will make clear the great usefulness of the law of superposition.

Burial   Burial of the dead is a depositional process. The first form of variability in burials is the treatment of the body or bodies. The basic types are *inhumation* or *primary* burial in the flesh, cremation, and *secondary* or *bundle* burial, in which the flesh is allowed to decay and the bones are then gathered up and interred. Within each of these types there is often selectivity in the burial of body parts. For example, when people are collecting the remains of a cremation, they often tend to pick up only the larger bones. In the case of decomposed bodies, skulls and long bones are sometimes saved by relatives and not buried at all. A form of this can even happen in inhumation, where particular body parts are cut off as trophies or relics and not included in graves. For example, the skulls in some Maya burials were sawed across and the facial portions removed. Some bodies are not buried at all. In a few cases, the dead are enshrined as socio-functional and ideo-functional artifacts: both V. I. Lenin and Mao Tse-tung, heroes of communist ideology, are on display in special chambers.

Burial position in inhumation is varied—face up, face down, flexed or extended, seated, or even standing. Archaeologists have often attributed great symbolic significance to whether the body is extended or flexed. Often, however, mundane explanations seem to work. Burial in the extended position usually occurs in soft soils; where digging is hard, bodies are often flexed to fit into small holes. Other characteristics of position include orientation of the body in relation to the cardinal directions and relation of the body to artifacts and to the grave itself.

The most obvious variability in burials is type of grave—whether it is a simple pit containing bones or a jar with ashes or whether it is an elaborate tomb or "family" crypt or even a whole pyramid or temple. Another form of variability is the location of burials. In some societies, where the dead are buried in structures still used by the living, you might well sleep on a bench containing your uncle; in other societies, of course, there are formal cemeteries.

The most intriguing variability occurs in the *grave goods* or *grave furniture* included with the body. One of the earliest general principles in archaeology deals with grave goods. Formulated in the 1840s by J. J. Worsaae, *Worsaae's law* states that items placed with a burial during the act of interment were in use at the same time. We will discuss this law again when we describe archaeological methods of dating (Chapter 9). Many of the famous archaeological finds were richly appointed burials—the frozen Scythian tombs from the Altai in Russia, Siberian horsemen buried with gold appointments (FIGURE 5-4); the tomb of King "Tut"; and the 2000-year-old tomb of Prince Liu Sheng, a Chinese nobleman and his wife, both encased in

<figure>FIGURE **5-4**

Vase with depiction of tooth pulling from tomb of a Scythian "warrior king" buried with his paraphernalia. This type of burial was common in the Russian Altai between 600 and 300 B.C. and probably reflects a political structure that was a patchwork of feuding tribes.</figure>

their own tailored jade body-stockings (FIGURE 12-6). Within most societies, the type and quantity of goods varies considerably from grave to grave.

What are the general causes of this variability? The rituals of burial, the characteristics of the mourners, and the artifacts involved reflect the deceased individuals' social standing, the sum of their social roles. The first principle of burials was succinctly stated by Christopher Peebles: persons who are treated differently in life will be treated differently in death. Most archaeologists assume that the amount and type of grave goods and the effort spent in preparing the grave are a direct reflection of an individual's social standing. For example, most burials at the Moundville site, in Alabama, dating between A.D. 1000 and 1500, had few grave goods. Peebles used the first principle of burials to infer that the few interments at Mound-

not nec. true

ville that had many exotic trade items were those of "chiefs." One obvious implication of the burial principle is that societies that have more ways of treating people in life—that is, more social roles—will have more ways of treating them in death. Lewis Binford has confirmed this prediction with a study of forty modern societies. He found that in bands, where age and sex are the primary determinants of social standing, there is little variability in treatment of the dead, while in chiefdoms there is far more variability, as in the case of Moundville, described above.

Variety in treatment of the dead increases in agrarian and industrial states. There is, however, a shift from ritual display and burial of objects to just ritual display. Thus, although the pomp of his state funeral was televised for the world, Charles De Gaulle, the French general and world leader, is buried in a rural cemetery wearing only his First World War uniform and a few medals. Joseph Tainter has concluded, on the basis of a comparative study of a number of living societies, that the total energy spent on *both* burial ritual and interment is the best direct reflection of an individual's social standing.

However, not all of the energy a society spends memorializing its dead is lavished on ritual or leaves material remains at the burial site. John Kennedy may have only a simple "eternal flame" in Arlington National Cemetery, but there are other monuments that indicate his social standing—airports, schools, and a national center for the performing arts. This reflects a change, seen in more complex societies, from taking goods out of circulation in the name of the dead to using goods for the benefit of society in the name of the dead. But the general principle still holds that the total allocation of goods and services—in ritual, in interment, and in memorials—reflects the social standing of the deceased.

Caches   Societies do not just bury objects with people, but sometimes intentionally bury artifacts by themselves. One source of such *caches* is ritual burial. The most familiar to us is the *dedicatory cache,* a set of objects deposited in order to dedicate a construction site. In our society, a comparable cache is usually included as part of a cornerstone in large buildings.

Archaeologists often excavate in front of the steps of Maya temples to find caches of pottery that will help them date a temple's construction. But how do they date the caches? The Maya also erected stone monuments, called *stela,* to mark particular events, such as the coronation of a ruler or the conquest of a town. Most stela have a date carved on them in Maya *glyphs* as well as a dedicatory cache under them. Thus, on the assumption that the erection of the stela and the placement of the cache were associated events, the date on the stela gives a date to the cached artifacts. When caches with similar kinds of artifacts are found in front of buildings, they are assumed to have been deposited at about the same time.

The purpose of caches is often difficult to determine. Perhaps the most dedicated and enigmatic cachers of all time were the Olmec, who buried thousands of tons of colored sands and carved stones in their sites along the Gulf Coast of Mexico between 1500 and 400 B.C. The most bizarre caches, even by Olmec standards, are two burials of serpentine (a type of stone) at the site of La Venta. In each cache 28 layers of cut serpentine blocks, which altogether weigh more than 1,000 tons each, were buried at the bottom of a pit 40 feet deep. A mosaic mask made of more blocks was used to cap the serpentine. The pits were then filled with layers of colored sand. The sand came from nearby coastal areas, but the serpentine had to be transported at least 150 kilometers from the Mexican highlands. Archaeologists still do not understand this cache. Some believe it was ritual, others believe that the Olmec were simply "banking" serpentine for future use.

Although the Olmec serpentine cache is problematic, other finds can confidently be described as *banking caches*. Examples from among the Duna farmers of highland New Guinea have been described in ethnoarchaeological terms by Peter White and Nicholas Modjeska. In clearing their gardens the Duna use polished stone axes that are obtained by exchange or trading over long distances. Extra axes are buried in a safe place for future use. Some informants reported sorrowfully that they had forgotten where they had buried their axes, which are now a part of the archaeological record. Similar explanations can be applied to ancient caches. One classic example is the treasure horde Heinrich Schliemann excavated at the site of ancient Troy in 1873.

Loss   The failure to remember and retrieve banking caches illustrates another depositional process—*loss*. Several factors affect rates of loss. One is object size. Generally, the smaller the object, the higher the loss rate; it is easier to lose a spearpoint than a 300-pound stone. A second factor is the nature of the surface on which loss occurs and the composition of the lost item. (A not uncommon memory for some is that of frequent pauses in high-school basketball games while players groped on their hands and knees for virtually invisible clear-plastic contact lenses.) Some surfaces, such as those with tall grass or sand, are more conducive to loss than others, and are, in effect, artifact "traps." A third factor is replacement cost. Although it is not unusual to see a person drop a penny, look at it, and then walk off, it is rarely the same case with a ten-dollar bill. Coins, most presumably lost, are the main artifacts used in dating Roman and Greek sites.

Together, these three factors—size, surface and composition, and replacement cost—explain many patterns in the archaeological record, particularly in the distribution of items still intact when found. The size of the object will affect how often items are misplaced and whether their loss is noticed. The surface will affect how difficult it is to retrieve objects. The replacement cost of the object will determine how much effort will be expended to retrieve it. These factors produced the patterns of pins that Stanley South found when he excavated the Public House/Tailor Shop in Brunswick Town, North Carolina, a colonial settlement. The tailoring activity resulted in the loss of pins (small items) through spaces in the floorboards (permeable surface); the value (replacement cost) of the pins was not sufficient to justify ripping up the floor to retrieve them.

Discard   In most sites the majority of items the archaeologist has to work with were intentionally discarded. They had either worn out, been broken, were waste products, or were no longer considered useful. Thus, in a real sense, much of what we know about the past is based on studying other people's trash. There are a lot of different kinds of trash and different ways to dispose of it. Some settlements have very little trash and some are awash in it. In some it is dispersed over a wide area; in others it is concentrated into *middens,* or large garbage dumps.

Because of their interest in discard practices, archaeologists have formulated two principles of refuse disposal. We can begin to discuss these by defining two kinds of refuse based on the location of discard within a settlement. *Primary refuse* is trash discarded at the location of use, while *secondary refuse* is trash deposited at other than the location of use.

The first principle of refuse disposal, recently confirmed by Patricia Murray in an ethnoarchaeological study of seventy-nine societies, deals with the quantities of these two refuse types that settlements produce. It states that, as settlements are occupied for longer periods of time, more secondary refuse results. A kill site used once to butcher game will consist largely of primary refuse; a Bushman camp occupied for several weeks will contain a mix of primary and secondary refuse; and a city such as ancient Ur, Teotihuacán, or even San Diego, will produce predominantly secondary refuse. In fact, one of the few places where primary refuse can be found in a city is vacant lots, where people don't bother to clean up after activities.

The second principle of refuse disposal states that as settlements become larger, specialized task groups are required to transport and dispose of refuse. Together, these principles have some clear implications. The larger and more permanent the settlement, the farther refuse will be moved from its location of use and the more it will be concentrated within specialized middens. Thus, in the largest settlements, such as modern cities, secondary refuse may be concentrated in a few "sanitary landfills" (modern jargon for dump). Artifacts in these locations provide almost no information on where activities were performed.

Even when refuse is regularly picked up from activity areas for discard elsewhere, some materials will remain behind as primary refuse. The factors that affect the nature of this primary refuse are similar to those influencing the deposition of lost items. The *McKellar hypothesis* proposes that small objects (under 4 inches in overall dimension—combined length, width, and depth) are most likely to remain behind as primary refuse (FIGURE 5-5). The hypothesis, originally proposed by Judith McKellar while she was an undergraduate at the University of Arizona, was found, by James O'Connell, to be applicable to Alyawara camps (p. 32) in Australia and was tested, with posi-

FIGURE **5-5** The McKellar principle at work in a drive-in theatre. At left, an assortment of trash deposited by theatre-goers near a speaker post. At right, the same area after cleaning, free of most large artifacts, but with many bottle caps and pop-tops remaining. The larger artifacts will be deposited in a sanitary landfill as secondary refuse; the smaller ones, left behind, have become primary refuse.

tive results, by Stanley South in parks in South Carolina. One of the most important implications of this principle is that very small items may be the only archaeological traces left behind to identify activity areas. (See the application of this idea in Chapter 8).

The *schlepp effect* is another important principle of deposition. In its simplest form it has two components: (1) the more butchering of an animal that occurs at a kill site, the more its bones will be deposited there; (2) the amount of butchering performed is directly proportional to the animal's size and the distance to the place of consumption. Thus, at a village or base camp one is likely to find almost complete rabbit skeletons, partial deer skeletons, but few bones of elephants. Naturally, the modes of transportation available will affect the operation of this principle.

Historical archaeologist Stanley South has proposed that there is stylistic variability in refuse disposal. In comparing colonial settlements, he found that German and British immigrants set aside different locations for dumping their secondary refuse.

One of the most obvious features of the archaeological record is that the materials in it can be counted. Archaeologists are now beginning to investigate the variables that influence the quantities of discarded items they find. One general equation that has already emerged from this study is

$$F_D = \frac{S}{L}$$

where F_D is the rate at which items are discarded, S is the average number of items in use, and L is uselife, the average time an item is in use. Simply stated, the rate at which items are discarded in a settlement depends on the number in use divided by the uselife of the item. Discard processes operate over time; the length of time discard has continued determines the accumulated quantity of discarded items. Our equation is easily modified, so that

$$T_D = \frac{St}{L}$$

where T_D is the total number of discarded items, and t the period of time discard has continued. The use of this equation can be illustrated by using Garbage Project (p. 34) data on pickups from 73 households recorded over a 5-week period. To determine the uselife of a 26-ounce container of salt, two assumptions were necessary: that, on the average, each house sampled was using one container of salt and that salt containers were discarded immediately after they were emptied. To simplify the example, we assume that a settlement consists of 73 households. Then T_D is 17 (the total number of salt containers discarded by the 73 households over the 5-week period), S is 73 (one per household), and t is 5 weeks. Substituting in the formula gives

$$17 = \frac{73(5)}{L}$$

$$L = \frac{73(5)}{17} = 21.5$$

Thus the uselife of 26-ounce salt containers in this example is estimated at 21.5 weeks, or a little over 5 months.

This discard equation shows that there is no single explanation for the frequencies of discarded items. For example, an item may be infrequently discarded because (1) it has a long uselife, or (2) there are a small number in use, or (3) it was popular for only a short time, or (4) any combination of those above. Clocks and pigs' feet make a good example. Almost every household in Tucson has at least one clock, but pigs' feet are eaten in only a few. Nevertheless, there are many more bones from pigs' feet than there are clocks in the Tucson sanitary landfill. Obviously uselife is the basic factor at work here. It is important to keep in mind the many causes of variability in the numbers of discarded items.

A further principle can be illustrated with the discard equation if we consider the length of time a settlement is occupied, or *occupation span*. Where occupation span is short, many items with high rates of discard will be thrown out; as occupation span increases, an ever greater variety of items having lower and lower discard rates will be deposited. This principle is known as the *Clarke effect*. Increases in a settlement's population will also result in a greater variety of items with low discard rates being thrown away.

There will be exceptions; a discard rate is an average. Although, for example, the discard rate of clocks may average one every fifty years per household, some clocks will break down much sooner and be discarded out of sequence. Thus, the Clarke effect is a *statistical law*. It will have exceptions, but it is a useful guide to general patterns.

Abandonment

What the occupants leave behind when they vacate an activity area, dwelling, or settlement is called *de facto refuse;* what they take with them is called *curate items*. Ethnoarchaeological studies have begun to identify the major factors that influence the decisions involved: (1) the means of transportation available, (2) distance to the next place they plan to occupy, (3) intention of returning, (4) the activities anticipated in the next location, (5) the conditions of abandonment (rapid, slow, forced, or planned), (6) the portability of the artifacts themselves, and (7) the replacement cost of specific items.

A number of principles can be derived by combining these factors. One states that when transport is limited to what can be carried, and when the next place of settlement is relatively distant, people will tend to leave as de facto refuse heavy objects, stationary facilities and structures, and easily replaced light objects (FIGURE 5-6). In our own society, where special artifacts and task groups are available to transport household possessions, people tend to leave much less behind. It is principles such as these that determine what is left on the floors of archaeological structures.

Pompeii, the Roman city in southern Italy that was buried in volcanic ash from the eruption of Mt. Vesuvius in A.D. 79, is a well known example of one extreme of the abandonment process. Many people anticipated the eruption that buried the city and took valued possessions with them; others left their possessions (FIGURE 5-7), and a few remained to be buried in ash with their worldly goods.

FIGURE **5-6**   De facto refuse on two room floors at Grasshopper pueblo. Obvious differences in the amounts of deposited material may be a result of abandonments under different conditions. Differences in kind of material are probably due to room function—with the one at top a storeroom, and the other a corn-grinding and food preparation room.

FIGURE **5-7**

A kitchen in Pompeii, Italy, preserved much as it was in A.D. 79, when it was covered by volcanic debris from the eruption of Mt. Vesuvius.

THE RECLAMATION PROCESSES

Pompeii can also illustrate the third major category of cultural formation processes—*reclamation*. Not everything that enters the archaeological record stays there. Some of the survivors of Pompeii returned to dig out their belongings from the volcanic ash. The same process occurs when survivors of floods, hurricanes, and fires return to "dig out." Reclamation processes thus include those activities that move objects from archaeological context back into systemic context.

Scavenging processes cover situations where the occupants of a settlement remove materials from archaeological context. In the Maya area, scavenging normally occurred immediately before a site was abandoned. Most of the tombs built during the last phases of the Maya Classic period (A.D. 700–820), probably those filled within the memory of the last residents, were broken open and stripped of valuables. Archaeologists digging the Late Postclassic city of Mayapán (A.D. 1100–1450) believe that the residents there followed a similar pattern and plundered most of the caches in the site. Court records and the records of religious societies attempting to preserve tombs intact show that tomb-robbing was a common practice throughout Egyptian history. In fact, the famous shaft grave near Deir el Bahri, containing a cache of mummies dating to the Middle Kingdom, was discovered by Egyptian antiquities authorities when the residents of a nearby town began selling jewelry from the tomb to tourists.

In many settlements more mundane items are scavenged. Building materials from abandoned structures often find their way into new construction. In fact, today in most industrial cities there is a thriving market in used bricks and plumbing fixtures. One principle of reclamation states that the more gradual the abandonment of a settlement, the more scavenging there will be of de facto refuse. Thus, one of the clearest indications of rapid abandonment of a settlement is great amounts of de facto refuse.

Collecting processes occur when occupants of one settlement remove archaeological materials from another. Modern Hopi potters collect potsherds from ruins to use as sources for designs. Nearly everyone has seen cigar boxes full of arrowheads or someone's brick from the Roman Forum. In prehistoric Southwestern pueblos, spearpoints have been found whose styles are typical of much earlier hunter-gatherer societies. Many archaeologists believe these were collected, probably for use in rituals.

Collecting behavior is patterned. "Pot-hunters" seek graves or caches where valuable whole or restorable objects are likely to be found. In fact, looters often know a great deal about the way sites are formed and use this knowledge to predict where booty can most easily be retrieved. They are aware, for example, that in Southwestern pueblos burials were often placed in middens, where the soil is easy to excavate. Thus, in the American Southwest, the first areas looted in pueblo sites are secondary refuse deposits, where graves and grave goods frequently occur.

When the easy targets, such as graves and refuse, are gone, pot-hunters will turn their efforts to the harder job of excavating room blocks, resorting to dynamite, bulldozers, or other mechanical aids. There are cases in southwestern New Mexico of entire pueblos having been laid waste by bulldozers for half a dozen whole pots (FIGURE 12-11). The basic characteristics of collection activities are that they are highly selective and they are undocumented.

Archaeological recovery stands in clear contrast to scavenging and collecting. It, too, removes things from archaeological context, but the goals and procedures are very different. Collectors and scavengers recover only formal information on some few items. Archaeologists record all of the dimensions of variability—formal, spatial, frequency, and relational—pertaining to the much wider range of artifacts that are recovered. No archaeologist would dig a site and recover only one class of artifacts. No archaeologist would dig a site without recording exactly where the finds came from. These differences arise because archaeologists view artifacts and sites as sources of information about human behavior rather than as mines for valuable or aesthetically pleasing objects. Chapter 7 examines the principles of archaeological recovery.

In some societies, particularly complex ones, archaeological materials are recognized to contain information about the past. Thus, the removal of materials from the archaeological record without documentation of their context is judged to be looting (Chapter 12). The perception of what is recognized as valuable historic and archaeological material is changing in our society today. As interest increases in preserving historic structures, many of the normal demolition and scavenging activities currently considered quite acceptable will likely be seen as looting in the future; in only a few years we may be referring to the "looting" of Ebbets Field.

Because both reuse and reclamation result in the conservation of materials, both are likely to increase when virgin materials become harder to obtain. A number of studies have shown, for example, that the amount of reuse and scavenging of chipped stone increases with distance from a source of raw materials. Thus, in the Ozarks in Arkansas, where chippable stone is readily available, many barely used tools were discarded in ancient times. In part of the neighboring Mississippi Valley, where stone is in short supply, discarded stone tools have been reduced to nubbins and barely a usable flake can be found. In another example, the reused items from Ebbets Field were those with the highest replacement costs, such as plumbing and electrical fixtures; chunks of concrete were discarded.

THE DISTURBANCE PROCESSES

The demolition of Ebbets Field was intentional. *Disturbance processes,* on the other hand, are the by-products of activities with other goals. One of the most prevalent disturbance processes is plowing and other agricultural activities. Plowing tends to move objects in small stages in the direction of the furrows until, after many years of cultivation, the distribution of artifacts becomes "blurred." The effects of plowing and other disturbance processes are not limited only to the direct movement of objects. Very often disturbance processes move artifacts and deposits into a position where they are subjected to a wider range of environmental alterations. For example, in the *plow zone,* bone and organic remains turned up and exposed to weather are more likely to decay rapidly than if left buried. In addition, plowed sites are eroded more rapidly by rain and irrigation water.

One of the better known archaeological principles—*the law of upward migration*—describes another effect of disturbance. It has been found that digging or bulldozing can bring previously deposited (hence earlier) objects to the surface, where they become mixed with or lie on top of later materials. Thus, it is assumed that a site with many pits or other evidence of disturbance is likely to show *reverse stratification*—that is, earlier materials overlying later materials.

Another widespread disturbance process results when people trample deposited materials. Trampling has several different effects. First, it abrades and breaks objects. Ruth Tringham and her students found that certain types of edge damage resulted from trampling chipped-stone flakes. A second effect of trampling is that it scatters objects. Robert Ascher studied Seri Indian settlements in Sonora, Mexico, and found that foot traffic had "smeared" the surface artifact distributions. The third effect—vertical displacement of artifacts—depends on the nature of the ground surface. In experiments with sandy soils, E. D. Stockton showed that trampling displaces large objects to the side while moving small objects downward. Trampling also contributes to the *fringe effect,* a tendency for artifacts to accumulate next to structures. The areas immediately adjacent to walls receive less foot traffic; thus, any objects that are kicked or dropped there are likely to remain. The gradual movement produced by trampling tends to add to the accumulation along the edges of buildings. Fringes will not develop in areas regularly cleaned. Thus, the presence or absence of a fringe can indicate the intensity of maintenance activities. Fringes also develop inside structures but are less pronounced because of more thorough housekeeping.

It is important to remember that disturbance processes are the inadvertent side effects of many other activities. Thus, when a foundation is built, when a field is cleared, when pots are looted, and even when people walk from place to place, we can expect archaeological materials to be disturbed.

THE PROCESSES AT WORK: TWO EXAMPLES

In this chapter we have examined several important processes that affect artifacts. We have, however, looked at these in isolation. The potential complexity of cultural formation processes is vastly greater than our discussions indicate because an item may be repeatedly affected over a long life history by a large and varied number of different processes. For example, we can imagine one tool's travels through time. Twelve thousand years ago, say, an Indian hunter butchered a deer with a chipped-stone knife until the tool became dull. The tool was then chipped into a drill or punch and used for leather-working (recycling). Next, it was abandoned (de facto refuse). Ten thousand years later another Indian found the ancient tool lying on the surface and returned it to his village (collecting), where it was used as a fetish in ceremonies (secondary use). Changes in ideology made fetishes obsolete, so the old drill was discarded (secondary refuse). After another thousand years the village site where the artifact lay was turned into a pumpkin patch, where plowing moved the artifact a bit now and then (disturbance). Fifty years later an archaeologist excavated the site (archaeological recovery) and deposited the artifact in a museum (conservatory process). In two hundred years that artifact may again be in archaeological context!

The concepts and principles discussed in this chapter furnish a sounder basis for the game of What will archaeologists find? than Joseph Greenberg had for forecasting the fate of Ebbets Field. We can construct for any item or structure a number of the more likely scenarios that lie ahead. Though these are not, of course, predictions, it is possible to sketch out likely occurrences based on some reasonable assumptions.

Let us imagine what would happen if you abandoned a house located in a big city. First, we assume that the house is ordinary and not likely to be the subject of efforts to preserve it as an historic landmark. Depending on your reasons for leaving the house, certain kinds of artifacts would be taken. For the sake of argument, we will assume it was necessary to "get out of town" in a hurry so that everything was left behind as de facto refuse. Twenty-five years from now how much of it will be in the context in which it was abandoned?

As soon as the neighbors realize the house is abandoned, scavenging will begin. The first raiding party will collect the more portable valuable items—radios, TVs, stereos, cameras, jewelry, clocks, liquor, collections of coins and stamps. A second party or the first on another trip will likely be better equipped for hauling large valuable objects—furniture, stoves, refrigerators, air conditioners—which are easy to remove if one has a truck and a few friends to help. This same pattern is followed by burglars.

But what happens when the easy pickings are gone? The thoroughness of scavengers is truly remarkable. The next parties will probably pick up most of the cheap knick-knacks and other small items of little monetary value. But the final phase of scavenging will strike at the guts of the house. Given time, it is almost certain that one by one—a toilet here, an air duct there—plumbing and electrical fixtures will be removed. Doors and unbroken windows and easily dismantled building materials will go next. Scavengers will also covet shingles and roof beams and floor coverings.

But while scavengers are taking, others will be giving. A vacant building becomes an activity area for special forms of play and relaxation for children and adults. One of the main activities is vandalism. Broken windows and spray-painted graffiti will be clear signs of the structure's altered function. Deposits of liquor containers, smokers' debris, food wrappers, and human waste will be added to the structure.

At some point in the processes of scavenging and deposition there will be a terminal event—one that puts a quick end to the house's slow dismemberment. It may be a fire set by vandals, a wino trying to keep warm, or a landlord aiming to collect the insurance. The house may be condemned for health reasons and bulldozed by the city. Either way, the remains will be taken to a city landfill. What an archaeologist in the future is most likely to find is a parking lot, carefully preserving beneath its asphalt the last remains of your house—a few nails, bits of glass, and lumps of charcoal.

Louis S. B. Leakey (1903–1972) and Mary Douglas Nicol Leakey (b. 1913)

Louis Leakey has been the source of two major controversies. One of these centers on Leakey's belief, based on the fossil evidence from Olduvai Gorge in East Africa, that 2 million years ago there were three kinds of humanlike creatures evolving separately. Only one of these, *Homo habilis*, is our ancestor; and, according to Leakey, *Homo habilis* may have hunted the others for food.   □   Leakey is also controversial because, though he has received most of the glory for the archaeological discoveries that are the basis of his interpretations, it was his wife Mary who conducted the Olduvai Gorge excavations. Visitors to Olduvai Gorge most often found Mary Leakey in a pit, digging implements in hand, smiling through a layer of dust. Louis was usually encountered strolling with a few Dalmatians or relaxing in a chair, in either case with thoughts of great moment churning in his head. Clearly, this most famous archaeological husband-and-wife team was an odd couple. Louis was brash and enthusiastic and bubbling over with exciting ideas. Mary is quiet and hard-working and meticulous. While Louis lectured and wrote, Mary dug. But no matter how different from each other, the Leakeys were a most remarkable team.   □   Louis was a white African born to missionary parents in Kenya. As a young man, he was made a member of the Kikuyu tribe and spoke Kikuyu and Swahili as well as he spoke English. Louis was trained in archaeology at Cambridge University in England, but returned to Kenya, where he spent most of the rest of his life searching for fossil humans. Aware that our earliest ancestors evolved in a changing natural environment, he went to great lengths to understand human evolution in its natural setting. He carefully studied the hundreds of feet of sediment exposed in Olduvai Gorge and wrote monographs on dating layers, on their geology, and on the animal bones they contained. All of this background was an advantage as Mary Leakey's careful excavations began to turn up fossil humans, often in association with stone tools and food debris. Mary's dedication to the details of day-to-day excavation and Louis' constant flow of interpretations and research reports have resulted in documentation of the origins of the human species in East Africa.   □   Today the Leakey family is still digging. Mary is quietly excavating at Olduvai and in Laetolil nearby. Son Richard is flamboyantly carrying on his father's tradition with excavations at other early sites and with a controversial book on the origins of aggression in human society.   □   We respect the Leakeys' single-minded—some say dogmatic—dedication to the discovery and interpretation of the remains of our earliest ancestors and the obvious teamwork that made possible their extraordinary accomplishments.

Louis Leakey and Mary Leakey, with their son Richard and numerous Dalmatians, excavating a site in Bed I at Olduvai Gorge, Tanzania.

6
ENVIRONMENTAL FORMATION PROCESSES

You have just considered (Chapter 5) the spectre of a house being dismembered by various human activities. While this nightmare is likely to come to pass only if the house is abandoned, other insidious forces are continually acting to erode our possessions. Even as you read this, the pennies in your pocket are oxidizing and the vinyl top on someone's car is becoming brittle from the sun, eventually to crack and peel, if it hasn't already. Gophers and ants infest lawns, and lightning sets fires. Rainwater soaks into and slowly weakens roofs and walls and washes soils from high spots in gardens into lower-lying areas. No wonder the Leakeys have had to search so carefully for the few traces of our oldest ancestors—traces that have survived 2 million years of exposure to the environment.

All human adaptive systems interact with their local natural environments. They exploit them for resources and respond to them when they change. Even when the adaptive systems have ceased to function, their material remains continue to be affected by their natural surroundings. Thus, the study of adaptive systems often begins with *paleoenvironmental reconstruction* of the environment with which past human societies interacted.

Archaeologists have two functions in paleoenvironmental reconstruction—to interpret the effect of the environment on human behavior and the effect of human behavior on the environment. To do this, however, they usually have to determine first the effects of past environments on the artifacts left behind by extinct adaptive systems. Thus, in this chapter we will emphasize the impact of *environmental processes* on artifacts in the archaeological record. In Chapter 8 we will mention other aspects of paleoenvironmental reconstruction.

Environmental processes are responsible for many changes in artifacts, particularly those in archaeological context. These changes greatly modify all four dimensions of variability and have a profound influence on what we can learn about the past. As an example, assume a twentieth-century wood-frame house on a hill in Georgia (FIGURE 6-1) has been abandoned to the elements together with the secondary refuse around it. In the Georgia hills this includes 50 inches of rain a year, high winds at times, and an abundance of plant and animal life. Of the many processes that will affect the artifacts of the house, we will mention only a few to illustrate changes in the four dimensions of variability.

The formal dimension will be quickly altered. Wood will stain, warp, and, most importantly, rot. Rot will occur most rapidly in the biologically active *decay zone,* which is the area from one foot above to one foot below the ground surface. It is in this area that the forest has a variety of workers —namely insects, fungi, and bacteria—to decompose fallen trees and other dead organic material. Within a few decades, the weakened wood of the house will give way and the house will collapse, altering its form considerably and bringing much of the remaining wood into the decay zone. As decay proceeds, wind, rain, and vegetation will alter the spatial dimension of the house. As elements of the house break up, large storms will wash some of those near the slope farther down the hill. This process will move objects differently depending on their size, shape, and weight. Vegetation will grow around and through the remains of the house and the refuse. At first these plants will stabilize the deposits, but as tree roots grow larger they also will move materials. Decades later, a lot of debris may be brought to the surface when trees die, fall, and become uprooted. As a result of these processes, the location at which an artifact is found may be considerably different from the place where it was originally deposited.

The frequency dimension will be affected by the different rates at which materials decay. Within a hundred years most wood and paper products will be gone, some metal objects will remain, others will only be stains in the ground. Most plastic items will have turned brittle and shattered into numerous fragments. Glass and pottery and asphalt shingles will remain, but the shingles will have cracked and crumbled. Because of their resistance to decay, glass and pottery will occur in relatively large quantities compared to the more vulnerable metals and organic materials.

At the same time that the house is losing some materials it will be gaining others that alter the relational dimension. Burrowing animals, such as gophers and squirrels, move materials—as illustrated in the Overton Down experiment—and when they die may leave their bones in association with the artifacts of the house.

modern counterparts; and stone tools made by humans were discovered deeply buried in gravel deposited by rivers. All of these finds gave the appearance of great antiquity, but the then accepted chronology for the earth's history was extremely short. Biblical scholars had spent centuries debating and calculating the exact time of creation. The most widely believed date was that devised by Archbishop Ussher, who pronounced the year of creation to be 4004 B.C.; in a later refinement, Dr. John Lightfoot pinpointed the time at 9 A.M. on October 23 (a Thursday). In order to explain the new discoveries, yet preserve the Ussher-Lightfoot chronology, scholars invoked a variety of catastrophic events. Earthquakes, volcanic eruptions, and floods were all blamed for the strange distributions of fossils, shells, and artifacts.

During the early nineteenth century, as more observations were made, *catastrophism* became less acceptable as a mode of explanation. What ultimately eroded catastrophism was research that showed that gradual geological processes could better explain the fossil record and the development of modern landforms. The most elegant treatment of the new approach was presented by Sir Charles Lyell in the 1830s. In his work *Principles of Geology*, Lyell defined the principle of *uniformitarianism*, which maintains that processes seen operating today also operated in the past. Lyell showed how slow and undramatic processes can, over long periods of time, create enormous changes in the face of the earth. Thus, the same kind of erosion that one can see going on today in the Colorado River, acting over millions of years, created the Grand Canyon. Uniformitarianism does not deny the importance of floods or volcanoes, but it places them alongside more mundane processes in a larger framework of explanation.

Glaciation   One of the most dramatic long-term environmental processes is *glaciation*. Although the causes are only now becoming known, during the past several million years large sheets of ice, or glaciers, advanced and retreated over vast areas of all the continents. Glaciation, which occurred several times, was identified in the nineteenth century and served as a major support of uniformitarian geology. Each glaciation lasted several tens of thousands of years and included many *interstadials*, times of partial retreat during a major glaciation. Between major glacial advances were *interglacial* periods, characterized by *eustatic changes*, rises in sea levels due to the addition of water from melted glaciers. Scientists now believe that major episodes of glaciation are caused by minor variations in the earth's orbit around the sun, as described by the Milankovitch theory. The *Pleistocene* is that geological time period, lasting about 4 million years, during which the most recent cycle of glaciation occurred. We are still in the Pleistocene, although some scientists prefer to call the last 10,000 years—which may be interglacial or interstadial—the *Holocene*.

Glaciations had several major effects. First, large areas were made uninhabitable. Second, temperatures in areas surrounding the ice sheets were greatly reduced. In North America, major *environmental zones* (regional

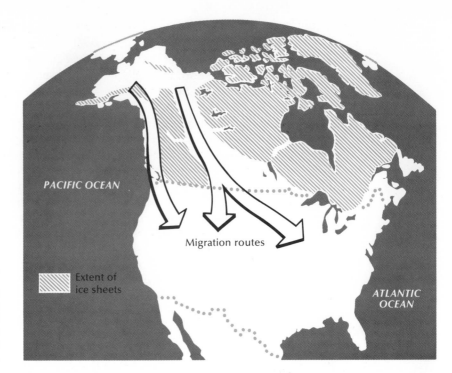

FIGURE **6-4**

A stage in a retreat of the
glacial ice sheets when
man could have entered
the New World. Arrows
indicate possible routes
of migration.

PACIFIC OCEAN

Migration routes

Extent of
ice sheets

ATLANTIC
OCEAN

plant-animal associations that are climatically determined) were moved
south to the extent that parts of the present Sonoran Desert in southern Arizona became woodlands that supported large grazing animals, including
mammoths and bison. In some cases, entirely novel plant-animal communities, found nowhere today, were formed by unusual combinations of temperature and precipitation.

When great amounts of water were locked up in massive ice sheets, the
sea level was much lower than today, so that the present Bering Strait, between North America and Asia, was then a land bridge between the two
continents. The New World was populated relatively late in the Pleistocene
by hunters and gatherers who crossed that land bridge. The exact time of
this colonization is hotly disputed. For people to enter the New World required not only a land bridge, but an ice-free corridor through Canada
(FIGURE 6-4). This condition occurred when the Cordilleran and Laurentide
ice sheets retreated, leaving a passage through the McKenzie Valley in Canada. (This ice-free corridor existed several times during interstadials in the
Wisconsin advance, the latest advance of glaciers in the Pleistocene.) Most
recently this occurred about 27,000 years ago, perhaps 18,000 years ago,
and again 12,000 years ago. We know that by 12,000 B.P. *Paleo-Indians*
were living throughout the continents of North and South America. Firmly

dated remains have been found as far south as Tierra del Fuego, the southernmost tip of South America.

Any evidence of earlier occupation that exists has been subjected to many environmental processes, including the direct and indirect effects of glaciation itself. Sites occupied in the paths of later glaciers would have been obliterated. Sites in low-lying coastal areas would now be under tens to hundreds of feet of water. In addition, the presence of glaciers would have determined where camps could and could not be made. Nearly all of the sites and finds that date prior to 12,000 B.P. are disputed, leaving the first use of the corridor by humans an open question. The best case for pre-12,000 entry is furnished by recent excavations at Meadowcroft Shelter (FIGURE 6-5), 35 miles southwest of Pittsburgh, Pennsylvania. There, in undisturbed strata, archaeologists James Adovasio and Joel Gunn have uncovered a sequence of occupations—with well-documented radiocarbon dates (Chapter 9)—that extend to at least 17,000 B.P. Because of well-dated sites like Meadowcroft, increasing numbers of archaeologists are beginning to accept remains dated

FIGURE **6-5**   Meadowcroft Rock Shelter—archaeology under the lights. The bright spots are markers used to label deposits.

FIGURE **6-6**

Landsat (satellite) composite photograph showing the Nile delta and Alexandria in Egypt.

to between 25,000 and 12,000 years ago as evidence of early human occupation in the New World.

Like glaciation, other geological processes create distinct landforms in the environment that affect where people live and the preservation of artifacts. Volcanoes, for example, build up mountains, fill in valleys, and sometimes preserve sites (as in the case of Pompeii). Rivers (see below) create fertile flood plains, abandoned channels, and great deltas (FIGURE 6-6). (See boxed item, The Overkill Theory, p. 152.)

Flowing Water   Flowing water is an environmental process that shapes the face of the earth and, to a large extent, influences human adaptations. People drink it, settle on rich soils deposited by it, irrigate with it, use it as a means of transportation and a source of food, and build machines to convert it to electrical and mechanical energy. At the regional scale the most important effects of water are erosion and deposition.

The erosive effects of water can be seen by examining a relief map of the United States and comparing the lofty, ragged peaks of the Rocky Mountains with the smoother (and much older) Appalachians. Water flowing down slopes and in rivers and streams has carried away over the millennia much of the Appalachians and deposited them in river valleys all over the eastern United States. Surprisingly, even many desert landforms, such as the Grand Canyon, have been shaped by flowing water. Erosion also cuts through layers of sediments, sometimes exposing long-buried sites. One of the most famous areas where this has occurred is Olduvai Gorge in Tanzania. There, Louis and Mary Leakey have scoured the slopes and crevices for over half a century, searching for remains of ancient humans and their campsites that have been exposed by erosion.

There are three major kinds of water deposition: (1) *colluvial* deposits, formed on slopes near sources of sediment, such as mountains; (2) *alluvial* deposits, laid down by streams and rivers in the channels themselves or on the broader flood plains; and (3) *lacustrine* deposits, formed by the settling out of materials in lakes. The particle size of sediments deposited by water varies directly with the velocity of the water. For example, large cobbles can be deposited only by swiftly moving water. On the other hand, fine clays will settle out only in stagnant water. Generally, alluvial deposition in river valleys, one of the forms most commonly dealt with by archaeologists, alternates between periods of erosion and deposition, creating characteristic *cut and fill cycles*. Erosion will cut through earlier deposits, often leaving *terraces* that may then be covered by subsequent depositions (FIGURE 6-7). By studying cut-fill episodes, it is possible to set up an *alluvial chronology* of depositional units which, especially in Pleistocene studies, is indispensible for chronologically ordering sites on terraces and other landforms.

Colluvial and especially alluvial deposition are worldwide processes that have the potential for completely burying archaeological sites. Sometimes such burial can take place quite rapidly, as a recent study in Kenya, East Africa, has shown. In 1974 ethnoarchaeologist Diane Gifford mapped a modern crocodile-butchering camp on a flood plain. Upon her return several months later, she discovered it had been buried by sediments washed in by two rainstorms. Her excavations disclosed 10 to 15 centimeters of sand and silt over some objects, while others had been completely swept away. Such sites have often been found by accident, as erosion has made them visible to passersby. Now, however, drawing on their knowledge of depositional processes in a region, archaeologists are building models to predict where important sites may lie and are excavating, usually with power equip-

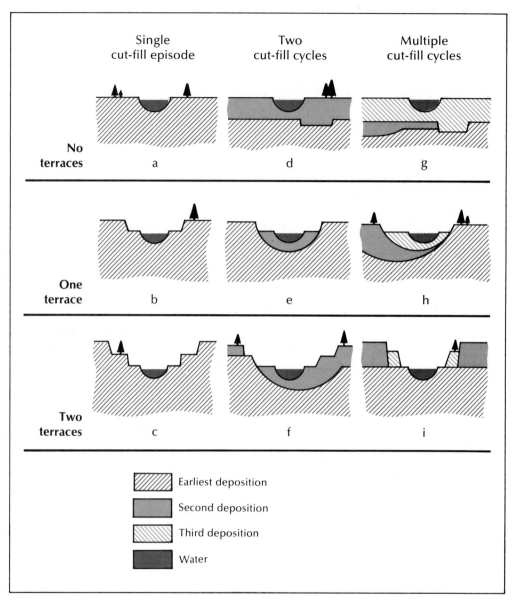

	Single cut-fill episode	Two cut-fill cycles	Multiple cut-fill cycles
No terraces	a	d	g
One terrace	b	e	h
Two terraces	c	f	i

Earliest deposition

Second deposition

Third deposition

Water

FIGURE **6-7**   A range of possible cut-fill cycles. Note that in *e* and *h* the earliest deposits are found at the highest elevations.

ment, to find them. Notable successes have been achieved. For example, Joffre Coe has found a number of Archaic period (10,000–3000 B.P.) hunter-gatherer campsites in North Carolina by trenching riverbanks likely to have been areas of human occupation that became overlaid with sediment.

Environmental zones are of great interest to the archaeologist. Plants and animals, like landforms, clearly influence the nature and location of human settlements, and the history and current condition of archaeological sites. This section deals with the effect of environmental zones on site visibility and the preservation of specific materials.

Many vegetation patterns offer problems and benefits to archaeologists. In the Maya area, rain forests obscure sites almost totally. On the other hand, the distribution of some specific plants, such as the ramón tree, provides an easy key to site location in a region. For decades, Maya archaeologists have found sites in the dense rain forest by turning their pack animals loose and following them to ramón trees, which tend to cluster at sites of ancient human habitation. This suggests a question about the cause of the association. Ramón trees bear an edible nut. Are current high densities around Maya sites a long-term consequence of cultivation, or do Ramón trees simply prefer to grow in the disturbed and nutrient-rich soils of ancient habitation sites? (For discussion of this question, see Chapter 9.)

Scale: Site-Level Processes

Soils and Sediments

Soils and sediments are most important to the archaeologist studying individual sites. Vegetation is one major factor in the formation of soils; the other is sediments or parent materials. A *soil* is a sediment that has been weathered and altered *in situ* (where it lies) to the extent that horizontal zones or *horizons* can be identified in it. Soil scientists identify three major horizons. The *A Horizon* is the uppermost zone, where plant materials decay and where there is a great deal of biological and chemical activity. This horizon is generally a dark, organic, humus-rich soil. The next, the *B Horizon*, is composed of materials removed from the A Horizon by the percolation of water. It is likely to be lighter and less organic than the A Horizon. The *C Horizon* is a zone of parent material in which there has been little or no chemical and biological alteration. In many cases it will be alluvial sediment or clay formed by weathering of underlying bedrock.

It is important not to confuse these natural horizons with strata resulting from human activities. This is easier said than done, because in many archaeological sites, soils form in and on the cultural deposits (FIGURE 6–8). Soil formation takes hundreds, or even thousands, of years. Thus, true soils are likely to be found only on ancient sites. That is why the "dirt" from sites is most accurately termed *sediments*. In some sites, one finds *paleosols*, which are soils formed during earlier environmental conditions and then buried by cultural or environmental processes. The study of the properties of soils, especially paleosols, furnishes important clues to past environmental conditions.

Two principal physical characteristics of soils and sediments are usually recorded in the field. The first, color, is measured by means of standardized color charts. (True "dirt archaeologists" will have their own *Munsell Color Chart*, which is similar to a paint sample book, with page after page of colors, each with its own code number.) The second important char-

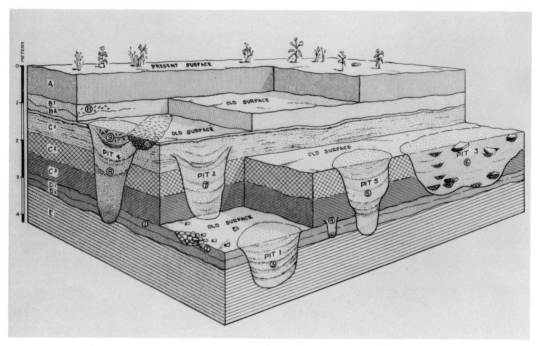

FIGURE **6-8**   In some sites, as in Cienega Creek, in East Central Arizona, deposits consist of a complex of cultural strata and soil horizons.

acteristic of sediments and soils is texture. When you pinch a bit of dirt, it may feel powdery, silky, or gritty, depending on the size of the grains—the individual particles of which it is composed. The makeup of a sediment in terms of grain sizes is called texture. Grain size categories are small and large, the former including grain diameters below 2 millimeters (clay, silt, and sand); the latter, all diameters above 2 millimeters, which are called *clasts,* and include granules, pebbles, cobbles, and boulders. By studying the texture of a sediment and the size and orientation of clasts, it is possible to infer many of the cultural and environmental processes that created the deposits. Many other physical and chemical characteristics of sediments and grains are routinely examined in the laboratory analysis of sediments. Archaeologists depend on specialists for these studies.

In considering the interaction between sites and the natural environment, it is useful to think of a site as a sediment deposit and of artifacts as clasts within the deposit. With this in mind we can discuss the most important natural processes that alter sediments, or in our case, sites.

Pedoturbation   The largest class of processes is known as *pedoturbations* and refers to the biological and physical mixing and disturbing of sediments. One of the most common is *faunalturbation,* soil disturbances caused by animals. Burrowing animals, such as mice, gophers, squirrels, rabbits, prairie dogs, and even armadillos, excavate tunnels (FIGURE 6-9). The major impact of burrowing is

Environmental Formation Processes □ **140**

to bring buried sediments and clasts to the surface. In addition, burrows can become filled with surface materials. Thus, reverse stratification is frequently produced. Fortunately, animal burrows can usually be identified because of their elongated, irregular shape and sediment differences.

Burrowing and tunneling activity is often quite extensive. For example, it has been estimated that in parts of California gophers annually transport 7 tons of soil to the surface of every square mile. Smaller animals, including crayfish and ants, termites, and other burrowing insects, are also important agents of soil mixing. Perhaps the most widely distributed small archaeological villain is the mild-mannered earthworm, which occurs in all but very dry or very acidic soils. Sir Charles Darwin, the father of evolutionary theory, took time to study the earthworm activity at Roman sites in England. The magnitude of their efforts is astounding. Worms burrow by ingesting soils and depositing them in their wake or on the surface. Darwin estimated that, in parts of England, 10 tons per year of "worm castings" are deposited on every acre. Earthworm activity has two primary effects. The first effect is the churning of the soil, which gradually blurs soil horizons and boundaries

FIGURE **6-9**   Evidence of the presence of burrowing animals at the site of Snaketown in southern Arizona. At left is the surface of a trash mound showing openings to numerous animal burrows. At right, a cutaway view of a trash mound after excavation shows tubular features, some oval and some more elongated, which are old animal burrows that have subsequently filled in with sediments carried by wind, water, and other animals.

between different archaeological strata. This can be clearly seen in the excavation of storage pits in worm-infested soils. At the top, where worm action is greatest, the boundaries are indistinct; the deeper parts of the pits are much more sharply defined. The second effect is that objects too big for worms to ingest are slowly buried under their castings. Because worm tunnels collapse, the combined effect is that large objects will slowly sink into the ground. Soil specialist Donald Johnson has had first-hand experience with this process. While spading his yard in Champaign, Illinois, he uncovered a brick patio buried under 3 inches of worm castings. Within a few weeks castings had again begun to accumulate on top of the bricks.

Floralturbation is the mixing of sediments and soils due to root growth and decay and tree falls. Root growth is the most prevalent soil mixing force in rain forests (FIGURE 6-2) and elsewhere: roots pushing through concrete sidewalks are a common sight. Tree roots move sediment, clasts, and even building stones, in many cases splitting open structures and dispersing facades and fill.

When dead trees fall or storms topple living trees, the roots, levered to the surface, carry sediments and clasts with them. The depressions they leave may become filled in with other materials. When the roots decay, the artifacts and sediment materials they pulled up are deposited on the surface. Although this process creates disturbances, it does have some beneficial side effects. In forests, where surveying is difficult, archaeologists often find artifacts in the soils caught in tree falls.

Cryoturbation describes a variety of processes that occur because of alternating freezing and thawing of the ground in cold regions. The most important of these is *frost heaving*. As sediments freeze, objects are often forced upward, depending on their thermal conductivity, shape, and orientation and on the rate of freezing and characteristics of the soil. Another important cryoturbation process is *mass displacement,* which takes the form of massive distortions (called *involutions*) resulting from pressures in the soil caused by freezing.

Graviturbation includes mud slides, avalanches, rock slides, as well as slower processes that mix and move materials downhill through the force of gravity. Mud slides not only mix materials, but can also cover and preserve sites. In western Washington State several mud slides buried the Indian village of Ozette during the last three centuries. Excavations have revealed a Pompeii-like wealth of de facto refuse, much of it well-preserved wooden artifacts (FIGURE 6-10). The effects of rapid gravity-driven processes are clear; the effects of slower processes are no less dramatic over the long run. *Solifluction,* one of the slower processes, is the very gradual downhill flow of soil that is saturated with water. *Frost creep* is the downhill movement of items that have been frost heaved on a slope. Because they are slow-acting, these latter processes are especially important in older sites.

While water has regional effects (see page 137), it is also an important agent at the site level. Erosion displaces objects on the basis of their size,

FIGURE **6-10**

At right, the Ozette site, in Washington state, which was covered by a mud slide about 1600 A.D. Note the use of garden hoses in excavation. Below are wooden objects from the site, which were waterlogged, and so particularly well preserved.

FIGURE **6-11**   The modern city of Erbil in Northern Iraq. Its predecessors, spanning the millennia, are responsible for these imposing accumulations of material. Most homes in the region have been traditionally built of mud brick, which adds to the height of the tell when it is eroded by rain or when old walls are leveled and used as foundations for new.

shape, and weight—generally, the smaller, the greater the displacement. Flowing water also deposits sediments; in some sites, for example, different occupations are separated by sterile layers of alluvium. Rainwater melts the mud bricks in the abandoned structures of Near Eastern settlements. Under the influence of other processes, this mud and that from similar structures built atop the remains of earlier structures (and, in turn, abandoned) accumulates to form *tells* or mounds, some of which have been occupied for millennia and are now small mountains (FIGURE 6-11).

Submersion in water saturates sites and may give the deposits a puddinglike consistency. In some cases, if sites are rapidly inundated, the organic artifacts may be unusually well preserved because the water has inhibited decay. Early Swiss villages, wooden foundations of which became exposed in lakes during periods of low water levels in Europe in the late nine-teenth century, are an example (FIGURE 6-12). Sometimes only the lowest levels of a site are submerged, usually because of high water tables. At sites like Koster, in Illinois, where the water table was encountered at 30 feet below the surface, pumps operated continuously to permit excavation.

Wind or *aeolian* action is especially significant where there is little or no ground cover. The mounds that mark some Southwestern pueblos consist largely of windblown sand trapped by standing walls. While excavating pueblos, archaeologists have found that during a weekend's absence, as much as 10 centimeters of sand can accumulate. Wind may also remove lighter sediments from deposits, thereby deflating or compressing the clasts that remain. Wind deflation is responsible for many sites that consist just of artifacts without a surrounding soil matrix.

At the site level, rapid processes such as earthquakes, mud slides, and large-scale erosion leave the most obvious traces and would seem to have the most dramatic effects. However, because archaeological sites are ex-posed to the natural environment for long periods, many slow-acting pro-cesses can have major effects on distributions of artifacts. Animal burrow-ing, tree growth and fall, and freeze-thaw cycles introduce a great deal of variability that is often difficult to detect or to make allowances for. This is also true for gradual erosion, wind deflation, and long-term burial in water. Although the effects of such processes may be subtle, with knowledge of the natural environment the archaeologist can usually determine if they have occurred. For example, even if obvious archaeological traces are lacking, sites in forests are likely to have suffered tree falls and the burrowing actions of animals, especially worms and insects.

Scale: Artifact-Level Processes

The finest scale of environmental effects is seen on artifacts. The interaction of artifacts and the environment results in the modification or disappear-ance of items in the archaeological record. Decay, weathering, oxidation, and corrosion are among the main processes at work. Experimental and eth-noarchaeological studies, such as Overton Down, are beginning to answer the question: What is preserved, what decays?

Decay or preservation depend on three sets of factors: (1) the material composition of the artifact, (2) processes that are active in the dep-ositional environment, (3) the length of time the artifact remains in archaeo-logical context. Here we will consider the effects of specific dep-ositional environments and durations on different types of artifacts.

Hard stones, such as granite, basalt, and flint, are perhaps the most du-rable materials. Nevertheless, when exposed to aeolian processes, freeze-thaw cycles, and rain, stone can be slowly modified. In arid areas where the winds carry particles through the air, stones can be rounded by natural sandblasting. In modern cities, pollutants in the air are a cause of both dis-coloration—known as *patina*—and deterioration, and special maintenance is necessary to preserve or restore structures.

FIGURE **6-12**　At top, some of the water-logged remains of a Swiss neolithic village that stood at the edge of a lake. Preserved by submersion in water, the village (shown as it may have looked, below) was exposed when water levels dropped during the famous European drought that began toward the end of the nineteenth century.

Buried stone is protected from weathering actions. Underground, only roots and a few minor chemical processes modify stone. Most chipped-stone tools are made from hard rocks, such as chert, flint, obsidian, quartzite, agate, and basalt. As a result, the edge of an ancient tool may be just as sharp today as when it was discarded 10,000 years ago. A subtle but important change occurs in stone containing silica. In such stone, when a new surface is exposed through a fracture, that surface will slowly take in water in a process known as *hydration*. The water forms a *rind* or *rim* on the new surface of the stone and slowly moves into the interior. The rate of movement depends on temperature and the specific composition of the stone. Rates of hydration for obsidian (volcanic glass) have been determined with great precision in regions such as western Mexico. It is now possible to measure the thickness of the rind on some obsidian tools and, on that basis, to assign a date to the manufacture of the artifact. As a result, *obsidian hydration* is becoming an increasingly important technique of archaeological dating. (See Chapter 9 for descriptions of dating techniques.)

Ironically, one of the most fragile items when whole is virtually indestructible when in pieces. Although ceramic artifacts are easily broken, the fragments or *sherds* persist, immune to most chemical, biological, and physical processes in almost all depositional environments (FIGURE 6-13). When they are exposed on the surface, weathering may take its toll on painted designs, sometimes leaving highly eroded sherds. Root action and other processes can cause surface discoloration, but through it all the potsherd remains essentially intact. The same basic description fits glass.

Metals have a great range of properties that affect their preservation. Iron and steel are very reactive chemically. In the presence of oxygen and moisture, they will rust. Even in historic sites from as recently as the nineteenth century, iron artifacts can be represented by little more than a reddish brown stain in the soil. Silver and copper are also reactive, but the reactions proceed much more slowly. Bronze, an alloy of copper and tin, is even less reactive than copper alone and can last thousands of years. Gold is almost entirely unreactive, and gold objects can appear today much as they did when they were made. Aluminum and some other industrial age metals are extremely durable—a factor in many of our present litter problems.

The shells produced by marine and freshwater mollusks are brittle and vulnerable to attack by acidic soils. In areas with good drainage and nonacidic conditions, however, shells and *shell middens* (built up as the result of numerous meals) are well preserved (FIGURE 6-14).

At first glance, bone seems to be hard and durable; and, indeed, it occurs in abundance in many archaeological sites. Like shell, however, bone will decay in acidic soils, and it is highly susceptible to weathering on the surface of sites. Recent ethnoarchaeological studies in Africa conducted by Anna Behrensmeyer have identified the regular stages of weathering in bone exposed to the elements. Additional experiments have shown that the denser the bone, the greater its resistance to decay and weathering. Under certain conditions bone becomes impregnated by minerals and fossilized. These fossils, such as those found by the Leakeys in Olduvai Gorge, are the basis for our knowledge of how the earliest humans looked. Ethnoarchaeologists have also discovered the important role that carnivores and other

FIGURE **6-13**   An underwater team exploring the remains of a Roman galley that had had a cargo of wine in amphorae, tall jars with pointed bottoms that fitted into racks meant to keep them from rolling during rough weather.

scavenging animals play in destroying and removing bones from archaeological sites. Hyenas, with their powerful jaws, will even crush (and swallow) large bones and then deposit them elsewhere. In fact, one of the most enduring debates in archaeological literature concerns whether bone fragments over a million years old in cave sites in South Africa are the products of the activity of scavenging animals or of humans who used them as tools. Archaeologists are now experimenting with different ways to break bones and are examining the bones collected by scavengers. Meanwhile, the origin of such "osteodontokeratic" (meaning literally "bone, teeth, horn") accumulations remains a mystery.

Plant remains—wood and foods—and plant products, such as cordage, textiles, and paper, are among the most fragile items in archaeological context because they are subject to thorough bacterial and fungal attack. For the most part, the following statements also apply to the fleshy parts,

Environmental Formation Processes □ **148**

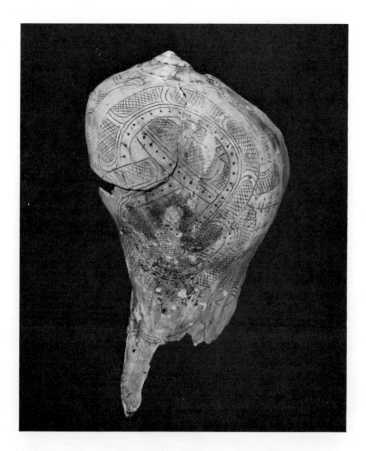

FIGURE **6-14**

An intricately carved shell—probably made around A.D. 1500—from the Spiro site in eastern Oklahoma. Shell in non-acidic contexts is often well preserved.

hides, and fur of animals. Unless the growth of bacteria and fungi are inhibited, plant remains will rapidly decay. A number of natural conditions, such as freezing, submersion in mud or other oxygen-free environments, and dryness, retard decay. It was not the mummification ritual accorded the ancient Egyptian elite that preserved their bodies, but the dryness of the desert—and this preserved both the rich in their tombs and the poor in their trash pits. Particular chemical environments may have the same effect. For example, remains deposited near copper may be preserved by copper sulfate that forms during the corrosion of the metal and is toxic to all animal life, including the bacteria that are agents of decay. In each of these cases conditions must remain stable. Variability—alternate freezing and thawing or dryness and moisture—will lead to rapid deterioration. In the United States, there are only a few places where perishable materials are preserved; in the dry rock shelters of the Southwest and the Ozarks, in the sinkholes of Florida, in sites covered by mud slides in the Pacific Northwest (such as Ozette), and in occasional caves elsewhere (FIGURE 6-15). Because these sorts of stable conditions are rare in the world, archaeologists attach particular signifi-

FIGURE **6-15**   Artifacts—probably from the period A.D. 1400–1600—found in a burial cave in northern Mexico. The dry conditions have preserved woven baskets and a mat, gourd dippers, wooden arrows, and a host of smaller objects.

cance to sites such as the dry caves in the Tehuacán Valley in Mexico, where plant materials are preserved in abundance.

Conditions relating to the preservation or decay of artifacts can be extremely variable. Even within a single site there will sometimes be great differences. For example, the presence of architecture may prevent the operation of some decay—and especially weathering—processes. In the Joint Site, a thirty-six room Southwestern pueblo, animal bone deposited inside rooms was at least a hundred times more likely to be preserved. In Maya sites each tomb will constitute a different depositional environment; some can hold cloth, cordage, and even bits of paper from sacred Maya books, while in others at the same site no perishables will be preserved. Conditions necessary for long-term preservation can be created, as in a tomb recently discovered in China where the body of a Han noblewoman, more than 2,100 years old, was so well preserved that her skin was still elastic. The tomb had been sealed with thick layers of charcoal and dense clay.

ENVIRONMENT AND THE FUTURE

This chapter has described the basic principles needed to understand the role of environmental processes in the formation of sites. With these in mind we can speculate, as we did in the preceding chapter, on what future archaeologists might discern about our civilization. Although our earlier speculations were in terms of a gap of about 100 years, we will use the figure of 100,000 years in this case because environmental formation processes are usually much slower-acting than cultural formation processes. We can speculate on three levels: that of artifacts, of sites, and of regions.

Artifacts

If a car were abandoned today on Route I-40 in Arkansas, could one find it 100,000 years from now? It would be difficult, not because it had been moved, but because so little of it would be left. The stately symbol of our social standing would be reduced to a scatter of ceramic spark-plug insulators, broken window glass, pieces of aluminum trim and engine parts, all nested in soils with a high iron content from degraded metals and a high organic content from the deterioration of plastics, textiles, and rubber. Our driver, if he had stayed, would be represented by the gold fillings in his teeth. While this is the general picture, lucky future archaeologists might find some flukes of preservation. For example, they might excavate the resort lodge of a Harry Truman, who refused to evacuate it when nearby Mount St. Helens was erupting in 1980. In May of that year, Harry, his lodge, and all his belongings were buried in a mud slide not unlike the ones that preserved Ozette.

Sites

Depending on their immediate environment, some sites will be better preserved than others. Assuming that our current sports palaces were not torn down to make room for housing, what vestiges of them could be found in the distant future? The remains of the Dallas Cowboys' home field would be plentiful, but probably covered with mature forest that would have engulfed concrete and Astro-turf alike. Further north, the remains of Chicago's Soldiers' Field would have been ground to small bits and slowly pushed through the Midwest by glaciers.

Regions

The fate of Soldiers' Field calls our attention to glaciation—perhaps the most important process in our predictions concerning the remains of our society 100,000 years from now. We must also remember the associated changes in climate, which will make some areas cooler and wetter and change regional patterns of preservation.

The Overkill Theory

Many megafauna of the New World—large game animals including mammoth and giant forms of bison—died out completely between 12,000 and 10,000 years ago. According to Paul S. Martin's "overkill theory" of what took place, when the first humans entered the New World, they found it teeming with these animals, which, never having developed survival strategies through previous encounters with hunters were relatively defenseless and were killed in large numbers. Furthermore, because they were large, these animals were slow reproducers. From their initial point of entry into the New World, human populations grew and expanded in a broad wave across the North and South American continents, with the result that ever larger numbers of game animals were consistently killed by hunters—to the point of extinction. By means of a computer simulation, Martin and his students have shown just how quickly this spreading wave of humanity could have eradicated a species.

If the overkill theory is correct, then the New World was first populated just slightly before the megafauna extinctions occurred. This expectation flies squarely in the face of mounting evidence for the much earlier settlement of the New World. The camp site at Meadowcroft Shelter (FIGURE 6-5), for example, has been dated to at least 17,000 B.P. Meadowcroft and a few other sites suggest that people and Pleistocene beasts coexisted for considerably longer than can be explained by the overkill theory.

Even were the evidence for pre-12,000 B.P. occupation to be overturned in the future, other weaknesses can be found in the overkill theory that suggest a need for drastic revisions. Despite discoveries of butchered mammoths, which gave rise to the characterization of early people as "big-game hunters," it is not at all established that the diet of these people was mainly large game. Given the difficulties of bagging even a "naive" five-ton mammoth, it is reasonable to suppose that mammoth kills were relatively infrequent and that a lot of time was spent collecting plants and hunting smaller game. On the other hand, if mammoths had contributed substantially to the diet, it is unlikely that any group of hunter-gatherers would drive its principal food source to extinction. Finally, zooarchaeologist Don Grayson has shown that quite a few species (especially birds), which were clearly not exploited to any degree by human populations, became extinct at the same time as the megafauna. (Although this suggests that broader environmental processes were at work to cause extinctions, it does not rule out some form of human influence.)

Despite its weaknesses, the overkill theory will probably survive in some modified form alongside a better understanding of the more general environmental processes that characterized the close of the Pleistocene. Most importantly, by providing a clear-cut, testable theory, Martin's work has stimulated important research and led to additional discoveries and questions. One of the most basic questions he raises is still unanswered: If hunter-gatherers were present in the New World for thousands of years prior to 12,000 years B.P., why have we found so few of their traces?

Afterword   While few of us worry about the coming of the next glaciation, or the long-term effects of the environment on our artifacts, many of our activities today are directed toward keeping the environment at bay, trying at all costs to prevent our precious artifacts from declining into some undesirable condition. We regularly paint and patch our houses to keep wood and masonry from deteriorating. We pull weeds from our lawns and gardens to maintain preferred but wholly unnatural plant associations. We wash and wax our cars to reduce corrosion and oxidation. We hire exterminators to spray our houses and yards with noxious chemicals so that we may retain sole possession of our territories. Communities and regional systems are no less active in the war with nature. They build dams and levees to prevent flooding, construct artificial channels for better drainage, and, in colder climates, remove snow with heavy equipment.

Sometimes we go beyond mere holding actions and engage in actual intervention. Canals are built to transport water as well as to carry cargo by ship. Forests are cleared to make way for settlements and agriculture or even for tree farms managed by foresters. Factories dump chemicals and other wastes in rivers, streams, and oceans. Our clothing, automobiles, and buildings create artificial environments to control temperature, humidity, and light. More recently, we have begun to develop products, such as Astro-turf, to replace nature altogether.

Throughout occupation and continuing until its excavation by archaeologists, a site interacts with its environment. When we abandon our settlements, as people did countless times in the past, the war against nature is lost. Slowly environmental processes claim our prized possessions and invade our sacred territories. It is an inevitable indignity that we and ours shall eventually return to dust.

General William Augustus Lane Fox Pitt-Rivers (1827–1900)   Many early archaeologists were wealthy, and General Pitt-Rivers was one of the wealthiest. Pitt-Rivers is remembered because he used his money to set new standards of excavation and recording. He required detailed drawings of the sides of pits as an aid to interpreting the way the observable layers had been formed. He was the first to publish "relic tables," which listed each of the artifacts recovered. These lists even included animal bones, which his contemporaries threw out as worthless. And his reports were innovative in their lavish use of illustration. General Pitt-Rivers is considered by many to be the "father of modern archaeology"; he is at least the founder of the British tradition of meticulous excavation and reporting.   □   Archaeology began as a hobby for William Augustus Lane Fox during his military career. His job was to train men in the use of rifles, and he became intrigued with the history of the weapons and, subsequently, the history of technology. These interests led him to construct sequences for the evolution of particular artifacts—especially firearms. In his later years he was apt to describe himself as one of the co-creators, with Darwin, of the theory of evolution.   □   Most of his fieldwork was done at Cranborne Chase, the estate of 27,000 acres he inherited (along with the name Pitt-Rivers) in 1880. For two decades he kept full field crews working steadily. His workmen were paid less than a pound a week—a fair wage for the time—which placed little strain on the estate's annual income of 23,000 pounds.   □   General Pitt-Rivers' standards for archaeology were high and were obviously set by himself. There was no need for him to fill out requisition forms for each trowel and shovel, to justify every hiring decision to three levels of bureaucracy, or to worry endlessly about raising funds to continue his research. Today, in an era when every archaeological project seems to be mired in red tape, we look back with envy at the freedom that Pitt-Rivers had to pursue his vision of archaeology.

General William Pitt-Rivers,
who was as properly Victorian
as this portrait would imply.

7
RECOVERY

Unlike General Pitt-Rivers, most archaeologists don't dig in their own backyards. In fact, they spend a lot of their time deciding where and how to look for sites and where and how to excavate those sites once they are found. The recovery of archaeological materials involves making informed decisions; it is not a haphazard process. The principles of *recovery theory*, which form the body of this chapter, are the principles that aid in making these decisions.

To begin with, archaeologists don't work blind. They make use of many types of information in their decision making, including existing knowledge of the environment of the study area, previous archaeological and historical research, and the practical factors of organizing people and equipment for fieldwork. In order to use this information in accordance with recovery principles, there must be a focal point—a particular research question or, more likely, set of questions, that the archaeological remains being sought will answer. Thus, the specific plans for archaeological research, known as *research designs*, are problem-oriented and are based on a careful consideration of a wide variety of information (FIGURE 7-1). The work of Richard MacNeish, described in Chapter 2, is a good example. MacNeish's question was, essentially, When and how did the first domestication of plants occur in the New World? Many of the corncobs he sought had long since decayed. In addition, because of limits on time and money, only a few regions could be intensively searched for likely sites, and only a

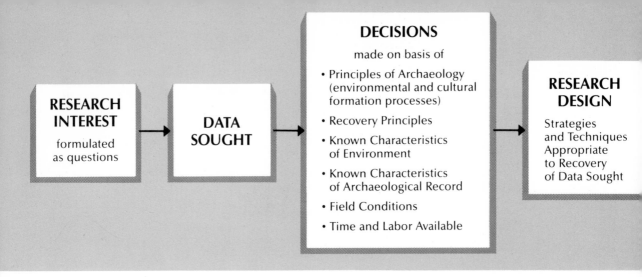

DECISIONS
made on basis of

- Principles of Archaeology (environmental and cultural formation processes)
- Recovery Principles
- Known Characteristics of Environment
- Known Characteristics of Archaeological Record
- Field Conditions
- Time and Labor Available

RESEARCH INTEREST
formulated as questions

DATA SOUGHT

RESEARCH DESIGN
Strategies and Techniques Appropriate to Recovery of Data Sought

FIGURE **7-1**

The process of choosing recovery techniques.

handful of sites could be excavated, none entirely. Marshalling the available information and applying the relevant archaeological principles led Mac-Neish first to dry caves in Tamaulipas and then to dry caves in Tehuacán, Mexico. The road from Tamaulipas to Tehuacán was long and, for all the success, there were also failures. The first domesticated corncobs, like many of the things archaeologists seek, are elusive prey. Every archaeologist faces similar difficulties, and each knows well that the way precious resources are used in the recovery phase of research determines what will be learned.

SAMPLING

All archaeological recovery is *sampling,* selecting from among the total possible regions and sites those areas to be surveyed and, within those sites, those areas to be excavated. Thus, sampling principles are the ones most fundamental to developing research designs. The problem under investigation defines the *universe,* or study area. This universe can be a region where archaeologists are looking for sites, or a site where archaeologists seek artifacts.

The whole set of materials an archaeologist wants to record in a study area, whether that set is made up of sites or artifacts, is called a *population.* We will illustrate the basic concepts and principles of sampling with a hypothetical drive-in theater (FIGURE 7-2), which will be treated as an archaeologist would treat a region or a site. The drive-in is our universe; it contains populations (of speaker posts, of pop-tops from beverage cans, and of other artifacts), and the specific characteristics of this universe are *population parameters.* For example, the number of screens and the number of speaker posts at the drive-in (in this case 1 and 356, respectively), are population parameters.

Any part or subset of a population is a *sample,* and each member of the population a potential *sample unit*—that is, a unit that is investigated or examined. The number of sample units surveyed or excavated is the *sample*

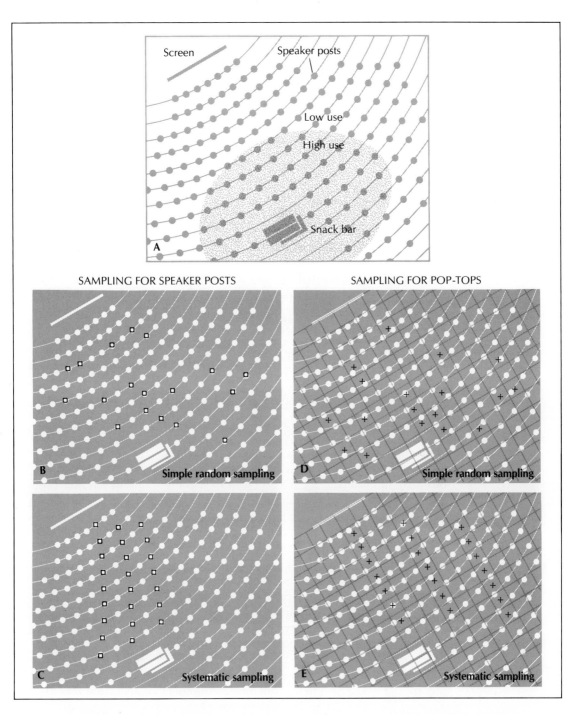

FIGURE 7-2   Archaeological sampling strategies as they might be applied at a typical drive-in theatre. At top center (A) is the basic plan of the theatre, showing screen, speaker posts, driving lanes, and snack bar complex. B and C show procedures when sampling from a list of elements, and D and E, when sampling space. Note the regularity of intervals between sample units where selection is on the basis of systematic sampling (C and E).

size. The characteristics of the sample are known as *statistics*. If we examined 10 posts (sample size, 10) and found that 5, or 50 percent, had defective speakers, these figures would be statistics that described our sample. The basic exercise consists of using sample statistics to estimate population parameters, such as using the percentage of defective speaker posts in a sample to estimate the number defective in the whole drive-in. This is a problem in statistical inference, and solving it depends to a major degree on the techniques used and the nature of the population sampled.

Every time we take something off a supermarket shelf we are, in effect, sampling. Our decision would be made according to one of two kinds of *subjective sampling techniques*—*purposive* (selecting tomatoes that met specific criteria of firmness, size, and color) and *haphazard* (taking tomatoes with no guiding system). In archaeology, purposive sampling is important: MacNeish, interested in preserved plant remains, did not waste much time at open sites, but went to dry caves, where preservation was more likely. In our example, if we wanted to study a few broken speakers, we could select them by quick visual inspection of any row of posts. A technique preferred by statisticians is *probability sampling,* which incorporates a random process in making selections. We are all familiar with random processes—flipping a coin, say—where the outcome (a head or tail) is totally a product of chance, and so, unpredictable. What makes random processes interesting and useful is that, if they are repeated many times, certain patterns or trends emerge. Thus, a coin flipped for several hours will have come up heads almost exactly half the time. It is these long-run regularities of random processes that make statistical inferences possible.

In *simple random sampling,* a popular technique, every member of a population, such as a speaker post, has an equal chance of being chosen as a sample unit. In this method, if we wanted to study use-wear on speakers (in our drive-in example), we would begin to select a sample of speaker posts (FIGURE 7-2*B*) by giving each post a number (from 001 to 356). Next, we would refer to a "table of random numbers" (one can usually be found lurking in the back of any statistical textbook), which is a list of randomly produced numbers (FIGURE 7-3). Starting anywhere in the table and moving in any direction—to left, to right, up or down—we would read off three digits in a row to get our first number. Continuing in the same direction additional groups of three digits are selected without skipping any digits. The resulting three-digit numbers would designate the speakers in our sample. We would continue in this way until we reached the desired sample size. (Numbers above our limit—356—are ignored.) The main advantage of simple random sampling is that many statistical techniques (for estimating population parameters) are available for data obtained in this way. Were we looking for pop-tops, it would be difficult and time-consuming to find and number them all. Here we come face-to-face with a major hardship in archaeological sampling. Just as we don't know how many or where pop-tops are in the drive-in, neither does an archaeologist know how many sites there are in a region

12651	61646	11769	75109	86996	97669	25757	32535	07122	76763
81769	74436	02630	72310	45049	18029	07469	42341	98173	79260
36737	98863	77240	76251	00654	64688	09343	70278	67331	98729
82861	54371	76610	94934	72748	44124	05610	53750	95938	01485
21325	15732	24127	37431	09723	63529	73977	95218	96074	42138
74146	47887	62463	23045	41490	07954	22597	60012	98866	90959
90759	64410	54179	66075	61051	75385	51378	08360	95946	95547
55683	98078	02238	91540	21219	17720	87817	41705	95785	12563
79686	17969	76061	83748	55920	83612	41540	86492	06447	60568
70333	00201	86201	69716	78185	62154	77930	67663	29529	75116
14042	53536	07779	04157	41172	36473	42123	43929	50533	33437
59911	08256	06596	48416	69770	68797	56080	14223	59199	30162
62368	62623	62742	14891	39247	52242	98832	69533	91174	57979
57529	97751	54976	48957	74599	08759	78494	52785	68526	64618
15469	90574	78033	66885	13936	42117	71831	22961	94225	31816
18625	23674	53850	32827	81647	80820	00420	63555	74489	80141
74626	68394	88562	70745	23701	45630	65891	58220	35442	60414
11119	16519	27384	90199	79210	76965	99546	30323	31664	22845
41101	17336	48951	53674	17880	45260	08575	49321	36191	17095
32123	91576	84221	78902	82010	30847	62329	63898	23268	74283
26091	68409	69704	82267	14751	13151	93115	01437	56945	89661
67680	79790	48462	59278	44185	29616	76531	19589	83139	28454
15184	19260	14073	07026	25264	08388	27182	22557	61501	67481
58010	45039	57181	10238	36874	28546	37444	80824	63981	39942
56425	53996	86245	32623	78858	08143	60377	42925	42815	11159
82630	84066	13592	60642	17904	99718	63432	88642	37858	25431
14927	40909	23900	48761	44860	92467	31742	87142	03607	32059
23740	22505	07489	85986	74420	21744	97711	36648	35620	97949
32990	97446	03711	63824	07953	85965	87089	11687	92414	67257
05310	24058	91946	78437	34365	82469	12430	84754	19354	72745
21839	39937	27534	88913	49055	19218	47712	67677	51889	70926
08833	42549	93981	94051	28382	83725	72643	64233	97252	17133
58336	11139	47479	00931	91560	95372	97642	33856	54825	55680
62032	91144	75478	47431	52726	30289	42411	91886	51818	78292
45171	30557	53116	04118	58301	24375	65609	85810	18620	49198
91611	62656	60128	35609	63698	78356	50682	22505	01692	36291
55472	63819	86314	49174	93582	73604	78614	78849	23096	72825
18573	09729	74091	53994	10970	86557	65661	41854	26037	53296
60866	02955	90288	82136	83644	94455	06560	78029	98768	71296
45043	55608	82767	60890	74646	79485	13619	98868	40857	19415
17831	09737	79473	75945	28394	79334	70577	38048	03607	06932
40137	03981	07585	18128	11178	32601	27994	05641	22600	86064
77776	31343	14576	97706	16039	47517	43300	59080	80392	63189
69605	44104	40103	95635	05635	81673	68657	09559	23510	95875
19916	52934	26499	09821	87331	80993	61299	36979	73599	35055
02606	58552	07678	56619	65325	30705	99582	53390	46357	13244
65183	73160	87131	35530	47946	09854	18080	02321	05809	04898
10740	98914	44916	11322	89717	88189	30143	52687	19420	60061
98642	89822	71691	51573	83666	61642	46683	33761	47542	23551
60139	25601	93663	25547	02654	94829	48672	28736	84994	13071

FIGURE **7-3** A typical page from a table of random numbers. In this case, random numbers are chosen by moving from left to right. The first number is 028. The last number is 226.

or how many stone artifacts there are in a site. In such cases, we could change our sampling units from pop-tops or sites or stone tools to something more manageable—we would sample space. We would divide our entire universe (drive-in, region, or site) into smaller areas. These pieces of space would become our population and we would number each and select our sample units from them. In our search for pop-tops, this method could be carried out by drawing a grid over the plan (FIGURE 7-2A) of the drive-in, numbering each square in the grid, and consulting a table of random numbers to select a sample of grid squares (FIGURE 7-2D). Each grid square in our sample would then be systematically searched for pop-tops.

One of the obvious problems with the simple random sampling of space is that sample units may cluster, leaving large areas unsampled. To get a more even coverage, archaeologists sometimes use *systematic sampling,* in which there is an equal interval between all sampling units. For example, we could choose every tenth grid square (FIGURES 7-2C and 7-2E). A serious problem with systematic sampling is the possibility that our periodic units may correspond to patterns in the distribution of artifacts. For example, it would be possible to select an interval between grid squares that would correspond to the distance between rows of speaker posts, ending with squares that represented mainly driving lanes and no parking spaces. Such a choice could severely bias the results of pop-top collection. Archaeologists are now experimenting with a variety of sampling designs that combine the advantages of simple random and systematic sampling methods.

Precision
The relative effectiveness of various sampling techniques is evaluated in terms of *precision.* Precision is a measure of how tightly the statistics cluster —that is, how nearly alike the totals obtained are—on repeated trials of the same technique. For example, let us assume that we have applied three different techniques to choose grid squares in which to recover pop-tops in our drive-in. Each technique is applied five times, with these results:

	Number of Pop-Tops		
Trial	Technique A	Technique B	Technique C
1	515	451	391
2	496	426	576
3	511	541	792
4	499	519	402
5	492	501	588

Clearly, Technique A, with its tight grouping of values (a relatively narrow range of 492 to 515), produces the most consistent and least varied results, followed by Techniques B and C in that order. Technique A is more "precise" and would, therefore, normally be preferred.

Sampling decisions can affect precision in several ways. The basic principle is that precision varies directly with sample size; the larger the number of sample units, the greater the precision. Let us assume we randomly selected and searched two sample units in our drive-in, and repeated this process ten times. The chances are good that on some trials we would select squares that had many pop-tops (for example, those at speaker posts) and that on other trials we would examine squares with few pop-tops (for example, in lanes). In the end, we would have quite varied results. If, on the other hand, we use thirty grid squares in each of ten trials, our results would be more likely to be consistent.

Another basic principle of sampling is that the more homogeneous the population, the smaller the sample needed to produce inferences having the same degree of precision. For example, if we wished to learn what items are associated with speaker posts (speakers and holders), a small sample of speaker posts (fewer than a dozen) would suffice because the population is very homogeneous—most posts have speakers and holders. On the other hand, were we interested in describing populations of artifacts deposited at the drive-in, a much larger sample of grid squares (say, 30–60) would be needed for precise estimates because of their greater heterogeneity: some squares have many items, some few; some have many types of artifacts, others are more limited in variety.

One of the easiest ways to take advantage of this principle is to *stratify* the population, dividing it into homogeneous subgroups (of sites, artifacts, or spatial units). Stratifying could be useful in a search for pop-tops, with all the grid squares in the snack bar area, the high-use area, and the low-use area treated separately—thus creating three *sampling strata* (different from depositional strata), which are then sampled separately. In fact, we could also make strata from the grid squares in lanes and from the grid squares in parking areas (FIGURE 7-2). Simple random sampling or systematic sampling can be used for selecting sample units within strata.

Three population characteristics—abundance, evenness of distribution, and size—also have an effect on precision and the choice of sampling techniques. In the case of abundance, the more common the element (relative abundance), the greater the precision, regardless of sampling technique. Thus, the techniques we have discussed are likely to provide precise statistics for pop-tops (a very popular element) but not for rare items, such as lost coins. The effects of evenness of distribution—the second important population characteristic—can be illustrated by the snack bar complex. Since all food preparation, display, sales, and restroom facilities are clustered in one location, their discovery will be hit or miss, much as with the rare but widely distributed coins. The third factor—size—also would affect discovery of the snack bar complex or the coins for, when sampling space, the larger the element on the ground, the more precise the results of any sampling technique. If our grid squares are relatively small and we sample a fair number, we are likely to consistently discover large complexes such as the snack bar.

The difficulty of obtaining precise estimates for rare, clustered, and small items is a particular hardship in archaeological sampling. There are always rare sites in a region that are of great interest, many sites are highly clustered, and some of the rare and clustered sites are small. Parallel problems are faced in sampling areas within sites. For example, some important kinds of deposits, such as de facto refuse and rich burials, are rare and perhaps clustered. Because precision varies directly with sample size, the archaeologist can attempt to improve the parameter estimates for rare and clustered elements by selecting more sample units. This is not a very efficient or realistic solution because one might have to sample almost the entire population in order to obtain precise statistics. Very often archaeologists turn to less costly—and less statistically elegant—techniques in these cases. For example, purposive techniques can be used: the snack bar might easily be found by visual inspection; if, from past studies, we know areas where coins are likely to be lost, these more limited areas can be systematically searched.

The Sampling Paradox

To determine the size of sample needed to estimate a particular population parameter, one needs to know some of the characteristics of the population, particularly homogeneity, rarity, degree of clustering, size of elements. This is the basis of the archaeological sampling paradox: How can archaeologists know *before* sampling starts the very thing they are trying to determine by means of the sampling? This problem can be illustrated by our drive-in. Were we investigating speaker posts, we could, because we know how many speaker posts there are, adjust our sample size accordingly. However, we don't know how many coins or pop-tops there are initially; as a result, we have insufficient information for designing a sample. Unfortunately, this is usually the situation in archaeological recovery. Archaeologists solve the sampling paradox by the use of *multistage* sampling. By this technique a first-stage sample is drawn, usually based on purposive hunches or simple random sampling. Parameter estimates are made from the results. On the basis of these estimates, the sample is redesigned and enlarged. There is no limit to the number of stages that can be used. There is also no "magic number" for how large a sample must be at each stage. The rationale behind the decision concerning sample size is extremely complex and is influenced by research questions, required degree of precision, characteristics of a population, and available time, personnel, and funds.

Because all artifacts are visible, even if they cannot be readily counted, our drive-in sampling example makes problems seem much less difficult than they usually are in the field. In many survey areas in forests, sites are obscured by pine duff and underbrush. Add to this the further dimension of depth of deposits, and the full difficulty of archaeological sampling becomes evident. Archaeologists excavate large tells in the Near East that are three stories high and composed of more than twenty building phases. In these cases, there are few surface clues to the characteristics of buried artifacts and structures. Moreover, the ideal sampling design for the top of the mound may not be at all ideal for the bottom. In constructing sampling designs in the real world, outside of our drive-in, archaeologists draw upon their knowledge of various principles, in addition to those discussed above, concerning the way the archaeological record was formed. In the remainder of this chapter we will discuss how such archaeological principles and sampling theory are used to design efficient and reliable recovery programs.

REGIONAL SURVEY: LOCATING SETTLEMENTS

No settlement is an island entire of itself. In order to understand human adaptation, we have to know how different settlements fit together into regional systems. Little can be learned about a past hunter-gatherer lifeway from studying just one camp; likewise, even an ancient city like Teotihuacán remains a mystery without information on its interactions with surrounding settlements. *Regional survey* is the activity of locating and describing the remains of past settlements as they exist in the landscape today. It is usually the first step toward understanding past regional settlement systems and answering more specific research questions. Such surveys are also the main means of gathering information relevant to land-use planning (p. 36).

The Virú Valley Project in Peru was one of the first studies to use an archaeological survey to describe human adaptation on a regional scale. Gordon Willey and James Ford together scrambled over every nook and cranny of the coastal valley, recording the remains of irrigation systems, hill forts, ceremonial sites, and small and large towns. Their data, when combined with the dating of sites by their pottery styles, or *seriation* (Chapter 9), produced a long-term picture of change in the settlement system as well as data on the diversity of settlements occupied at any one time (FIGURE 7-4).

Surveys are carried out in archaeological study areas. Study areas can be defined on the basis of topographic criteria (a river valley), the distribution of a type of artifact (the area of a particular style of pottery), or even administrative convenience (a national forest or a highway right-of-way). These areas tend to range in size from a few acres to many thousands of square miles, depending on the purpose of the study. Study areas usually contain dense clusters of artifacts or archaeological sites, such as Near Eastern tells and Maya temple centers, and more widely scattered remains, including, for example, items lost on hunting trips or water jars broken near a spring.

Pedestrian Tactic

Archaeologists have available a large arsenal of survey techniques to use in sampling the archaeological record. The most widely employed survey technique is the *pedestrian tactic*—systematically walking over the ground with set intervals between surveyors. Within sample units there can be variations in intensity (the effort devoted to inspecting the ground surface), which is directly related to the distance between surveyors. Variations in intensity have important practical consequences. The greater the intensity, the better

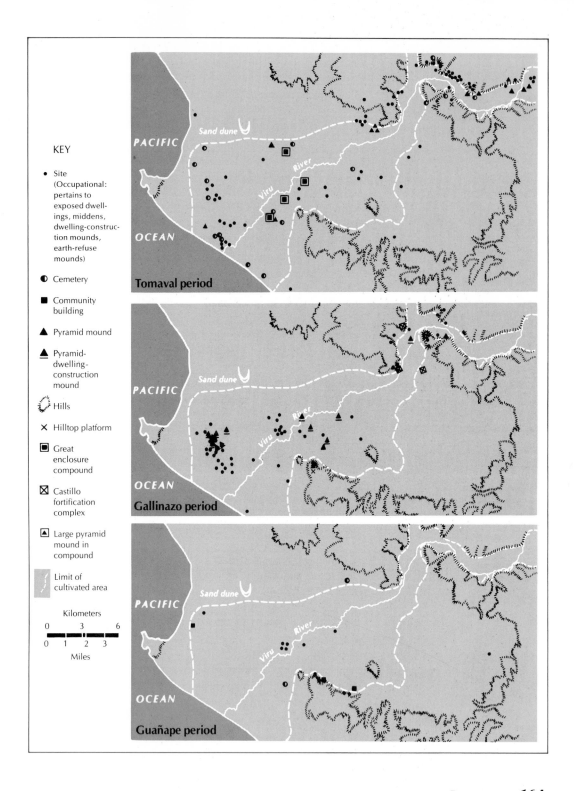

KEY

● Site
(Occupational:
pertains to
exposed dwell-
ings, middens,
dwelling-construc-
tion mounds,
earth-refuse
mounds)

◑ Cemetery

■ Community
building

▲ Pyramid mound

▲ Pyramid-
dwelling-
construction
mound

⦚ Hills

✕ Hilltop platform

▣ Great
enclosure
compound

⊠ Castillo
fortification
complex

◣ Large pyramid
mound in
compound

▨ Limit of
cultivated area

Kilometers
0   3   6
0   1   2   3
Miles

PACIFIC

Sand dune

River

Viru

OCEAN

Tomaval period

PACIFIC

Sand dune

Viru River

OCEAN

Gallinazo period

PACIFIC

Sand dune

Viru River

OCEAN

Guañape period

the precision. This means simply that more kinds of sites and artifacts, especially small ones, will be found. Obviously, it is desirable to increase intensity, but for every doubling of intensity there is almost a doubling of fieldwork costs; archaeologists, therefore, must make many painful compromises regarding level of intensity.

Choices must also be made about the size and shape of the sample units. To determine optimum sizes and shapes of sample units archaeologists have done a number of experiments using information from surveys having 100 percent coverage. Findings were that small units, because there are more of them, are preferable from the standpoint of sample size. However, the more units there are, the more the effort spent finding them and moving crews from one to another. Thus, from a logistical standpoint, fewer but larger units are preferable. Although unit sizes vary greatly from study to study and even among stages within a project, they generally average about a tenth of a square mile. The smallest units are normally used in high-intensity surveys that focus on isolated artifacts.

The unit shapes commonly employed in surveys are a square (called a *quadrat*) and an elongated rectangle (known as a *transect*). Quadrats provide good information on site clustering and associations among types of sites. Transects, on the other hand, are often easier to lay out and survey. In addition, when placed across environmental zones, transects can disclose associations between types of sites and plant and animal communities.

The bases of decisions concerning intensity and unit shape and size are not simple. No configuration of units and intensity is ideal for all problems and areas. Usually the archaeologist is trying to balance gains in precision against greater field costs. Thus, each decision reflects the application of basic principles in the context of specific field situations.

The Reese River Valley Project furnishes an example of the effective use of probabilistic sampling and pedestrian tactics to answer specific research questions. David Thomas began this project in the Great Basin region of the American West in the late 1960s. In this desolate area of north-central Nevada, Thomas sought to test Julian Steward's model of the long-term adaptation of Indians to an arid environment. Steward's model was derived from his research in the 1930s among then-surviving Indian groups, such as Paiute and Shoshone (FIGURE 3-4). His classic descriptions were, however, based less on observations of actual behavior than on the memory of aged informants, who recalled "how it used to be" before major changes caused

FIGURE **7-4**   (Facing page) Three main phases of settlement in the Virú Valley: In the earliest, the Guañape phase (1800–900 B.C.), there is one simple temple or public building; in the Gallinazo (200 B.C.–A.D. 600), there is, on the alluvial plain, a large cluster of adobe buildings and pyramids, constituting one of Peru's earliest cities. (The four forts at the upper end of the valley were probably built to protect the large irrigation network constructed in this phase.) In the Tomaval phase (A.D. 600–1000), population is concentrated into large compounds (See FIGURE 8-23).

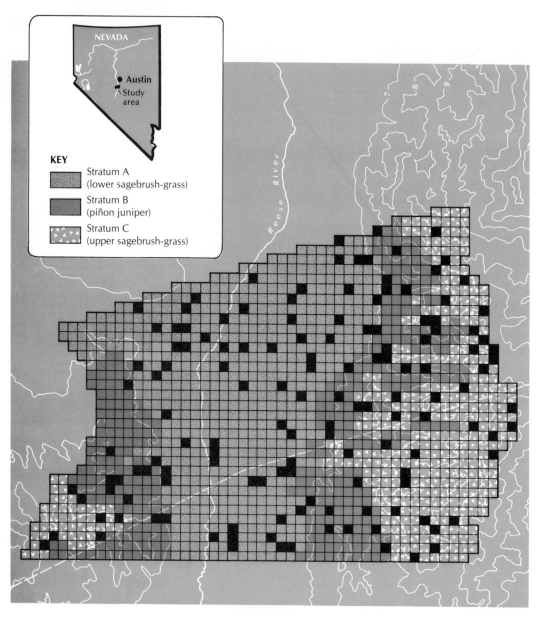

FIGURE **7-5**   The Reese River Valley project. Map shows portion of Reese River Valley studied; photograph (on facing page), a view of the valley. (Note zonal vegetation differences, which formed the basis of the sampling strata used in the research design.) In the grid, which shows the scheme for stratified random sampling of space, each filled square (quadrat) was selected randomly within one of the three major strata: lower sagebrush-grass (*A*), pinon-juniper (*B*), and upper sagebrush-grass (*C*). Quadrats selected comprise a sample of 10 per cent of the study area.

by European diseases and settlements. Steward's model is now familiar as the "seasonal round" of hunter-gatherer bands, the movement during the year from place to place as different plant and animal resources become available. With Steward's model as a guide, Thomas used a computer simulation to predict the kinds of artifacts that should have been deposited in different environmental zones during different seasons.

To check the simulation predictions and thereby test the model, Thomas designed a survey for his 135-square-mile study area that relied on stratified random sampling. He defined three major strata based on different environmental zones (FIGURE 7-5). He selected quadrats 500 meters on a side as his survey unit and assigned six crew members to each. Spaced about 20 or 30 meters apart, they could survey one or two units per day. After several seasons of work, he had accumulated 140 sample units, or about 10 percent of the study area. His crews recorded both ancient and modern sites —of which there were precious few—and collected artifacts such as arrowpoints, scraping tools, used cores, and grinding stones, which made up the major part of the archaeological record. His analysis supported the Steward model and implied a great stability (from about 5000 B.C. to A.D. 1850) of adaptation to the arid environment.

Although Thomas made good use of pedestrian survey, it cannot be applied everywhere. Two factors of the study area influence the practicality of the pedestrian tactic: (1) visibility, the ability to detect by visual inspection archaeological materials on the ground or indications, such as depressions or humps, that archaeological materials lie below the ground, and (2) accessibility, the difficulty of getting around such obstacles as impenetrable brush, bodies of water, and sheer cliffs. Pedestrian techniques are most profitably applied in areas of high visibility and easy accessibility, such as deserts, fallow fields, and lightly wooded areas. Not all archaeologists are as fortunate as Thomas was in working in areas where artifacts are visible on the surface and crews can easily move from one area to another.

Exposures

Archaeologists use a variety of techniques to overcome problems of poor visibility and low accessibility. In forests and areas of recent natural deposition, two major approaches have been employed to find sites. Existing exposures such as dirt roads, rodent burrows, cattle paths, and tree falls are searched out and inspected for artifacts. In other areas archaeologists are now creating artificial exposures by means of garden rakes, shovels, posthole diggers, and even specialized coring and boring tools. Once sample units are chosen, one or more of these types of exposures are made at regular intervals on the ground. Small-diameter coring tools (less than 3 inches) may not be reliable for finding sites unless artifact density is extremely high or unless the number of exposures is extremely large. In fact, experiments with small corers at known sites have failed to produce artifacts. In some cases, buried sites have been discovered through systematic trenching in deep alluvial deposits with a backhoe—a kind of power scoop or excavator. The likelihood of discovering a site with existing or artificial exposures varies directly with: (1) site area, (2) artifact density, (3) artifact size, (4) surface area exposed, and (5) number of exposures. Existing and artificial exposures make site discovery under bad field conditions possible; regrettably, it is difficult to make precise parameter estimates from these discoveries.

Remote Sensing

Other techniques are now available to provide supplementary information about sites, even in inaccessible areas. Aerial photography and other *remote sensing* methods have supplied increasingly sophisticated techniques for spying on the archaeological record. First used in 1906, when a British lieutenant, F. H. Sharpe, photographed Stonehenge from a hot-air balloon, "observation and recording at a distance" has expanded to include a wide range of devices from cameras mounted on kites and U-2 spy planes to earth-orbiting satellites.

Remote-sensing techniques in archaeological research have been used mainly for site discovery. Archaeologists find aerial photography indispensible in the field for plotting finds and sometimes for finding themselves. Aerial photographs are often converted, by photogrammetric techniques, into conventional maps (FIGURE 7-6). In aerial photographs archaeologists seek various traces of human behavior on the landscape, such as pueblo walls in the Southwest or large tells in the Near East. Subtle traces that may elude

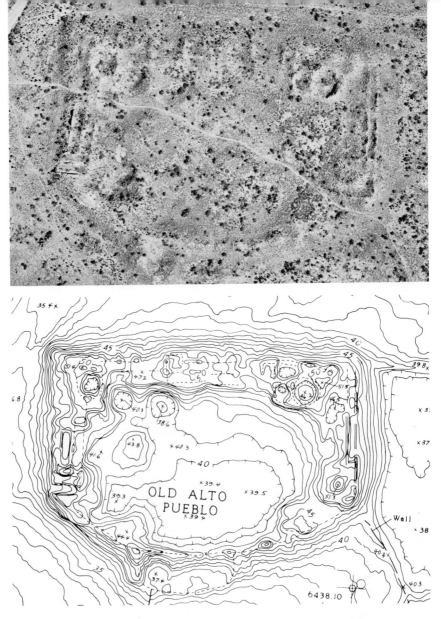

FIGURE **7-6**   At top, an aerial photograph of Pueblo Alto in Chaco Canyon, New Mexico; below, a contour map drawn by computer from a pair of stereo photographs.

the surveyor on foot—such as silted-in irrigation canals and trails or roads (FIGURE 7-7)—are sometimes readily observed on aerial photographs. Stereoscopic photographs—images of the same area taken from slightly different points—can often show, in a three-dimensional image, slight differences in elevation and low-lying alignments of rocks, which disclose sites. Sites can even be found in this way in inaccessible areas, such as military bomb-

Aerial photograph of the ancient Nahrawān canal and its radiating branches, looking southeast from Quantara weir, near Baghdad, Iraq. The tents at right, center, give an idea of the scale of the project.

ing ranges and tracts of land where surveyors are denied entry (sometimes at gunpoint) by owners.

Major types of subtle traces detectable by aerial photography are shadow marks, soil marks, and crop marks. *Shadow marks,* cast by irregularities in elevation, are recorded best by photos taken when the sun is low on the horizon. *Soil marks* indicate differences in soils created by human behavior. For example, the introduction of organic wastes, such as household garbage, will darken soil to a degree recognizable from the air, and canals, trails, and dirt roads can destroy the A-horizon (Chapter 6), leaving the lighter-colored B- and C-horizons exposed. *Crop marks* are differences in vegetation patterns caused by underlying artifacts. Such archaeological materials can either retard or promote plant growth by affecting drainage and soil characteristics. Plant growth above buried walls is often stunted, and it is this fact that allows fairly detailed mapping of buried structures

FIGURE **7-8**

Crop marks, which can sometimes disclose the outlines of buried features, can be seen in this aerial photograph of the remains of a Roman settlement near Salisbury, England.

(FIGURE 7-8) from aerial photographs. Crop marks are most readily seen on grain fields, but any vegetation has the potential to respond to variations in growing conditions introduced by artifacts.

Different features in a study area may reflect different wavelengths of light, a phenomenon that photographic films with different spectral sensitivities will detect. For example, panchromatic film (ordinary black-and-white film), which has the same light sensitivity as the human eye, is a good general-purpose film for site detection. Panchromatic aerial photographs are available from federal and state agencies for almost every region of the United States and many areas in foreign countries. Black-and-white infrared film records the visible portion of the spectrum as well as infrared radiation. It is especially sensitive to differences in vegetation and in water content of soil. Normal color film is potentially more sensitive than standard black-and-white, but is expensive and rarely used. Color infrared film, extremely sensitive, responds to green, red, and infrared radiation; the images produced are startlingly unnatural, but are especially useful in environmental studies for delineating vegetation, soil, and topographic zones.

New techniques of remote sensing are continually being developed by the National Aeronautics and Space Administration and the Defense Department. Many have archaeological applications; for example, side-scanning radar, developed to penetrate dense jungle foliage during the Vietnam War, is now being utilized to hunt Maya canal systems in the rain forests of lowland Guatemala and Mexico.

Remote sensing also has a place in the large arsenal of techniques employed to find rare, small sites. The process begins with location of potential resources (for example, outcroppings of chippable stone) on aerial photographs. Surrounding areas can then be intensively searched for otherwise "invisible" quarry and workshop sites. This kind of formulation of predictive models on the basis of environmental variables is an especially effective way to locate quarries, shrines, rock art, and other hard-to-find sites likely to be associated with particular environmental features. Such predictive models are sometimes used as a shortcut, permitting survey of only those areas where sites are expected. Such shortcuts, however, have shortcomings; although limited searches will certainly produce sites, they leave unanswered the question of the population of sites in an entire region. The absence of sites in some places often reflects only the absence of survey.

Historical Sources

Historical data in archives are useful in finding historic sites. Even legends and folklore provide important clues to site location. Heinrich Schliemann used Homer's account of the siege and fall of Troy to lead him to the modern tell of Hissarlik, where he discovered "Priam's treasure." In a similar manner, in the 1890s, Jesse Walter Fewkes followed Hopi migration legends south from the modern Hopi towns to large abandoned ancestral pueblos such as Homolovi in northern Arizona.

Archaeologists have found it valuable to consult amateur archaeologists and residents likely to be familiar with local sites, especially rare ones. This procedure often saves valuable time and effort as well as establishing a beneficial rapport with local landowners.

REGIONAL SURVEY: RECORDING SITES

Once located, sites must be recorded and mapped, and very often artifact collections are made. Within a single project, standardized recording forms streamline the recording process and ensure that the same observations are made at each site. A number of observations are generally made regardless of specific research questions: land form, soil texture and color, vegetation, types of material remains, surface area over which they are distributed, present use of the site, and evidence of recent disturbance such as pot-hunting. On sites with visible architecture, sketch maps with pace measurements are commonly prepared.

Once archaeologists have observed and recorded the most obvious characteristics of a site, it is time for them to get their hands dirty. One important part of most surveys is the collection of surface materials. Obtaining a surface collection is a sampling problem. The archaeologist can visually examine the surface remains and obtain preliminary information on the variety and abundance of materials and on their spatial distribution. This information helps in determining appropriate strata, grid units, and sample sizes. For example, on a quarry and workshop site, an archaeologist observing that a small number of artifact types occurred in high frequency would conclude, if the distribution of materials was uniform, that there is no basis for stratifying the surface. Because of the low variety and the abundance of artifacts, only a small number (about twenty) of relatively small units (2×2-meter squares) would need to be collected to obtain a fairly precise sample. On the other hand, where there is a great deal of variability in artifact types, frequencies, and distributions, it would be useful to stratify the site into high- and low-density zones and sample a large number of units (perhaps several hundred or even a thousand), mostly in high-density zones. The majority of real sites fall somewhere between the extremes just cited, and sampling decisions are always difficult.

Archaeological materials are collected from *recovery units,* the building blocks of fieldwork. The basic problem in surface collection is how to plot clearly and quickly the outlines of the surface recovery units in the field. Land surveying instruments, such as the transit, alidade, and Brunton compass, are sometimes used, but archaeologists are often willing to sacrifice the accuracy obtainable with these instruments for more rapid recovery by less precise methods. With the *dog-leash technique,* which is one of the most common of rapid methods, a sturdy marker is driven into the center of a grid square. The end of a rope attached to this marker is used to trace the boundary of a circular recovery unit. This is a quick method that requires only one collector, but the resulting units are difficult to mesh with a grid system such as might be used in later excavations. In the *furrow technique,* a quick-and-dirty shortcut of systematic sampling, collectors in plowed fields pick up all the materials in, say, every fifth or tenth furrow. (In areas of poor visibility these methods would have to be modified. For example, in a forest a fieldworker might have to rake the pine duff from a recovery unit before collection.) Another technique, applicable where there are few trees, involves the use of long ropes that are knotted or taped at regular intervals. When these ropes are laid out at right angles to each other with the aid of a compass, the corners of any unit in the resulting grid system can be quickly and easily found. The potential variety of collection techniques is enormous; in fact, in practice, there are almost as many techniques as there are surveys.

To recover rare items, such as ornate potsherds used for dating sites, archaeologists often use purposive techniques of surface collection, with crew members scouring the surface of sites for items.

SITE EXCAVATION

Because excavation is so costly, archaeologists rely heavily on surface collections in regional studies. There are, however, definable relations between surface and subsurface materials, so that information concerning the latter can be inferred from the former. Such surface-subsurface relations are also important in that they help determine the location of major deposits of artifacts, and so, the places at which to excavate.

Surface-Subsurface Relations

The relationships are not all simple and direct; what you see on top may not be what you get underneath. On one extreme are sites such as Koster, in southern Illinois, where more than 30 feet of deposits accumulated over the last 10,000 years. Since each occupation was sealed shut by colluvial deposits (p. 137), materials from early occupations are not represented on the present surface. On the other extreme are shallow lithic sites, such as those in the eastern United States, where artifacts are concentrated within 10 or 20 centimeters of the surface. Plowed, these sites often show a close correspondence between surface and subsurface artifacts.

There are three basic approaches for determining what lies below the surface. In the first, predictive models are developed from information on previous archaeological work in the region, the site's environment and surface, and archaeological principles. For example, let us suppose that a Southwestern archaeologist is investigating the nature of household organization in pithouse villages. On the top of a bluff, the archaeologist finds pottery and other artifacts indicative of a pithouse village, as well as distinct roundish depressions of the surface. Because the site is atop a bluff in a forest, there has been little deposition of natural sediments. Each depression is exactly what should be found after the collapse and deterioration of a pithouse. Thus, the presence of pithouses is highly predictable. Another site is found where the right type of artifacts are visible in the backdirt (excavated earth) of rodent burrows, but there are no depressions. This site is on a slope where colluvial deposition has probably occurred regularly since site abandonment. Thus, even though there are no surface traces, the archaeologist would be justified, on the basis of artifacts and environment, to predict the occurrence of buried pithouses.

Electronic aids form the basis for *prospection techniques,* the second approach to detecting subsurface remains and structures. One frequently used device is the *magnetometer* (a descendant of the mine detectors of the Second World War), which operates by detecting modifications of the earth's magnetic field that are produced by any magnetic materials in a vicinity. Many materials have magnetic properties, and others become slightly magnetic after heating; thus, concentrations of sherds (often of cooking vessels) and of hearths are easily detected with the magnetometer. Readings taken at small, regular intervals (every 2 meters, for example) are plotted on a map in order to determine if there are any anomalies of magnetic intensity in an area (FIGURE 7-9). Lightweight, portable magnetometers are now readily available.

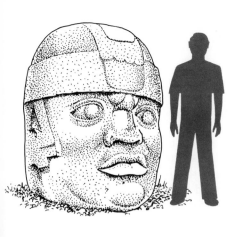

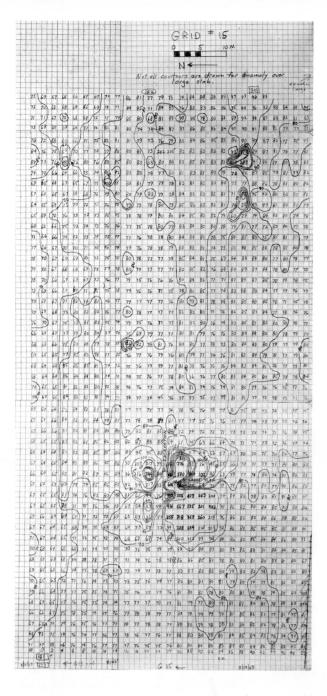

FIGURE **7-9**

A magnetometer survey of San Lorenzo, Mexico, revealed some 500 anomalies, such as those obvious at the center of the map of Grid 15 (at right). Note that readings in the vicinity of the anomalies are often more than five times those of background readings. At upper left is an Olmec sculpture similar to those found on excavation of the anomalous areas. (Map was completed by Sheldon Breiner and Elizabeth K. Ralph.)

Michael Coe surveyed San Lorenzo—an Olmec site in the Gulf Coast lowlands of Mexico dating from 1500 to 700 B.C.—with a cesium magnetometer. The Olmec are known for their large basalt sculptures—often in the form of huge human heads—weighing as much as 50 tons each. Coe, surprised to find more than five hundred anomalies in the site's large central mound, was even more surprised that the anomalies were aligned in rows. His biggest surprise, however, came when he excavated twenty anomaly locations and found stone sculptures at each. (Why these sculptures were buried is an anomaly of another sort.)

Electrical resistance is the basis of the surface-subsurface inferential method of resistivity surveying. Because artifacts and filled-in pits may contain more or less moisture than surrounding soils, they will have correspondingly different electrical conductivity. Thus, in this method, probes are placed systematically in the soil, and the electrical resistance of the ground between them is measured. As with the proton magnetometer, anomalies (of resistance, in this case) are plotted on a map, sometimes with the aid of a computer. Although resistivity is more cumbersome than proton magnetometer survey because of the need for probes, it is especially effective in discovering buried linear features such as walls.

A host of other devices is being subjected to experiment, including radar systems, metal detectors, and small probes fitted with cameras (which can be lowered into tombs). Acoustic holography has the potential of providing three-dimensional images (of buried artifacts) made with sound waves.

Predictive models and electronic aids can take the archaeologist just so far. The final approach to finding what lies below the surface is the most direct, accurate, and costly: excavation. The first stage of excavation, known as *testing*, is normally undertaken to evaluate the predictions of models of site formation, interpretations from electronic aids of data and surface collections, and plain archaeological guesswork. The results of these tests help the archaeologist define prime areas for further sampling.

Sampling within a site, like regional survey, suffers from the sampling paradox. One or two stages of test excavations can help resolve this by furnishing the provisional information on population parameters (homogeneity of deposits, abundance and clustering of artifacts, and particular types of deposits) needed to design a major program of excavation.

Deciding Where to Dig: In-site Sampling

In-site sampling is based on the same principles as survey sampling, but, because of the added dimension of depth, is more complex. The use of sampling strata and multistage designs becomes indispensible. Thus, where concern is with changes in subsistence activities through time, the first excavation stage would sample to determine the locations of subsistence remains. If interest were in the conditions under which a site was abandoned, sampling would be for the areas occupied last, perhaps containing de facto refuse. Once first-stage investigations have defined the appropriate sampling strata, probabilistic sampling can be used to determine the excavation units in the next stage.

The following three examples show some archaeological approaches to the sampling problems in (1) large, complex sites (2) smaller sites with architecture visible on the surface, and (3) sites with no architecture and where sampling strata cannot be easily defined.

FIGURE **7-10**   A small portion of the Tiahuanaco site in Bolivia. Such large urban sites present difficult sampling problems.

The interplay of theory with specific sites allowed Wendell Bennett to solve an extremely difficult problem imposed on him by the government of Bolivia. The archaeological sequence for highland Peru and Bolivia had been constructed from surface collections of potsherds through the technique of seriation, which arranges artifact styles into a logical order (Chapter 9). In the 1930s, Bennett was interested in finding deposits that spanned the entire archaeological sequence so that he could see if different artifact types occurred in the order predicted. For this purpose he chose the site of Tiahuanaco. Located near the shores of Lake Titicaca in highland Bolivia, famous for its monolithic Gate of the Sun, the site was once the center of a large pre-Inca empire in the Andes (FIGURE 7-10).

The Bolivian government limited Bennett's excavations to ten pits, with an area no greater than 10 square meters. Today, a neophyte archaeologist confronted by the same problem might be tempted to grid off the site's surface and reach for a table of random numbers to select excavation units; this would probably be futile. Although the site covers some 450,000 square meters, it is likely that only a small portion of it contains the rare types of deposits relevant for testing a long-term sequence. Bennett, employing his knowledge of cultural formation processes and previous maps, tests, and exposures made at the site, carefully selected those areas most likely to contain deep deposits of secondary refuse. A railroad line had been built across the site, and several units were located where construction cuts had exposed deep trash accumulations. Three areas were also chosen because local workers, familiar with the region, identified them as the "richest" in Tiahuanaco. Another pit was placed in a flat stretch between the ruins of a temple and a hill fort because it seemed a likely area for a garbage dump.

Bennett's excavation strategy was a great success. In fact, two units contained ceramic types that represented all the phases in the Andean archaeological sequence—and in the correct order from bottom to top. As they were at Tiahuanaco, artifacts are sometimes concentrated into deposits of fairly limited extent. As in regional sampling, these rare, clustered units are most efficiently found by purposive techniques, those that incorporate all the information available, and so allow investigators to raise the probabilities of discovery.

The following example of a smaller site, with some visible architecture, shows how probability sampling can be used effectively. Pursuing an interest in room functions and in social organization led James Hill to the surface remains of a pueblo in east-central Arizona called Broken K. In the first stage of excavation, crews cleared surface rubble in order to outline room walls, on the basis of which a map was made of the ninety-five rooms of the pueblo. Two sampling strata were immediately defined—architectural and nonarchitectural areas. Within architectural areas a simple random sample of rooms was drawn. Because this was one of the earliest uses of probabilistic sampling, some opportunities were lost; Hill could have stratified further on the basis of obvious differences in room size, differences that he later showed were a product of room function.

Ironically, many sites that seem to present the most problems are the easiest to sample. For example, throughout the eastern United States there are many shallow lithic sites in forests (in which electronic aids are largely useless) without architecture, so that there is little information with which to define sampling strata. Vegetation obscures most of the surface, making visible only a light, apparently homogeneous, scattering of artifacts. In such cases, archaeologists usually lay out a simple grid and draw a random sample of squares to excavate. This is the approach John House employed to investigate the occupational history at the site of Windy Ridge in South Carolina. The first stage of excavation used a probabilistic sample that produced information on the types of artifacts present and their distribution. The second stage was purposive: excavation units were placed in "hot spots," or areas of relatively high artifact density disclosed by the probability sample (FIGURE 7-11). This technique allowed House to show that the site was not homogeneous and that different parts of it were occupied at different times.

Although archaeologists are improving their sampling techniques all the time, some kinds of sites defy the most earnest efforts. In small caves, for

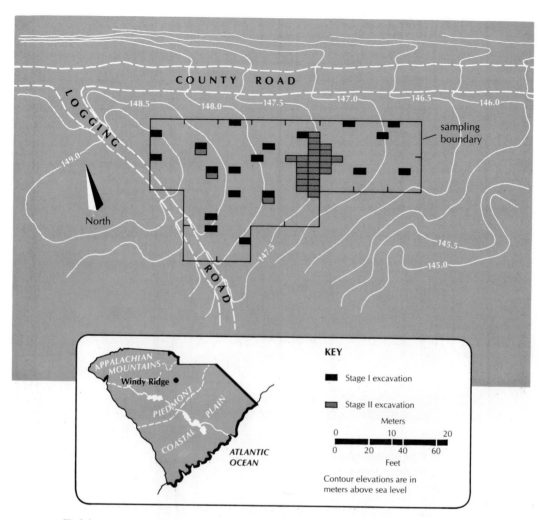

FIGURE **7-11**   Map of the Windy Ridge site in South Carolina showing recovery units from two stages of excavation. Grid shows "hot spots" (areas of relatively high artifact density) which were the focus of the second stage.

example, sheer physical constraints may dictate where the archaeologist can dig safely. In very large, deeply stratified sites, such as tells, one pit will cut through many levels and, most likely, many different kinds of archaeological deposits. Finding what an archaeologist seeks at the bottom of such a pit—perhaps 50 feet deep—is largely a matter of luck, and the larger the site, the more luck needed. Archaeologists have been excavating at the site of Nineveh (home of the biblical Jonah) in Iraq most seasons since 1842 and their giant trenches are only nicks in the surface of the tell, which is more than 7 miles in circumference (FIGURE 7-12).

FIGURE **7-12** Large trenches and pits, dug by persistent German archaeologists in more than 70 field seasons, barely scratch the surface of the site at Nineveh, which was occupied for seven millennia beginning around 6000 B.C.

Even under the best of conditions, in-site sampling is difficult, but each new excavation provides more information and a better basis for the principles useful in designing future excavation projects.

Recovery Techniques   Excavation is the process of recovering artifacts from archaeological context by digging, with the recovery units and their contents painstakingly recorded. Records are, above all else, what distinguishes scientific research from looting and pot-hunting. The dimensions of artifact variability, especially relational, which are documented during excavation, provide the foundation for archaeological analysis and inference.

The recording process is set in motion before the first shovel touches the ground. In order to locate precisely every recovery unit to be excavated, a grid is mapped over the site. At the center of the grid, at a corner, or even at some distance, a fixed reference point of known elevation is established. This *datum point,* which is often a steel bar set in concrete, is the one to

Recovery □ **180**

which all other measurements and locations refer—both horizontally and vertically. (See the boxed unit, "Measuring-in a Point," p. 193.)

Ideally, excavation of a recovery unit is the process of removing depositional strata (p. 110) in the reverse order in which they were laid down. In practice, two factors hinder the full realization of this ideal: (1) because of cultural and environmental processes, single depositional strata may be difficult to recognize, and (2) although depositional units are three-dimensional phenomena, at any given moment excavation proceeds in two dimensions. We will discuss these problems and, in turn, the solutions archaeologists have devised to deal with them.

Differences in sediment texture and color and the artifacts present are the basis for defining depositional strata. A depositional stratum can be a single deposit of ash that appears as a thin lens in cross section, or it can be a 5-foot-thick block of mound fill made up of sandy sediments and artifacts that appear totally homogeneous. In delineating depositional strata, archaeologists attempt to discern the traces of past events and formation processes. These are used to account for what we see in the archaeological record today. For example, the archaeologist must be careful not to confuse well developed soil horizons with culturally deposited strata, or mistake an intentionally filled pit for a pit filled in by natural processes. (See "Stratigraphy," boxed item, p. 192.) As a result, excavation is not just the removal of dirt and the recording of sediment changes and artifacts; it is an intellectual exercise by which the archaeologist attempts to unravel the specific cultural and environmental processes responsible for a given site's characteristics. Thus, on the basis of careful observation and analysis in the field, the archaeologist delineates depositional strata and defines boundaries between them (FIGURE 7-13).

Two general strategies for excavation have evolved: *vertical exposures,* which provide a continuous vertical face for recording the details of deposition (FIGURE 7-13), and *horizontal exposures,* designed to reveal detailed patterns in the spatial associations of artifacts (FIGURE 7-14). The strategy used will be a mix of the two approaches, in proportions dependent on the research questions and the nature of the deposits. Arthur Jelinek's excavation of Tabun Cave in Israel is an example. Tabun was occupied over the last 100,000 years. Previous excavations had revealed the skeletal and artifact remains of Neanderthals dating to over 50,000 years ago. During this long occupation, about 80 feet of deposits accumulated. The site of Tabun presented serious excavation problems. Not only were the deposits warped and distorted by the percolation of water, but the artifacts were embedded in a matrix almost as hard as concrete. To help untangle this stratigraphic nightmare, Jelinek employed an ingenious system of excavation. The basic recovery units were 1-meter cubes dug in an alternating pattern. By the time a given cube was excavated, its top and several sides were usually already exposed by the excavation of previous cubes (FIGURE 7-15). With several cube faces visible, it was possible to carefully chisel off consolidated depositional strata one at a time.

FIGURE **7-13**   Complex stratification visible in the vertical face of a recovery unit at the site of
Tabun, Israel (occupied on and off ca. 100,000 B.P. to the present). On facing page is
a profile drawing of the face typical of the kind prepared in the field.

Recovery □ **182**

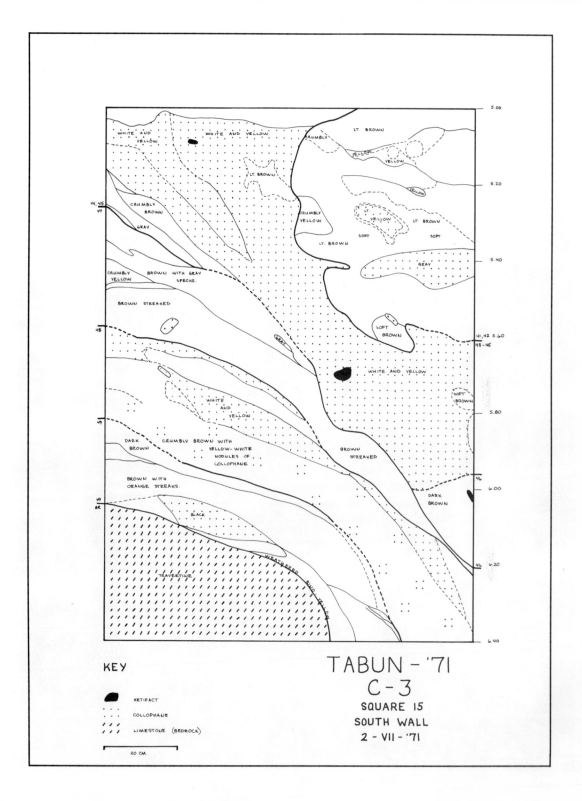

KEY

ARTIFACT

COLLOPHANE

LIMESTONE (BEDROCK)

20 CM.

TABUN - '71
C - 3
SQUARE 15
SOUTH WALL
2 - VII - '71

FIGURE **7-14**

Photograph (facing page) and typical archaeological rendering or plan of a horizontal exposure; here, an excavated room at Grasshopper Pueblo, Arizona (ca. A.D. 1350), showing artifacts and features in association with a floor.

FIGURE **7-15**   Excavating alternate cubes at Tabun Cave, Israel.

Recovery Units   Excavation recovery units are called *pits* and come in a variety of shapes and sizes. One common unit is the *trench,* or *cut* — in plan, an elongated rectangle. Trenches are used primarily for exposing vertical faces and as a way to locate clusters of artifacts and structures. For example, *step trenches* (FIGURE 7-16) are a relatively inexpensive means of uncovering sections of a large mound from top to bottom. *Slit trenches* are small and narrow and can, in rows, be used to trace the locations of canals or embankments, stockades, and other similar constructions.

Another common excavation unit is the *test square,* usually a 2×2-meter pit in the Americas. This unit, typically used in open sites, is now frequently a component in probabilistic sampling because of its compatability with grid squares and with any excavation design that requires coverage of widely dispersed areas of a site.

Once artifact clusters and/or structures and occupation surfaces are located by trench or test square, *area excavations,* or full horizontal exposures, are often called for by research designs. This type of excavation is expensive and regrettably, seldom practical in deeply stratified sites. Some sites, however, are important enough to justify the expense, and the results are often worth the effort, providing a unique glimpse into the past. For example, in 1964–65 Emil Haury excavated extensive areas of the site of Snaketown, a large Hohokam village just south of Phoenix. During a seven-hundred-year period the Hohokam Indians had cut canals to draw water from the Gila River to irrigate their crops of corn, beans, squash, and cotton, and had built and rebuilt their pithouse dwellings. The largest excavation exposure, almost the size of a football field, revealed a mosaic of more than sixty house floors, many superimposed (FIGURE 7-17). It is only

FIGURE **7-16**   Archaeologist Martha Rolingson (right) inspects a just-completed step trench at Mound B of the Toltec site (A.D. 700–1000) near Little Rock, Arkansas.

FIGURE **7-17**   Horizontal exposures reveal a complex history of pithouse occupation at
Snaketown, Arizona (A.D. 500–1200). The rows of small holes—curved and straight—
are post holes that outline individual houses. Figures at left of photograph and truck
at top give some idea of the large scale of the horizontal exposure.

through such large-scale excavation that the complex history of house construction at Snaketown could have been dissected and then synthesized into
a history of occupation.

*Recording
Procedures*   Regardless of the research questions and the nature of the site, the archaeologist makes use of three fundamental *recording units:* levels, features, and
occupation surfaces. A level is a three-dimensional segment of deposit. *Natural levels* correspond to depositional strata; *arbitrary levels* are determined

by convenience or convention. Thus, thick depositional strata that seem the same from top to bottom would be removed and recorded in arbitrary levels, a segment at a time.

A *feature* is a designation given to any phenomenon, other than a level or an individual artifact, that the archaeologist feels should be recorded as a unit. Features have some integrity that would be lost if they were not isolated in the field and recorded separately. Thus, a cluster of sherds that may be from the same pot would be recorded as a feature. Other common examples include burials, caches, hearths, trash-filled pits, and rodent burrows.

An *occupation surface* is a boundary between depositional strata upon which activities were carried out; room floors, stairways, roofs, and plazas are examples. Very often, depositional strata build up on occupation surfaces. For example, abandoned rooms rapidly fill with trash; constant sweeping is needed to keep dirt off sidewalks. Because we are particularly interested in the activities carried out on occupational surfaces, it is especially important to distinguish between items that were deposited during the occupation of a surface and those deposited after it was abandoned. Often this is difficult.

There are many different ways to record the find spots, or *proveniences*, of artifacts. The recorded provenience of an artifact or feature or structure documents its archaeological context. Usually, exact three-dimensional location of each object, or *point provenience*, is reserved for artifacts in contact with occupation surfaces or those associated with features such as burials. For most artifacts *bulk proveniences* are more practical (FIGURE 7-18). Such artifacts are labeled according to their associated feature or level and pit (recovery unit). Artifacts from the same bulk provenience are grouped and placed in bags by type of material—lithic, ceramic, animal bone. Bulk bags are labeled with date, site, excavators' names, type of material, pit, and unit of recording—levels, features, or occupation surfaces.

Section and *plan* drawings (as shown in FIGURES 7-13 and 7-14) are two basic means of recording depositional strata and provenience. A section, also called a *profile*, is the record of the vertical faces or sides of a pit. It is in these sections that archaeologists record the characteristics of depositional strata and carefully mark the boundaries of natural strata or arbitrary levels. A plan is a drawing of a horizontal exposure. Commonly, plans are made of occupation surfaces, the top of arbitrary levels, and features. Photography is an important part of the recording process. Pictures are taken during all stages of excavation. Features, occupation surfaces, and stratigraphic profiles are all recorded, usually on 4 × 5 black-and-white and 35-millimeter black-and-white or color film. This permanent record provides objective documentation for the archaeologist's subjective notes and drawings. Photographs are also used in illustrating reports.

For every recovery unit or pit, careful records are kept of the samples taken (for example, sediment), artifacts receiving point provenience, bulk artifact bags, plan and section drawings, photographs, techniques of excavation, personnel, and time spent on recovery. In addition, archaeologists

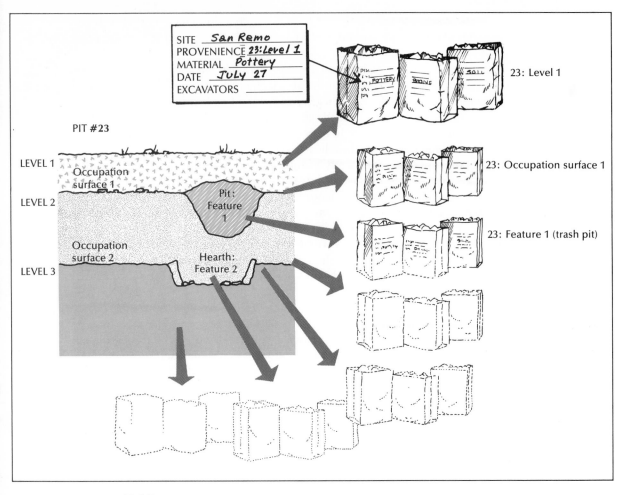

SITE _San Remo_
PROVENIENCE _23:Level 1_
MATERIAL _Pottery_
DATE _July 27_
EXCAVATORS _____

PIT #23

LEVEL 1
Occupation surface 1
LEVEL 2
Pit: Feature 1
Occupation surface 2
LEVEL 3
Hearth: Feature 2

23: Level 1
23: Occupation surface 1
23: Feature 1 (trash pit)

FIGURE **7-18**   Bags—one for different material types for each level or occupation surface set in an excavation unit—provide bulk proveniences for all artifacts not given point provenience.

keep a detailed diary of each day's work. This great redundancy of the recording process makes it possible to correct the inevitable errors—mislabeled bags, lost samples—that occur under the stressful conditions of the field.

Stratigraphic Interpretation   Although most interpretation occurs when artifacts are analyzed in the laboratory and after excavations are finished, the interpreting process must begin in the field. In stratigraphic analysis the archaeologist is trying to answer the questions: What events and processes are responsible for the characteristics of the deposits? What are their chronological relationships? In particular, stratigraphic analysis or *stratigraphy* is carried out to enable (1) the recognition of depositional strata and the designation of proveniences, (2) decision making about how and where to dig next, and (3) formulation of an initial chronology of events for the site. (An example of stratigraphic interpretation is provided in the boxed unit, "Stratigraphy," on p. 192.)

Field Tools and Equipment

The choice of tools is mainly dependent on the local conditions at specific sites as well as on the excavator's research questions. Dental tools, ice picks and small paint brushes are used for detail work, such as removing dirt around fragile bones or other artifacts. Heavy root cutters, axes, and saws are indispensible in wooded sites. Shovels are important multi-use tools. Though generally for coarse removal of soil, when sharpened they can skim off thin layers, enabling the archaeologist to detect features such as the outlines of deteriorated posts (*post molds*) or of burial pits. Once such features are discovered, the archaeologist's most trusted field companion, the *Marshalltown trowel,* comes into use. The trowel is the single most versatile earth-moving tool. It is especially suited to shaving away soil a few millimeters at a time (for defining the boundaries between strata) and to prying the last few centimeters of sediment from occupation surfaces. The trowel is the surgeon's scalpel of the skilled fieldworker; it is no wonder archaeologists spend so much time sharpening them (FIGURE 7-19). Specially made gold and silver trowels are sometimes presented to archaeologists at important rites of passage in their professional careers.

Archaeologists also use power equipment—such as backhoes, bulldozers, and roadgraders—when large quantities of dirt need to be moved, as in removing the *overburden* from a site deeply buried under alluvium. (A widely-held pessimistic belief concerning deposition of such backdirt is expressed in the mock principle that, regardless of how carefully laid out an excavation is, backdirt will always have to be moved because nearby excavation units will inevitably disclose important structures or features underneath it. A similar principle states that important and usually complex finds are always made in the waning days or even minutes of the field season, when it is too late to follow them out carefully. These two principles can be termed the first and second nemeses of excavation.)

To improve recovery of artifacts, archaeologists often put excavated dirt through screens. Although ¼-inch mesh hardware cloth is generally used, experiments have shown that even finer meshes are sometimes necessary for adequate recovery of very small remains such as fish bones, tiny beads, and minute flakes of stone. Screening may be carried out wet or dry; wet screening, where dirt is washed through screens, provides the most gentle and complete recovery. At the Lubbock Lake site, a series of early hunter-gatherer settlements in the panhandle of Texas, some extending as far back as 12,000 years, archaeologist Eileen Johnson is wet-screening the entire deposit.

Stratigraphy

Stratigraphy is a chronological ordering of the events and processes responsible for the observed stratification or layering of deposited material. Although the law of superposition plays a central role in stratigraphic analysis, it accounts for cases of deposition only; other principles apply where removal of materials has occurred. In fact, a host of principles and a familiarity with local artifacts and formation processes are needed to practice stratigraphy. Stratigraphic analysis begins with profile drawings on which depositional units and the traces of other processes, such as erosion, are marked. Each unit is described as to sediment color and texture and the nature of clasts, if applicable. These are the basic data for chronological interpretation, the process of which is best shown by example, as follows; numbers indicate order of *excavation*.

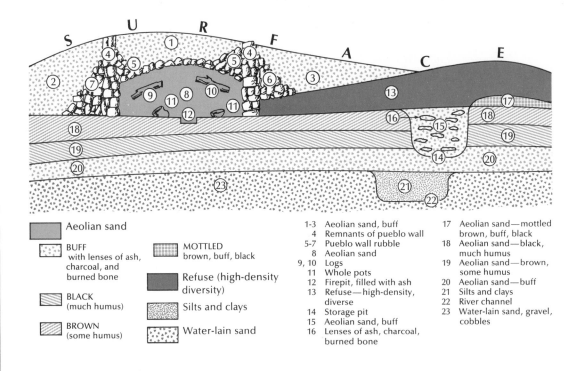

Aeolian sand		1-3	Aeolian sand, buff
		4	Remnants of pueblo wall
BUFF with lenses of ash, charcoal, and burned bone	**MOTTLED** brown, buff, black	5-7	Pueblo wall rubble
		8	Aeolian sand
	Refuse (high-density diversity)	9, 10	Logs
		11	Whole pots
BLACK (much humus)		12	Firepit, filled with ash
	Silts and clays	13	Refuse—high-density, diverse
BROWN (some humus)		14	Storage pit
	Water-lain sand	15	Aeolian sand, buff
		16	Lenses of ash, charcoal, burned bone

17 Aeolian sand—mottled brown, buff, black
18 Aeolian sand—black, much humus
19 Aeolian sand—brown, some humus
20 Aeolian sand—buff
21 Silts and clays
22 River channel
23 Water-lain sand, gravel, cobbles

The alluvial sediments in Unit 23, were laid down first by a moderately rapid flow of water. Next, Unit 22 was formed by a downcutting (eroding) stream or river. When stream flow became sluggish, silts and clays began to be deposited; these eventually filled in the channel, creating Unit 21. Units 18–20 were laid down next by the process of aeolian (wind-blown) deposition. Vegetation took hold on the top of Unit 18 and persisted long enough for soil development to take place. (Unit 18 is the A-horizon, Unit 19, the B.) On stratigraphic evidence alone, one cannot determine which came next, the storage pit (Unit 14), the pueblo walls (Unit 4), or the fire pit in the room (Unit 12). If one can infer that all were associated in one occupational episode, then the order is likely to have been pueblo room, fire pit, storage pit. Dirt from the excavation of the storage pit was deposited in Unit 17. The storage pit rapidly fell into disuse; lenses of refuse (Unit 16) were deposited sporadically as aeolian processes also contributed sand to the pit fill (Unit 15). Occupation generated a deposit of secondary refuse (Unit 13). After this the pueblo was abandoned, the occupants leaving behind several whole pots as de facto refuse (Unit 11). Aeolian sand entered the abandoned pueblo through roof hatch, accumulating on the floor (Unit 8) and covering the de facto refuse. The pueblo roof began to collapse (Units 9 and 10) and sand (Unit 8) continued to blow in. Further collapse formed Units 5–7. Finally, aeolian sand covered the ruin (Units 1, 2, and 3).

Measuring-in a Point

Vertical locations are recorded in terms of distance above or below the *datum plane,* an imaginary horizontal surface that runs through the *datum point* and the entire site. Horizontal locations are also measured from the site datum point. When a decision is made to excavate at a given place, two corners of the planned recovery unit are "sighted in" from the datum—that is, located optically by an instrument (usually a surveyor's transit or theodolite) set up at the datum—or its location is measured from other known points. From that time onward, locations within the unit can be recorded conveniently by means of a tape measure, string, and *line level,* the string being attached to a fixed point and extended to a position directly over the object whose location is being determined. The line level is used to keep the string horizontal, and the tape is used to measure the vertical distance between the string and the object and the horizontal length of the string (see FIGURE). For added precision a plumb bob (a pointed weight hanging from a string) can be used to find the point on the string that is directly above the object, and additional horizontal measurements can be made between the object and the sides of the recovery unit.

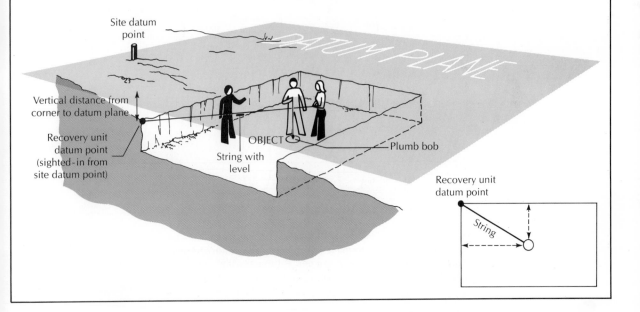

Site datum point

DATUM PLANE

Vertical distance from corner to datum plane

Recovery unit datum point (sighted-in from site datum point)

String with level

OBJECT

Plumb bob

Recovery unit datum point

String

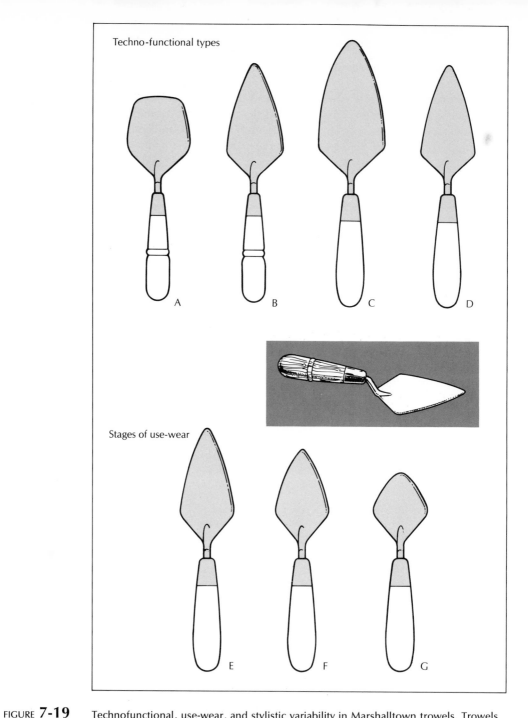

FIGURE **7-19**   Technofunctional, use-wear, and stylistic variability in Marshalltown trowels. Trowels are often cut or filed to make them more suitable for shaving or chopping in a downward motion (*A*), scraping and cutting at a high angle (*B*), and cutting at a low angle (*C*). *D* is a general-purpose, unmodified trowel. *E* is a trowel that has had little use; *F*, moderate use; and *G*, heavy use. Handles of trowels *A* and *B* have two rings, which show them to be of an older style.

Special Recovery Techniques

The recovery of other important materials requires the consistent use of additional special techniques. To collect pollen, for example, fresh soil surfaces are exposed using clean tools, and dirt from these surfaces is promptly placed in plastic or paper bags for laboratory analysis. Within sites, archaeologists also seek out seeds, stems, and leaves. The success that archaeologists have in recovering plant remains depends on their knowledge of formation processes and the use of specialized recovery techniques such as *flotation*. This process involves mixing soils with water and skimming off and drying the materials that float to the surface; for heavier, denser items, such as bones, a fluid with a higher specific gravity is used (p. 18). For many years chances to recover seeds were routinely missed. As archaeologists began to consider some simple cultural formation processes (that in food preparation some food will be burned and discarded) and environmental processes (that carbonized food remains will be preserved in most environments), fine-mesh screens and flotation began to be used to examine debris from hearths and other ashy deposits. The result was the recovery of literally millions of plant parts. For example, at Ali Kosh, an early farming village in the Near East, the first excavations produced few seed remains. After the introduction of flotation on ashy deposits, however, tens of thousands of seeds useful in documenting the change in domesticated cereals were recovered.

Many specimens that the archaeologist finds, such as waterlogged organic remains, require special handling and first aid. Techniques for preserving artifacts have been developed by museum specialists and applied by archaeologists. Waterlogged wood, because of deterioration of its fine cellulose structure, becomes more porous and soaks up water like a sponge. The wood then becomes very heavy and, if improperly handled, can easily crack across the grain. Furthermore, if the wood is allowed to dry without being specially treated, the weakened cell walls, once held apart only by the presence of the water, will collapse, and the specimen will warp, shrink, or otherwise be damaged beyond repair. Thus, in the field, waterlogged wooden objects must first be raised on some rigid support and then kept wet until they reach the laboratory for treatment.

Two effective laboratory techniques for removing the excess water and strengthening the structure of waterlogged wood are the alcohol-ether method and the injection of polyethylene glycol wax. In the first, alcohol replaces excess water, and ether then replaces the alcohol. When the ether evaporates, the cellular structure of the wood is left intact. In the second method, removal of excess water and consolidation of the wood occur in one operation.

Recovered documents that are of clay present no special problems. However, paper or papyrus offer a great challenge to conservators. The Dead Sea Scrolls were particularly difficult. Hidden for almost 2,000 years in caves above the Dead Sea, these important early Judeo-Christian documents were preserved by the arid conditions. The initial steps of conservation included slowly humidifying the brittle parchment so that it could be painstakingly sliced into strips and, thereby, "unrolled" and examined.

Field Laboratory	Once artifacts are dug up they are prepared for analysis in the field laboratory. The first laboratory chore is washing. Chipped stones, ceramics, shells, and bones can usually be washed in water without harm, though overzealous workers have been known to scrub designs from potsherds. Some specialists prefer to delay the washing until the materials are brought to their laboratories, because bits of plant and animal material that may adhere to the edges of stone tools can offer useful information. In the laboratory each tool is cleaned separately and residue is saved for study to identify that tool's techno-function.

The second laboratory chore is cataloging and labeling. Each bag of material brought from the field, regardless of whether it holds one artifact or one thousand, is recorded on a master list of finds. Also recorded on the master list are artifacts with point provenience and special samples, such as pollen and those for flotation.

Ideally, in order to avoid confusion in further sorting for analysis, artifacts should be individually labeled with their provenience. This provides insurance against the inevitable broken bags and other accidents of handling. Labels are usually in code. For example, "C-18:119:3" means that the artifact bearing this code came from site 18 (or "Buena Vista") on Cozumel Island, Mexico, recovery unit 119, level 3. Codes will vary from dig to dig and the different codes must be learned in order to study the material. In practice, artifacts in bulk provenience are often not labeled individually.

The third laboratory chore is sorting artifacts into the groups that will be used in analysis. Usually these groups are based on the material composition of artifacts. Once sorted and packed, the entire *assemblage*—all the artifacts excavated at a site—is shipped to the laboratories where analysis will take place. (Chapter 8).

OTHER RECOVERY METHODS	Fieldwork for some archaeologists does not mean digging. For them, data recovery takes place in a variety of different settings, from modern villages and cities to libraries and archives. As is the case with those who do dig, there are basic concepts that help such ethnoarchaeologists and historical archaeologists obtain the information needed to answer research questions.

Ethnoarchaeological Fieldwork	Ethnoarchaeology is carried out in industrial societies like our own and in nonindustrial communities such as those of !Kung Bushmen and Kalinga villagers. Archaeologists who excavate can record events only in terms of their material traces. Ethnoarchaeologists document events from two perspectives: the artifacts involved, and associated behaviors and beliefs. These two perspectives are essential, in that they are the source of many of the principles used by archaeologists, who dig to infer past behaviors and beliefs from material traces.

The ethnoarchaeologist's first concern is with quantitative recording of behaviors, attitudes, and associated artifacts (through the use of direct observation of activities and artifacts and of interviews and questionnaires). A convenient example is the ethnoarchaeological study of Kalinga pottery by Longacre (Chapter 4), who undertook a detailed, house-by-house census of the people and pottery in an entire village (FIGURE 7-20). More than six hundred pots were described through direct observation. In interviews, members of each household were asked who made each pot, who trained the potter, which task group the potter belonged to, the functions of the pot, and when the pot was made. Each pot was tagged and, when any broke, Longacre or an assistant was notified, and cause of breakage and the actual disposal of the pot were recorded. These activities, which took a year for Longacre and two Kalinga assistants, provided a unique record of a life cycle of pottery.

Michael Schiffer's Reuse Project in Tucson, Arizona, is another example of a study combining observation and interviews. The purpose of the research was to determine the importance of the circulation of used items among households, and to establish the relations between socio-economic characteristics of households and reuse behavior. In the first stage of the project, student researchers visited swap meets, yard sales, thrift shops, auctions, and antique stores to observe transactions in used artifacts directly. This procedure documented a variety of reuse processes and how they work. In the second stage of research, an interview survey was devised that sought information on basic household characteristics—such as age and sex of members, income, and type of dwelling—and a total inventory of furniture and major appliances that included when and where they were obtained. Students who administered the surveys generally had good cooperation in completing the questionnaires, though a few respondents feared that the survey was a pretext for "casing" their homes for a future robbery and refused to divulge information. The major difficulty, however, was the informants' pleasure in the process and their consequent reluctance to have the question session end. Some results of this study are presented in Chapter 12.

An ethnoarchaeologist encounters all of the problems that an *ethnographer* (a cultural anthropologist who studies living societies) does: good relations must be developed with members of the community being studied, an exotic language often must be learned, and stomachs must be galvanized against unfamiliar food habits and bacteria. Beyond these problems, the ethnoarchaeologists must strive to avoid two temptations.

The first temptation is trying to reconstruct from information elicited from "old-timers" the way "primitive" societies functioned before the arrival of European technology and influence. (There are no pristine "primitive" societies. Longacre found in a remote Philippine village that the grandson of one of his Kalinga informants was a dentist now living in California; and O'Connell (p. 32) sometimes joined the Alyawara in shooting kangaroos from the back of a pursuing pickup truck.) To appreciate the diffi-

FIGURE **7-20**   In the Kalinga Village of Dangtalan, Philippines (far left, facing page), a potter (near left) works on a vessel. At bottom left, a research assistant records the shape of a vessel like those (bottom right) stored on a shelf in a typical Kalinga house, whose interior is shown above.

culty with using *oral history* as an adjunct to the other techniques of archaeology, consider what people are likely to know or remember about their society: a cobbler would remember how he made shoes, and this would be useful knowledge for an archaeologist. But would he remember—did he ever know—how much meat was eaten in his community each week, how often pots were broken, or how many of his neighbors owned more shell jewelry than he did? Thus, answers to many ethnoarchaeological questions are probably beyond the experience or recall of informants, hence the advantage of having a living society where the required observations can be made.

The second temptation is that of trying to eliminate all influences of modern technology from study and to concentrate exclusively on what seem to be traditional activities and artifacts. The ethnoarchaeologists who give in to this temptation miss an opportunity to study how societies and artifacts change. Although the particular changes may be from a gourd penis sheath to Fruit of the Loom underwear, rather than from one style of pot to another, if there are general principles that govern change, they will be the same regardless of the specific items involved (FIGURE 7-21).

FIGURE **7-21** Change in a New Guinea community: Above is shown an important ceremony with participants in their finest regalia in the 1930s; at left, in New Guinea in the 1970s, a young girl wears a necklace of light bulbs as a sign of her modernity.

Historical Research The recovery of documents often requires unique types of digging through libraries and archives. Many documents, such as official records from censuses and court cases, and deeds, travelers' accounts, diaries, and letters, lie on shelves and in crates, buried under strata of dust and bureaucratic red tape. Hundreds of descriptions of New World civilizations at the time of the Spanish Conquest remain unread deep in archives in Seville, Spain. Archaeologists of colonial North America are finding that probate records contain valuable inventories of household artifacts, and in the Near East, unfired clay tablets with texts written in *cuneiform* have been recovered by the hundreds of thousands, the majority remaining to be studied carefully. Old photographs, too, constitute a valuable resource.

Proper analysis of recovered written materials requires more than the documents themselves. The purpose of such documents from past societies was not particularly the enlightenment of historical archaeologists. Therefore, the bias of a document, or the point of view of the writer, must be determined. Some biases are obvious: one of the first functions of writing was to trace the achievements and family lines of rulers to legitimize their rule. Thus, practically no early records report the lives of common people, and the accomplishments of the upper class are often greatly exaggerated. For example, Egyptian texts describe their victory over the Hittites at Qadesh, around 1300 B.C.; as might be expected, the Hittite texts claim victory in the same battle. We do not know who won.

Some biases are less obvious. For example, the practice of cannibalism, reported in many hundreds of diaries, travel accounts, and anthropological reports, seems to be well documented. In his book *The Man-Eating Myth,* however, William Arens argues that almost all these accounts are the result of bias. Arens found only one report to be based on first-hand observation of cannibalism; all others were accusations by one group of another. Many, quite fanciful, were reported by colonial administrators to justify their rule and by adventurers to enliven their travel accounts. Arens concludes that cannibalism was never a widespread phenomenon; in fact, the general rarity of archaeological examples of cannibalized bones tends to support his argument.

Proper interpretation is also made difficult by the fact that documents recovered are only a sample of all those that existed. Consider how different an interpretation of our society would be were it based on recovery of books from a university library as opposed to a grade-school library, or on books from a drugstore as opposed to a health-food shop. Thus, there is a special need for thoughtful sampling in sites where written materials are likely to be found in rare and highly clustered deposits. Detailed documentation can help to determine the nature of some obscure biases. Scholars have long pondered, for example, the tremendous number of variants found on ancient Near Eastern tablets inscribed in cuneiform. A once widely held interpretation was that these represented accepted variations in texts. Today, scholars hold that many of the differences are due to "dictation errors" that occurred as student scribes attempted to learn their trade. Carefully documenting the archaeological contexts of tablets excavated in the future will aid in sorting out the legitimate texts and help modern scholars correct errors made 4000 years ago.

Historical research often turns up useful photographs. For example, archaeologists working in sites of the mid- to late nineteenth century can sometimes find photographs of structures, people engaged in activities nearby, house interiors, and even family sittings. Although old photographs are usually sought in historical societies, museums, and special archives, they can turn up in strange places. The oldest known photograph of the White House was found in 1972 at a California flea market. Many families maintain photograph collections of immense historical importance. Photographs from one's childhood, or—better yet—from one's parents' childhood often offer a material record of artifacts, buildings, and behaviors seldom seen today (FIGURE 7-22).

FIGURE **7-22**   Old photographs are important resources for the historical archaeologist: On facing page, at left, Mulberry Street in New York City in 1888; at right, a trolley line (with baby) in 1912 California; below, a photograph of Paris taken from a hot-air balloon in 1862. Above, a street in San Francisco in 1850.

Afterword   In this chapter we have discussed a variety of ways in which archaeologists recover data to answer specific research questions. Above all else, it should be clear that archaeological fieldwork, whether "dirt" archaeology, ethnoarchaeology, or the archaeology of historic documents, is more than simple manual labor or the rote application of techniques. Fieldwork is a complex process of decisions based on research questions and the application of archaeological principles. Before archaeologists enter the field, they choose a mix of purposive and probabilistic sampling techniques and weigh costs against expected gains in precision. These decisions are followed by actual regional surveys, surface collections, and/or excavations, all of which are both physically and intellectually demanding. At each step in the recovery process, the archaeologist must carefully document both the research decisions made and the information that is recorded.

Tatiana Proskouriakoff (b. 1909)   Tatiana Proskouriakoff has an unusual background for a Maya archaeologist. Her father, a purchasing agent for the czar of Russia, brought his family to the United States in 1916 on a buying trip and never went back. Tatiana became an illustrator and eventually found herself drawing Maya art and artifacts for A. V. Kidder and the archaeologists of the Carnegie Institute. In 1946, the Carnegie published a complete collection of her architectural reconstructions, *Maya Art and Architecture,* which marked the culmination of her career as an illustrator.   □   Memorable as her paintings are, Proskouriakoff will be remembered by archaeologists as the one who solved the riddle of the Maya glyphs. The riddle was decades old. What was the meaning of these curious signs carved in stone? In the sixteenth century, Bishop Diego de Landa found that the glyphs recorded time and astronomical observations. Nothing much else was added in the next four hundred years of study. Able to translate only dates, Mayanists believed that the remaining glyphs on the carved stone monuments represented calculations concerned with astronomical events. This view persisted until the 1960s, when Proskouriakoff published a series of revolutionary articles.   □   Before Proskouriakoff, scholars who had labored over the glyphs had made a crucial error, looking at the glyphs alone or at their patterns of occurrence within inscriptions. She took a whole new approach, placing inscriptions in their total archaeological context by examining their distribution within sites, such as Quirigua and Piedras Negras. She found that monuments grouped together shared certain dates in patterns that suggested a record of events in the lifetime of a single individual. From this simple start an avalanche of translations followed—of "name" glyphs, "birth" or "naming-day" glyphs, "ascension" glyphs, "marriage" glyphs, "captor" glyphs. Today, there are some dozen Mayanists busily piecing together the life histories of rulers that, Proskouriakoff had discovered, the glyphs commemorated in stone.   □   The study of glyphs had been at an impasse for four centuries; Proskouriakoff set it moving again through her admirable thoroughness, patience, and respect for the data of Maya archaeology. While every such achievement involves insight, most noteworthy is the years of laborious analyses that Proskouriakoff undertook before her demanding standards of proof were met.

Tatiana Proskouriakoff.

8

ANALYSIS

Our drive-in archaeologist (from Chapter 7) has spent a few days picking up trash as an archaeological surface collection, and it is now all in the laboratory in bags labeled by provenience and material: metal, glass, paper, other organic materials (such as popcorn and chicken bones), and miscellaneous (for those few surprises people always leave behind, such as a child's sock and a "living" bra). How does an archaeologist make sense from all these bags of debris that anyone else would immediately recognize as worthless? They follow in the footsteps of Proskouriakoff, using analysis—studying the four dimensions of artifact variability in order to answer research questions.

Analysis, the next stage in the process of archaeological research, is the basis for the final steps of inference and explanation, and involves describing and organizing the formal, spatial, frequency, and relational variability in artifacts. It begins with classification, by which artifacts are designated as to type. Types are abstract categories based on characteristics or attributes —observable properties such as length, hardness, color. Each attribute can have different values, or states: red, green, blue, and brown are common states of the attribute "color." (The states of "red" color, "firm" texture, and "thin" skin are among those that define a type of vegetable, the tomato.) A set of related types forms a *typology*, as a set of types of cars— sedan, hardtop, convertible—is a car typology.

The starting point for building a typology is a general research question. Our drive-in archaeologist might ask: What subsistence strategies do people use for a night at the drive-in? In other words, what kinds of foods and beverages are consumed at drive-ins? This general question could be rephrased more specifically in ways relevant to certain kinds of artifacts; for example, what kinds of beverages are consumed that are packaged in metal containers?

The physical analysis begins when an archaeologist spreads the finds out on a table to see what kinds of variability are present. The bags of metal artifacts will hold such treasures as a few beverage cans, some small car parts such as bolts and washers, a very few coins, and extremely large numbers of pop-tops and bottle caps. The coins and car parts may be set aside as having no relevance to the question at hand. At first, cans might seem to be the most useful artifacts to analyze in detail, but a knowledge of formation processes suggests something quite different. Because many beverage cans are valuable aluminum, people save them for recycling. Also, because drive-ins are swept up every morning, the cans in the archaeologist's bags represent only those left from the night before the collection was made. Thus, a one-night sample is not adequate. Recall, that, according to the McKellar hypothesis, small items are likely to remain in activity areas as primary refuse (FIGURE 5-5). Recall also that pop-tops are made exclusively from aluminum, which is virtually indestructible in the natural environment. Thus, drawing upon principles of cultural and environmental formation processes, one may assume that the pop-tops represent remains accumulated over weeks, months, and even years.

In the next step, formal variability in pop-tops is examined. After the pop-tops are sorted according to form, the archaeologist will consult patent records, catalogs, and company documents, to determine if different forms of pop-tops were used on cans of different brands and kinds of beverages. The end result of this process would be a typology of pop-tops identifying the formal characteristics of each type and the brand and kind of beverage it represents (FIGURE 8-1). Some types are very distinctive, such as that of Coors beer; some show only subtle differences. On the basis of this typology, pop-tops can be sorted into two groups—those from beer cans and those from soft-drink cans. However, cans for the same brand and beverage may also have different pop-tops if they are manufactured in different parts of the country, so that this typology is applicable only to Tucson, Arizona, and to those nearby cities supplied by the same breweries and soft-drink manufacturers.

Once the pop-tops in each bag are identified and counted, totals for beer and soft-drink cans can be compiled for the sample and extrapolated to

FIGURE **8-1**   (On facing page.) Pop-tops from beverage cans exhibit a variety of combinations of shape and color. The typology shown here is valid only for Tucson, Arizona; one for Boston or Milwaukee might differ considerably, since different canning plants use different can designs.

BEERS

COORS

SCHLITZ LIGHT

CARLING BLACK LABEL

BUDWEISER
MICHELOB LIGHT
ANHEUSER-BUSCH NATURAL LIGHT

OLYMPIA GOLD
HAMM'S

MICHELOB

SCHLITZ
OLD MILWAUKEE
SCHLITZ STOUT

PILSNER LIGHT
MILLER HIGH-LIFE

MILLER HIGH-LIFE

BURGIE
PABST BLUE RIBBON

SCHLITZ (16 OZ.)

FALSTAFF

HEINEKEN
BUCKHORN

MODELO ESPECIAL

SOFT DRINKS

COKE
MR. PIBB
SPRITE
FRESCA
TAB
RONDO CITRUS

RONDO CITRUS

NUTRAMENT

OCEAN SPRAY CRANAPPLE JUICE

KEY   Color of Tabs

 GOLD
FRONT

 GOLD
BACK

 LIGHT GOLD
FRONT

 LIGHT GOLD
BACK

GOLD FRONT
AND BACK

DARK GOLD
BACK

WHITE
BACK

SILVER FRONT
AND BACK

GATORADE

BORDEN YOGURT SHAKE

KERN'S FRUIT NECTARS

the whole drive-in. The results from our drive-in collections indicate that canned beer is ten times more popular than canned soft drinks.

But pop-tops that this figure is based on were deposited over some unknown span of time. How can we be sure that there haven't been changes over time in the popularity of beer relative to soft drinks? The widespread crushing of pop-tops (by foot and auto traffic) in the drive-in will help us answer this question, for older pop-tops should show more damage. Thus, our drive-in archaeologist will need to subdivide beer and soft-drink pop-tops into two further categories—pop-tops heavily damaged and those lightly damaged. There will now be four piles of pop-tops for each provenience bag: heavily damaged, beer; lightly damaged, beer; heavily damaged, soft drink; and lightly damaged, soft drink. The archaeologist now computes two ratios: heavily to lightly damaged beer pop-tops and heavily to lightly damaged soft-drink pop-tops. If the two ratios are more or less the same, there has probably been little change over time. If the ratios are different, the archaeologist should be able to tell from them the direction of change. But how long a time do the pop-tops represent? At present, we do not know. But archaeologists could try to find out by salting drive-ins with tagged pop-tops whose movements can be tracked over time.

We are familiar with our own artifacts, so constructing pop-top typologies is relatively easy. Archaeologists are seldom in this advantageous position, however; when analyzing ancient artifacts, it is difficult to determine the causes of variability and what attributes are most relevant to a particular research question. This is why archaeologists joke, for example, that future colleagues, finding train cars marked "smokers" and "nonsmokers," might take these divisions to signify the presence of two basic social classes. Fortunately, ethnoarchaeology, experimental archaeology, and historical records sometimes provide information on the sources of variability in artifacts that can help us establish relationships between specific attributes and specific research questions.

TYPOLOGIES

Archaeologists, then, start out with a question they are attempting to answer and a basic understanding of the cultural and environmental causes of variability in the artifacts they are analyzing. Drawing upon this knowledge, they select a set of relevant attributes and define their states. These attribute states are combined into types, which in turn form typologies. There are several types of typologies.

Temporal typologies are composed of types of artifacts manufactured at different times. Although the types composing them are most often based on stylistic attributes, utilitarian attributes can be included so long as they change with time (Chapters 1 and 4). In television receivers, for example, there is a progression through time from round to rectangular screens. (FIGURE 8-2). We could divide this continuum into several types, each of which was manufactured during an identifiable era. The shift, in television

FIGURE **8-2**

Some temporal types of televisions: At top left, a 1940s set, appreciably smaller than its successors, and with a round screen; at top right, a 1950s General Electric, which introduces a new screen shape; and at right, one with the squared-off ellipse shape typical of the 1970s.

circuitry, from vacuum tubes to transistors could also be the basis of a temporal typology. Useful for coarse dating of sites and very easy to construct, temporal typologies are usually the first devised in an unexplored area.

Technological typologies include types based on techniques and stages of artifact manufacture. These typologies are also easy to construct because of the availability of experimental information from archaeology and other sciences. Attributes selected are traces of specific manufacturing acts and stages. In our television example, at least two major manufacturing processes have been used to build receivers—hand-wiring (traces include insulated wires soldered to components to make connections) and printed-circuits (traces include components attached to a plastic board and connected by thin, metallic films).

Techno-functional typologies are made up of types based on attributes such as shape and size and those related to use-wear. These are designed to study the human behavior that takes place in activity areas and to study the activities carried out in different settlements in regional systems. Televisions can easily be categorized according to techno-functional type—big-screen types, used in bars; consoles, usually found in "family rooms" or "living rooms"; and portables, which can be found just about anywhere, but are most common in bedrooms and kitchens.

Socio-functional typologies include types whose attributes symbolize behavioral components and individual roles and social standing. These attributes usually include differences in material (such as gold, jade, clay), differences in design elements, and subtle differences of shape and size. These are used to identify individual manufacturers, social units of manufacture and use, the social standing of individuals, and social classes within a society. There are many ways to construct socio-functional types for the television example. Within the techno-functional type "console," we could look at screen size, cabinet materials, whether black-and-white or color, and presence of remote control. While there will be exceptions, types based on combinations of the more expensive attributes will occur in the highest frequencies in upper-income neighborhoods.

Ideo-functional typologies are based on attributes that symbolize ideas and beliefs. The specific attributes are similar to those used in socio-functional types. In fact, socio-functional and ideo-functional types often overlap, as in the case of the Seal of the President of the United States, which represents a social role (president), a social unit (the White House), an institution (the executive branch of the United States government), and the concept of the United States itself. Development of socio-functional and ideo-functional typologies is in its infancy, but attempts have been made for most kinds of artifacts. In the case of the television example, it is not individual attributes, but the objects themselves that symbolize attitudes. Thus, the complete absence of a television in a household strongly expresses a family's commitment to a certain life style.

Native typologies are comprised of types recognized as such by the members of the society. For example, the television is so central an artifact in our society that we have developed a number of native types we all recognize. These types are combinations of an array of brands and stylistic and utilitarian attributes. Some of the types already mentioned—such as "console," "portable," "black-and-white," and "color"—are native types. Ethnoarchaeologists record native typologies to study the relationship between native categories and various kinds of archaeological types.

All archaeologists share certain problems and need to be able to use the data of other investigators. Therefore, while each investigator will most likely have devised a few specialized typologies, each also uses a temporal typology that is employed widely throughout a region. Beginning in the 1930s, archaeologists in the Southwest created a number of temporal types, many of which resembled each other. For convenience these types were grouped together into large typologies, such as the type-variety typology of

White Mountain Redwares, pots with a red slip painted with black and/or white geometric designs (FIGURE 8-3). St. Johns Polychrome, with black designs on the inside and white on the outside, is a "type" of White Mountain Redware. What makes this type-variety typology most useful is its ability to accommodate new discoveries. For example, if an archaeologist finds pottery identical to St. Johns Polychrome, but with a white line added on the inside, this could be defined as a new "variety" of the St. Johns Polychrome type.

It is interesting to note the relationship between the sociological model of style (pp. 72–74) and the type-variety system. The sociological model of style states simply that the degree of resemblance between styles is related to the amount of social interaction. In a type-variety typology, similarities between types are assumed also to be due to social interaction, which is further assumed to have occurred among potters living at about the same time period in a region (FIGURE 4-5)—similar pots should have a similar date of manufacture.

Type-variety typologies are useful for some purposes other than dating. Because archaeologists at a number of sites are using the same system for naming pots, it is possible to observe the spatial distribution of types, useful in studying patterns of trade and social interaction among the communities in a region.

Building Typologies

Once an archaeologist decides on the problems whose solutions require a typology, the next step is to build one. In some cases it can be fabricated from available typologies, such as an existing type-variety system; in others one must start from scratch. The most widely used and trusted method is the *lab table approach*. In this, the first step is to write the provenience directly on each artifact (if it hasn't been done). Next, the archaeologist separates the materials, such as ceramics, into piles of items that are deemed similar on the basis of attributes considered relevant to the research questions. Many comparisons—for example, of ceramic color or design—can be made using simple visual inspection. Others—hardness, chemical composition, and tensile strength—are made through more complicated tests. The specific attribute states shared by the items in a pile compose a type. Types produced by this process are known as *monothetic*—those in which each included artifact has the same set of defining attribute states.

A second, more objective, approach for constructing monothetic types is paradigmatic classification, made popular by Robert Dunnell. The starting point is a listing of all relevant attributes and their states. The possible combinations of all these attribute states comprises a *paradigm*, or an exhaustive set of theoretically possible types. The actual occurrences of specific attribute combinations, some portion of the total possibilities, become the types. Because the number of possible types increases dramatically with each new set of attribute states, paradigmatic classification forces the analyst to identify speedily, in a logical manner, the attributes most relevant to a research question.

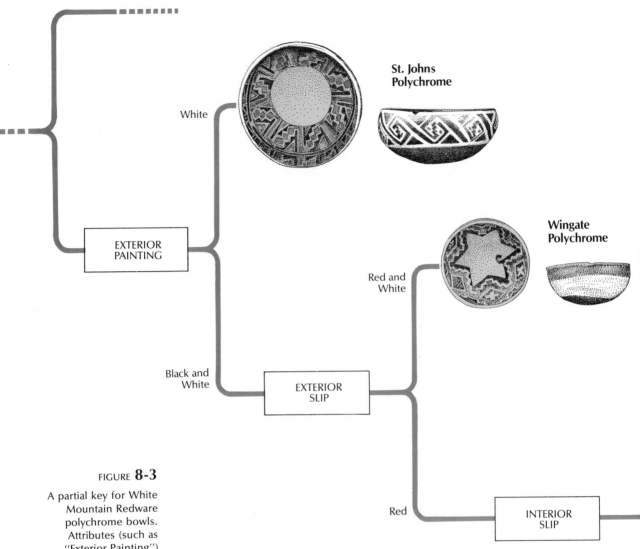

**St. Johns
Polychrome**

White

EXTERIOR
PAINTING

Wingate
Polychrome

Red and
White

Black and
White

EXTERIOR
SLIP

Red

INTERIOR
SLIP

FIGURE **8-3**

A partial key for White
Mountain Redware
polychrome bowls.
Attributes (such as
"Exterior Painting")
branch into specific
states (such as "Black
and White"); thus, by
following the branching
from left to right, one
could identify a bowl
with the attributes
*black-and-white exterior
painting, red exterior
slip, and white interior
slip* as a bowl of the
Showlow Polychrome
type.

Monothetic types have several useful characteristics. Once constructed, they can be formalized and explicitly defined by a listing of attributes and their states. These in turn can be arranged into a *key*, a step-by-step model describing the order in which attributes are examined in the process of classifying specimens as to type (FIGURE 8-3).

Albert Spaulding has made the point that attribute clusters or types can be discovered statistically. During the past twenty years many archaeologists have followed Spaulding's suggestion. For such studies, the relevant attribute states of each artifact must be recorded. Analysis often involves dozens of attributes on tens of thousands of artifacts. Statistical procedures needed for such extensive analyses have become widespread only recently, with the increasing availability of computers. Computer analyses consider a large number of attributes simultaneously and identify those that most clearly differentiate classes of objects into types. Perhaps because of the recency of their introduction, these techniques have done little more than validate existing typologies. In a few cases, some highly sophisticated techniques, such as cluster analysis and factor analysis, have generated potentially useful *polythetic* types—groupings of items on the basis of *overall* similarity. Members of polythetic types do not share a list of defining characteristics. To be a member, an object need only be more similar to other objects in a group than to objects in another group. While statistical studies are provocative, their ability to surpass the archaeologist as a generator of types remains to be demonstrated.

The processes of analysis discussed above are carried out on every major kind of material recovered by the archaeologist. Several of the most common kinds are examined below.

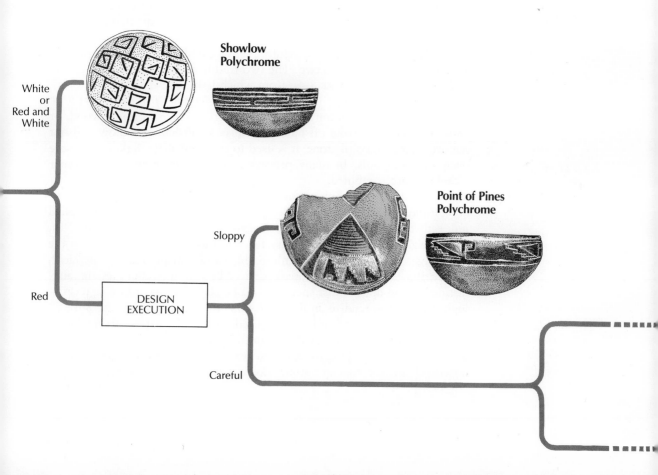

MATERIALS FOR ANALYSIS

Chipped Stone

Analysis of chipped stone often begins with studies to identify the source of the raw material. This is sometimes done by visual inspection or through neutron activation, in which minute differences in the chemical composition of materials according to their sources can lead to relatively positive identifications. These studies sometimes turn up surprises; for example, obsidian in Hopewell Indian burial mounds (in Ohio) was found to have come from sources in what is now Yellowstone National Park, in Wyoming—1800 miles away.

The major part of chipped-stone analysis is technological, especially that involved in studies of the tools of early hunters and gatherers. As a result of experimental studies by people like Bordes and Crabtree, it is becoming possible to identify attributes and attribute states produced by particular manufacturing techniques (FIGURE 8-4). *Hard-hammer percussion* is an old and versatile technique in which one stone, the *hammerstone,* strikes a second stone to produce fractures (FIGURE 4-11). Hard-hammer techniques vary greatly in complexity. The earliest humans, who left deposits at Olduvai Gorge, simply struck one pebble with another repeatedly to produce a ragged but sharp cutting or scraping edge. The *Levallois technique* is a more sophisticated form of hard-hammer percussion. In it, the knapper strikes off a series of *flakes* from a nodule of flint, removing the *cortex,* or outer surface, and forming a specialized core that resembles a tortoise shell. Striking this core at one end detaches a flake of predetermined shape that is immediately serviceable as a tool. A third hard-hammer method is the *split-cobble technique.* Here the knapper carefully aligns a cobble so that when struck by a hammerstone it splits in two. The two freshly fractured surfaces become *striking platforms* (FIGURE 8-4), from which flakes are struck.

Another major chipping technique is *soft-hammer percussion* (FIGURE 4-11). In this case, a baton of resilient material—such as bone, wood, or antler—is used to strike off flakes. Because a soft-hammer blow will not remove a large mass of stone, it is used to trim and shape flakes into more finely finished tools. In many processes, hard-hammer and soft-hammer techniques are combined.

The last major technique for working chippable stone is *pressure flaking* (FIGURE 4-11). In pressure flaking no blow is struck, and force is applied indirectly through another tool. In the case of the chest crutch (pp. 89–90), body weight supplies the necessary force to push off a large blade; in the final stages of shaping a projectile point, hand-arm pressure is sufficient. The attributes of flakes and cores produced by various techniques are fairly distinctive and allow most specimens to be classified according to technological type by specialists in lithic, or stone tool, analysis (FIGURE 8-4).

Once a tool is made it is usually used. Traces of wear occurring during such use can often be detected, a point that Soviet archaeologist Sergei Semeonov has been making for decades. Several major kinds of such wear are observable on the edges of stone tools, including microflaking, striations, and polish.

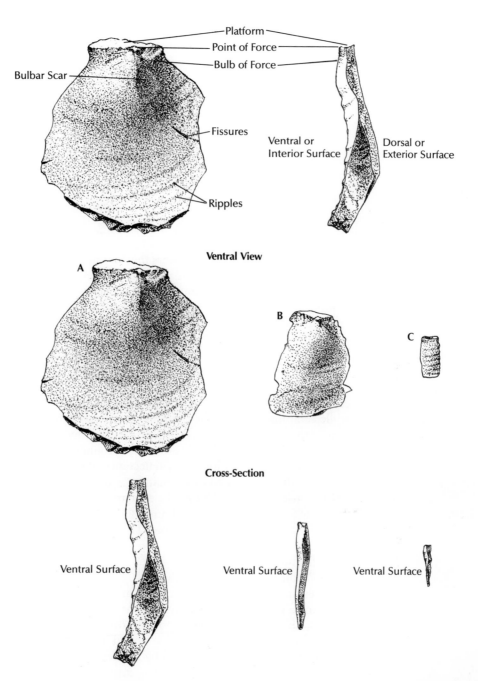

Platform
Point of Force
Bulb of Force
Bulbar Scar
Fissures
Ventral or Interior Surface
Dorsal or Exterior Surface
Ripples

Ventral View

A

B

C

Cross-Section

Ventral Surface

Ventral Surface

Ventral Surface

Ventral Surface

FIGURE **8-4**   At top, important characteristics of chipped-stone flakes; below, flake types produced by three basic techniques of flake detachment: *A,* hard-hammer percussion, which produces the largest size and thickness and the most prominent bulb of force; *B,* soft-hammer percussion, in which flakes are usually not more than 3 or 4 cm long, have relatively flat bulbs of force, and, sometimes, near the point of force, have a small lip; *C,* pressure flaking, producing flakes usually not more than 2 or 3 cm long and relatively flat and thin bulbs of force. These technological flake types are defined in exclusive terms; in actuality, many flakes have characteristics of more than one type.

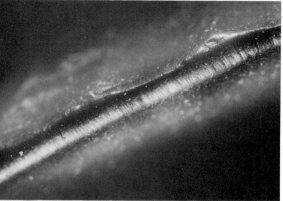

Microflakes are tiny flake scars that can be seen on a tool's edge, sometimes with the naked eye, but usually requiring low-power magnification (FIGURE 8-5). Ruth Tringham and her students have shown that scraping motions produce flaking on only one side of a tool edge, while cutting motions produce flaking on both sides. Unfortunately, a variety of processes in addition to use can produce microflaking, including manufacture, trampling, and even careless handling.

Striations are scratches formed by abrasion. The orientation of striations on tools indicates the direction of motion during use. For example, cutting and sawing motions produce striations parallel to the cutting edge, while scraping and chopping motions leave distinctive perpendicular striations. Striations are also easily observed under low- or medium-power magnification. Extensive abrasion produces a rounding of the edges.

Polish is relatively high light-reflectance of a surface. Exactly how it develops in the use of a tool is a matter of debate, but that it occurs as the result of use is certain. Among the remains of early agricultural societies in the Near East, polish has been found on the flakes once glued into wooden handles to make crude sickle tools. This striking *sickle sheen,* visible at a glance, is the result of harvesting grains. Lawrence Keeley has used high magnification on experimental stone tools to describe the attributes of "meat" polish and "antler" polish.

Despite the rudimentary state of use-wear analysis, many studies of prehistoric tools have yielded important and sometimes surprising results. For example, the symmetrical, pointed tools customarily termed projectile points (in the belief that they once tipped arrows and spears) were found, through microscopic examination by Stanley Ahler and others, to have been used in a variety of tasks, including cutting and scraping. Most of these projectile points probably were multi-use tools; some may even have been arrow- or spearpoints.

In some cases, the materials worked leave a deposit or residue on the tool edge. If the conditions of preservation are favorable and enthusiastic

FIGURE **8-5**

Several types of lithic use-wear under the microscope: On facing page, at left, microflaking, in a tool used experimentally to scrape soapstone; at right on facing page, striation, in a tool used by Eskimos to scrape hides; and, at right, polish, in a tool used experimentally to cut bracken fern.

laboratory workers do not scrub artifacts clean, the nature of the residue may be determined. For example, Frederick Brieur, working with tools from a dry cave in Arizona, was able to show, through chemical analysis, whether tools had been used most recently on plant or animal tissue.

The angle of the working edge, or *edge angle,* also provides clues to tool use. Sergei Semeonov has proposed that tools with an acute edge angle (below 35°) were used for cutting soft materials such as skin and muscle. Tools with edge angles above 60° were used for cutting or scraping hard materials such as wood and bone. Tools with intermediate angles (35°–40°) were possibly used as whittling knives.

After use, stone tools may be resharpened by *retouching* or further chipping. Archaeologists such as George Frison have shown that tools may be used in one set of activities until they become worn out, at which time they can be resharpened or even retouched into a different tool. Obviously, these maintenance and recycling processes create additional formal variability. In the eastern United States, a number of projectile point types assumed to be temporal types were shown by Albert Goodyear to be simply various stages in the resharpening process of knives (FIGURE 8-6).

FIGURE **8-6**

Postulated stages in the uselife of the Dalton point. At left, is its first stage—as a wide-blade serrated knife. Resharpening by pressure flaking along the working edges gradually narrows the point. In its final form, at right, the point probably could no longer be used as a knife, and may have been reused as an awl for piercing hides.

Ceramics   Ceramic studies, like lithic studies, tend to start with sourcing, and, again as with stone, neutron activation can be used to identify sources. In petrographic analysis, also widely used, minerals present are identified by microscopic examination of a thin slice or section cut from a sherd. Petrographic analysis is especially useful for identifying temper, the nonplastic material such as sand or crushed shell that is added to clay to assure more even drying and less (and more even) shrinkage. The results of such analyses can be used to describe patterns of trade and exchange—sometimes with surprising outcomes. In fact, in the 1930s, most archaeologists refused to accept Anna Shepard's petrographic analyses, which showed that the majority of the pots at several thirteenth- and fourteenth-century pueblos were imported. At that time, Southwest archaeologists envisioned ancient pueblo communities as largely self-sufficient. Today, with our better understanding of trade in tribal societies, these results are accepted, although the reason for this heavy importation of bulky pots is not known.

Techniques of manufacture have long been documented in ceramic analysis. There are five common ones: (1) *modeling,* hand-shaping a lump of clay into a desired form; (2) *coiling,* building vessels by joining rolls or strips of clay one atop another, sometimes in spirals, sometimes in rings; (3) *molding,* pressing clay onto or into a rigid form, from which it is removed when dry; (4) *throwing,* shaping a ball of clay as it rotates on a horizontal surface or wheel; and (5) *slip casting,* pouring slip, or clay with the consistency of mud, into plaster molds, in which it solidifies. This last process is used for mass-producing modern pottery.

In many cases, these techniques leave traces for the archaeologist. The place where coils join can often be seen on the inside or bottom of vessels. Sometimes these joints are obscured by smoothing with a wooden paddle and a stone anvil, (the potter holds the anvil stone against the inner wall of the pot while gently paddling the outside). This technique leaves its own distinctive marks. Molding and slip casting are identifiable by the exact repetition of forms and by uniform thickness of vessel walls. Identification of particular techniques can also result from finding the tools used in manufacture and the waste products.

Once the basic form of the vessel is achieved, the potter may employ one or more techniques for finishing the surface and decorating it. The more common techniques include burnishing, scraping, incising, carving, painting, stamping, impressing, appliquéing, and slipping (painting a watery slip onto the surface of a pot). The completed pot is then fired (baked in intense heat).

Such techniques of surface treatment are often extremely important elements in temporal and socio-functional typologies, which concentrate on such features as slip color and design layout. As we saw in Chapter 4, Longacre used the actual distribution of specific design elements on pots in his attempt to identify matrilocal residence at Carter Ranch Pueblo; Hill has studied minute differences in design elements to identify individual potters.

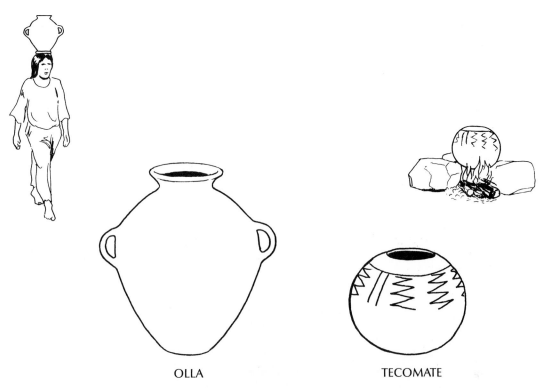

OLLA

TECOMATE

FIGURE **8-7** Two familiar techno-functional pottery types in Mesoamerica: at left, the *olla,* or necked jar, used today for carrying water and common in the highlands; and, at right, the *tecomate,* or neckless jar, found more often in lowland coastal areas, where it is used today in cooking shellfish stews.

Most of the ceramic typologies we use in everyday situations in our society are techno-functional and based on vessel shape. When archaeologists construct techno-functional types, they are often built on our own native categories, such as plate, bowl, vase, bottle, jar, mug, pitcher, and ladle. Our native categories, however, are not sufficient to describe all of the relevant variety. For example, jars in Mexico come in two common types: those with necks and those without (FIGURE 8-7). That we have no specific names for these two forms is one reason for the use of Mexican terms such as *olla* for the necked jars, which usually hold water, and *tecomate* for the jars without necks, which are most often used as stew pots. At present, archaeologists are trying to develop techno-functional typologies that use geometric shapes as basic units rather than native types.

Most of the pottery archaeologists recover is in the form of potsherds. In order to record shapes, archaeologists must extrapolate attributes of whole vessels from pieces. A number of ingenious techniques have been devised. For example, rimsherds are used for determining the shape of vessel walls as follows. The rim of most bowls and jars (turned upside-down) will lie flat on a floor. Thus there will be only one way that a rimsherd can orient itself so that its top edge fits flush against a flat surface. That orientation is most likely the orientation of the rim to the rest of the vessel. With this knowledge, one can easily learn something about the shape of a vessel from just one sherd.

Rimsherds also furnish clues about vessel size. Most apertures in pots are circular. Determining the diameter of a rim simply requires calculating the arc of the circle. As a shorthand aid to this, archaeologists, using charts which are drawings of a number of concentric circles, merely slide a rimsherd to the place where its curvature matches the curvature of one of the circles. It is then a simple matter to read off diameter.

Method of surface treatment is often assumed to relate to use. Richly decorated pots are not likely to have been placed in cooking fires; while rough and undecorated ceramics are not likely to have been used for serving food. In addition, pots that have been placed over a fire may have carbon deposited on the vessel walls. Residues in and on pots also provide additional information. In some Southwestern sites, for example, enough corn kernels have been found in pots to identify a seed jar.

Tests of resistance to breakage and of porosity can also contribute to techno-functional analyses. Papago Indians use highly porous vessels for holding drinking water because the "sweating" of the pot serves to cool its contents. Tests on ollas from Mexico, usually assumed to have been water containers, show them to be extremely porous.

Several new directions are being taken in the functional study of ceramics. Christy Turner and Laurel Lofgren measured the volume of whole serving bowls and cooking jars excavated in the Hopi area of the Southwest and dating from A.D. 500 to 1700. The volume of serving bowls remained stable, but that of cooking jars declined. On the assumption that the volume of the latter was a function of family size, Turner and Lofgren postulate a decrease in average household size from 7 to 4.5 persons.

Ethnoarchaeologists have found that some pots have a long uselife, on the order of ten to twenty years for large storage jars. During this long period the scars of use accumulate, and these can be readily seen on sherds. Although few extensive use-wear studies have been done on ceramics, there are some preliminary results. For example, one study has reported that among painted pots those most carefully painted show fewer traces of wear, suggesting that these fancier pots had important socio-functions.

Pottery decorated with figural representations offers a unique picture of an ongoing society as seen by its artisans and political figures (FIGURE 8-8). Two of the best-known examples of this ceramic art are Classic Maya figural polychromes and effigy vessels of the Moche civilization in Peru (A.D. 200 to 700). Michael Coe has studied scenes on Maya burial pottery to substantiate the considerable antiquity of the myth (recorded during the Spanish Conquest) of the Maya "hero-twins" who, in a story not unlike the Greek myth of Orpheus, journeyed into the underworld to confront the

FIGURE **8-8**

The snail collectors—a
Moche pot, whose
decorations demonstrate
why Mochica artisans are
famous for their portrayal
of nearly every aspect of
daily life in the Moche
Empire of Peru (A.D.
200–700).

gods. Elizabeth Benson has concentrated on the earthly views of life and
death provided by Moche pottery.

Another ceramic-like material with a history of production from at
least 3400 B.C. in Egypt is glass. Glass is formed by melting sand in a furnace, then blowing or casting the molten glass into its final form. The earliest glass was handblown; a small percentage still is today. Color in glass is
imparted by impurities that can be identified by chemical analysis. Today,
color usually relates to techno-function. The vast majority of beer bottles
are brown glass, while those of soft drinks are green or untinted. With glass
objects, shape is both stylistic and utilitarian. Within techno-functional categories—such as soft-drink containers—socio-functional types can be distinguished that identify manufacturers. The shape of Coca-Cola bottles is
especially distinctive. The shapes of many beer, wine, and medicine bottles
are equally indicative of their contents (FIGURE 8-9).

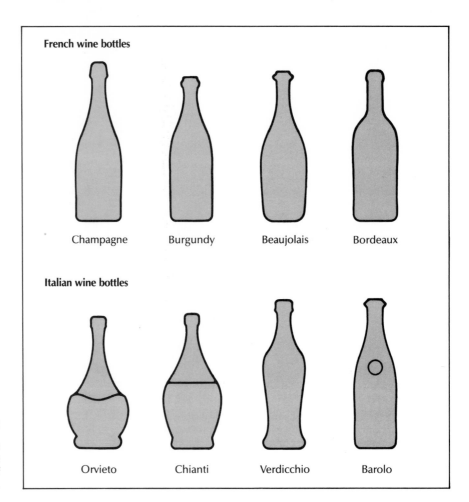

FIGURE **8-9**

Many wine bottles indicate by their shape the general category of the wine they contain.

French wine bottles

Champagne Burgundy Beaujolais Bordeaux

Italian wine bottles

Orvieto Chianti Verdicchio Barolo

Metal Objects

Another important artifact material is metal. Metal marked the last two "ages" in the three-stage system of prehistoric cultural development, formulated in the nineteenth century: stone, bronze, and iron. Metallurgy was developed in the Old and New Worlds independently. Somewhat surprisingly, the first items in both hemispheres were socio-functional and ideo-functional—jewelry and other symbolic commodities. This remained the case in the Americas until after European contact in the sixteenth century; but in the Near East, iron was invented in the second millennium B.C. and was soon formed into plows, chisels, swords, and other tools and weapons.

Many archaeologists analyze metal to determine production processes and so add to the history of technology. The simplest technique is *cold hammering,* or beating the metal into the desired shape. Of the few metals that exist in nature in a metallic state, copper and gold were the most commonly exploited in this fashion. In North America, one prehistoric society, the Old Copper Culture of the Great Lakes area (ca. 1000 B.C.) was named for its use of the cold-hammering technique on locally available copper. Some band groups still use this technology on metal items they receive from more technologically advanced societies. For example, the Canadian Eskimos cold hammer iron items they salvage from shipwrecks.

The next stage in metalworking involved melting and casting metals. Smelting, the use of high temperatures to reduce ores to metallic elements was a more advanced technique practiced in the Balkans and Near East by 4000 B.C. and in Peru by 200 B.C. The results included the production of tin (and arsenic in Peru), which, when combined with copper, formed bronze, an *alloy,* or the physical mixture of two or more metals. In the New World no further technological breakthroughs occurred. The Hittites of the Near East are credited with the first systematic smelting of iron in the middle of the second millennium B.C. Ironworking spread widely and became the technological base for farming and warfare in many later Old World societies.

Metals have distinctive compositions according to their place of manufacture. Techniques such as neutron activation can be used in pinpointing production locations and tracing trade networks, and microscopic analysis of the crystal structure of metals can reveal the details of how an artifact was produced. The analysis of metallurgy also involves experimentation. During an ethnoarchaeological study of the Haya in Tanzania, Africa, Peter Schmidt and Donald Avery asked their hosts to demonstrate the traditional technique of iron-working, which was no longer practiced because of the availability of modern trade items. The older men built a furnace and fashioned metal ingots. The capability of the furnace to produce extraordinarily high temperatures was confirmed during a later experiment by a battery of monitoring devices, and a chemical analysis showed the resulting ingots, to almost everyone's amazement, to be of a high-carbon steel. Using the experimental furnace as a model, Schmidt and Avery identified the remains of ancient furnaces and now argue that the first production of high-carbon steel was not a nineteenth-century American achievement, but an African one of much greater antiquity (FIGURE 8-10).

Tin cans have been intensively studied by historical archaeologists. First invented for Napoleon to preserve food for his wandering armies, cans have gone through a series of technological changes—from soldering on tops and sides to modern rolled-steel techniques. These innovations are well documented and were rapidly adopted by manufacturers, forming clear horizon markers useful for building temporal types. For example, the first canned soda appeared in "cone-top" cans in 1953 and the first pop-tops appeared about a decade later. Cans can also be analyzed in terms of use. Historic-sites archaeologists record the size and shape of cans to determine what they held. The easiest to identify are sardine cans, whose unique shape has remained the same for well over a hundred years. Sometimes the archae-

FIGURE **8-10**   Nyunge villagers of the Haya tribe in the West Lake region of Tanzania operating a smelting furnace that produces high-carbon steel. Eight bellows are operated up to 8 hours in the process.

ologist has historical records to help interpret formal attributes—for example, the Census of Manufacturers and the National Canners Association Package Statistics records, kept since 1904, of what quantities of what commodities were packed in what types of containers.

Animal Bones   Animal bones provide information on a variety of subjects and are intensively analyzed, usually by specialists known as zooarchaeologists. As a first step, the zooarchaeologist identifies the kind of animal and the anatomical part or *element* represented. If possible, each element is assigned an age and sex. The next step often involves calculating, for each kind of animal, a quantity known as the *minimum number of individuals* (usually written as MNI). Basically, the MNI is the lowest number of individual animals needed to account for the observed number of elements.

Faunal or animal bone data are used to describe important behaviors, such as the prominence of different species in the diet; hunting, butchering, and cooking practices; season of occupation of settlements; past environments; trade patterns; and ritual uses of animals. Inferences about animal procurement depend on knowledge of animal behavior in specific environments. For example, where the bones of ocean fish that live in 200 feet of water are found in late prehistoric California sites, it is likely that boats and hook-and-line fishing were part of the procurement technology. Acquaintance with animal behavior is also required for inferences about season of occupation of settlements. Bones from migratory birds, for example, would be clues to when, during the year, procurement (and thus occupation) took place. Bones may also be classified according to the environment the animals once inhabited. Such classifications help the zooarchaeologist reconstruct past environments.

Many faunal studies require special typologies of bones. For example, the kinds of cooking (such as boiling and roasting) leave characteristic traces on bone (discoloration and cracking). Studies of ancient diets require some knowledge of the amounts of meat typically obtained from different kinds of animals. In order to make estimates of these, zooarchaeologists experiment to determine the ratio of meat weight to total animal weight. By knowing the number of animals butchered (the MNI), and assuming a particular average size for animals, the weight of meat obtained can be inferred. Olsen-Chubbuck, in Colorado, is a site where, 9,000 years ago, bison were stampeded into a dry creek bed and then butchered (FIGURE 4-12). From the bone remains, Joe Ben Wheat calculated that 190 animals were killed, described in detail the butchering activities, and inferred how much meat was available for processing. Because most animals mate and give birth in a regular seasonal cycle, he was able, on the basis of the number of bones of immature calves found at the site, to determine the time of year the massacre occurred—late May or early June.

Faunal data are also a source of information on animal domestication —keeping animals and controlling their breeding, rather than hunting them. Animals that are bred undergo behavioral and biological changes. Thus, the bones of animals that have been domesticated for many generations will show minute differences from those of wild animals (FIGURE 8-11). For example, because the muscles of domestic animals are less robust, the bones themselves are correspondingly so. In addition, in some species, brains and jaws become smaller. However, the identification of the *earliest* stages in the domestication process is difficult. One approach has been to determine ratios of mature to immature animals—on the assumption that hunters would bag a full range (in age) of animals, while among domesticated animals large numbers of young males, which neither breed nor provide milk, would be culled from herds and slaughtered. Differences between domesticated and wild forms are also being sought through microscopic examination of thin sections of bone and horn cores.

Animals figure prominently in a society's ceremonies. The kitchen middens of the Olmec, who left the unexplained serpentine caches at San

Lorenzo in Mexico (Chapter 5), were full of the bones of the small *Bufo marinus* toad. The meat of this amphibian is poisonous, but the bufotenin in the sacks behind its ears is a natural hallucinogenic drug, much like LSD. Such drugs were widely used by priests and shamans in prehistoric Mexico to alter consciousness and produce euphoric highs and violent illness, both a part of ritual cleansings.

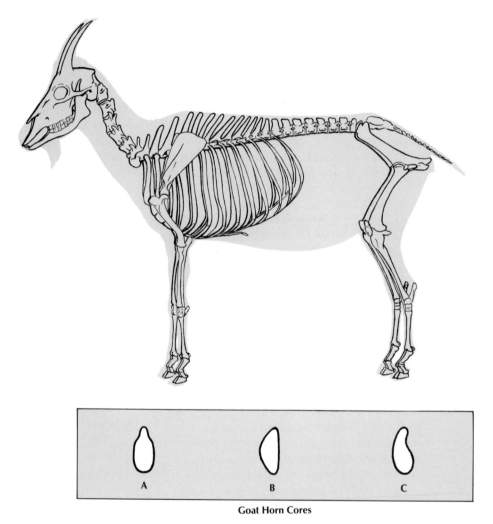

Goat Horn Cores

FIGURE **8-11**   Cross-sections of goat horns can indicate the degree of domestication of the animal. Those shown are from goats that were *A,* semidomesticated, *B,* descended from many generations of domesticated animals, and *C,* of even longer domestication than those of *B.* The reasons for the differences are not well understood. The goat skeleton indicates the many bones that an animal can contribute to sites.

Plants   Plant remains are analyzed by specialists in *paleobotany,* whose skills fill a gap between archaeology and botany. Experts in identifying plants from fragmentary, often charred, remains, they also usually have a broad knowledge of the variety of human uses of plants.

Plants or plant materials occur in a number of different forms in archaeological context: pollen, seeds and leaves, food remains, wooden tools, lumber, textiles, and charcoal. One of the most ubiquitous forms is pollen, the microscopic, nearly indestructible, male sex cells of plants. Pollen is introduced into sites by animals, wind, human activity, and on-site plants. Extracted from soil samples by use of acid baths and flotation, it is occasionally identified even to the species level with the aid of microscopes. Pollen data from archaeological sites give us information on the variety of plants people used. Pollen, like bone, can be classified according to the environmental zone where the plant grew. As a result, pollen data from natural sedimentary deposits, such as bogs or lake bottoms, are most valuable for reconstructing the nature of past environments. In these reconstructions, changing pollen frequencies clearly indicate changes in plant communities (FIGURE 8-12).

The recovered remains are useful in studying plant structure and especially the changes in plant form that accompanied domestication. Intensive analysis of seeds recovered from caves in the Midwest and South has shown that certain native North American plants, such as sunflower and sumpweed, were probably the first plants domesticated in the eastern United States, dating back to at least 2500 B.C. Past diets can also be reconstructed from plant remains. The data, however, must be interpreted with caution because of the haphazard way in which they enter the archaeological record —as the result of burned dinners, spills, and occasional fires in storage areas.

Archaeologists have used a variety of extraordinary data to reconstruct ancient meals. One specialized source of information is prehistoric feces, or *coprolites.* MacNeish, in his corn domestication study (pp. 19–26), leaned heavily on the analysis of such preserved fecal specimens. As in other areas, experimental archaeology has a role to play. Vaughn Bryant and Glenna Williams-Dean fed themselves pollen and then checked the preservation of different types after it had passed through their digestive systems. Where bodies are well preserved, in dry caves or bogs, analysis of stomach and intestine contents has provided direct data on one or two meals. In the 1960s, the stomach contents of one bog-man (the so-called Tolland Man) were analyzed, and two archaeologists—Sir Mortimer Wheeler and Grahame Clark—ate a gruel made with the ingredients identified; their reaction to the meal provided one possible explanation for Tolland Man's demise.

Plants are made into products that archaeologists sometimes find: baskets, sandals, textiles, wood cabins, ceremonial objects, and musical instruments. Wooden artifacts are frequent finds in historic sites, and typologies have been applied to lumber to identify manufacturing techniques (FIGURE

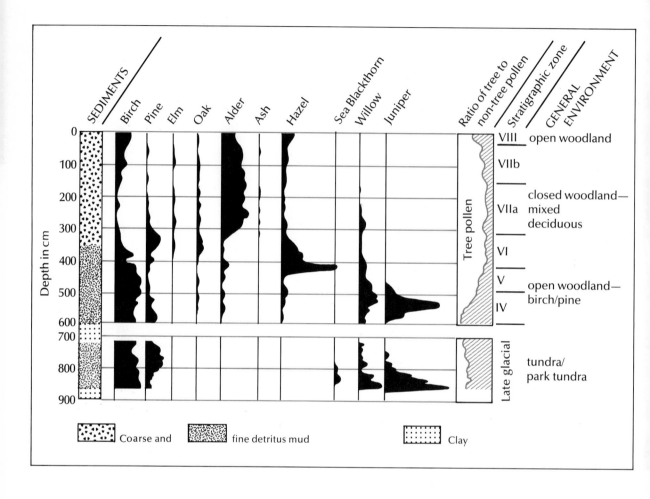

FIGURE **8-12**   Differences in the frequency of occurrence of certain pollens in lake-bottom deposits at Nant Ffrancon, North Wales, indicate changes through time in the environment. Views of the environments similar to those listed here are shown on facing page where *A* is open woodland; *B*, closed woodland—mixed deciduous; *C*, open woodland—birch and pine; and *D*, tundra/park tundra.

A

B

C

D

8-13). Construction materials also furnish evidence about the impact of communities on their local environments. Jeff Dean's study of roof beams at Kiet Siel Pueblo, in northeastern Arizona, showed that there were changes over time in the species of tree used in construction, local trees being replaced by those that grew in difficult-to-reach locations in deep coves and well-watered cliff ledges. Dean believes that builders turned to more inaccessible trees only after exhausting those easy to reach.

Items such as baskets and textiles exhibit a lot of utilitarian and stylistic variability that can be analyzed. One archaeologist, James Adovasio, believes that he can identify the work of individual weavers. James Deetz has studied the baskets of the historic Chumash Indians of Southern California to identify the distinctive weaving styles of different communities. The use of some plants even indicates differences in social class: in ancient Oaxaca, Mexico, upper-class families burned charcoal made of oak and pine cut from mountainsides, while the lower classes foraged for whatever they could get near their residences.

The symbolic use or representation of plants in ceremonies and ritual tells archaeologists something about the significance of plants to a society. The corn motif is common in Mexico and the United States' Southwest. Wheat and other plants are pictured in Egyptian tombs and on palace tableaux in Egypt and the Near East. Although morning glories do not grow in the Teotihuacán Valley, they are a continually repeated design element and

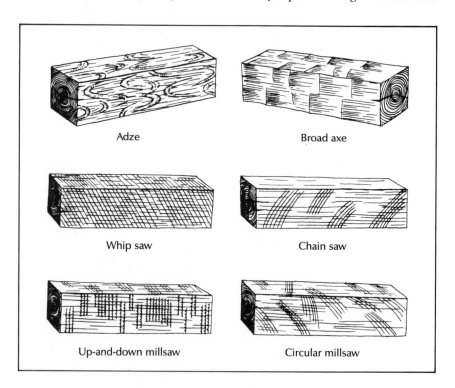

Adze

Broad axe

Whip saw

Chain saw

Up-and-down millsaw

Circular millsaw

FIGURE **8-13**

Differences in the traces left by various lumber-shaping techniques.

FIGURE **8-14**   A "priest" in a Teotihuacán mural with flowers on a vine. The three flowers (hanging upside down at bottom center) are morning-glories, which are not native to the Teotihuacán region and which may have been used as a source of an hallucinogen.

component of costumes in the murals at the ancient city of Teotihuacán (FIGURE 8-14: see FIGURE 3-2). At the time of the arrival of the Spanish, the Aztecs were reported to have used morning glories to make an hallucinogenic drug. The frequent occurrence of that plant, which had to be obtained at some distance from Teotihuacán, suggests some antiquity for this practice.

Burials   There are innumerable ways to dispose of a dead body and archaeologists have seen and recorded just about all of them. Each burial usually has three components: a body or bodies, a grave or burial site, and, often, accompanying artifacts (See Chapter 5).

Where bones are preserved, they are an important source of information on the health and longevity of the original population. These bones are usually studied by specialists known as human osteologists. The age of individuals is determined from tooth eruption and wear, the degree of fusion of the several parts that make up a bone, and other skeletal traits (FIGURE 8-15). The size of bones and the prominence of muscular attachments are

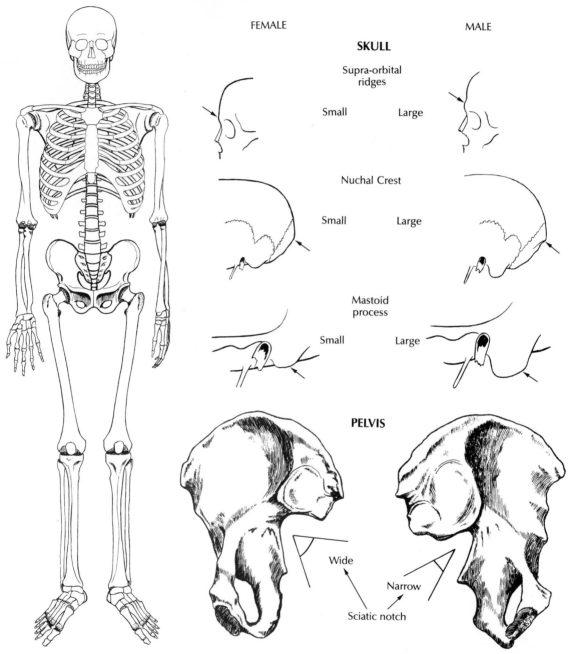

FEMALE   MALE

SKULL

Supra-orbital
ridges

Small   Large

Nuchal Crest

Small   Large

Mastoid
process

Small   Large

PELVIS

Wide

Narrow

Sciatic notch

FIGURE **8-15**

Attributes of the pelvis and skull in the human skeleton
are especially useful in determining the sex.

clues to sexing of skeletons; but ideally sex is determined by the angle of the sciatic notch in the pelvis, the angle in the female pelvis being greater. Skeletal remains permit estimation of even the number of children a woman has borne—from the wear patterns on the pubic symphysis, a part of the pelvis.

From age and sex information, archaeologists can construct statistical lifetables, which show patterns of longevity. Closely related are attempts at *paleopathology,* studies of diseases that afflicted extinct populations. While a few such studies are done on mummified bodies, the majority are done on bones. In some diseases, such as arthritis, later stages are characterized by calcification of the joints; others leave less obvious signs. Frank Saul has identified spongy perforations in bones from Classic Maya burials that he believes are the result of Vitamin C deficiencies. These pathologies show up consistently in burial populations from 300 B.C. to A.D. 850. How scurvy can occur in the middle of a rain forest full of fruit is a question not yet answered.

Osteology is also the crux of "the Great Syphilis Controversy." Some contend that syphilis was confined to the Old World until introduced into the Americas by European explorers; others believe it was a New World disease brought back by them to the Old World. While advanced stages of syphilis do attack bones and leave lesions, so do other diseases, and osteologists are groping for the answer in burial grounds.

Osteological analyses often tell us about health care in ancient societies. Before aspirin, one method of treating headaches was trephining, cutting holes in the skull. Many examples, which show "fresh" cuts, indicate that the headache was permanently relieved; others show signs of healing.

Tooth decay was not a problem for many populations before the advent of refined sugar, but dental mutilation was a common practice among the Classic Maya, who seem to have conceived of filing and inlaying teeth as a form of decoration that perhaps even symbolized social standing or task group membership—such as a functionary for a particular temple (FIGURE 8-16). Although archaeologists first assumed that the filing was done after death, wear studies and patterns of healing soon showed that filing was done on live subjects.

The construction and layout of the grave are of major concern to archaeologists. Again the variety of forms is boggling—shaft tombs; logtombs; crypts; scaffolds; lined cists; burials under benches, temples, pyramids, doorways, stairways; and, of course, the simple pit burial. The body itself may be flexed or extended, face up or face down, and oriented in any direction. Orientation, taken as the direction of the spinal axis and skull, has no clear practical function and is likely to vary with belief systems.

Grave goods are recorded painstakingly in drawings and written descriptions. The form of analysis used on them (and on the graves themselves) depends on the particular interest of the archaeologist. For example, the association of particular techno-functional items with burials of different ages and sexes can disclose patterns in the division of labor. These are

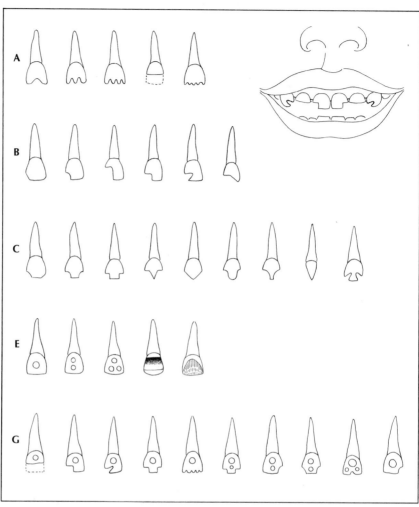

FIGURE **8-16**   Filed teeth found in Maya burials. The set of teeth above exhibits a common pattern known as the "sun god motif." (After Romero, 1958.)

especially obvious in simpler societies where age and sex are the most important characteristics in defining social roles. Unfortunately, the simplest societies are of the highly mobile hunter-gatherer type, among which it is the practice to leave the dead behind. Concentrations of burials and cemeteries are associated with sedentism and increasing social complexity. Nevertheless, in these societies age/sex differences are still clear. For example, in Classic Maya burials, *spindle whorls* (small round clay weights placed on stick spindles and used to spin thread) are usually found in the burials of females; spearpoints are more common in burials of males. With increased complexity in the Maya area, occupation was still an important component in defining social roles symbolized in burials. For example, some burials have produced shaman tool kits, including deer toe bones, crystals, and carved bone objects, all associated ethnohistorically with the role of diviner and curer.

But along with these job-related items in the Maya area are items whose primary function is ornamental, such as necklaces and earplugs. The occurrence and frequency of socio-functional types can be used to identify different social roles. Archaeologists assume that if there is unequal access to social roles, there will be unequal access to material goods and that, in many societies, these differences will show up in burials. In fact, the primary way archaeologists infer social inequality is by recording the degree to which grave goods are unevenly distributed among burials—how many burials have no pots or necklaces or cutting tools, how many have one, two, twenty, thirty of these objects, and so on. In addition, they record not only how many pots are in a grave, but which are decorated and with what symbols; not only how many necklaces, but which are made of clay and which of gold or jade or turquoise. Evaluations of socio-functions are often based on two obvious factors: the material from which the object was made, and the amount of work involved in production. Underlying both of these is the single concept of replacement cost. Thus, much more time and labor would be required to manufacture a plate from gold than one from locally available clay, or to make a ceremonial serving pot with painted figures and glyphs than a crude pot for everyday cooking. While these differences are obvious, many times the archaeologist, finding it difficult to rank items in terms of replacement cost, turns to experimental archaeology, ethnoarchaeology, or history for help. For example, to rank tin items and silver items in Near Eastern burials, archaeologists can refer to ancient records kept by traders in which actual ore purchase and transport costs were listed.

Replacement cost is important because it is a standard concept that can be used to compare burials having very different types of grave goods. The same concept can also be used to evaluate different types of grave constructions, from vaulted masonry tombs to simple pits in soft earth. Applying the concept of replacement cost to grave goods and grave construction provides a quantitative way of describing differences in the disposal of the dead. Compare the range of burials from the ancient state of Ur to the range from the Grasshopper site in Arizona. From an examination of FIGURE 8-17 it is not hard to tell which society exhibited the greatest social inequality.

Skeletal remains have been examined as independent evidence of social inequality. For example, Bill Haviland found that at Tikal individuals in tombs were, on the average, taller than persons placed in housemound fill, perhaps reflecting differences in diet due to social standing. It is only in combining evidence from the human, artifactual, and construction remains that a fairly complete picture of social organization emerges.

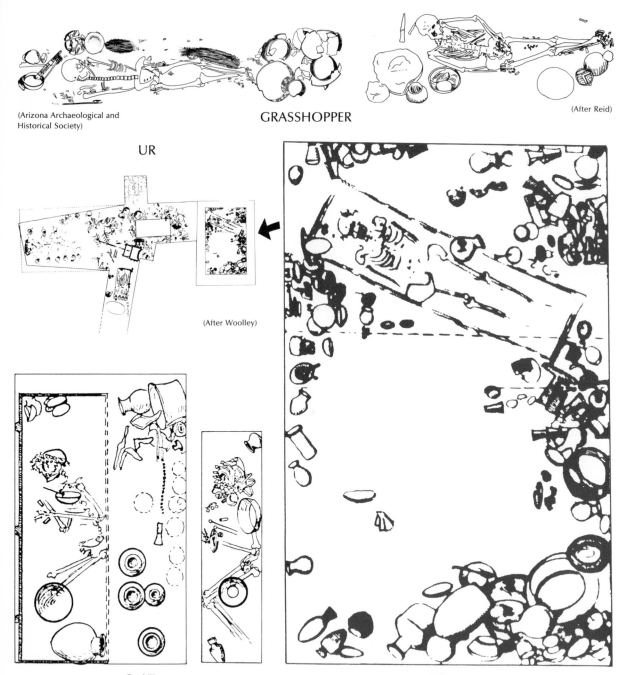

GRASSHOPPER

UR

FIGURE **8-17** Burials from Grasshopper Pueblo, Arizona (ca. A.D. 1350), and Ur, Iraq (ca. 2400 B.C.). Scale is approximately the same for all the burials shown. The arrow indicates the relation of the Ur burial at right to the whole grave, which included a chariot and a large chest. Among the smaller items in the Ur burials are bronze axes, copper razors and mirrors, gold rings, silver and gold hair ornaments, silver cups, and lapis lazuli cylinder seals. These show a greater range of materials and greater difference in distribution than the offerings in the rich Grasshopper burial, which consist mainly of ceramic, chipped stone, and bone artifacts.

Architecture   Another area where societies invest substantial amounts of labor and materials is architecture. The remains of structures are generally available and furnish information on a variety of subjects. Identifying how materials were obtained, manufactured, and used on construction is fairly straightforward, although sometimes there are surprises. One intriguing example is appropriately named "Casa Grande," an amazing four-story adobe building southeast of Phoenix that was erected by the Hohokam about A.D. 1350 (FIGURE 8-18). First reported by Father Kino in 1694, there has been speculation ever since on how the adobe walls have lasted so long, withstanding even earthquakes. As a result of chemical and mechanical analyses of small chunks of the wall, the surprising answer has only recently been pieced together by John Andresen. The walls are not adobe, but a mixture of local soil, clay, and ground-up *caliche* (a rock-hard layer in the soil), which was formed into a primitive concrete. Unlike adobe, which readily melts in rain, the Casa Grande walls have lasted for more than six hundred years. Will our sidewalks do as well?

FIGURE **8-18**   Casa Grande ruin, near Phoenix, Arizona, which was built (ca. A.D. 1350) of a primitive concrete. This historic photograph was taken prior to 1903, the year in which the National Park Service built a roof over the ruin to protect it from rain.

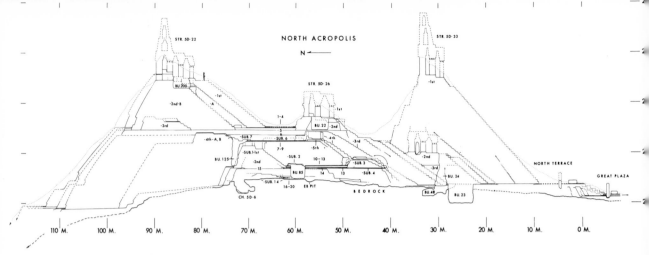

FIGURE **8-19**   Section of a trench cut through the Tikal North acropolis shows the remains and reconstructions of 1000 years of Maya civilization, which began well before Christ and ended around A.D. 820.

FIGURE **8-20**   Kiet Siel Pueblo, Navajo National Monument, Arizona. Walls and roofs shown were preserved by the dry conditions afforded by the cliff overhang. The plan (on facing page) shows rooms and the patterns of wall bonding and abutments used by archaeologist Jeffrey Dean to discriminate between core and accretion units.

Analysis □ **238**

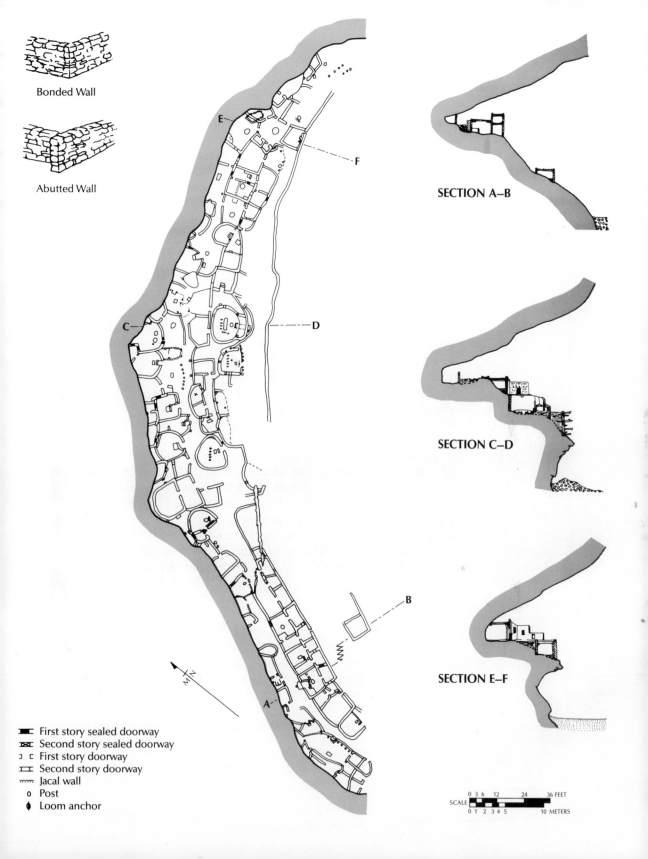

Bonded Wall

Abutted Wall

E

F

C

D

B

A

N

SECTION A–B

SECTION C–D

SECTION E–F

First story sealed doorway
Second story sealed doorway
First story doorway
Second story doorway
Jacal wall
o Post
Loom anchor

SCALE

0 3 6   12   24   36 FEET

0 1 2 3 4 5   10 METERS

Identifying sequences of construction activities is often difficult. In our discussion of the McDonald's fast-food chain (Chapter 1), we pointed out that older restaurants are sometimes remodeled to accommodate new utilitarian and stylistic features. Architectural analysis dissects the end product of such alterations into its construction units—individual construction episodes—and orders these in time. Many of the structures archaeologists find are far more complex than McDonald's restaurants, the result of dozens or even hundreds of construction episodes (FIGURE 8-19).

Structures change in two ways. First, they grow upward, principally by two processes: old structures are torn down or deteriorate and their remains become the foundations for new structures, and additional stories are added to existing buildings. Thus, archaeologists can use the law of superposition to order construction units from first to last. But second, buildings also change by growing outward, through additions. To get a horizontal stratigraphy, or the sequence of additions and deletions, archaeologists make use of the fact that, in building additions, people usually save effort by attaching the new construction to existing walls. Thus, what is actually added is incomplete in and of itself. These incomplete units can be identified by the ways walls are attached—whether by *bonding* or *abutting*. Units that are bonded are assumed to be part of the same construction episode. Hence, archaeologists often spend a great deal of effort digging out room corners to determine whether two walls bond or abut. In this way, construction episodes and resulting architectural units are isolated. Units complete in themselves are called *core construction units,* and additions are called *accretion units.*

These principles have been elegantly applied by Jeff Dean in his analysis of the pueblo cliff dwellings of Kiet Siel (FIGURE 8-20) and Betatakin. Because of their protection from rain and other destructive agents, the rooms of the pueblos are remarkably well preserved; most, in fact, still have standing walls and roofs. In terms of architecture, these sites have changed little from when their occupants abandoned them some seven centuries ago.

Dean studied the patterns of bonding and abutting, identified core and accretion units, and determined the occupational history of the two pueblos. He was able to accomplish this with unusual precision because of the availability of a large number of roof beams, which could be accurately dated (Chapter 9). These sites, which are about the same size, largely contemporaneous, located in the same canyon, and built using the same construction materials and techniques, might be expected to have had similar occupational histories. Instead, Dean found that Kiet Siel had expanded through the accretion of many small units, probably built at different times; in contrast, Betatakin was the result of several major construction episodes. From these patterns Dean went on to offer a number of hypotheses concerning differences in migration patterns, community planning, and the size of local task groups.

Once basic construction sequences are worked out, archaeologists often attempt to understand the organization required for building episodes. For example, it is obvious that the task of building the larger units at Betatakin took more planning and organization than putting up the small units of Kiet Siel. Specific labor-energy requirements are sometimes calculated, and these are sometimes tested through experimentation or ethnoarchaeology. When they have been, the results have often been surprising. For example, Maya archaeologists estimated that hundreds of men would have labored for decades to build the Nunnery Quadrangle, the largest building complex at Uxmal. Charles Erasmus hired modern Maya laborers, and, on the basis of their work (complete with coffee breaks), he calculated that 1200 laborers, each working only 40 days a year, could have built the Nunnery Quadrangle in under 15 years.

Some longstanding mysteries of construction have been solved by the application of a little ethnoarchaeology. For centuries, explorers, archaeologists, and sensationalists have puzzled over how the great stone heads of Easter Island were transported several miles from their quarries and placed upright. Estimates of the work force necessary for both tasks were in the thousands, drastically exceeding the number that would have been locally available, and assumed advanced engineering knowledge, skills, and tools. When Thor Heyerdahl and his team studied Easter Island, however, Heyerdahl asked the local mayor how it might have been done. "We'll show you," replied the mayor, and the next morning two hundred men dragged a stone head across the island. The mayor then chose 18 men who, in a week, had succeeded in standing the 12-ton stone head upright. Their only tools were wooden poles, used as levers, and small rocks used as supports (FIGURE 8-21). Asked why he had not divulged the secret of the stone heads earlier, the mayor simply replied, "No one ever asked me."

Variability in the formal properties of structures is assumed to relate to the nature of the social groups that occupy or use them. For example, archaeologists often assume that the size of residences relates to the number of inhabitants. Some go so far as to propose that even in a complex society there is a constant amount of "roofed space" taken up by each individual. It is clear that in our own society, the number of occupants is only one of several variables that determine size of residence. The foremost of these is the social standing of the household, as measured by wealth or income. In fact, in Tucson we have found that income is more strongly related to dwelling size than the number of people in the household. Other ethnoarchaeological studies in the Philippines and Iran have come to similar conclusions.

Because the activities of the social unit that puts up and uses a building greatly affect the building's form, studying the formal properties and associated features of rooms can often reveal their special functions. For example, James Hill was interested in learning if the people of Broken K, a pueblo site occupied in the thirteenth century in eastern Arizona, had room types

FIGURE **8-21**

One of the massive stone heads on Easter Island being re-erected by contemporary Easter Islanders.

similar to those of modern Pueblo Indians. Hill first studied modern pueblos. He found that habitation rooms were relatively large and included built-in features such as mealing bins (for grinding grain), fire pits and, very often, ventilators. Storage rooms were small and featureless. *Kivas* (ceremonial rooms), of variable size, usually round, and often semisubterranean, contained distinctive features, such as benches, fire pits, ventilators, and a *sipapu* (a shallow cylindrical hole in the floor symbolizing the "navel of the earth"). Hill's analysis of Broken K was based on 59 excavated rooms, representing slightly more than half the site. Rooms with a floor area of more than 6.6 square meters were designated "large," and less than this area, "small." Larger rooms were associated with habitation features expected on the basis of their presence in modern pueblos, while small rooms were mostly featureless. Five rooms conformed similarly to expectations concerning kivas. Hill decided to use artifacts as an additional, independent test of his room function inferences. On the basis of activities, Hill predicted the kinds of materials that would be deposited as primary and de facto refuse in each room type. His analyses of the distribution of pollen, animal bone, potsherds, chipped-stone tools, shells, and other artifacts showed a surprisingly close match to his expectations.

Since Hill's pioneering studies in the 1960s, additional refinements have taken place. For example, at the Grasshopper site, a 500-room multistoried pueblo occupied between A.D. 1275 and 1400, work by Richard Ciolek-Torrello and J. Jefferson Reid has disclosed more complex patterns of space usage, with more than a half-dozen types of rooms, including varieties of habitation rooms as well as those for workshops and specialized storage. The investigators hypothesize that these room types were combined in

FIGURE **8-22**

Reconstruction by Tatiana Proskouriakoff of a palace structure at the Maya site of Uaxactún in Guatemala.

various ways by households differing in size, wealth, and stage of development. As a result of all this variety, studies of room function have become complex, even in the Southwest, where such studies are normally relatively easy.

Rooms in Maya palaces (FIGURE 8-22) are among the more difficult in assigning functions. Although some are easy to designate—such as public audience rooms (with built-in thrones overlooking stairways and plazas)—most have few if any features or have "problematic" ones, such as benches that could have been used for storage or sleeping as well as sitting. In addition, most Maya rooms were stripped clean of artifacts, the few found being those of late squatters camping in then largely abandoned structures.

Where few artifacts are found in structures, archaeologists sometimes resort to identifying functions at a more abstract level. One useful concept is degree of accessibility to spaces within architectural units. In these sorts of analyses, the archaeologist assumes the role of a rat in an ancient maze, trying to find out which rooms would have been most and least accessible to someone entering from outside. In a large settlement, these overall patterns can provide clues to function and social organization, the general principle being that, as social inequality increases, there will be an increase in the number of places that are hard to get to. For example, in a community where everything is easily accessible there was probably little social inequality. On the other extreme are sites such as Pampa Grande and Chan Chan in Peru, where, although both sites are large, relative differences in social organization can be found through architectural analysis. Pampa Grande, dating to the Moche Period, is clearly more open to access than Chan Chan, built several centuries later (FIGURE 8-23). Areas of more restricted access imply

FIGURE **8-23**   Maps of Pampa Grande (ca. A.D. 980) and on facing page, Chan Chan (ca. A.D. 1400), both located in coastal valleys in Peru. Note the differences in formal planning and accessibility of interior areas.

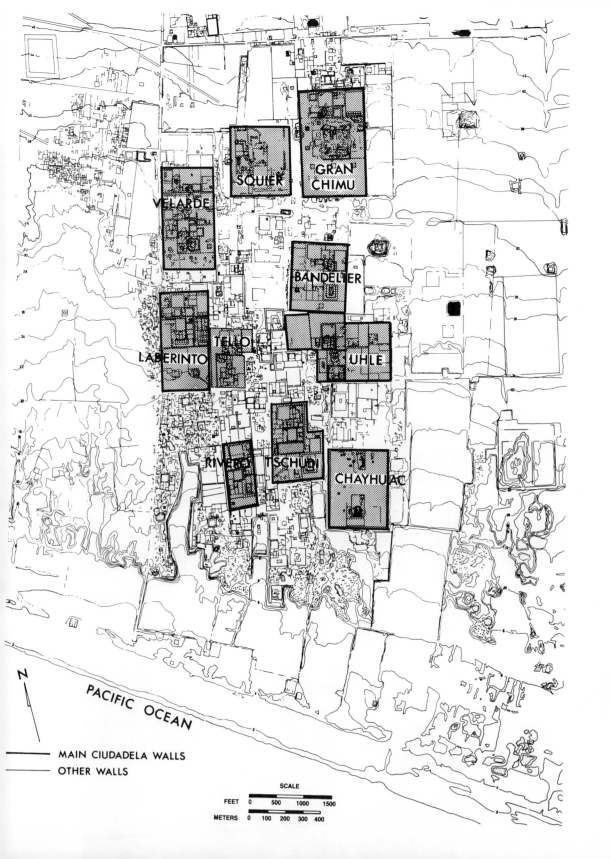

VELARDE

SQUIER

GRAN CHIMU

BANDELIER

TELLO

LABERINTO

UHLE

RIVERO TSCHUDI

CHAYHUAC

N

PACIFIC OCEAN

—— MAIN CIUDADELA WALLS

— OTHER WALLS

SCALE

FEET 0 500 1000 1500

METERS 0 100 200 300 400

FIGURE **8-24**

Aerial and ground views of Stonehenge, Salisbury Plain, Wiltshire, England. This ruin, the most famous of European "megaliths," (Chapter 9), may have been used for making astronomical observations. Its earliest stages were built ca. 2500 B.C.

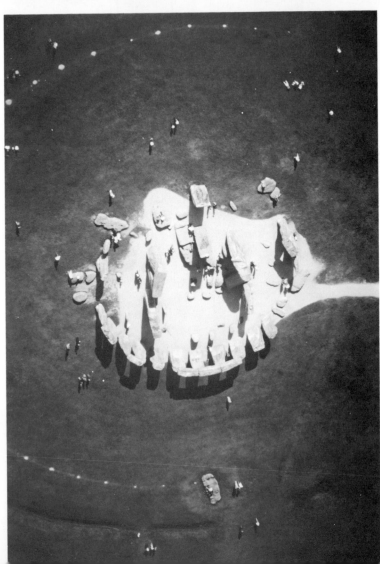

increased specialization, perhaps including high-level administrators insulated by layers of lesser officials.

Many structures that archaeologists have known for a long time defy interpretation and generate endless discussion. The giant *megaliths* of Western Europe are examples, and Stonehenge is a case in point (FIGURE 8-24). A famous curiosity as early as 1675, the first interpretations explained Stonehenge as a feat of Merlin's magic. Later it was associated with druids and other bizarre religious sects. At the beginning of the twentieth century, an energetic young Flinders Petrie began the tradition of analytical research at Stonehenge by measuring every nook and cranny. Later interpretations focused on Stonehenge as a Mycenaean outpost because of the general similarity of Stonehenge to megaliths documented in the Mediterranean area, a similarity between a dagger form carved on a stone upright at Stonehenge and daggers excavated from Mycenaean Greece, and because of a general assumption that ideas spread from the Near East to Europe rather than vice versa.

Other recent interpretations have concentrated on the function of Stonehenge rather than on identifying the builders. Astronomers and archaeologists have collaborated to produce a new and startling interpretation—that Stonehenge was an astronomical computer. Careful measurements of stone alignments were compared to astronomical charts of the sky and horizon of 2000 B.C., and it was found that a number of alignments coincided with significant solar and lunar events, especially solstices. These alignments, together with a series of enigmatic features that may have been markers, could have been used to predict lunar eclipses. At present, it is not known whether the full potential of Stonehenge was realized by its builders. Nevertheless, this first detailed quantitative analysis started a flurry of similar research that has now become known as *archaeo-astronomy* or *astro-archaeology*. Without doubt, architecture, a highly diverse and visible part of the archaeological record, will continue to stimulate new analyses and inferences.

Afterword So far, we have tracked the archaeologist's study through analysis. At the most basic level, analysis involves constructing types in order to describe and organize the variability in material remains that relates to specific research questions. As a part of the analysis process, artifacts are divided for study into broad categories such as chipped stone, faunal remains, and architecture. Analysis requires low-level inferences about the life cycle of artifacts, such as methods of manufacture and patterns of use. Although interesting and valuable, normally these inferences are not the final goal. In the next phase the archaeologist attempts to combine separate analyses into reconstructions of population size, subsistence base, degree of social inequality, and other fundamental aspects of past life. These higher-level inferences are necessary for testing models of changes in behavior and organization in human societies. Making such inferences is the subject of the next chapter.

Vere Gordon Childe (1892--1957)   After V. Gordon Childe turned sixty, he methodically set about tying up the loose ends of his career. He completed several major books, including *Piecing Together the Past,* which outlined the principles he used to interpret the European archaeological evidence. He also wrote several articles critically reviewing his lifetime of archaeological research. At age sixty-four he retired and left England for his native Australia, which he had not seen for thirty-five years. There, although complaining of ill health, he managed a considerable amount of mountaineering, and it was after one such excursion that his body was found at the bottom of a 1,000-foot cliff. Whether he fell or jumped is still debatable. Thus, in death as in life, Childe was the center of controversy, much of which stemmed from the fact that he was a Marxist.   □   Childe seems to have achieved most of the goals that archaeologists set for themselves. He published more than a dozen books, which pulled together the disjointed pieces of the prehistory of Scotland, England, Europe, and the Near East. In still other books he wrote about cultural evolution, archaeological inference, and the general findings of archaeology. In view of the copiousness of his writing, Childe is usually envisioned as the ultimate armchair archaeologist, spinning out ideas from a comfortable seat in his office. In reality, although he did not like fieldwork, he spent many seasons digging in Scotland and published as many site reports as his colleagues.   □   The breadth of Childe's interests and the complexity of his ideas created a potential for a great variety of interpretations of his writings. Most remarkable about Childe is that, more than a quarter century after his death, his ideas still make us think and debate. But the ideas of anyone who writes as much as Childe need to be carefully sorted. As Bruce Trigger wrote: "Childe clearly did not take all of his ideas equally seriously. He was devoted to some, tried others on for size, and may have regarded still others as jokes or bits of whimsy. Yet even today archaeologists cannot agree which of his ideas fall into which category."

V. Gordon Childe
at the site of Skara Brae
in the Orkney Islands,
Scotland.

9

INFERENCE

$\mathbf{C}$orrect inferences—conclusions arrived at by reasoning from observed evidence or facts—can involve difficult, intricate processes
even in the simplest situations. To illustrate this, let's suppose that,
after a tedious analysis of look-alike potsherds has put you to sleep, you
awake to find yourself transported into America's past. You are alone in a
strange house and, being an expert on twentieth-century American artifacts,
your first question is: How far back? Since there is no one around to answer
your question, the answer will have to be based on inference—in this case,
inferences drawn from thousands of items present in this as in any house.
Off in a corner, a radio in a 4-foot-high wooden cabinet attracts your attention. You know it was manufactured in the 1930s. Over the table hangs a
handmade Tiffany lamp, a product dating several decades before the radio.
Next to the table is a 21-inch black-and-white console television. On the
basis of the cabinet design and the shape of the picture tube, you recognize it
as a 1957 model.

From these three very different dates you can infer that you have gone
back in time no farther than October 1956, when the first 1957 televisions
went on sale. The Tiffany lamp is probably an antique, and the radio has
most likely had a long uselife.

You are still afloat in time—somewhere between the present and 1956
—so you keep seeking evidence. There is a 45-rpm record on a 1950s-style
portable phonograph. The record is "Sherry," which was recorded by the

Four Seasons and reached its peak popularity in September 1962. A letter drops through the mail slot in the front door. Although the date on the hand cancellation is unreadable, the stamp is a 4-cent one; anytime after January 1963, it would have been a 5-cent stamp or more. Now you know: you are probably somewhere between July and December 1962.

All the evidence fits, but, to test your inference, you explore your surroundings further. You know that pop-tops were not used on canned beverages until 1963, so that, if your inference is correct, there should be none in the refrigerator. Sure enough, all of the steel cans of soft drinks and beer must be opened by a pointed implement known as a "church-key." As you sit back and sip your Pabst, you are cheered by the thought that, if you really are in 1962, you can get all the gasoline you want for twenty-five cents a gallon.

Although analysis of specific artifacts (such as that by our time-traveling archaeologist) can tell us about limited types of behavior, like conditions of manufacture, use, and discard, general models of human behavior and social organization cannot be derived from, or tested by, one kind of data alone. The more complex inferences at these higher levels are achieved by pooling information from as many analyses as possible. Some examples follow.

INFERRING TIME

Chronology building is the process of combining numerous lines of evidence to create a dated history for a region. These lines of evidence, discussed below, consist of three principal kinds of dating techniques: (1) relative, such as stratigraphy, seriation, and cross-dating; (2) chronometric, including biological and chemical dating methods; and (3) absolute, which has two techniques—tree-ring dating and the use of historical documents. The following example of chronology building in Europe embraces several of these techniques and illustrates how they are used in making inferences.

Seriation and Cross-Dating

In Europe, as elsewhere, stratigraphic excavations provided the first clues for chronology building. By the end of the nineteenth century, Europe was a crazy-quilt of archaeological sequences, unconnected to calendar dates or even to each other. Further east, in the cradles of the first Mediterranean civilizations—the Sumerians and Babylonians of Iraq, the Egyptians, and the Greeks—archaeologists found another line of evidence. These literate civilizations kept histories and records and even inscribed dates on artifacts and buildings. The first problem—of translating the scripts and of relating ancient calendars to our own—was rapidly solved; the second was to link more common undated artifacts, such as pottery, to already dated events and objects. One of the first to succeed in doing so was Sir Flinders Petrie, who, in 1890, excavated nearly 2,000 burials in an early Egyptian cemetery. Since few burials were found on top of one another, there were no clear stratigraphic relationships. To overcome this problem Petrie invented the tech-

nique of *seriation* (which he called "sequence dating") and used it on pottery from the burials.

In seriation the archaeologist first constructs temporal types on the basis of stylistic attributes (FIGURE 9-1). (Stylistic attributes are used rather than utilitarian ones on the assumption that the former are more likely to change rapidly and systematically through time than the latter.) Next, the archaeologist records the frequency of these temporal types for each assemblage—be it a grave lot, surface collection, or the secondary refuse in an excavated room. The next step is to order assemblages relative to one another (FIGURE 9-2). The most basic principle in such ordering is that the more similar the assemblages, the closer they are in time of deposition. Thus, the greater the similarity between assemblages the closer to each other they are placed in the sequence. The frequency law (Chapter 4) describes the life cycle of artifact types and is the basis of another criterion of a good seriation. It postulates that every type first steadily grows in popularity and then declines similarly (rather than fluctuating wildly). Thus, a good seriation will show gradual changes through time in the frequency of artifacts in each type.

One of the most convenient ways to arrange assemblages and create a seriation is James A. Ford's graphical method (FIGURE 9-2). In this method the archaeologist begins by recording the percentage of temporal types for each assemblage as a separate strip of paper. Each temporal type is represented by a bar on the strip of paper; the greater the percentage, the longer the bar. Next, the strips of paper are compared and those with bars of similar length are placed adjacent to each other. Finally, minor adjustments are made to smooth out the curves formed by (actual or imaginary) lines connecting the adjacent bars until the best ordering is achieved.

The technique of seriation has undergone continuous elaboration—especially recently, with the use of computers to make rapidly the many comparisons necessary to assess similarity and construct orderings. Seriation cannot be used to give specific dates to assemblages because the rates of change in stylistic attributes are variable and usually unknown to the archaeologist. In addition, the technique cannot determine which end of the seriation is the recent one.

Seriation must be used with caution. There are many sources of variability in archaeological materials that are not related to time. For example, differences in assemblages can result from differences in the function of settlements, the deposits sampled, preservation, and local stylistic preferences. Thus seriations require large numbers of artifacts, from similar kinds of de-

FIGURE **9-1**

Stylistic changes in pottery (the latest at the top) that formed the basis of Petrie's seriation of predynastic burials at Nakada, Egypt (ca. 4000–3000 B.C.). Note the changes in vessel shape and size and in the handles. (After Petrie 1901.)

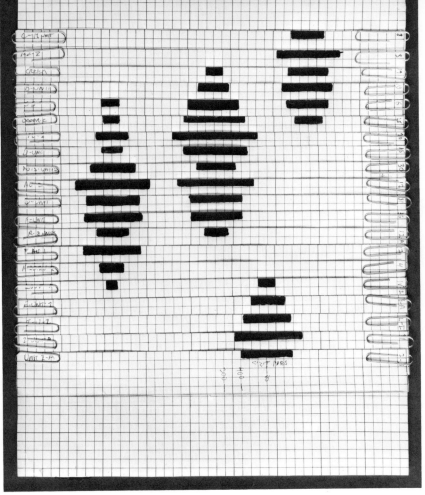

FIGURE **9-2**   A stage in one method of constructing a seriation—in this case, the one shown completed in FIGURE 4-19. Assemblages are represented by individual strips of paper, which are attached to a sheet of graph paper in a way (here, paper clips) that permits them to be rearranged easily. Bars inked on the strips show, by their length, the percentage of occurrence of a particular type of artifact (here, a style of gravestone).

posits in functionally equivalent settlements within a limited region. Where these conditions were met, excellent seriations have been produced.

Petrie wanted his seriation to order *grave lots* (the contents of individual graves) on the basis of similarities in the pottery offerings included in them. Relying on Worsaae's law (Chapter 5) he inferred that the contents of each grave lot had been in use at the same time. Next, he developed a method for mathematically assessing the similarity between grave lots and then placing them in sequence. Once the grave lots had been placed in an order, Petrie had to determine which end was up—that is, which was most recent in time. To solve this problem, he employed *cross-dating*, a method for using items of known manufacture date to help assign dates to associated artifacts. Greek pots, probably traded to Egypt, were found in a few grave lots. Fortunately for Petrie, archaeologists in Greece had found similar pot types associated with dated monuments and thus knew their periods of manufacture. The Greek vessels in Egypt, however, could have been heirlooms, could have taken a long and circuitous route to the graves, or could have been in use for decades before burial. As a result, Petrie could not give specific dates to graves. He could, however, determine that a grave lot was created *no earlier* than the manufacture date of the Greek pot it contained. By this process Petrie linked Egypt with the Aegean and determined which end of his seriation was probably most recent. Petrie and other archaeologists went on to test his seriation in stratigraphic excavations and to link it to dated monuments in Egypt. With minor modifications, this seriation, which spans some 2,000 years, is still the basic sequence for ancient Egypt.

Childe:
The Diffusionist
Model

European archaeologists were also eager to cross-date their many local archaeological sequences with the better-dated sequences of the classic civilizations of the eastern Mediterranean. But for most of prehistoric Europe, including the British Isles, there were few trade items that could be traced to the Near East. Without such direct material evidence, archaeologists had to rely on more vague stylistic similarities and on assumptions about how these similarities originated.

One artifact pattern widely shared in Europe is the architecture of megaliths—stone circles and rings, mounds, burial cairns, and "temples" made of massive blocks of cut stone (FIGURE 9-3). These megaliths could be related to each other in time in an infinite number of ways. They could, for example, all be roughly contemporaneous—either local developments or rapidly spread from a single area; on the other hand, each type (stone circle, mound, cairn) could have been invented in a different location and time. The megalith problem attracted the attention of V. Gordon Childe, who, mainly concerned with the problem of matching the European sequences, saw in the megaliths a possible solution.

Childe assumed that very complex artifact types would be invented only once, and therefore, complex architectural forms like megaliths probably had one place of origin. (It was well accepted already that complicated technologies, such as copper smelting, were beyond the capabilities of "primitive" Europeans and must have spread or *diffused* from the more sophisticated civilizations of the eastern Mediterranean.) Childe reasoned further that the origin of megaliths could not be with the "barbarians" that Caesar found in western Europe, but must also have occurred among the earliest civilized societies far to the east. From the eastern Mediterranean, the practice of megalithic architecture would have diffused outward, according to Childe, until hundreds or even a thousand years later it would have arrived in the farthest reaches of barbarian Europe.

In 1924 Childe published his scheme for matching the sequences of Europe and the Near East; the sole unifying assumption was diffusion, the

FIGURE **9-3** Some major megalithic monuments in Western Europe. Although their function is still in doubt, many alignments have been correlated with use in astronomical observation. Note in the inset map (lower right) the white arc, which is the dating "fault line," or break in the assumed diffusion of complex artifacts from the Near East. This is, in part, a result of the finding of copper metallurgy at Vinča, Bulgaria ca. 4500 B.C., well before metallurgy was introduced in Greece.

slow replacement of "European barbarism" by "Oriental civilization." This model became the unchallenged foundation of European chronology. Megaliths were assigned later dates the farther they were from the Aegean Sea. Childe's diffusionist assumption, designed to simplify dating, became the basis for interpreting European prehistory as only the pale reflection of the classic civilizations of the eastern Mediterranean. And so it stood until the mid 1950s and the first major test with the newly developed method of *radiocarbon dating*.

Libby: Radiocarbon Dating

In 1949 a startling development by Willard Libby, a University of Chicago chemist, revolutionized chronology building for archaeologists. By Libby's technique of radiocarbon dating, scientists could determine how long ago any once-living organic (carbon-containing) material had died.

Radiocarbon dating can be applied to anything that once lived: charred and uncharred plant remains, hair, flesh, the protein fraction of bone, and even shell. (The latter two materials present special dating problems, however, that sometimes result in erratic dates.) The technique is based on the fact that carbon is the building block of life, found in all living things. In the atmosphere, both normal carbon-12 (C^{12}) and its unstable, radioactive isotope carbon-14 (C^{14}) occur in carbon dioxide. Carbon dioxide is converted by plants into protoplasm, which later is ingested by animals and incorporated into their tissues. Thus, the proportion of C^{14} to C^{12} in the atmosphere is duplicated in living plants and animals.

When organisms die, they no longer take in C^{14}, and what remains in their tissues decays at a fixed rate known as the *half-life*. The half-life of C^{14} is $5,730 \pm 30$ years, the ± 30 years indicating statistical precision (see below). Thus, after the passage of that many years, half of the C^{14} atoms in a dead organism will have decayed, emitting a beta particle and, thereby, changing into nitrogen-14 (N^{14}). Half of the remaining radiocarbon will decay in the next $5,730 \pm 30$-year time segment, and so on. Obviously, the older a sample, the less radiocarbon it will contain and the fewer beta particles it will emit. Libby's major contribution was in building a device to count the decays, or beta rays, produced by disintegrating radiocarbon atoms. The number of decays per gram of sample is usually recorded over a period of about a day to determine how much C^{14} remains relative to C^{12}. From this ratio, the age of the sample in *radiocarbon years* is readily calculated.

Radiocarbon dates come from the laboratory expressed in radiocarbon years B.P. (Before Present), but the present used is always 1950! Use of this arbitrary year permits comparison of C^{14} dates without knowing the year in which the dates were calculated. In addition, the date is actually expressed as a range—for example, 950 ± 105 B.P. Because C^{14} atoms decay in random fashion, the date is really a statistical estimate; in fact, there is one chance in three that the true sample age falls outside of the stated interval of 845 B.P. to 1055 B.P. in our example. To improve these statistics would require much longer counting periods, at vastly greater cost. Today (1981) the average cost of obtaining one date is $250.

Because the amounts of radiocarbon get very small very fast, the technique presently is not useful for organic materials more than 50,000 years old. However, recent developments in the direct counting of C^{14} atoms promise to extend its range considerably and to improve its precision. Among other limitations, radiocarbon dating was based on the crucial assumption that the amount of C^{14} in the atmosphere has been constant over the past 50,000 years (p. 258).

When C^{14} tests were applied to the European chronology it passed with flying colors. Only the chronologies for Egypt and the Balkans flunked. In the Balkans, the dating of strata containing copper artifacts and stone carvings seemed clearly too early, being more than 1,000 years earlier than similar items from the Aegean. The radiocarbon dates for Egypt were several centuries more recent than hieroglyphic dates on associated artifacts. Thus, an artifact dated historically at 2000 B.C. might date at 1500 B.C. by radiocarbon. At first these cases and other minor anomalies were explained away by both chemists and archaeologists, who quietly blamed each other. But as more dates accumulated, explanations became more contorted, and soon it was clear that something fundamental was wrong.

Douglass: Dendrochronology

On the other side of the world in the arid United States Southwest, a new application of *dendrochronology,* or tree-ring dating, was about to come to the rescue. Tree-ring dating is one of archaeology's oldest methods for obtaining calendrical dates. The father of dendrochronology was A. E. Douglass, an astronomer at the University of Arizona interested in the effects of sunspots on weather. What he needed for his study was a sensitive indicator that documented weather patterns from before the development of rain gauges, thermometers, and modern record-keeping; what he used was tree-rings. Each year a tree adds a ring of new growth. When there is ample moisture, the ring is thick and light in color; when there is not, the ring is thinner and darker. Thus, the sequence of thick and narrow rings seen in cross-section in the trunk or limbs of trees furnishes a record of rainfall changes in a region. The most weather-sensitive trees in the Southwest are various species of pine, Douglas fir, and oak. (Some species are *complacent,* meaning not very sensitive to environmental variation; still others, such as juniper, are erratic in the production of rings.)

Each region's sequence of good and bad years, recorded as thick and thin tree rings, is unique. Douglass began with presently growing trees and worked backward by matching the earlier rings of a specimen with the later rings of the next earlier specimen, and so on (FIGURE 9-4). By 1929 Douglass and his archaeological collaborators had constructed a master chronology that went back over 1,500 years and permitted ready dating of many archaeological wood samples. With this chronology, a roof beam that includes the last ring added by the tree can furnish the date when the tree was

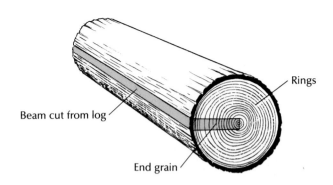

Rings

Beam cut from log

End grain

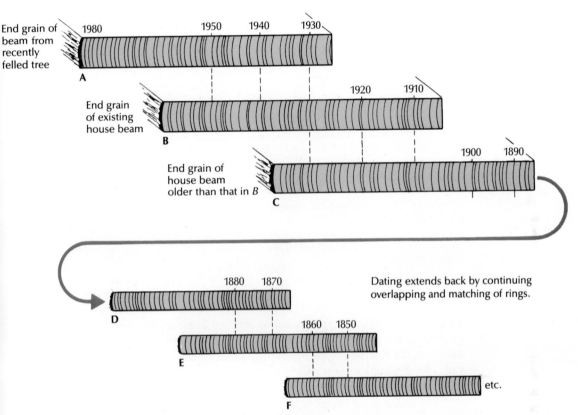

End grain of beam from recently felled tree

1980 1950 1940 1930

A

End grain of existing house beam

1920 1910

B

End grain of house beam older than that in *B*

1900 1890

C

Dating extends back by continuing overlapping and matching of rings.

1880 1870

D

1860 1850

E

etc.

F

FIGURE **9-4**   Building a master chronology with tree-ring dating. Once the sequence of rings has been determined, new specimens can be readily dated by matching their ring sequence with that of the master chronology.

felled. And one can infer, from the pattern of dates obtained from a roof, when the roof was built (Chapter 8, p. 239).

Once a ring is formed, for all practical purposes it is dead and, therefore, no longer incorporates radiocarbon from the atmosphere. With this as

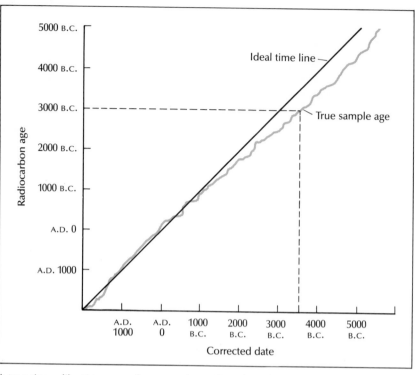

FIGURE 9-5 A tree-ring calibration curve for correcting radiocarbon dates. The straight diagonal represents the ideal time-line. To use the chart, one determines where a horizontal line from the specimen's radiocarbon age (left-hand scale) intersects the wavy diagonal (true sample age). A vertical line from that intersection meets the bottom scale at the correct date.

a basis, tree-ring dating was used to test the accuracy of the radiocarbon method. In the actual test, dendrochronologists constructed a 5,000-year sequence using the long-lived bristlecone pines of eastern California and Nevada. Ring samples from this sequence whose ages were precisely known were then dated by three radiocarbon laboratories.

The radiocarbon dates returned from the laboratories were largely consistent but disclosed the major flaw in radiocarbon dating—that the C^{14} content of the atmosphere has fluctuated through time. Radiocarbon results match tree-ring dates moderately well until about 1000 B.C., when they begin to diverge consistently, making C^{14} dates increasingly too close to the present. Thus, a bristlecone sample from a tree that died in 3000 B.C. would have a date of 2200 B.C. in radiocarbon years. Tree-ring checks of radiocarbon dating not only disclosed the flaw, but provided the solution—a curve (FIGURE 9-5), or correction chart, constructed from a long series of tree-ring samples subjected to C^{14} analysis.

Obsidian Hydration Dating

Obsidian is a volcanic glass that was frequently used for the manufacture of cutting and scraping tools. The technique of obsidian hydration dating is based on the ability of obsidian to adsorb (physically incorporate) water from its depositional environment, creating a distinctive hydration layer or *rim*. The rim, created by microfracturing due to stress, is visible microscopically in thin sections cut from obsidian artifacts. The hydration process begins in the surfaces newly formed at the time of an artifacts' manufacture. The thickness of the rim depends on three major factors: the time since the surface was created, the chemical composition of the obsidian, and the temperature of the depositional environment. Thus, if composition and temperature are held constant, the thickness of the rim can furnish a relative dating technique. With suitable independent dating evidence and controls on the rate of hydration, the technique can yield chronometric dates. First developed in 1960, it has been extensively applied in Mexico and California and new applications are continually being found.

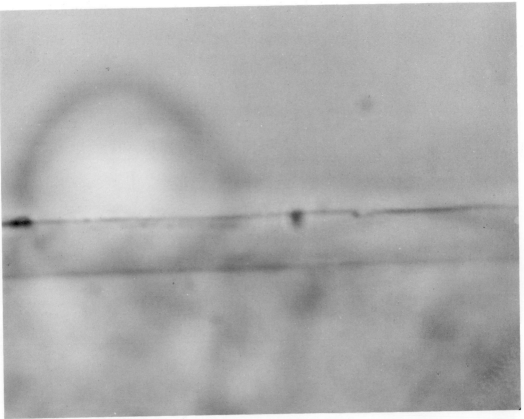

Photograph of a section of an obsidian specimen showing the hydration rim.

Archaeomagnetic Dating

The principles of archaeomagnetic dating are simple. Scientists have determined that the earth's magnetic field has changed over the years; in particular, the location of the magnetic north pole has wandered. Many artifacts and soils contain magnetic materials such as iron-containing minerals. If these are heated sufficiently, the magnetic particles in them will align themselves with the prevailing magnetic field of the earth and retain that positioning when the material cools. Determining the positioning and comparing it to the record of local magnetic orientation gives a chronometric date for the last heating of a specimen. To be datable, however, a specimen must have been found in exactly the position in which it was heated. Stationary objects that have been heated—such as hearths and burned walls—best meet this condition.

The taking of archaeomagnetic samples is laborious. Eight or ten blocks of material from the feature being studied are encased in plaster cubes that have been precisely oriented with a compass. (The figure shows the two steps: *A*, plaster is about to be poured in a square mold that has been placed around a hearth specimen left in its original position; *B*, using a Brunton compass to record the magnetic orientation of the specimen now encased in a white plaster block prior to its removal from the site.) In the laboratory, the magnetic alignment of the samples is measured with a special magnetometer and then correlated with the history of local alignments, which is derived from samples whose ages are known through radiocarbon dating, tree-ring, or other evidence.

A

B

In the rapid shuffle that ensued to recalibrate dates and adjust regional chronologies, there were more than a few surprises. British archaeologist Colin Renfrew recognized in the changes a pattern that would slay the diffusionist dragon that Childe had turned loose on Europe. First and foremost, the new corrected dates were in perfect agreement with the Egyptian historic dates. The archaeologists, Renfrew gloated, had been right! Second, the new dates pushed back the development of copper metallurgy in the Balkans to 4500 B.C., clearly predating supposed forerunners in the Aegean by nearly 2,000 years. Third, the impressive megalithic architecture in western Europe, including Stonehenge (FIGURE 8-23) and Avebury, was now dated to before 2000 B.C. This placed their construction several hundred years before the birth of the first Mycenaean craftsman whom Childe supposed had ventured westward to enlighten the European barbarians (FIGURE 9-3).

European archaeologists, for the first time in decades, are now struggling to explain the evolution of complex societies—such as those that built the stone monuments of Europe—in local terms. Repudiating the vague concept of diffusion, they are focusing on the effects of population growth, soil exhaustion, warfare, and the demand for trade goods.

Other Dating Techniques

Dating techniques other than radiocarbon and dendrochronology have produced equally dramatic results and far-reaching implications for the study of human behavior. *Potassium-argon (K-A) dating* is responsible for establishing the antiquity of early humans in East Africa more than 4 million years ago. K-A dating, useful in areas (such as eastern Africa) where human remains are either sealed under or overlie volcanic deposits, identifies the time when volcanic rocks formed. Most rocks contain the element potassium (K^{39}), and a small amount of its radioactive isotope K^{40}. By the process of radioactive decay, K^{40} slowly changes into argon (A), a gas that is trapped within the rock matrix. When the rock is melted, as in a volcanic eruption, the argon is driven off. After the new rock cools, the conversion of K^{40} into A begins again. Thus, since the rate of conversion is known, determining the amount of K and A in a rock can tell us how long ago the rock formed. The time range over which K-A dating can be used is rather longer than for radiocarbon dating, as the half-life of K^{40} is 1.3 billion years. K-A dating reliably covers the range from about 1 million years ago to the beginnings of the universe (20 billion years?). (For other important dating techniques, see boxed items "Obsidian Hydration Dating" and "Archaeomagnetic Dating" on p. 259 and 260, respectively.)

Interpretation of Dates

Archaeologists, then, use three kinds of dating techniques. The oldest set of techniques, including stratigraphy, seriation, and cross-dating, allows us to determine the sequence of events or processes. Stratigraphy tells us the order in which strata were deposited; and seriation indicates the order in which temporal artifact types were manufactured. These *relative dating* techniques do not produce calendrical dates. They help the archaeologist determine whether one event or process preceded or followed another. Today the most common dating techniques are *chronometric*—those, such as radiocarbon, K-A, and archaeomagnetism, that place the death of an organism or another physical event within a specific range of dates on a calendrical time scale. Except for historic records, tree-ring dating, which produces unambiguous calendar years, is the archaeologist's only *absolute dating* technique.

The process of inference does not stop when a date is assigned to an artifact in a laboratory or a stratum in the field. A fragment of charcoal from a hearth dated by tree rings to A.D. 1275 tells us that the hearth was in use some time in or after A.D. 1275. We cannot, however, be sure when the charcoal we have dated was burned, since the wood thrown onto the fire could have been, for example, old driftwood or a reused roof beam. How much earlier or later the hearth was in use cannot be determined from the charcoal date. Frequently, dates provide little more than the information contained in this charcoal fragment (though sometimes that is enough for the dating problem at hand). Furthermore, a laboratory date usually refers not to some behavioral event of interest to the archaeologist, but to an isolated biological or geological event. (Radiocarbon, for example, dates only how long ago an organism died.) The interpretation of a date requires that the archaeologist establish a link between a date and an event or process of interest—say, a radiocarbon date on a wooden lintel linked to the building of a temple. Because of the pitfalls inherent in linking dated materials to specific behavioral events (and because of the different limitations of each dating method) archaeologists use all applicable techniques in making such interpretations. Thus, to determine the period during which a pueblo was occupied, archaeologists have used concurrently tree-ring and C^{14} methods, archaeomagnetism, stratigraphy, seriation, and cross-dating. Once again, as it was in the case of Europe's chronology, inference is a process that integrates a number of diverse lines of evidence.

Archaeological-Culture Classifications

Before the era of modern dating techniques, archaeologists like Childe were inventive in using artifact variability to build chronologies. Their basic tool was the diffusionist assumption that change comes about largely through people and ideas that move out from a small number of "creative centers" (p. 253). This view gave birth to the age-area hypothesis, according to which objects spread gradually outward from points of origin (Chapter 4). The concept held that artifacts, once created, had a kind of irresistible life of their own, moving (with other items) in groups. These distinctive artifact groups were thought to represent the products of people who shared similar ideas and values, the *cultural norms* of a society. This *normative approach* focused on the sets of artifacts by which sites or regions could be distinguished from one another. Fixed combinations of artifacts that typified specific regions at particular times were thought of as *archaeological cultures*. These archaeological cultures were given colorful names such as the "Red-on-buff culture" of the Southwest and the "Bell-beaker folk" of Europe, both named for their distinctive pottery. Thus, archaeologists using the normative approach rarely studied the details of artifact and assemblage variability within regions; instead, they concentrated on comparing the broad similarities in assemblages between regions.

The dropping of a few items and the introduction of new ones in a region often provided archaeologists with enough evidence to conclude that one cultural group had replaced another. For example, migration and diffusion were used to explain a change in ceramic technology and ceremonial architecture around A.D. 1000 in the southeastern United States. Specifically, temple mounds replaced burial mounds and *shell temper* replaced other types of temper in pottery. This change from "Woodland" to "Mississippian" cultures was thought to have been spread throughout the Southeast by people and ideas emanating from a core area in the Mississippi Valley near St. Louis (FIGURE 9-6). This example illustrates how cultural development was seen largely as a history of the interaction of archaeological cultures—migration of people, diffusion of ideas, and (only rarely) invention. This normative approach was the basis of the *culture historical school* of American archaeology (also called historical particularism p. 302), which was dominant during the first fifty years of this century.

The diagnostic artifacts that were used by such culture historians were called *traits*. Traits were vigorously formalized into culture typologies, such as the *midwestern taxonomic system,* which archaeologist W. C. McKern codified. Starting with the artifacts deposited at a site during one time period, a hierarchy is built that is composed of increasingly generalized descriptions of traits. The end results are regional cultures, defined by a few very general traits, and local variants, which can be contrasted through time. *Trait lists* (sometimes called "laundry lists") are the tools used to place actual archaeological assemblages into archaeological culture categories.

With the development of C^{14}, tree-ring, and other sophisticated dating techniques for chronology building, the heyday of archaeological culture classifications passed. As it became possible to date artifacts independently of their formal similarities, it was soon evident that similar artifacts did not always date to the same period. In addition, patterns of artifact distributions between archaeological cultures were not as neat as once assumed. Megalithic architecture, once thought to have spread steadily outward from a single source, was found on a continent-wide scale to be a rather more erratic development. In the southeastern United States, variability began to be recognized in the material remains of sites that had been lumped together as Mississippian culture. Archaeologists are now busy trying to explain these differences in terms of adaptations to local environments.

Thus, better chronologies have called into question the utility of the normative concept of culture. Today, archaeologists seek to go beyond diffusionist models to explain how and why changes occurred. Nevertheless, the concept of archaeological cultures still furnishes useful descriptions of

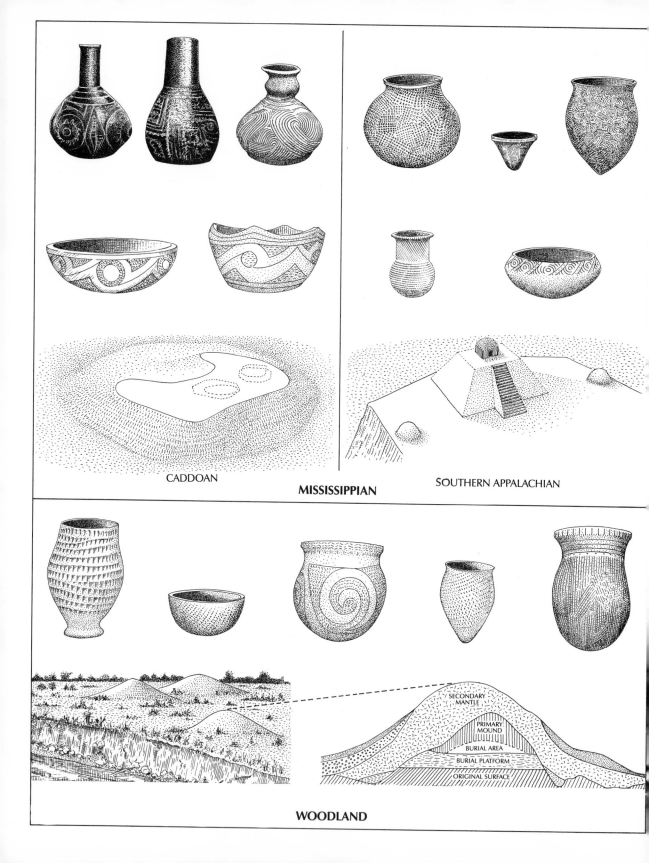

CADDOAN

MISSISSIPPIAN

SOUTHERN APPALACHIAN

SECONDARY
MANTLE

PRIMARY
MOUND

BURIAL AREA

BURIAL PLATFORM

ORIGINAL SURFACE

WOODLAND

FIGURE **9-6** (On facing page.) Differences in pottery and mound styles characteristic of three cultures from the prehistory of eastern North America: the Woodland culture (ca. 1000 B.C. to A.D. 1000) and two varieties of Mississippian culture (ca. A.D. 1000–1700)—Caddoan and Southern Appalachian. Archaeological cultures are defined by complexes of traits, often those of ceramics and architecture. Portions of the drawings after Ford and Quimby, 1945; Wedel, 1943; and Ford and Willey, 1940.

large-scale similarities in regional patterns of artifacts. While these rather large and vague units are a start, contemporary archaeologists begin to build most of their inferences at more concrete levels.

INFERRING BEHAVIORAL COMPONENTS

From activities and activity areas we can reconstruct behavioral components. For example, when we find structures on a site that occur in abundance and contain evidence for the entire range of domestic activities, we can be confident that we have recognized households. On the other hand, a number of structures with relatively uncommon features and manufacturing waste is evidence for task-group workshops. What archaeologists usually draw from such studies is a picture of settlements comprised of activities and activity areas.

Activity Areas

Using information from activity areas to build complex inferences concerning behavioral components requires the skillful piecing together of different lines of evidence. If all artifacts were deposited as primary refuse and if we knew their functions, it would be a simple matter to make inferences about activities. This ideal situation is not usually the case. Primary refuse is rare in the real world. Tools are not often discarded after a single use. In large settlements, the debris from activities is systematically collected and redeposited as secondary refuse. Even in smaller settlements, such as a hunter-gatherer base camp, there is a mix of disposal practices, and primary refuse may still be fairly scarce. Another element that may add to the confusion is variability in the abandonment processes. If, for example, one of two identical settlements is abandoned rapidly (in the face of an impending disaster) while the other is abandoned over a five-year period, they will have very different de facto refuse. Add environmental processes and scavenging behavior to these sources of variability and it is easy to see why inferences about activity areas demand great care in assembling the data.

One of archaeology's increasingly popular efforts is identification of activity areas according to the sex of those working in them. William Longacre and James Ayres recorded the material remains of an Apache wickiup abandoned two years earlier. They found that, with the exception of a single axe-head found outside the wickiup, few items in primary and de facto refuse seemed related to male activities (FIGURE 9-7). Informants who had visited the site while it was occupied in 1962 and 1963 confirmed that the adult male of the family occupying the wickiup had been away cutting juni-

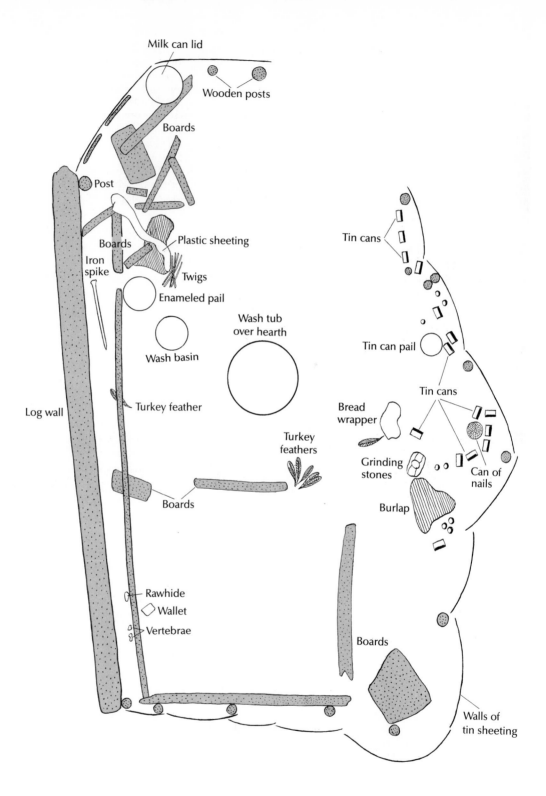

Milk can lid

Wooden posts

Boards

Post

Boards

Plastic sheeting

Iron spike

Twigs

Enameled pail

Wash tub over hearth

Tin cans

Log wall

Wash basin

Turkey feather

Turkey feathers

Tin can pail

Bread wrapper

Tin cans

Grinding stones

Can of nails

Burlap

Boards

Rawhide

Wallet

Vertebrae

Boards

Walls of tin sheeting

FIGURE **9-7** The modern Apache wickiup studied by Longacre and Ayres in their ethnoarchaeology project; above, the exterior, built against the remains of a collapsed log ranch house, and on facing page, a diagram of the floor with associated artifacts.

per posts for weeks at a time, while the adult female maintained the camp with their two children.

Marcus Winter and Kent Flannery believe that they have similarly identified the tools and work areas of men and women in houses excavated at Oaxaca, Mexico, that dated from 800 B.C. In modern households in highland Mexico, men's tools cluster around the house altar, women's around the hearth. Winter and Flannery found that if they divided excavated houses along the mid-line, what they assumed to be men's tools tended to occur on one side and presumed women's tools on the other. Although these patterns in actual households are suggestive, there was an overlap of women's tools

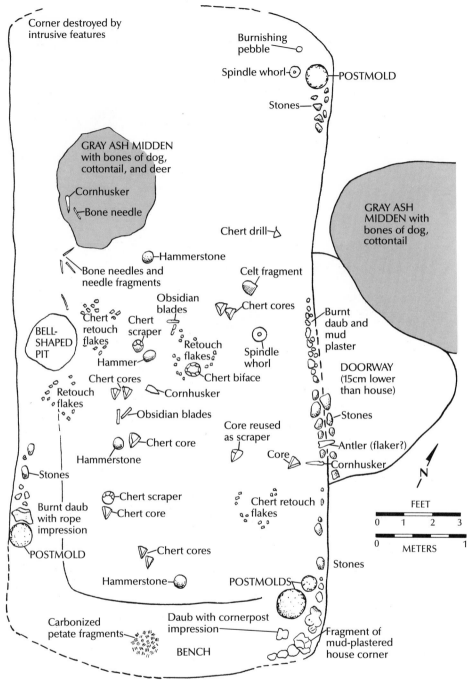

FIGURE **9-8** Debris—rare in abandoned Mesoamerica houses—in an Oaxaca house from about 900 B.C. The excavators concluded that the north half was used primarily by women for cooking and sewing, and the southern half by men for toolmaking. Such a spatial division of male and female household chores is common today.

in men's areas and vice versa. (Note the cornhusker and chert pebbles in FIGURE 9-8.)

The examples mentioned so far depend on the analysis of primary and de facto refuse. When these ideal deposits are not available, archaeologists turn to careful examination of secondary refuse. O'Connell (Chapter 2) has shown that, although the activity areas in the vicinity of the hut and hearth in Australian aborigine households are kept free of large artifacts, the resultant secondary refuse is not carried far. Thus, it is possible to associate specific refuse areas with nearby activity areas. But this situation is rarely encountered, especially in more complex settlements, in which secondary refuse is transported to dumps. Perhaps one of the most discouraging discoveries for the archaeologist of complex societies is the empty room. Was it a sleeping area? a storage area? a prison? an administrative office? Such rooms are common in the ancient cities we unearth.

A similar circumstance is common to large Maya settlements, where rooms often have several layers of plastered floors, each layer of which seems to have been swept clean before the next one was added. How might one approach this kind of unpromising deposit? Even with the specialized array of cleaning tools available to the modern housekeeper—vacuums, mops, brooms—some debris is left behind. Crime laboratories have developed highly sophisticated methods of retrieving and analyzing minute scraps of evidence, and archaeologists can call on even more refined techniques for recovering what Maya brooms left behind. For example, we can recover minute flakes of stone, bone, and organic residues by carefully peeling off the surface of each floor and subjecting it to flotation processes, fine screening, and chemical analyses.

By itself, this kind of micro-archaeological evidence does not produce final answers. To supplement these tantalizing hints, we can attempt to coax other patterns out of secondary refuse. Maya archaeologists have conceded that it is extremely difficult to relate specific middens to specific earth platforms on which houses were built, called *housemounds*. Nevertheless, while they have lost this battle, they won't concede the war. Housemounds are usually found in groups around one or more plazas, each group ringed by a scatter of dumps. Secondary refuse also makes up a large portion of the dirt fill in house platforms. Studies by T. Patrick Culbert at Tikal have shown similarities in the artifacts found in dump and fill refuse from individual house clusters, indicating a common source. Culbert has even reconstructed individual pots from sherds taken from different locations—a dump and housemound fill.

Comparisons show that house cluster refuse is totally different from refuse from Tikal's main ceremonial plaza. For example, 80 to 90 percent of the potsherds from the plaza are decorated, but only 30 to 40 percent from housemounds. If we assume that decorated pottery was for display, this difference in distribution would confirm the obvious—that plazas were special activity areas where such display items were used and discarded in high frequencies. Thus, in some large settlements we can relate secondary refuse to activity areas and make inferences about what went on in them. These novel types of information produced by Culbert can then be matched with traditional analyses of the function of architecture and the frequencies and distributions of architectural units and associated burials (p. 231). For example, Temple 1, on the east side of Tikal's main plaza, was dedicated on May 4 A.D. 682. The inaugural feast for Tikal's Ruler A, probably Temple 1's illustrious burial occupant, was surely an occasion for the use of large quantities of decorated pottery, some of which would have been broken and swept off the edge of the plaza the next morning.

Characteristics of Behavioral Components

Information about activities, activity areas, and settlements is used to reconstruct the characteristics of behavioral components. We will concentrate on communities and regional systems, which are usually the most easily identified behavioral components and make convenient units of study for testing models of change.

Settlement Systems

Archaeologists begin by attempting to infer which settlements make up a community and which communities make up regional systems. These inferences are made on the basis of a number of lines of evidence. The first is survey data identifying the range of sites in a region. Temporal types from those collections can be seriated and cross-dated (p. 252) to determine which sites were occupied at the same time. If the archaeologist is lucky, chronometric or absolute dates are obtained from items found in excavations. Further, surface collections can be classified according to techno-functional type in order to determine differences in activities among contemporaneous sites. These differences can be used to infer settlement types, such as hunting camp, farming village, city, lithic quarry. Another line of evidence brought in to add depth to the picture is the location of particular types of settlements in relation to farmable lands, navigable rivers, prime areas for deer hunting, outcrops of chippable stone or other such resources, and even neighboring settlements. In the Southwest, large pueblos with diverse artifact inventories tend to be located by relatively permanent sources of water; while, on the other hand, very small contemporaneous pueblos with almost no artifacts are often found near pockets of arable land at some distance from major water sources. Archaeologists have inferred that these two settlement types represent permanent villages and seasonal field houses, respectively. On the basis of the inferred activity differences, the archaeologist formulates models of how functionally different settlements formed a settlement system—whether, for example, sites were occupied year-round and, if not, the seasons during which they were inhabited.

Inferences of *seasonality* from excavated plant and animal remains rest on the assumption that people lived in a settlement at least during the seasons when those particular resources were available. Thus, the bones of mi-

FIGURE **9-9**   Papago Indians of Southern Arizona harvesting the fruit of the sahuaro cactus with long poles fashioned from parts of the plant.

gratory birds are often evidence of season of occupation. So are antlers and the bones of young animals whose stages of growth are seasonal. Since the fruit of many plants ripens for only a short time, plant remains, including pollen, can indicate time of occupation; so can techno-functional analysis of artifacts. For example, drawing upon ethnographic observations, archaeologists have identified strange long sticks from Arizona sites as sahuaro-fruit pickers (FIGURE 9-9). Because the giant sahuaro cactus ripens in early summer, it is assumed that these sites were probably occupied during early summer.

A settlement's function can provide inferential clues to patterns of occupation. For example, a quarry site containing no habitation debris indicates short visits. Storage facilities, depending on their size, can suggest year-round occupation. Architecture too provides clues to seasonality; it is often assumed that more substantial structures indicate year-round occupation. Recall (Chapter 5) that methods of refuse disposal vary with the permanence of a settlement—in large villages and cities, specialized areas are set aside for the disposal of secondary refuse.

Inferring Behavioral Components □ **271**

None of these individual indices of occupation is conclusive by itself. There are general reasons why this is true. First, for any particular bit of evidence, there are always alternative explanations. For instance, because of storage and transport, items can be consumed and discarded in places and at times when they were not available in the local environment. Second, any single line of evidence is limited to only a small portion of a community's activities and cannot prove conclusively that other activities did *not* occur. In many environments, during the winter very little procurement goes on and people eat stored foods. Thus, in such environments, plant and animal remains will only indicate occupation from spring through fall; occupation during the rest of the year will leave durable evidence of a different type—storerooms, large jars, substantial houses, mounds of secondary refuse.

The model of a settlement system for each time period (determined in the first step, described above) includes (1) the types of settlements used by a community, (2) where they are located, (3) the seasons in which they were occupied, and (4) the activities associated with each. This procedure is elegantly illustrated by Howard Winters' study of the Riverton culture (Wabash River Valley, Illinois). On the basis of key temporal types, especially variously shaped projectile points, Winters first identified sites occupied during the Late Archaic period (ca. 3000 to 1000 B.C.), then developed techno-functional typologies of stone tools and other artifacts. On the basis of the relative frequencies of occurrence of tools in three categories (general utility, weapons, and fabricating-processing-domestic) at different sites, Winters pictured a hunter-gatherer lifeway composed of four different settlements, including seasonally occupied base camps and extraction loci.

Population The most fundamental property of communities and regions is people. Over the decades, the goal of identifying the population size of communities has produced a kaleidoscope of techniques, from counting rooms to counting potsherds or bodies. Raoul Naroll's formula, which relates the amount of sheltered area to the number of sheltered people, is most often applied to obtain rough population estimates. Naroll's formula asserts that, on the average, each person requires 10 square meters of roofed floor space. This formula was derived from an analysis of eighteen living societies worldwide. Ethnographic data compiled by Sherburne Cook and Robert Heizer suggested that for California Indian societies a figure of 1.86 square meters per person is more accurate.

Such formulas are based on the incorrect assumption that population is the only variable that affects roofed floor space. Other variables influencing the floor area in a community include climate, wealth and social inequality, building materials, residential mobility, and the uses of structures. Thus, while in a worldwide sample the number of inhabitants may be the most important variable, there is still great potential error when such formulas are applied to specific archaeological sites. As in the case of Cook and Heizer, when local factors are considered, more accurate formulas can be built.

A more fine-grained level of analysis is possible when the individual dwellings of households can be identified in a settlement. For example, James Hill attempted to count the households in a Southwestern pueblo using a method based on an archaeological principle formulated by K. C. Chang. Chang, who derived his principle from a study of a diverse sample of small agricultural communities, concluded that the best indicator of a household dwelling is a hearth or fireplace. Hill counted the number of large rooms with hearths at Broken K Pueblo. The question then became: How many of the household dwellings would have been occupied at any one time? Ethnographic data suggested that, on the average, 22 percent of the dwellings in a modern Southwestern pueblo are vacant. From the same data source, Hill calculated an average of six people per household. Putting this information together, Hill arrived at a peak population estimate for Broken K of 120 persons, a figure that most archaeologists consider reasonable.

Population estimates can require even more convoluted processes in complex societies. Teotihuacán, for example, reached an area of 8 square miles, or 22 square kilometers. René Millon, who headed the team that mapped Teotihuacán, estimated the city's population in its heyday. He faced a much more difficult task than Hill. Architectural units were highly varied, ranging from workshops and temples to large storage areas, apartment units, and structures of unknown use. To complicate the situation further, few hearths were found in the living quarters. Cooking and heating were apparently done with brazier-like portable ceramic hearths. Millon attempted to identify another indicator of households—"sleeping rooms" within excavated apartment compounds. Sleeping areas were defined as rooms with no distinguishing features, completely enclosed, with the exception of one or more doorways. On the basis of size, sleeping rooms were estimated to have accommodated 1–3 people. By studying maps of Teotihuacán's excavated apartment compounds, Millon calculated the average number of sleeping rooms per apartment. Finally, using his map of the compounds that were known to have been occupied during the city's peak, Millon estimated total sleeping-room capacity to be 125,000 persons (FIGURE 9-10). This is considered a conservative estimate.

Since every site or group of sites presents unique problems for making population estimates, a number of specialized techniques have been devised. Some, exemplified by Jeffrey Parson's survey of the Texcoco Valley in the Basin of Mexico, attempt to estimate population by measuring the area over which potsherds are distributed. Others derive population from food debris, such as shells or—in historic mining towns—even tin cans. All of these methods assume that there are constant rates of production per person for specific items such as potsherds or clamshells. These methods are difficult to apply because of all the added information that is required, such as specific rates of discard and the exact length of time a settlement was occupied. Although experimental and ethnoarchaeological researchers are beginning to supply discard rates, inferring precise occupation spans is still difficult.

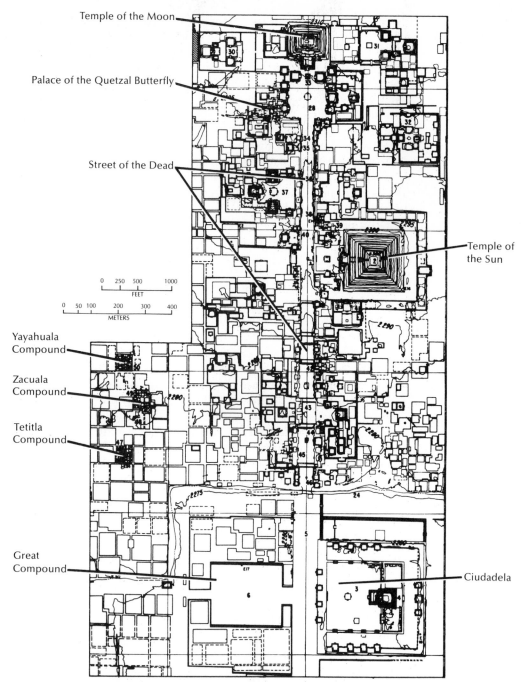

Temple of the Moon

Palace of the Quetzal Butterfly

Street of the Dead

Temple of the Sun

Yayahuala Compound

Zacuala Compound

Tetitla Compound

Great Compound

Ciudadela

FIGURE **9-10** René Millon's map of Teotihuacán, Mexico, shows a city impressive by any standards. At A.D. 600 population may have reached 200,000, and area, 20 square kilometers. The city seems to have been a focus of attraction for rural populations, which reached a low point at this time. (Detail of map from *Urbanization of Teotihuacán, Mexico*, V. 1:1, Austin, © René Millon, 1973.)

For any given site there may be a number of ways to estimate population and perhaps even changes in population during site occupation. Some techniques are likely to produce more reliable results than others; but rarely will an archaeologist obtain definitive numbers for population. Careful weighing of evidence and comparison of results from different techniques, however, may yield a reasonable approximation.

If population estimates for specific sites seem difficult, consider the problem of inferring how many people lived in a region. The foremost problem is that survey data must be the basis of such population estimates, since few sites in a region are ever excavated. Archaeologists have developed creative methods for using survey data. Working in eastern Arizona, Fred Plog was testing an economic model of social change that required the measurement of population sizes through time. He decided to use as his basic measure changes in the number of occupied pithouses and pueblo rooms, but vegetation and windblown sand made it difficult to discern individual pithouses and pueblo rooms from the surface.

To overcome these visibility handicaps, Plog turned to reports of excavated sites that had surface indications (sherd scatters and rubble mounds) similar to those in his area. Using the data reported for the excavated structures, Plog derived two formulas—one for pithouse villages and one for pueblos: for example, the number of rooms in a pueblo is equal to one-tenth the site area (area—in square meters—of the rubble mound prior to excavation) plus four. With today's emphasis on regional studies, techniques such as Plog's are becoming more common.

Subsistence A population eats to survive, and so another major area of inference in studying archaeological communities concerns their subsistence base. The questions of most interest are: What plants and animals were a part of the subsistence base? and, What was their relative contribution to the diet? The first line of evidence is the actual remains of the plants and animals. A high standard of analysis was set by J. G. D. Clark, a British prehistorian, in a report of his work at Star Carr in Yorkshire, England. Excavations revealed a small Mesolithic encampment (ca. 9000 B.P.) on a loose platform of birch brushwood beside a lake. The bones of 276 individual animals, mostly red deer, were uncovered. Body weights of the animals were estimated from bone size. Using modern ratios of meat to body weight, Clark calculated the quantity of meat represented at the site for each of five species of animals and inferred their relative contribution to the Star Carr diet.

Although there were plant remains at Star Carr, little was done beyond noting that they may have contributed to the diet. In making quantitative inferences about food, plant and animal remains cannot be considered in the same way. Bones are often preserved, especially the larger, denser bones, while plant remains survive less often. In addition, when an animal is consumed, the bones are left; when plants are consumed, there may be nothing left. While it is possible in principle to rank animal species in terms of their

contribution to the diet (on the basis of bone remains), it is doubtful that the same can be done using plant remains.

When particular plants, especially domesticated species, form a major portion of the diet, specialized tools and facilities—such as grinding stones, hoes, storage structures, field boundary markers, and dams and canals—are often developed. Thus, in those cases, even in the absence of plant remains, estimates of the utilization and sometimes even of the relative importance of plants can be made. For example, long before archaeologists found actual plant remains at Cochise sites in southern Arizona and northern Mexico (occupied between 8000 B.C. and the time of Christ), the presence of numerous grinding stones had indicated the importance of plants in the diet.

Many additional lines of evidence, such as paintings and carvings, folklore and ethnohistory, and current subsistence practices in an area, are sometimes available. The murals of ancient Egyptian tombs, which often depict everyday activities such as planting, harvesting, threshing, fishing, and hunting (FIGURE 9-11), are one of the joys of Egyptology and the envy of other archaeologists.

An independent line of evidence can be derived by comparing community population size with the resources available in the environment. For example, archaeologists infer—from its large population and its location at the source of a number of springs now used for irrigation—that the city of Teotihuacán was heavily dependent on irrigation agriculture for its subsistence. Also based on population size and local resources is Jerome Schaefer's determination that a number of Byzantine settlements (A.D. 500–700) in the desolate Negev Desert of southern Israel must have depended on trade for a major portion of their subsistence.

Some ecological archaeologists use quantitative models to estimate what resources were utilized (and in what proportions) by hunter-gatherers. These models are based on various theoretical assumptions about how hunter-gatherers would have had to behave for the most efficient exploitation of the resources in their territories. Michael Jochim, for example, has built a general model of hunter-gatherer exploitation of animals in cold forested regions. The model assembles a variety of information about the types of large game available in an environment, including (1) their abundance and distribution during different seasons, (2) the effort required to find and kill these animals with a simple hunting technology, and (3) the returns of meat and hides and other by-products from each. Using the efficiency assumption, Jochim's model predicts where hunter-gatherers would camp and what mix of animals they would hunt at different times of the year. Such models are still in their early stages of development and testing.

The attempt to infer the subsistence strategy of lowland Maya civilization is a good example of the need to examine every available scrap of evidence in such efforts. In fact, the subsistence base of this colorful civilization is still a mystery. One reason is that most traditional sources of information are unavailable. In the tropical rain forests of the southern Maya lowlands, few plant remains survive in archaeological context. In the absence of preserved plants, archaeologists have had to resort to less direct lines of evidence. The presence of artifacts such as manos and metates—grinding stones—builds a strong case for reliance on corn. Descriptions by explorers and missionaries of sixteenth-century descendants of the ancient Maya, which survive as ethnohistoric documents, record a clear dependence on corn grown by the *slash-and-burn* method. The method, in which fields are cut from the forest, cleared by burning, planted a few years, and then abandoned, is still common throughout the Maya area. In addition, corn today is a major focus of ritual, a role that can be traced back to the Classic period, as evidenced in depictions of corn plants in prominent positions in paintings and sculpture from that time (FIGURE 12-9). Thus, all the obvious evidence led to an unremarkable conclusion: that the ancient Maya were slash-and-burn corn farmers just like their modern descendants. For many years archaeologists were comfortable with this conclusion, though their satisfaction later declined as estimates of Maya population were steadily revised upward. Eventually, population estimates reached a level where it was clear that slash-and-burn agriculture could not have supplied the needed food.

How was the shortfall made up? Was food imported? Were there undiscovered resources or exotic modes of production? These questions have stimulated a great deal of research over the last two decades. Dennis Puleston, looking for the answer in supplementary foods, became intrigued by the *Ramón nut.* He was interested in this large nut first because its seed, like corn, could be ground into a meal and made into tortillas. He was interested also because Maya sites are usually associated with heavy stands of Ramón trees; in fact, early explorers located Maya sites obscured by dense foliage by watching for Ramón trees.

In order to substantiate this archaeological folklore, Puleston compared the distributions of ancient housemounds and of modern Ramón trees in a two-kilometer transect through the outskirts of Tikal. He found that housemounds and trees usually occurred together. On the basis of this evidence, Puleston suggested that the Classic Maya tended large orchards of Ramón trees. However, though intriguing, the housemound/Ramón association was a weak line of evidence. The specific trees Puleston recorded had obviously not existed during the Classic period, and their modern distribution could have been due to favorable growth conditions in the refuse-rich soil around housemounds.

In searching for more supportive evidence, Puleston investigated another Maya puzzle pondered for decades—the function of large pits cut in limestone, called *chultuns,* that dot Maya sites. It occurred to him that, rather than being sweat baths or water reservoirs, they might have been used for storing food. To test this he wrapped quantities of corn, beans, and Ramón nuts in leaves and sealed them in a chultun. At the end of several months the corn and beans had been destroyed by mold, but the Ramón seeds were still edible, showing that chultuns were suitable for storing Ramón nuts. Whether or not they had this function is still an open question, as is the mix of techniques and foods that composed Classic Maya subsistence.

Puleston was also one of the first Maya archaeologists to identify *ridged fields* near some Maya sites. The ridges were formed by digging long ditches and piling the earth from them in adjacent rows for planting. Puleston noticed these in the small flood plains of rivers. When the rivers flooded, water would have filled the ditches and irrigated the ridges. Few Maya sites, it was thought by Mayanists, are near rivers large enough for these types of fields to be of much importance. A recent series of aerial photographs, taken at sundown so that shadows would be accentuated, shows a remarkably regular series of ridges covering the Bajo Santa Fe, a huge swampy low-lying area northeast of Tikal. About half of all the land in the central Maya area is *bajo,* which has been considered unfit for agriculture of any kind. If the Bajo Sante Fe and other such areas were, indeed, huge complexes of irrigated fields, then the ancient Maya could have dramatically increased their production of corn and surpassed the population limits set by slash-and-burn techniques.

As archaeologists bring more lines of evidence to bear, the picture of Maya subsistence is likely to change even more. Customarily it is thought to be easy for archaeologists to make inferences about subsistence. In fact, it is a long and complicated process of finding new kinds of evidence in order to refine our models of subsistence behaviors.

Trade   Subsistence goods and resources are often obtained through trade. Archaeologists ask two basic questions in relation to trade: What was traded? and, How was it traded? Trade items are identified by the battery of techniques discussed in Chapter 8. For example, source analysis can be used to pinpoint areas where raw materials or manufactured items originated. Items found to have originated at a distance from their place of deposition are usually assumed to have been traded. The next job is to infer the type of social interaction responsible for a pattern of trade.

Archaeologists have developed a simple typology of ways that trade may be organized. Colin Renfrew, for example, distinguishes two major types of trade at the regional level: *down-the-line trade* and *directional trade*. Down-the-line trade is defined as the movement of goods over long distances through a number of short-distance exchanges between individuals in nearby communities. In contrast, in directional trade, goods are moved in bulk over long distances by merchant groups without intervening short-distance exchanges. These different patterns of trade can be identified in the archaeological record using the *law of monotonic decrement,* which is related to the gravity model (Chapter 4). This law states that, when items are exchanged from hand to hand, rates of acquisition will decrease as distance from the source increases. The archaeologist identifies the source of trade goods and plots their distance from that source to see whether there is a pattern of gradual fall-off. If there is, then down-the-line trade is inferred. The gradual fall-off seen in down-the-line monotonic curves is disrupted by large trade organizations, which can easily leap-frog quantities of goods between distant settlements through directional trade.

To translate these expectations from systemic to archaeological context requires a host of assumptions and inferences. Because acquisition patterns are related to the population and occupational history of settlements, these must be taken into consideration. Similarly, measures of distance cannot simply be calculated in conventional units, but must be based on the concept of *effective distance,* which takes into account differences in effort required to cross rivers, mountains, plains, or forests.

Because of these obvious difficulties, few archaeologists have succeeded in drawing the real curves of trade patterns. Instead, gross approximations based on obvious differences in the relative frequencies of occurrence of trade items are used to separate trade patterns that actually differ from each other in extreme and complex ways. Studying early Near Eastern villages (ca. 7000 B.C.), archaeologists identified a regular fall-off (with distance from sources) in the percentage of obsidian in chipped-stone inventories

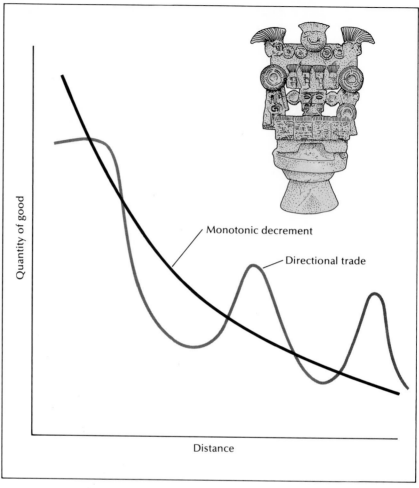

FIGURE **9-12**   Monotonic decrement—the fall-off of occurrence of trade items with distance from their source—and directional trade—the pattern of distribution resulting from movement of goods in bulk by merchants over long distances. Directional trade accounts for the distribution of Teotihuacán incensarios (see also FIGURE 4-7).

(FIGURE 4-6). In Mesoamerica, the distribution of Teotihuacán incensarios is clearly very different, with high densities in both Teotihuacán itself and along the Pacific coast of Guatemala, and low frequencies in the 800 kilometers between (FIGURE 9-12).

Archaeologists have been tempted to equate types of trade with types of societies—down-the-line with bands and tribes, directional with agrarian and industrial states. As more and more types of trade goods have come to be studied, such simple equations have collapsed. For example, Randall

McGuire and Christian Downum have studied trade goods that moved between the vicinities of present-day Flagstaff and Phoenix in Arizona between A.D. 700 and 1100. They recorded the distribution of both decorated pots that moved south and shells that moved north from their origin in the Gulf of California. The distribution of pots followed a down-the-line fall-off pattern; the distribution of shell did not. McGuire and Downum explain those patterns as reflecting differences in demand. Shell was in demand as a symbol of wealth by people of high social standing in large communities all over the Southwest. Thus, the trade of shell largely bypassed small settlements. The need for decorated pottery was more widespread and could be filled from a variety of sources including local manufacture. The lesson from this example is clear. There is no one-to-one correspondence between type of society and type of trade. Archaeologists must examine the distribution of each trade item to determine how it was moved. Eventually, the results of these separate studies can be combined in a search for patterns in the ways societies make use of different kinds of trade.

Warfare   Warfare—any armed conflict between communities or larger social groups —can be divided, according to the tactics and outcomes, into two very broad types—*ritualistic* and *imperialistic*. At one time or another, most small societies engage in ritualistic formal combat or raids against other communities. Fighting is sporadic and does not involve long-term mobilization or sieges. The effects of ritualistic warfare tend to be undramatic. Few are killed and few resources change hands. Imperialistic war, fought by specialists, involves large-scale mobilization of resources, long-term fighting, and sieges. Its effects are dramatic in terms of body counts and captured lands and other resources.

Some features in the archaeological record—such as large retaining walls and ditches, caches of weapons and mutilated body parts taken as trophies—are clear indications of violence. This sort of evidence is fairly common among archaeological societies. The expansion of the Roman Empire into Britain provides an example. Sir Mortimer Wheeler's excavation of Maiden Castle has produced a graphic picture of Romans storming an Iron-Age British hill-fort. Drawing on brief statements in historical sources and the archaeological evidence from excavations, Wheeler was able to piece together the sequence of events of the battle and its bloody aftermath.

While it is sometimes possible to reconstruct specific episodes of violence, inferring the overall patterns of warfare from these is much more difficult. In the case of Maiden Castle (FIGURE 9-13), our inferences are strengthened by historical data. Usually, the total evidence available is far less conclusive, and archaeologists are left to ponder the meaning of a few ditches, scattered spearpoints, or mutilated human bodies.

We know from written sources and the wide distribution of Roman military paraphernalia and architecture that the Romans were skilled practi-

A

B

C

FIGURE **9-13**   Four "defensive" sites: *A*, Maiden Castle, Dorset, England, an Iron Age settlement taken by the troops of Roman Emperor Vespasian about A.D. 47. *B*, Machu Picchu, Peru, a highland Inca site that contained military, governmental, and religious structures, dates to the Late Horizon period (A.D. 1476–1534), just prior to the Spanish Conquest. *C*, One-Tree Hill, Auckland, New Zealand, a *pa* or fortified hill—in this case, a terraced volcanic cone—was probably occupied by a Maori community in late prehistoric times (ca. A.D. 1450–1800). *D*, Fortified Hill Site, Gila Bend, Arizona, a Hohokam village occupied during the early Classic period (ca. A.D. 1200–1300), is located atop a butte regarded as a "defensive" site although excavations disclosed no obvious evidence of warfare.

D

tioners of imperialistic warfare. But what about the Britons who were overrun at Maiden Castle? The area of transition from ritualistic to imperialistic warfare is fuzzy, especially when written records are not available. Part of the problem is that societies may practice both types of warfare. The Aztecs, for example, used their armies to conquer and extract tribute from vast areas of central and southern Mexico. These same armies also fought ritual battles with those from nearby communities in what was known as the "War of the Flowers." Its major function was to give warriors a chance to take captives, which increased their social standing and provided priests with sacrificial victims.

Another part of the problem in inferring patterns of warfare is that although developed imperialistic warfare leaves distinctive traces, such as specialized military outposts, garrisons, and fortifications, there are few known types of materials to identify early imperialistic stages or different forms of ritualistic warfare. In fact, there are few material remains of Aztec warfare, either imperialistic or ritualistic. If archaeologists did not have the written observations of the first Spaniards in the New World, they might well have missed the evidence of the Aztec military empire, which lasted only thirty years.

On the other hand, in some places the most prominent artifacts of entire societies are those related to warfare and military preparedness. We are all familiar with the landscape of Europe, dotted with medieval hill-forts and castles, and the history of small and large wars there. This pattern of social conflict seems to have great antiquity. Shortly after the farming lifeway spread through Europe, much of the continent became an armed camp. Settlements built in defensible positions such as hilltops were often fortified. Social standing was clearly tied to trappings of war. As early as 500 B.C., the graves of community leaders bristled with chariots, battle axes, daggers, and armor. Despite this welter of evidence, the exact nature of early European warfare is unknown. We do not know the effect it had on the daily life of the people, the frequency of battles, the patterns of alliance, or the nature of spoils. Such details are necessary in assessing the role of warfare in cultural evolution. Archaeologists are now attacking this problem from their own trenches.

Social Differentiation and Integration

Every society includes divisive behavior patterns that tend to set people apart from one another, as well as patterns that hold people together, integrating them into a workable society. Archaeologists use the concept of *social differentiation* to describe those aspects of society that make people different—such as occupational specializations and various social roles and behavioral components. The greater the number of these in a society, the greater the differentiation. If not balanced by other behavior patterns, differentiation would break societies into useless pieces. Archaeologists use the concept of *social integration* to describe behavior patterns that arise to counteract the divisions created by differentiation. These include marketing-

and-distribution systems, political bureaucracies, the use of widely shared symbols, and participation in large-scale religious and social activities. The larger the number of widely shared material items and behavior patterns, the greater the social integration.

Although it is difficult to measure social differentiation and integration precisely, they permeate a community and, hence, its artifacts. Attempts to infer these organizational characteristics can be illustrated with a variety of examples.

Specialization   One basic measure of social differentiation is the number of occupational specialties and specialized task groups. Archaeologists often begin a study of specialization by focusing on the organization of production. For example, an artifact shows traces of manufacturing behavior. Highly standardized items are usually assumed to reflect the existence of specialized task groups of mass production. Individual specialists in craft production are identified on the basis of artifacts whose manufacturing traces indicate that they were produced one at a time and required a high degree of technical skill (FIGURE 9-14). Ethnoarchaeological analysis is needed to identify the subtle differences among the products of various forms of in-household production and part-time specialization that fall on the continuum from full-time craft specialists to full-time mass producers.

To further describe specialization, archaeologists are beginning to examine societies according to their range of products and to characterize societies by differences in manufacturing patterns. This task is complex because all societies use a mix of methods. Although most of the people of a tribe will know how to make pots, the majority are made by the more skilled potters. Even in our mass-production society there are numerous part-time and full-time craft specialists. Many of the handicrafts sold at our street fairs are made by part-time specialists, and the world's fastest computers are made of mass-produced components hand-assembled by craft specialists.

While specialization, by definition, leads to differentiation within a society, it can lead to a kind of integration. As farmers, obsidian chippers, weavers, priests, and bureaucrats become increasingly specialized, they become dependent on exchanging their own wares or services for the wide variety of those they need. In a very small society, specialists can trade directly with one another. As the number of specialists grows, face-to-face exchanges become impractical, and a host of new organizations, such as markets and merchant groups, arise to move goods from producers to consumers.

Bureaucracies within religious, business, and political institutions develop to manage the relations between groups of diverse specialists. In much the same way as the organization of manufacture leaves its marks on artifacts, so are the organizations behind the movement of goods and social interactions reflected in the distribution of artifacts. Similarities in the com-

FIGURE **9-14**

At top, a detailed, hand-painted, Near East bowl from the Halaf period (6000–5000 B.C.), which is of a kind that was superceded by simpler mass-produced wares such as beveled-rim bowls (at bottom), typical of the Uruk period (3600–2800 B.C.). Such shifts from craft to mass production are seen in many areas of the world.

modities found from household to household or community to community imply integrative institutions that equalize access to a society's manufactures. For example, many brands of processed food and health and cosmetic products can be found in households from one end of the United States to the other. A nationwide, in some cases worldwide, network of wholesalers, distributors, and supermarket chains make these products generally available. Other marketing organizations integrate regions (for example, milk companies) and even single communities (most city newspapers).

Archaeologists have examined the distribution of artifacts for traces of social integration. Michael Spence, using neutron activation to link the obsidian debris of workshops at Teotihuacán to four specific volcanic flows, divided the workshops into two types. Large workshops were clustered along the main avenue (the impressive "Street of the Dead") while smaller workshops were scattered through the rest of the city (FIGURE 9-15). He further noted that the products of the two types of shops differed. At the bigger shops he found more specialized tools and ceremonial implements, while smaller workshops apparently produced an assortment of more generalized household tools. Most interesting of all was the discovery that the large workshops had similar mixes of raw materials—in direct contrast to the highly varied types of obsidian found in the smaller workshops. Spence hypothesized that the small workshops were run by entrepreneurs, each of whom obtained his own obsidian, and that a centralized trade organization within Teotihuacán controlled the large workshops and procured their obsidian for them. Further research is likely to produce new evidence with which to test this hypothesis.

With the right evidence, the specific nature of an integrative mechanism can be defined, sometimes through a process of trial and error. A series of cuneiform texts from the site of Lagash, Iraq (ca. 2000 B.C.), recorded numerous economic transactions within an integrative *temple community*. The first translations were made by Father Demiel in the 1930s. According to the model he constructed from the texts, priests served the whole community both as religious functionaries and as managers of the flow of goods between farmers, fishermen, metallurgists, weavers, herders, and the other specialists needed in a large city. In effect, all economic activity in Lagash was viewed as being dominated by a priestly class. Demiel's model of a monolithic theocracy has influenced most subsequent interpretations of archaeological data from Near Eastern sites. In fact, it is a view that is still found in most history textbooks. However, when additional translations of the Lagash tablets were made in the 1950s, the theocracy model was overthrown and the temple community was assigned a more modest role. It became clear that the Lagash texts were the records of a temple that was only one small, relatively independent, institution in the community of Lagash. References were found to a royal palace, to the estates of nobles, and to the farmsteads of freemen, revealing the same messy complexity we see in present-day societies of comparable scale.

FIGURE **9-15**   Teotihuacán's main street, the "Street of the Dead," was laid out at the beginning of the site's long history. It was, no doubt, a focal point of community activity; the largest of the city's 500 obsidian workshops are found near this causeway. (See also FIGURE 9-10.)

Sometimes the distribution of artifacts at several sites furnishes clues to integrative organizations that operate at a regional scale. For example, during late prehistoric times (ca. A.D. 1200–1500), a number of large settlements with temple mounds were scattered in the river valleys of the southeastern United States. Some of the burials at the larger sites contained similar sets of ornate artifacts clearly produced by full-time craft specialists. These sets included copper gorgets, elaborately carved copper breastplates, carved shells, mica cutouts, and other worked exotic items that shared many design motifs, including "eagle warriors" (FIGURE 9-16). Early investigators dubbed this the Buzzard or Southern Cult. In so doing they recognized that some sort of regional integrative organization had been at work, one that included a religious burial cult. Today, an economic function has been proposed. According to this view, the Southern Cult maintained ritual ties between mostly independent agricultural communities. From time to time tornadoes, hurricanes, and floods would badly damage a community's crops, creating the potential for hardship and starvation. At such times, affected communities could have used their ritual ties to secure resources from more fortunate communities. Such an economic use of the Southern Cult has not yet been substantiated.

Investment
of Resources

A second set of measures of differentiation and integration involves examining the way resources are invested in artifacts. One of the main functions of artifacts is to symbolize social differentiation or the differences in social standing among people. Usually, high social standing is expressed in scarce artifacts, which are the product of great amounts of labor and/or exotic materials. Thus, while everyone buys clothes, some will buy hand-sewn Yves St. Laurent designer gowns, while others purchase mass-produced copies from J. C. Penney. Both types of people are expressing their social standing. Such symbolic functions of artifacts are critical because, in every activity and location, people need cues to differences in social standing in order to know how to behave toward each other. Information on social standing is symbolized by virtually all of our artifacts and furnishes the archaeologist with ample evidence for inferring social inequality. Hence these patterns can be used as an index to social differentiation.

One form of evidence on social differentiation is provided by comparing residences within communities. Ancient Near Eastern cities are good examples. Their residential neighborhoods are usually composed of dense mazes of tiny rooms crowded along narrow walkways. Palaces, such as that at Mari (FIGURE 9-17), stand in stark contrast. Their regular plans, spacious rooms, and open plazas attest to the large quantity of resources used to support the life style of the palace's occupants. This obvious differentiation in social standing within a community contrasts markedly with that of large Southwestern pueblos, such as Grasshopper (FIGURE 9-17). Intensive analysis there by J. Jefferson Reid and his colleagues has found very little residential variability that cannot be explained by household size or stage of household development. In contrast to Grasshopper and even the ancient city of Ur (FIGURE 9-17), the housing in our own society—mansions, custom-built mid-size homes, tract housing, mobile homes, and more—shows even greater differentiation in social standing.

Differentiation in social standing also ought to be reflected in inventories of household products and regularly consumed subsistence goods. Thus, household refuse can be an important source of evidence of differences. It is, however, sometimes difficult to collect relevant data in this way because of the complex formation processes in large settlements. At many large sites there is little or no de facto refuse other than a few storage jars or potsherds, and secondary refuse is mixed in huge dumps. On the other

FIGURE **9-16**

Some "Southern Cult" artifacts, found in
burials in the eastern United States
from the period A.D. 1200–1500.

A

SCALE

0   25   50 METERS

0   50   100 FEET

FIGURE **9-17**   Contrasting plans of three sets of structures: *A*, the Palace of Mari (ca. 1800 B.C.) in Syria; *B*, a residential section of the city of Ur, in Iraq (as it looked at about 1750 B.C.); and *C*, the plan of Grasshopper pueblo (ca. A.D. 1350). All are drawn to the same scale.

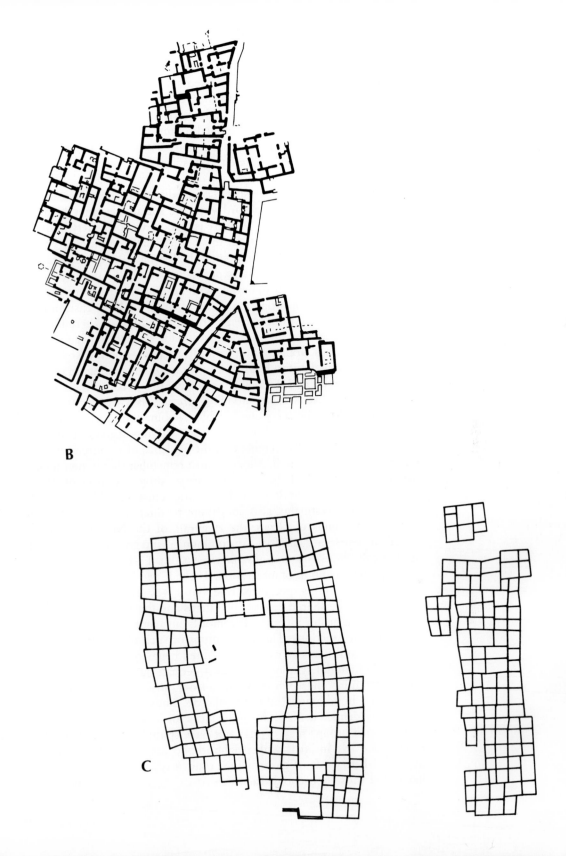

B

C

hand, at Grasshopper almost two-thirds of the excavated rooms had some de facto refuse, though most of it consisted of bulky pots and heavy grinding stones (FIGURES 5-6 and 7-14). Items that reflect wealth, such as jewelry and other portable valuables, were probably carried away. Although secondary refuse had been dumped into abandoned rooms, it cannot be traced back to specific households at Grasshopper. Thus, refuse analysis remains a weak line of evidence for inferring differences in social standing at present, though it is likely to be developed in the future.

Burials are uniquely expressive of social differentiation because individuals are treated in death in accord with the social roles they held in life (Chapters 5 and 8). For example, there is a good deal of variety in the burials at Grasshopper—ranging from those in specially prepared crypts with eighty pots, dozens of projectile points, shell jewelry, turquoise beads, and carved bone ornaments to ordinary pit graves with half a dozen pots and a shell or turquoise necklace, to burials with nothing that has been preserved. As we might expect, the burials at the city of Ur, in the Near East, show even more differentiation. At one extreme are the Death Pit—where forty-three women wearing jewelry and headdresses made of gold, other metals, and semiprecious stones, drank poison from silver cups—and the Royal Tombs, with special rooms built to house a king's ransom, including, in one hall, a chariot, two horses, and three fully armed guards. Between these spectacular burials and those with no surviving offerings is a vast array of burials with what seems to be every conceivable combination of grave goods. The patterns at Ur and at Grasshopper indicate varying degrees of differentiation (FIGURE 8-17). When combining the evidence of resources invested in residences and burials, archaeologists must remember that in non-industrial societies burials are likely to be much more sensitive indicators of social differentiation than are dwellings and domestic refuse.

Resource investments also contribute to integration. The temples of Tikal, the pyramids of Gizah, the ziggurats of the Near East, the Eiffel Tower of Paris, are all foci of community integration—what Roland Fletcher calls *monstrous visual symbols* (FIGURE 11-13). Items do not have to be big, to be symbols of integration. The jade pendant a Maya high priest wore was a sign of his specialized role, but it was also a symbol of integration, representing shared beliefs. Such items and the associated ritual define and symbolize group identity. The motifs on common pottery may have served similar functions. The distributions of such objects indicate groups sharing material items as well as associated behaviors and ideas.

Single material symbols, such as American flags, have two functions. They differentiate those who have them from those who do not; in addition, they form a bond among all those who do. Thus, distributional studies of stylistically defined artifacts form the basis for identifying integrated social groups. Such groups may or may not have spatial integrity. For example, people who live in areas with neighborhood associations are expected to maintain their yards or gardens in certain ways. On the other hand, it is likely that those households in which American flags are found today are not all in a single neighborhood. The distribution of a single object may symbolize a group, but rarely provides much information on its nature. The more shared objects, the more we can decipher about the nature of the groups. In some sense, when boundaries of artifact and design distribution are drawn, integrated groups are, to a certain extent, being defined.

Social Interaction A third measure of differentiation and integration focuses on social interaction or rates of interpersonal contact. Archaeologically, differentiation is indicated by "private spaces" in architecture—spaces created by partitions and doorways or even city walls. Areas with limited access indicate restrictions on social interaction and corresponding degrees of inequality. Many ancient societies built large structures with few entrances and rat maze interiors. It is clearly possible, from study of the amount of highly restricted space in these (FIGURE 9-17), to rank communities according to social interaction (FIGURE 8-23). Integration can also be broadly measured by quantifying those "public spaces" designed for large numbers of people to view political, religious, and entertainment spectacles; examples include St. Peter's Square in Rome, the Great Plaza at Tikal, the Superdome in New Orleans, and the Roman Coliseum. Again, the integration of societies can be ranked on the basis of the percentage of area allotted to such public spaces.

Differentiation and integration are fundamental concepts in inferring the nature of past societies, but they are fundamental only in so far as they help us to investigate the basic qualities of human existence—specialization in jobs, access to goods and services, and patterns of social interaction. The ultimate indicator in describing and comparing societies is contrasts in the conditions of life for people of different social standing. Thus, archaeologists are attempting to make the abstract concepts of differentiation and integration real by representing them in terms of actual behavior.

Afterword The archaeologist who has been successful in inferring behavioral components and behavioral properties—population, subsistence, trade, warfare, differentiation and integration—needs to combine these into a model that will offer a view of a society that is apt to be unlike, in particulars, any that exists today.

Obviously, the energy and resources necessary to complete such a model of a past society are immense, and in terms of most past societies we are far from meeting this objective. Nevertheless, the inferences that we have achieved give us invaluable glimpses into the many unfamiliar lifeways of our predecessors. The questions they raise—how and why societies have evolved as they have—are the basic focus of explanation in archaeology and the subject of our next chapter.

Lewis R. Binford (b. 1930)   Lewis Binford is surely one of the most dynamic and controversial archaeologists of recent times. Many people would say that in the 1960s he single-handedly created a "new" archaeology, the central focus of which was a conceptual scheme built on the ideas of Steward and White—the latter, one of Binford's professors when he attended the University of Michigan. □ Binford's own research has focused on explaining differences in artifact assemblages. He has stressed techno-function as an explanation of variability (Chapter 4) and was a pioneer in using computers to test his hypotheses. These studies have drawn him into confrontations with archaeologists who excavated the European and African Stone Age tools Binford chose to analyze. Analyses of the tools were inconclusive, so Binford turned to the plentiful animal bones associated with the stone tools. Together, the stone tool and faunal evidence presented an even more confusing picture. As a result, he initiated a long-term ethnoarchaeological study of the Nunamiut Eskimo of Northern Alaska. Binford and his students patiently followed reindeer hunters, observing how animals were butchered, where and when meat was stored, and the way bones were deposited in the archaeological record. Initial findings—making up a surprisingly complex picture—were published in 1979 in *Nunamiut Ethnoarchaeology* and in 1981 in *Bones*. □ Archaeologists often find it difficult to discuss Binford or his ideas without getting into shouting matches. Binford is more than a match for them; in fact, because of his verbal skills, his aggressive style of arguing, and his constant flow of new ideas, he never lacks for an attentive—and necessarily silent—audience. After one dinner with a number of graduate students at which Binford totally dominated the conversation, he commented with a puzzled look, "For a bunch of bright graduate students, they sure didn't have much to say."

Lewis R. Binford
conducts a class
in archaeology.

10

EXPLANATION

Two thousand B.C. The heart of the Yucatán Peninsula is an uninterrupted sea of rain forest. By 500 B.C., small islands of human settlement have intruded on the jungle. Their temples breaching the forest canopy, the islands multiply and push outward in waves. At A.D. 800, the middle of the Yucatán Peninsula is one of the most populous centers of high civilization in the world. A mere half-century later, the temples are still, the people gone, and the rain forest swallowing what was left of Maya society. Today we ponder the question, Why?

When the information from separate analyses of archaeological materials is combined to form inferences, we can often be fairly certain of *what* happened. But archaeologists want to know *why* it happened. They are not satisfied knowing a past society's population size, subsistence base, or means of social integration; they want to know *why* these changed through time. They want to explain variability in human behavior and artifacts. Archaeologists have drawn inspiration for their explanations from the societies they know best—those in which they live. Slowly, using models inspired by the present, they have built more and more rigorous and satisfactory explanations of the past. The more we experience change in our own society, the more insight we bring to explaining changes in the past.

THE EMERGENCE OF ARCHAEOLOGY AS A DISCIPLINE

Archaeology was born in Western Europe just after the beginning of the Industrial Revolution. It was an era of miraculous change. During the first half of the nineteenth century, evidence of the pace of that change was clearly visible to Europeans and to Americans—the first steam locomotives and railroads (FIGURE 10-1), gaslights, photographs, lighter-than-air balloons and other airships, and the telegraph. In fact, the pace of technological and social innovation had reached so high a pitch that, perhaps for the first time in history, the experience of constant change became an awesome reality for individuals. By the time adults of one generation began to raise their children, the world of *their* childhood had been transformed. By the time they had grandchildren, it had changed again. Within this rapidly evolving world, new concepts were forming about the natural history of the earth and its inhabitants.

Beginnings: Nineteenth-Century

At the opening of the eighteenth century, it was generally believed that the biblical account of Creation was literally correct. A common preoccupation was tracing back the genealogies in the Bible to determine the date of Creation. (Recall from Chapter 6 the contribution of Archbishop Ussher and Dr. John Lightfoot.) Thus, the early eighteenth century thought of itself as a special creation only a few thousand years old. The world had been created

FIGURE **10-1**   The DeWitt Clinton, an early-nineteenth-century locomotive with passenger cars.

FIGURE **10-2**   Excavating the remains of prehistoric man at LaGrange, Les Eyzies, France, in the 1800s.

once and was unchanging. Whatever anomalies turned up, such as fossils of unfamiliar animals or seashells found high in mountains, were explained away by claiming a succession of catastrophes, of which Noah's Flood was the best known.

By the 1800s, more and more anomalies were accumulating that led to more and more fanciful explanations. However, the build-up of evidence that was inconsistent with a short history was not ignored by everyone. Geologists were the first to offer new explanations, and the contributions of Sir Charles Lyell were among the most comprehensive and convincing. By rigorously applying the basic principles of stratigraphy and uniformitarianism, Lyell produced a new history of the earth (Chapter 6).

For those seeing the arrival of the first train and the flicker of the first gas lamp, radical changes in their view of the past became plausible. They became reality through archaeological discoveries (FIGURE 10-2), particularly those in the Somme River gravels, near Abbéville in France. There, Boucher de Perthes scouring the ancient terraces laid down by the Somme River, found, many feet below the ground surface, crude, bifacially-chipped core tools, called *handaxes,* sometimes in association with the bones of extinct animals. Boucher argued that the gravels were very ancient. This was just one of many anomalies, which, when related to the principle of uniformitarianism, established the antiquity of humankind. Boucher's work was the first to be certified to the satisfaction of the skeptical scientific community—when John Evans and Joseph Prestwich reported on their evaluation of his research to the Royal Society of England. Boucher's triumph came in 1859, the same year that Charles Darwin published *On the Origin of Species*. That these two highly visible events occurred in the same year testified to the fact that the evidence had accumulated to a point where it could not be ignored. Darwin's theory provided the rationale for searching for our ancestors and established the relevance of the data of prehistory.

The continued relevance of archaeological investigations was also supported by another development in evolutionary thought. The "Age of Discovery"—as it came to be known—had shown a diversity in human societies that was embarrassing for theologians and social thinkers to contemplate—from Pygmies hunting elephants in an African rain forest to South Sea Islanders who ate strange root crops and tattooed their entire bodies. Viewed from the heights of the technological supremacy of Western Europe, the existence of "simpler" societies was explained in two ways. The theologians ascribed the "savage" state of some to a tragic fall from grace. Ironically, while they could not admit evolution, the theologians were willing to countenance devolution. The other interpretation, one which was gaining favor among academic social thinkers, was that primitive societies were simply stalled along the path of development. They had, for various reasons, failed to evolve. It was the people who held this view, such as Britishers Edward B. Tylor and John Lubbock and American Lewis Henry Morgan, who founded the young discipline of anthropology, the behavioral science that arose to explain the diversity of human races and societies.

Cultural Evolutionism

By the time these men were writing—in the 1870s and 1880s—the theory of biological evolution had been widely accepted. Much of their work was aimed at finding an equally elegant theory of cultural evolution. In an attempt to reveal the past stages of cultural evolution (Chapter 3), scholars invented the comparative method, in which contemporary societies were ordered from simple to complex. This method and theory was anthropology's first conceptual scheme; and this scheme of the development of societies into "higher and higher" stages, or what was called "progress," reinforced the Victorian view of England as being at the pinnacle of "mankind" in a day when the sun never set on the British Empire.

No one had witnessed a society evolve out of savagery into barbarism, as Morgan alleged all societies had done. The evolutionary scheme was plausible, but little more than that. What it really needed was archaeological evidence to demonstrate that societies had actually changed in the proposed manner from simple to complex. Testing the theories of biological and cultural evolution demanded a prehistoric archaeology.

The study of human biological evolution through archaeology is today called paleoanthropology. It has followed a course from the Somme gravels and from the first Neanderthal skull, found in Germany in 1856, to the current discoveries of 5 million-year-old fossils in Ethiopia and Kenya. What sets paleoanthropology apart from archaeology is the emphasis on the skeletal remains of our ancestors. Thus, most paleoanthropologists are trained in the biological sciences and leave tools and their behavioral implications to their archaeologist brethren.

Because most evolutionary models concentrated on features of language and social organization, the developmental stages that social theorists proposed could not always be readily substantiated archaeologically. Material items were used to distinguish between stages in only a few instances, as—in Morgan's scheme—in the case of the bow and arrow, domesticated animals, and iron tools.

As a result, archaeologists formulated their own stage models, which concentrated on artifacts and technological change. One early example was C. J. Thomsen's three age system, a stage model that organized ancient tools in the National Museum of Denmark into exhibits labeled "Stone Age," "Bronze Age," and "Iron Age." Archaeologists in the late 1800s worked toward constructing more refined technological schemes. They spent a great deal of their time conducting stratigraphic excavations and organizing their findings into models of regional evolution. As a result of this effort, nineteenth-century archaeologists succeeded in confirming the most general evolutionary prediction: societies developed from simple to complex.

Once the broad outlines of change in past societies were established, archaeologists attempted to fill in the details. They very quickly learned that evolutionary generalizations, hatched in armchairs, could not explain the diversity in past cultures. The experience of Victorian scholars was simply too limited to explain the variety of artifacts excavated daily. It was at this time that archaeologists turned to those anthropologists who spent their time studying nonindustrial communities. The prehistorians hoped to learn from cultural anthropologists, who studied living societies, some useful principles for explaining the development of dead ones. This relationship has lasted to the present day. In much of the English-speaking world, and especially in the United States and Canada, archaeology is viewed as a part of anthropology, that part dealing with the unwritten history and the artifacts of human societies.

In America the relationship between archaeology and cultural anthropology was particularly close because archaeologists were excavating the material remains left by the ancestors of living Indians. In fact, many of the early archaeologists in the Southwest spent a great deal of time recording the behavior of tribes such as the Hopi and Zuñi. In the early 1880s, for example, Frank Cushing lived at the pueblo of Zuñi for more than four years. He not only became a member of the tribe, but was inducted into the sacred war society of the Bow Priests (FIGURE 10-3) as well. In 1886, seeking the ancestors of the Zuñi tribe, Cushing conducted the first scientific excavations in Arizona at the large site of Los Muertos (FIGURE 10-6).

As researchers ventured into the field to observe "primitive" societies first-hand, they found that their evolutionary generalizations were incorrect.

FIGURE **10-3**

Frank Hamilton Cushing at Zuñi Pueblo, New Mexico, in the late nineteenth century. He is wearing Zuñi clothing.

It became evident that these generalizations had often been based on misinterpretations, superficial comparisons, and inaccurate descriptions based on information supplied by early explorers.

Historical Particularism

The attack against cultural evolutionism was led by Franz Boas, who helped establish the conceptual scheme we now call *historical particularism*. This perspective identified several basic historical processes that were used to explain specific instances of change. Not surprisingly for a German immigrant to the United States during a time of massive movements of people in Europe and America, Boas saw *migration* as a major historical process. Similarly, given the immense impact of Western ideas and artifacts on the simpler societies anthropologists were studying, *diffusion* was considered a second historical process, while a third was *invention*—which, as embodied by Alexander Graham Bell and Thomas Edison, was a fundamental part of the "American Dream."

Because archaeologists could see these processes at work in their own society and because of the emerging complexity of the archaeological record, the conceptual scheme of historical particularism seemed to furnish a ready-made framework for explaining the past. In order to use this scheme, archaeologists first borrowed the concept of culture, in this case used to refer to the distinctive mass of beliefs, ideas, values, institutions, customs, and artifacts that set one society apart from another. To use the concept archaeologically, sets of traits that commonly occurred together were assumed to indicate archaeological cultures (Chapter 9). Specific distributions of traits were explained by reference to the three fundamental historical processes—migration, diffusion, and invention.

Archaeologists began explanations of past cultures by establishing sequences of traits in their chosen areas. In such a framework, what required explanation were the new traits that appeared through time. The first step was to determine if the new traits occurred earlier in adjacent areas. If they had, then either diffusion or migration were taken to be responsible. If new traits had appeared suddenly, in a cluster, then migration was the explanation; if they trickled in slowly, then diffusion was the cause. If the traits could not be found elsewhere, invention was invoked.

Most cases were not clear-cut. One of the flaws with historical particularism was that there were no standard rules for choosing among the possible explanations. Ultimately, most explanations depended on the specific assumptions that individual archaeologists made about human behavior. Some investigators believed that people are basically uninventive, and that important ideas are dreamed up only once. The most famous example is the Heliocentric school of Grafton Elliot Smith, which considered ancient Egyptians to be the founders of all other civilizations. The followers of Smith saw evidence of Egyptian influence everywhere. Other diffusionists assigned a similar role to the mythical lands of Atlantis and Mu. In science, the heyday of such extreme diffusionism was the early decades of the twentieth century. These ideas still persist in the public media (Chapter 12).

In recent decades, historical particularists have taken an optimistic view of human capabilities and have placed more stress on invention. Today, archaeologists recognize at least half a dozen centers in the New World in which pottery-making was independently developed. Routes of diffusion have been traced from each of these centers into surrounding communities and regional systems. For example, pottery-making begins in sites along the Gulf coast of Georgia around 2500 B.C. During the next several millennia the new technology spread throughout eastern North America. The earliest spread was easily traced because of a distinctive fiber temper in the pottery.

From the point of view of a historical particularist, once a historical process has been identified, explanation is complete. From our modern perspective, this is not enough. As we know from recent experience with Vietnamese and Cubans, migrations occur all the time; some have few effects, others profoundly influence recipient societies. Simply invoking migration does not answer the basic question: Why does change occur in one place and not another? Similarly, societies are always exposed to innovative ideas and new artifacts, but only some are adopted. Of these, many are modified; some artifacts even acquire new functions. Again, the question remains: Why does a society adopt one and not another idea or item? For example, the "explanation" that pottery diffused from Georgia does not tell us why it spread very slowly and erratically. To explain why a particular group adopted pottery-making at a particular time, we have to understand the functions of ceramics in societies. At 2500 B.C. eastern North America was inhabited by hunter-gatherers with little use for pots. The diffusion of pottery is likely to be a good marker of changes in subsistence and residential mobility among these groups.

Historical particularism does not have the principles needed for answering the "why" questions about change. Nevertheless, this conceptual scheme served as the basis for building chronologies and describing archaeological cultures and changes in their distribution through time. Although few archaeologists today would claim to be historical particularists, this school of thought has had a major impact on the archaeology of the twentieth century.

The New Conceptual Scheme

The first half of the twentieth century could be called the Age of Historical Particularism; the following age is not as easily named, but like its predecessor it is based on changes observed in our own society. In the aftermath of the Second World War, specialization increased. The division of labor separated experts in the study of technology from experts in the study of social groups. This division also often separated those who believed change originates with technological development from those who believed important changes are the result of new ideas and attitudes.

This same polarization occurred within the discipline of anthropology, splitting the conceptual scheme of archaeology from cultural anthropology. Where once great "Renaissance men" such as Alfred Louis Kroeber and Florence Hawley Ellis roamed easily between archaeology and cultural anthropology, post-World War II specialists chose one or the other. The basic differences in the data of archaeology and cultural anthropology attracted people who would apply different conceptual schemes to the respective disciplines. For example, if you were interested in the impact of ideas as an explanation of change, artifacts would not provide the best results. This process of selection, separating those who study artifacts from those who study ideas, has reached a point where there is a general homogeneity in conceptual schemes within archaeology. The reason for this homogeneity is partly a function of demographic trends: 99 percent of all the archaeologists who ever lived are alive today; the majority were trained after 1970.

The homogeneity is expressed most clearly in four orientations of current archaeology: (1) it is materialist. Perhaps largely because of archaeology's data base and methods, behavioral change is seen as a response to alterations in the material conditions of life, such as the size of the population or the availability of arable land or the impact of new labor-saving devices.

(2) It is concerned with the process of evolution, identifying the underlying patterns and trends behind change. This is an orientation that seeks to establish general principles and, therefore, (3) it uses the scientific method. (4) It is becoming eclectic. Rather than deriving principles exclusively from cultural anthropology, it freely seeks inspiration from other disciplines and from our own society.

Because of this new eclecticism within archaeology's basic conceptual scheme, there is room for a diversity of opinions. For example, within the evolution segment, some archaeologists emphasize the role of population growth and some the role of irrigation. Within the eclectic interdisciplinary segment, some borrow from geography and some from ecology. The result is often exciting debates over explanation within a set of established ground rules. The remainder of this chapter is devoted to a discussion of some modern approaches to explanation.

Steward and White

Cultural ecology, one of the earliest modern conceptual schemes, was formulated initially by Julian Steward. He began writing in the 1930s, when historical particularism was still dominant. Cultural ecology is built around the concept of *functionalism,* derived from British cultural anthropologists. Functionalism states that societies are not a hodgepodge of traits, but are like living organisms, in which each activity and social unit has a function or role. For example, Egyptian religion placed a great emphasis on tracking the star Sirius. It is probably no coincidence that the movements of Sirius foretell the annual floods of the Nile River. Thus, Egyptian religion functioned in part to rationalize the study of astronomy, which contributed to maintaining agricultural production. For Steward, functionalism alone was not enough. He added materialism to give it causal direction. Drawing inspiration from Karl Marx, Steward proposed that the nature of a society's social organization and ideology are strongly influenced by its technology and by the requirements of adaptation to its environment.

In two influential books, *The Science of Culture* (1949) and *The Evolution of Culture* (1959), Leslie A. White (p. 42) codified these ideas still further. For him, societies could be represented in a layered model. Technology, White argued, is a society's foundation. It captures energy from the environment and channels it into production. Technology, in turn, requires that people be organized in certain ways and thus determines the next layer, social organization. This social order is maintained by the top layer, ideology. The nature of each level is largely a product of the levels below. Thus, White argued that the most basic and important changes begin with technology and work their way up. Nevertheless, White acknowledged that the direction and rates of change were influenced by all the levels.

Although White is widely regarded as the foremost materialist of his time, it was Steward who showed how these principles operate in real societies. His most elegant illustrations of cultural ecological explanation were focused on hunter-gatherers from the Great Basin of the United States. His painstaking analyses clearly revealed the way features of social organization related to patterns of resource procurement and seasonal mobility. From this case study emerged the general concept of band society. Bands (Chapter 3) were defined by Steward as a form of organization that allows hunter-gatherers to exploit environments with scattered, sparse resources.

Steward also tried to apply cultural ecology to the development of political institutions in complex societies. This time he borrowed the *hydraulic hypothesis* of Karl Wittfogel, a historian of China. On the basis of data gathered in China, Wittfogel suggested that the building and maintaining of large-scale irrigation systems required managers organized in powerful political institutions. Thus, Wittfogel believed that the adoption of irrigation brought about complex societies. In the early fifties Steward assembled a number of experts, mainly archaeologists, to test this model worldwide. The results were inconclusive, and the debate was on.

The basic question was simple: Which came first, centralized political authority or large-scale irrigation? Obviously, many early civilizations were heavily dependent on irrigation. However, in order to support the Wittfogel model, the development of water control technology must have occurred before or at the same time as the centralization of political authority. Archaeological testing of this hypothesis was difficult because very accurate chronologies were needed. Despite the difficulties, Robert Adams made some headway by drawing on both historical records and archaeological surveys from the Near East. He argued convincingly that large canal systems were built only after the appearance of centralized political institutions.

Another line of evidence came from comparative studies of ongoing irrigation-using societies. René Millon reviewed the literature on fourteen such societies, from Bali to the Sonjo of East Africa. He concluded that not all hydraulic societies had powerful political authorities. In a later study of Millon's societies plus six others, Wayne Kappel reached altogether different conclusions. First, arguing that Millon had no clear definition of political power, Kappel developed one based on the number of people involved in decisions over water control and whether or not such decisions could be appealed. Second, where Millon had looked only at community organizations, Kappel included regional systems in his study. The end result provided a new twist to the old argument. Kappel found no correlation between political authority and irrigation systems within small societies; however, he also found that in irrigation societies of more than 5,000 people decision-making was highly centralized. Kappel's provocative conclusions have only served to create more interest in the irrigation debate set off by Steward. Today, this "hydraulic" hypothesis is one of many explanations that archaeologists are attempting to test.

Many of the explanations that archaeologists are exploring focus on changes in social complexity, which is measured in terms of differentiation and integration (Chapter 9). Increased numbers of social roles (more specialists of different kinds) and more types of behavioral components (new kinds of task groups and institutions) are taken by archaeologists to indicate more differentiation and an increase in social complexity. Increased numbers of integrative artifacts and activities as well as more energy spent on these integration devices are also taken by archaeologists to indicate an increase in social complexity. It is often difficult to quantify precisely the difference in degree of complexity between two very similar societies. Nevertheless, using the principles of inference (Chapter 9), archaeologists can recognize major differences in differentiation and integration. They have concentrated, therefore, on explaining changes from hunter-gatherer bands to tribal farming societies and from chiefdoms to agrarian states.

PRIME CAUSES

Like the hydraulic hypothesis, many current explanations for changes in complexity rely on one *prime cause.* (In fact, the hydraulic hypothesis itself has been expanded to explain *all* complex societies, whether they had irrigation or not. Those without irrigation were termed "secondary hydraulic states" and were assumed to have developed through contact with "primary hydraulic states.") The irony of the prime-cause position is that, as will be seen below, there are many prime causes championed by archaeologists; they can't all be right.

Population Pressure/ Agricultural Intensification

Population growth is currently the most fashionable of prime causes. Many archaeologists trace their interest in population to the 1965 book *The Conditions of Agricultural Growth,* by economist Ester Boserup, or to a series of articles by cultural anthropologist Robert Carneiro. Boserup drew interest by answering a question raised by the hydraulic hypothesis: Why irrigate? Using data from developing countries, she argued that irrigation as a form of intensive agriculture is a mixed blessing. On the one hand, the crop yields are greater; on the other hand, individual farmers have to work longer hours building and maintaining canals and fields, and so make the decision to irrigate reluctantly. According to Boserup, what tips the balance is usually population pressure, an increased number of mouths that cannot be fed through the old agricultural technology. Furthermore, with an excess population, labor is cheap, and this labor can be invested in more intensive agriculture—including irrigation—to increase food production. To coordinate this complicated technology, Boserup's followers postulate that societies establish new management institutions and become more complex.

William Sanders has identified Teotihuacán as an irrigation civilization. It is located next to a set of springs that today supply modern canals with water. Sanders has argued that irrigation must have been used at Teotihuacán because without it, the large population in the city could not have been fed. Establishing when the canal network was built relative to when Teotihuacán became a large and complex city has been difficult. The first few archaeological traces of local ancient canals were identified only in 1976.

FIGURE **10-4**

Figure from Stela 31, Tikal, Guatemala. The shield or cloth on his arm depicts Tlaloc, the goggle-eyed diety of Central Mexico. In his right hand is a spear-thrower, a weapon not seen elsewhere in Classic Maya art.

Population Pressure/ Warfare

Robert Carneiro's early articles established that large populations are associated with complex organizations, as we have seen in Chapter 3. More recently, he has identified another route to complex organization, one open to societies whose populations are outstripping their resources. Instead of agricultural intensification, Carneiro emphasizes the role of conquest warfare. According to his *circumscription hypothesis*, population growth is a normal condition in favorable environments. In some regions, as population pressure grows, people are prevented from migrating into adjacent areas by natural barriers such as mountain ranges and large bodies of water and by the presence of other societies. As populations continue to increase in these circumscribed areas, competition for resources becomes more intense. Rather than put additional people to work farming, some societies build armies for conquest. According to Carneiro, when one society achieves military superiority, neighbors will be subjugated and needed resources will be taken as tribute. The conquerors and the conquered become social classes within a single, more complex society.

Believers in the circumscription hypothesis would be likely to explain the rise of Teotihuacán by pointing to the chain of volcanic mountains that surrounds it in the Basin of Mexico. The many distant areas in which Teotihuacán architecture was copied and in which Teotihuacán artifacts were found in large numbers have led archaeologists to speculate that the city was the center of a military empire. Dating the rise of imperialistic warfare is difficult. Massive fortifications are absent as are caches of weapons or the mass graves likely to ensue from large battles. In their absence, much of the existing data are ambiguous. For example, the Teotihuacano pictured on Stela 31 at Tikal could as easily be a priest, trader, or politician as a military commander (FIGURE 10-4).

Trade   A third prime cause is trade. Many resources useful to societies must be imported. The resulting trade may stimulate the growth of complex management organizations. Colin Renfrew in Europe, Carl Lamberg-Karlovsky in the Near East, and William Rathje and Barbara Price in Mesoamerica are among those who argue that demands for imported goods stimulate the rise of trade organizations. People are willing to pay for imports; thus, there will be a reward for those entrepreneurs who establish trading groups that move goods efficiently at low costs. This reward will be especially high if the trading organization monopolizes some resource, whether natural or manufactured. In fact, whenever supply and demand are geographically separate, opportunities are created for middleman organizations to spring up that service both producer and consumer. As trade organizations become larger and more central to the economy, they stimulate craft and mass production and the expansion of political institutions. As a result, the society in which they are growing becomes more complex.

Promoters of the trade hypothesis, such as Barbara Price, have argued that much of the rise of Teotihuacán can be attributed to the city's apparent monopoly of the obsidian trade and its extensive export of locally manufactured pottery (FIGURE 4-7) and other goods. They point to the numerous large obsidian workshops along the main ceremonial avenue and to the pan-Mexican distribution of green obsidian from Pachuca, a source apparently controlled by nearby Teotihuacán. They also infer that Teotihuacán controlled the major obsidian sources in Guatemala through the city of Kaminaljuyu, where a miniature Teotihuacán was built over 800 kilometers from its obvious model.

Dating Teotihuacán's trade activities is crucial. The main unanswered question is whether Teotihuacán became complex by expanding its role as a center of trade or expanded trade after it became complex from other causes. In addition, the volume of trade has yet to be established, as has the exact nature of the merchant organizations involved.

FIGURE 10-5

The round pyramid at Cuicuilco, Mexico, which is the only part of the site that protrudes from the lava that covered it when the volcano Xitli erupted around the time of Christ. The cataclysm removed Teotihuacán's main competitor.

Environmental Stress

Another popular prime cause is environmental stress. Advocates argue that in some parts of the world environmental changes caused fluctuations in harvests and in the ease with which resources could be obtained. For example, early frosts might destroy crops in low-lying fields of a valley or a reduced flow in a river might leave downstream settlements with insufficient water to irrigate their crops. In areas where the environment causes such variability in resources, there is an advantage for communities to form large complex regional systems. In these systems, which integrate diverse communities, cooperation and sharing of resources evens out imbalances caused by nature. Using environmental stress as an explanation requires first determining that a change occurred, and second, determining just how stressful that environmental change was.

Natural disasters are one obvious cause of environmental stress. Until about 2500 B.C. the Euphrates River in Iraq flowed in two branches. Along each was a line of regularly spaced small villages. Then the river flooded and, when the flood waters receded, one branch had ceased to flow. McGuire Gibson has proposed that when people from the stranded communities (those on the now dry branch) migrated to neighboring settlements, the result was instant population pressure, which led to more complex societies. Within a few decades the pattern of settlements on the river branch that still flowed was drastically changed. Instead of a series of small villages, there were the city of Nippur and several large satellite communities.

The rise of Teotihuacán has also been explained by environmental stress. Just before the time of Christ, Cuicuilco was the dominant settlement in the Basin of Mexico, and Teotihuacán was a relatively minor community. Not long after, the volcano Xitli erupted and buried the hapless Cuicuilco under 20 feet of lava (FIGURE 10-5). Some archaeologists argue that Teotihuacán's growth as the hub of an empire was only possible after—and as a result of—the untimely demise of Cuicuilco.

MULTICAUSALITY

As noted above, by definition, there can be only *one* prime cause, and believers in a particular one must, therefore, also believe that it explains every case of change—whether rise or fall, whether in Mexico or China. Conversely, as we have noted, at one time or another *every* prime cause has been used to explain the rise of Teotihuacán. The many prime causes—and long lines of archaeologists behind each prime cause—seem to indicate that there are *none*. Most archaeologists now realize that many factors are always involved in any change and influence its outcome. In order to explain changes, archaeologists must identify the most important factors and the particular effects that each is likely to have. During the past two decades archaeologists have concentrated on prime causes; as a consequence, they have already been studying the effects of several of the most important factors involved in change. Today, the emphasis is on combining these individual causes into *multicausal explanations,* which involves a return to the general model of adaptive systems and their six basic elements: population, technology, social organization, ideology, and the natural and social environments (Chapter 3). Most archaeologists have come to believe that a single very general principle describes how the basic elements of adaptive systems change. As the functionalists—Julian Steward, Leslie White, Lewis Binford, and others—argue, in all societies the basic elements are adapted to one another. The general principle is simply this: Because the basic elements of society are fitted to each other, when one element is altered, changes in other elements necessarily follow. For example, as population grows, social organization expands and becomes more complex and new forms of social organization lead to new ideologies. Because of the connections among society's elements, the explanation of any change process requires the consideration of many causes and the way they affect one another.

Where Does Change Begin?

To simplify the study of change, archaeologists recognize two fundamental questions: (1) Where does change begin? and (2) How does change move from element to element in adaptive systems? In answering the first of these two questions, most archaeologists take either an *externalist* or an *internalist* position.

The Externalist View

Those in the externalist group argue that factors outside the adaptive system, such as natural and social environments, are the primary causes of change and strongly determine the course it takes. Societies are viewed as being relatively stable unless disturbed by outside forces. Archaeologists who subscribe to this external view are likely to study the environment intensively and borrow many concepts from ecological theory. The above-mentioned example of the flood of the Euphrates River and the rise of the city of Nippur is an obvious illustration of how an archaeologist would approach the explanation of a change using external factors.

Some archaeologists see patterns in the kinds of environments in which complex societies develop. *Nuclear areas* are regions where large, complex societies arise again and again, in contrast to those areas where they develop once or never at all. For example, the basin of central Mexico is a nuclear area. It produced the large Preclassic community of Cuicuilco; Teotihuacán, the largest population center in Classic period Mexico; the Aztec capital of Tenochtitlán; and modern Mexico City. Rome has played a pivotal role in Italy since the beginnings of written history. Several major cities in the Orient, such as Karachi and Peking, are located near the capitals of ancient states. The modern capital of Arizona is built on the remains of Hohokam irrigation societies and even draws water through some of the ancient

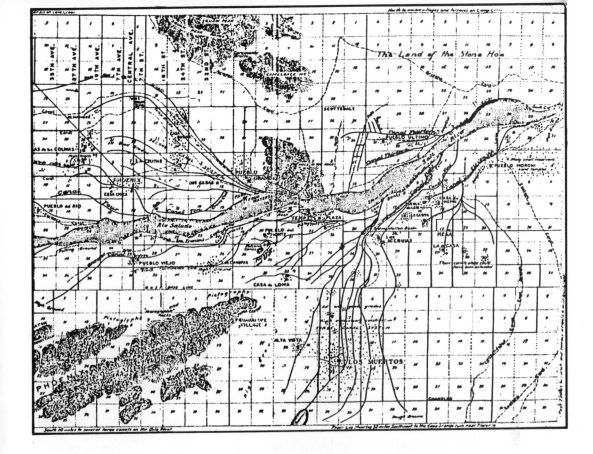

FIGURE **10-6**

On facing page, aerial photograph of Phoenix, Arizona, metropolitan area. Superimposed in white is a portion of the map (above) by Omar Turney of the ancient Hohokam ruins and canal system (ca. A.D. 800–1450). Scale is about one-quarter inch to a mile.

canals. Its name, Phoenix, referring to the mythical bird that would rise from ashes, was given to the town by early settlers who were very conscious of the many impressive ruins around them (FIGURE 10-6).

In explaining nuclear areas, archaeologists have identified a number of features common to them. Although they are not necessarily near other desirable resources, they are usually situated in regions with large expanses of easily farmed land. This may be essential to a nuclear area because food, being perishable, is one of the most difficult resources to move long distances. Nuclear areas also tend to be located at communication and transportation crossroads. While the growth of population centers obviously draws traffic, nuclear areas occur at important points on rivers or trade routes where traffic would be heavy regardless of local conditions.

While archaeologists see these characteristics as promoting the growth of complex societies, some see the other side and view external variables, such as the environment, as a major limitation on the development of complex societies. Betty Meggers attributes the Maya collapse to an impoverished environment. She believes that the lowland Maya rain forest could not long sustain the population levels necessary for the growth of complex societies. Thus, although complex societies did develop in the Maya lowland, according to Meggers they were doomed from the start. As is probably clear, this externalist explanation resembles earlier prime-cause models. In fact, in extreme forms, externalists do nothing more than use the environment as a prime cause.

The Internalist
View

Those in the internalist group argue that the seeds of change originate in internal variables, such as various forms of social organization. Proponents of the internal view see growth and change as a natural part of all societies. Thus, changes come from built-in patterns in organization, which archaeologists attempt to identify and which take the form of developmental cycles. (Chapters 4 and 11). External variables are usually seen as unpredictable, chance events, not worthy of much attention.

One example of an internalist approach is Norman Yoffee's explanation of the collapse of an empire that he derived from analysis of administrative records. These texts, from the Old Babylonian period (ca. 2000 to 1600 B.C.) in the Near East, provide a record of a bureaucracy expanding while the society it is trying to manage crumbles. For example, beginning in 1700 B.C., more and more agricultural officials were appointed to oversee production on plots of land divided into ever smaller administrative units. At the same time, it was getting more difficult to find enough laborers to work the fields. Not only did the bureaucracy fail to manage resources efficiently, but its growth placed an increased burden on those resources available to it. Ultimately, what was left of the Babylonian Empire collapsed under its own bureaucratic weight. Yoffee and others, such as Kent Flannery, trace this result to patterns inherent in the management of complex societies. Although details remain elusive, a general pattern seems clear. Bureaucracies take on the added function of self-perpetuation as well as the functions of management they were designed to carry out. This is one of the reasons that complex adaptive systems eventually fail to respond to new problems.

T. Patrick Culbert's *overshoot model* is an internalist view of how complex societies often fail to respond to a typical problem—a rapidly growing population (FIGURE 10-7). The overshoot model is based on the assumption that there is always a time lag between the appearance of a problem and a society's response to it. The lag becomes more harmful the more rapid the changes. For example, where a quickly expanding population "overshoots" food supply, there may already be too many people to feed before the problem is recognized. In this case, once the food shortage is finally perceived, the solutions a society adopts will tend to be stop-gap attempts to manage the immediate crisis. Such shortsighted measures can ultimately strain organization and ruin the society's economic base. The end result may be nearly total collapse of organization and large-scale loss of population. This overshoot model emphasizes that population size, or growth, itself may be less important to explaining collapse than how quickly population increases in relation to the ability of societies to find long-term solutions.

Culbert uses this model to explain the collapse of Classic Maya societies around A.D. 800. It also furnishes an internalist explanation for the collapse of Lagash, in Iraq. The decision makers of the city, faced with the problem of declining crop yields and a growing population, opted for the short-term solution of cutting fallow time in order to put more land under cultivation at any one time. Inadequate fallowing resulted in the long-term problem of even greater declines of productivity. This is discussed below (pp. 320–23) in more detail.

Internalist views are also expressed on a more grandiose scale. For decades, people have noticed that large agrarian and industrial states have risen and fallen in remarkably similar ways. In the early 1900s, Oswald Spengler proposed that such large states followed patterns of growth and decay similar to biological organisms. While this direct biological analogy is no longer fashionable, other internalist models of the developmental cycle of societies have taken its place. One recent model was proposed by Carroll Quigley in two mammoth volumes on the evolution of empires. According to Quigley, the basic component of a growing state is an *instrument of expansion,* such as trading groups or political units. Instruments are the heart of vigorous empires. They promote surplus production and invest it in new technologies and organizations that lead to expansion. The key internal change Quigley identifies is the transformation of instruments into bloated bureaucracies, which are incapable of sustaining growth.

Quigley identifies several stages in this transformation process. During "mixture" (I) the presence of a surplus and an instrument leads to a new civilization. "Gestation" (II) is a period of investing surpluses that leads to

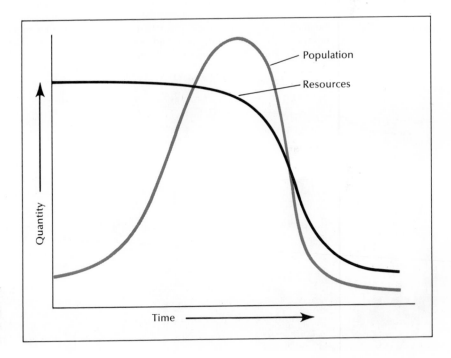

FIGURE **10-7**

The overshoot model applied to population in relation to resources.

an "expansion" (III) in the economy, population size, and territory. A period of "conflict" (IV), both internal and external, is replaced by a "golden age" (V). During this time of peace and prosperity, the instrument stagnates and a period of "decay" (VI) results, often followed by "invasion" (VII). This developmental cycle can be seen in the history of the Roman Empire, from a dynamic republic into a sluggish behemoth ruled by dictators and vulnerable to the invasions of barbarian hordes. It can also be seen in the development of aggressive and innovative businesses into multinational corporations that invest funds in improving existing products rather than risk their wealth in the development of new products.

What makes Quigley's scheme so unusual is its flexibility, which accommodates a number of different sequences of change. For example, in Stage VI (decay) the instrument can be reformed and a society can revert to either Stages III or IV. Also, Quigley makes predictions based on a society's stage of development. When two civilizations come into conflict, the winner, according to Quigley, will be the one closest to Stage II or III. Once an empire is identifiable, Quigley's model describes its general developmental cycle, but it does not explain when, where, or why this particular type of adaptive system will arise. Nevertheless, models such as Quigley's are useful to archaeologists trying to understand patterns in the remains of ancient empires (FIGURE 10-8).

FIGURE **10-8**   Events reflecting the developmental cycle of the British Empire: Below Sir Francis Drake is victorious in battle (late 1500s); on facing page at top is a scene in the bustling London of the mid-1700s, when it was the hub of an empire "on which the sun never set;" below, the "thin red line" of British troops marches bravely against American guerrillas fighting for freedom (1777).

Clearly the externalists and internalists consider important, but differing, aspects of change. A fuller view of the rise and fall of adaptive systems awaits the development of multicausal models that integrate external and internal aspects of change. In their present incomplete form, external models seem to be more useful for explaining patterns in simpler societies while internal models are more successful in handling complex societies.

Those who study trade are caught between these approaches. Demand for trade items is due to "internal" needs for "external" resources. The *colonial model of trade* is an example of internal/external causality. In order to export goods most efficiently and to receive imports in return, a society dependent on trade must establish outposts or colonies. Colonies help create markets in new areas and organize the flow of raw materials back to home base. These colonies can develop their own capacity for production and trade to the point that they become independent political entities and even competitors of the society that established them. Depending on their social and natural environments, they may even go through the same developmental cycle as their founding society (FIGURE 10-8). The British Empire furnishes an example of this colonial process. Our original thirteen colonies were first founded to supply European demands for raw materials. To pay for these resources the British sent back their own manufactured goods—ceramics, silver services, furniture, and others—as well as trade goods from elsewhere in the world, such as tea and spices. As the colonies prospered, organizations arose to manufacture goods from local raw materials, and colonial traders began to compete with the British in foreign markets. In response the British established tariffs to make goods produced in America or sold by Americans as expensive as those produced and sold by the British. It is no wonder that America's founding fathers include a silversmith and several well-known smugglers (FIGURE 4-9).

The United States "empire" is now well on its way through its own developmental cycle. We are all painfully aware that the process of colonial independence is continuing as we lose control of "our" foreign oil supplies. Clearly, this colonial scenario of change must include both internal and external variables. In fact, so must every useful explanation. For example, Quigley's internalist model describes general patterns in the way empires rise and fall, but it says little about where they will be located. The externalist nuclear area concept explains where empires will arise again and again and where they won't, but it says nothing about their internal structure or development. Both models furnish important, but incomplete, insights into change.

**How Does
Change Move?**

Our previous discussion of externalist and internalist viewpoints aimed to answer the first of the two fundamental questions: Where does change begin? To answer the second question—How does change move from element to element in adaptive systems?—archaeologists focus on the links between elements. To illustrate how such studies are conducted, we consider below some of the more likely scenarios of change.

Population
Scenarios

We begin our scenarios with changes in population size. Even though we seldom know why populations grow or decline, we do know that changes in population size dramatically affect the other elements of adaptive systems. For example, when population increases in a stable environment, the other elements of the adaptive system may respond in several ways. The most obvious possibility is that excess population can simply migrate. A second is that production can be intensified in order to increase food and other resources. Intensification, in turn, will involve new forms of technology, social organization, and ideology.

Binford combines both possibilities—migration and intensification—to explain why plants were domesticated. Just after the end of the last glacial advance (about 10,000 B.C.), Binford proposes, hunter-gatherers in the Near East began to establish more permanent communities by settling in coastal areas and exploiting shellfish and other sea animals available year-round. Freed from the rigors of constant travel, women gave birth more often and children had a better chance of survival. As populations increased in coastal areas, adaptive systems began to be strained to capacity. Binford suggests that under these conditions, where local resources were being exploited to their limits, surplus people migrated to neighboring zones. These regions were already inhabited, so that the additional population quickly strained carrying capacity (the number of people the environment could support) in these less-favored areas as well. This time, however, there was no release valve for excess people. The resulting stress, Binford believes, provided the impetus for experiments in domestication, such as the planting and tending of wild crops outside their normal habitats.

Over several millennia, domesticated plants became a larger portion of the diet, and populations continued to expand. Associated with these trends were identifiable changes in technology, social organization, and ideology (FIGURE 10-9). The archaeological remains of the technology of these early farming villages in the Near East include agricultural tools, granaries, ceramic cooking and storing containers, and dwellings with stone foundations. The technology of farming required new forms of social organization, including larger task groups required by agricultural work and new social relations in accord with the necessities of more permanent settlements. The new kind of organization that emerged was a farming village with its cluster of dwellings.

The change to this kind of settlement can be seen in the general shift through time from round or oval dwellings to square or rectangular ones. Ethnoarchaeological research suggests that circular structures, often portable tents, are usually built by nomadic or seminomadic groups, while square structures are used by fully sedentary communities. The reasons for this pattern relate to ease of construction. Nomadic groups usually prefer round

Multicausality □ **319**

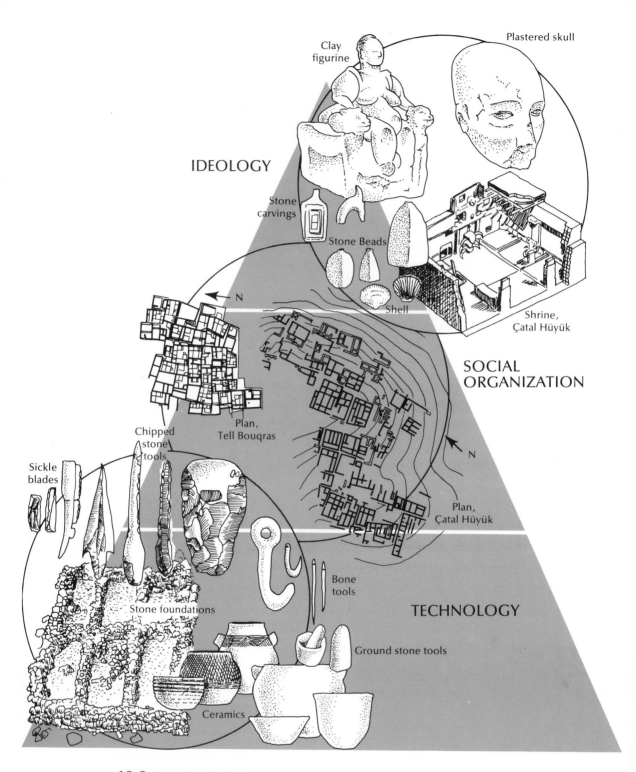

IDEOLOGY

Clay figurine

Plastered skull

Stone carvings

Stone Beads

Shell

Shrine, Çatal Hüyük

SOCIAL ORGANIZATION

N

Plan, Tell Bouqras

N

Plan, Çatal Hüyük

Chipped stone tools

Sickle blades

Bone tools

TECHNOLOGY

Stone foundations

Ground stone tools

Ceramics

FIGURE **10-9**   Related technology, social organization, and ideology in early tribal farming villages in the Near East.

houses because building them requires little effort. Square dwellings are worth the added effort in more permanent settlements because, among other things, as social units (and the corresponding need for housing) grow, additions can be made more easily. Thus, this change in dwellings is expectable as social units build more housing in response to the demands of a farming technology.

With the development of farming villages, land probably became a scarce resource subject to social controls affecting its ownership and transfer. Ethnographic research suggests that in such situations land would have been controlled by groups of families related by kinship. These social groups would have had shared values and an ideology and would have reinforced them through ritual and material symbols. The production of such material symbols would also have been encouraged as groups became more sedentary and material possessions no longer had to be moved frequently. Thus, it is likely that symbols of ideology would appear in the archaeological record of early farming villages. It is extremely difficult to separate socio-functional from ideo-functional artifacts, especially at this early time horizon; nevertheless, some artifacts strongly suggest ideo-functional uses. For example, at the site of Jericho, an early farming village in the Jordan Valley (ca. 7000 B.C.), human skulls were found carefully placed in the corners of some rooms. The skulls were covered with mud that was modeled into human faces with cowrie shell eyes (FIGURE 4-16). Although these curious items could function in a variety of ways, it is not difficult to envision them as cult objects, perhaps associated with ancestor worship, war rituals, or other arcane rites. Whatever they were, they were surely neither tools nor personal adornments.

The first part of this scenario, Binford's explanation relating population to carrying capacity and technology, remains to be tested. Archaeologists have yet to develop a satisfactory measure of carrying capacity. Further, there are no estimates of regional population size or evidence for migrations at this early period. The second part of the scenario, which begins after the process of plant domestication was underway and which links the material remains of technology to those of social organization and ideology, is more secure. We do know that technology, social organization, and ideology changed concurrently. Thus, while we still have not identified the causes behind agriculture, we have some idea of its consequences.

There are additional population scenarios. While intensification of technology may at first provide more resources to growing populations, it may eventually cause population collapse. For example, some modes of agricultural intensification may lead to the loss of soil nutrients, acceleration of erosion, or other results of "over"-exploitation. An example of this scenario may also be drawn from the Near East, where records in the form of baked clay tablets furnish evidence (FIGURE 10-10). Lagash was a growing city, one of the many that developed early along the Euphrates River in Iraq. Then, as now, rapid urban growth comes from rural populations attracted

FIGURE **10-10**

A tablet with cuneiform text, a writing system that flourished in the Near East between 3000 B.C. and the time of Christ.

by the more diverse economic opportunities of a city. As Lagash grew, more and more people were employed in community services, including the manufacture of items for trade and for the local elite. At the same time, more people worked on extending the city's irrigation network to help feed the rapidly increasing population. Cuneiform texts from 2300 to 1700 B.C. record that the burden of this increasing population weighed heavily on the land that supported it. A major problem created by canal irrigation is that the water table rises, increasing the concentration of salts in the A and B soil horizons. Very few crops grow well in saline soils of this type. The only way to solve the problem is to allow fields to lie fallow long enough for the water table to lower and for other natural processes to slowly carry away the salts. In the case of Lagash, this periodic resting of fields seems to have fallen victim to the need for additional food. The result was predictable. The production records show a downward trend in crop yield and the growing popularity of salt-tolerant crops. Ultimately, even these plants yielded too little for the human effort involved. The decline in productivity set in motion population decrease and organizational collapse. By 1600 B.C., where once there were miles of green fields and a bustling city, there was only an inhospitable desert and ruins (FIGURE 10-11).

A third population scenario is possible—decline due to changes in the social environment. We might expect that, as population decreases, so will its capacity to maintain complex technologies and social organizations. The historical record from the southeastern United States furnishes an example of this process. In the year 1539, the Spanish explorer Hernando Soto (commonly called De Soto in grade-school history books) landed in Florida with 600 men, 200 horses, and a herd of pigs. For several years Soto explored large areas of the southeastern United States. Throughout the journey his party encountered large communities at a chiefdom level of organization subsisting on a mix of agriculture and hunting and gathering. The Soto expedition had two effects on this indigenous population. The first was the death of large numbers of people through warfare and the introduction of European diseases. The second was the use of great quantities of stored corn for food. Soto's men and pigs ate everything, including the seed corn for future crops. These predations seriously affected a number of societies. Population reduction and loss of resources led some communities to abandon agriculture and return completely to hunting and gathering. Among these groups, social organization became correspondingly less complex.

Other
Scenarios
There are many additional scenarios that archaeologists are documenting in order to trace specific links through adaptive systems. Some interesting questions and potential answers concerning the causes of change are also being investigated. For example, archaeologists have found that the same causes can have different effects on different adaptive systems—some societies recovered from Soto's visit, some did not. Other studies show that different causes can have the same effect; populations declined both at Lagash and in the historical southeastern United States, but for different reasons.

These instructive cases return to us the question. In any given society, what course will change take? At present we cannot answer this question with any certainty. Most archaeologists believe that our explanatory impotence is due to the fact that additional factors, some of which we haven't identified, some of which we don't yet know how to measure, influence changes. Combining internalist and externalist positions and building workable multicausal models remains to be accomplished. Perhaps one of the readers of this book will do it.

FIGURE **10-11**

At top, a representation of part of the surface of an alabaster vase from the ancient Sumerian city of Warka, in Iraq, showing a land of plenty, the result of irrigation; at left, a detail from the actual vase. On facing page, a view of Warka today, an arid desert that resulted from mismanagement of resources.

Explaining Modern Change

It is obvious that archaeological explanation is incomplete. Some think that this is because archaeology's perspective is limited to artifacts. In fact, archaeologists have looked with great envy on behavioral scientists who study modern society, believing that they have been successful in understanding human behavior. But if the goal of behavioral science is to explain and predict behavior, then the many failures of applied behavioral science clearly indicate it is far from succeeding. Pruitt Igoe, a multimillion-dollar urban

FIGURE **10-12**   Part of The Pruitt-Igoe Housing Complex in St. Louis, Missouri, at the moment of demolition.

renewal project in St. Louis, testifies to that. Built with the best intentions of providing low-cost housing for the poor, it was widely hailed as a showplace of urban renewal; it even won awards for its intelligent design. Unfortunately, the planner's expectations of the residents' behaviors were at odds with reality. Insufficient trash containers, easy access for vandals, poor design for upkeep, and similar flaws made life less than idyllic in Pruitt Igoe. As conditions deteriorated, distrust and fearfulness grew among the residents. Eventually the situation became intolerable; the few tenants left were evacuated and the entire complex was demolished—blown up before a national television audience in 1973 (FIGURE 10-12).

We may know something about behavior and its relation to beliefs and artifacts, but not nearly enough. To cope with gas shortages we need to know more about how people use cars, to conserve resources we need to know more about how they are wasted, and to avoid disasters like Pruitt Igoe we need to know more about the developmental cycles of low-income households and their relationship to artifacts, activities, and activity areas.

All elements of society are interrelated. Although, as archaeologists, we are most interested in the relation between artifacts and human behavior, we recognize that no perspective by itself is complete. Let us suppose, for example, that food waste in a certain neighborhood was found to be 10 pounds a week per household according to the Garbage Project (Chapter 2), and only 1 pound per week by an interview survey. Is the Garbage Project information closer to reality than the interview-survey data? No, both sets of data describe real elements of an adaptive system. In order to "explain" food waste behavior, both elements are essential. In this case, that people do not realize how much food they waste (a fact that derives from taking *both* sets of data together) may be one explanation for why the waste continues. It is often such interactions as these between beliefs, activities, and artifacts that influence the direction of change.

Managing a complex society requires looking at human behavior from many points of view. A new conceptual scheme is forming that focuses on understanding the interaction of the beliefs, behaviors, and artifacts of societies in order to anticipate changes. Now, when artifacts are such an important part of our adaptation—and the only certainty we face is rapid change—the archaeologist's perspective is particularly important. For the new conceptual scheme (Chapter 12) archaeologists can provide long-term data on trends in human behavior; furnish methods, manpower, and basic concepts to record artifacts and behavior in modern societies; and investigate basic principles of change. It is clear that, whether archaeologists work in the dirt or in our cities, they are studying the same thing. When we ponder the fall of the Maya, we are mulling over possible scenarios of our own civilization's demise.

In order to tell which scenario is in our future, we need to examine the record of past changes and identify the long-term trends carrying forward today. It is to some of these trends that we turn in Chapter 11.

Gordon Randolph Willey (b. 1914)   Gordon Randolph Willey has earned his position as one of the most respected archaeologists of our time. In 1942 Willey began a long career of surveying and excavating at archaeological sites strewn across North, Middle, and South America (including Peru, Ecuador, Panama, Guatemala, Honduras, and Belize) and the southeastern United States. He has led an expedition into the field in every year but three of the last 38.   □   In the midst of this heavy schedule, Willey has been a pioneer in giving direction to archaeological method and theory. He has written more than thirty books and monographs, and in 1953, he published the classic *Prehistoric Settlement Patterns in the Virú Valley,* which won him a Viking Fund Medal and formed the basis for settlement pattern studies that are a cornerstone of contemporary archaeology. Also in the 1950s, he produced, with Philip Phillips, *Method and Theory in American Archaeology,* the first systematic summary of the discipline.   □   Digging shellmounds in Panama or sorting potsherds at Maya sites could not keep Willey from reading staggering numbers of archaeological reports in his search for the large patterns of prehistory. His book on method and theory showed that the archaeological sequences of North, Middle, and South America had similar stages of development. His most monumental work of scholarship—*An Introduction to American Archaeology*—expanded on this idea in a synthesis of the archaeology of the New World. This two-volume opus, which places detail within a grand scheme, has earned him the title of "great synthesizer" in archaeological myth.   □   One further accomplishment deserves brief mention. In 1933, as an undergraduate track star and captain of the University of Arizona track team, Willey won the 150-yard dash in the record-setting time of 14.7, which remains unbeaten; his archaeological records may be just as hard to beat.

Gordon R. Willey in the Virú Valley.

11

THE COURSE
OF CULTURE

Americans tend to look back on the decade of the fifties as a golden age, when life was more fulfilling and less complicated. Other societies have had their golden ages as well. The classical Greeks' shining image of their past gave the Golden Age its name. The Aztecs envied and worshipped their Toltec predecessors. In Britain some still bask in the glory of an empire where once the sun never set.

In our case it is usually forgotten that those "happy days" included the Korean War, McCarthyism, some of the bleakest periods of the Cold War, and blatant racial discrimination and sexism. The reality of other golden ages was often equally distorted. Plato's temples of solid gold would have been impossible to construct, and both the Toltec and British empires were built on unrestrained colonial exploitation.

Naive beliefs about the past, innocent enough on the surface, are often cited as historical precedents for present-day policies and actions of far-ranging effect. Early explorers in what is now the eastern United States discovered spectacular burial and temple mounds and other remains of older and more complex societies (FIGURE 11-1). By the early nineteenth century, explanations for the massive earthworks abounded, though none attributed them to the ancestors of historic American Indians. While candidates came and went—wandering groups from the Phoenicians to the lost tribes of Israel were given credit for the constructions—the basic scenario remained the same: the Mound Builders represented a golden age that had mys-

FIGURE **11-1**

Serpent Mound, Ohio, a monumental earthwork of the Woodland culture (see FIGURE 9-6), has long been the subject of speculation as to its builders.

teriously vanished before the arrival of the American Indian. Because of archaeology, we now know that the ancestors of historic Indian tribes did, in fact, construct the mounds.

The Mound Builder myth was not a harmless belief; in robbing Indians of their past it fit well with the prejudices of early nineteenth-century America that Indians were inferior. And this belief, in turn, was the justification for those who exterminated Indians and drove them from their lands. Thus, since policies of great significance are often influenced by our understanding of the past, it may be that the most important application of archaeology is in making that understanding as complete as possible.

Since archaeologists study behavior from artifacts, and since all societies, past and present, use and leave behind artifacts, the entire sweep of cultural evolution falls within our grasp. When the whole history of human societies and artifacts is on view, the difficulties of doing archaeology are dwarfed by the clear trends of change that are made visible. By taking a long-term perspective, we see ourselves not as voyagers adrift in time, but as part of the wave of history on whose crest we ride.

In this chapter, in order to see the trends in cultural development, we put aside our examination of methods and emphasize general results, summarizing patterns in human history.

CULTURAL DEVELOPMENT

As early as 1836, Christian Jurgensen Thomsen noted that there were obvious differences among the artifact inventories of ancient societies in his native Denmark. The earliest societies produced tools made only of stone. In later ones some tools were fashioned of bronze. Iron-working was added still later. Many similar markers of change have been described; their accumulation has given us more detail than Thomsen's original three-age system. Even at the grossest level, in both the New and Old Worlds, we now

have five-age systems. For the Old World, the ages are Paleolithic, Mesolithic, Neolithic, Bronze Age, and Iron Age. (This simply subdivides Thomsen's Stone (lithic) Age into Paleo-, Meso-, and Neo-lithic.) The New World
stages are Paleo-Indian, Archaic, Formative, Classic, and Postclassic. Old
World and New World stages are in close correspondence; we will use them
as a framework in the following overview of the evolution of human societies. To illustrate change, we will focus on tools, energy sources, subsistence
patterns, community size and distribution, and social differentiation and integration.

Great controversies rage around the few fragmentary fossils of our
most remote ancestors. Those from Olduvai Gorge, the Omo Basin, and
Lake Turkana indicate that humanlike creatures appeared in East Africa
about 5 million years ago. The Paleolithic, however, begins with the first
crude tools, which date to 2 million years ago. We leave to paleoanthropologists the arduous task of reconstructing our evolutionary tree, and turn to
the more plentiful evidence of early toolmaking.

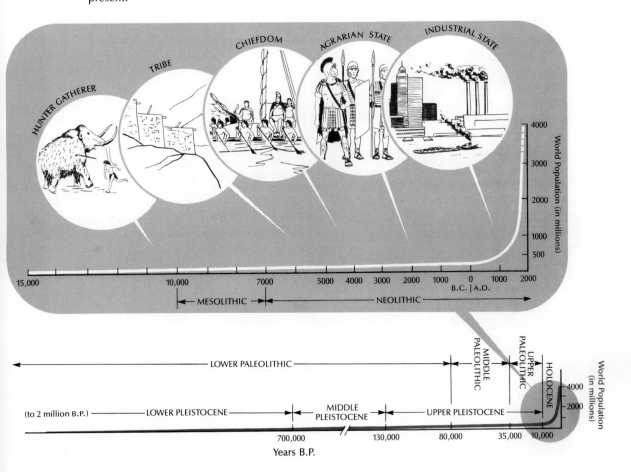

FIGURE **11-3**   Australopithecines in an artist's reconstruction. Most archaeologists believe that these human-like creatures were responsible for the Oldowan artifacts.

Paleolithic/ Paleo-Indian   The Paleolithic (Old Stone Age) can be divided into three periods—Lower, Middle, and Upper (FIGURE 11-2). Within the Paleolithic there were four major glacial advances and retreats; their effects on the course of cultural change are unclear. Nevertheless, when the three periods are reviewed in terms of the variables we have chosen to consider, there are major differences in the lifeways that characterize each.

Lower Paleolithic   The *Lower Paleolithic*, a huge expanse of time that covers most of human history, is further divided into the *Oldowan* and *Acheulian* periods. The Oldowan artifacts, made by humanlike creatures called *Australopithecines* (FIGURE 11-3), are found mainly in the tropical areas of Africa and Asia; those of the *Acheulian*, made by populations of *Homo erectus* (FIGURE 11-4), show a wider distribution that includes the colder, temperate zones of Europe and Asia.

The pebble tools of the Oldowan are exactly that—pebbles with a few flakes struck off to form a simple cutting edge (FIGURE 11-5). Although pebble tools and flakes do not fall into neat techno-functional types, they no doubt were used for a variety of tasks including cutting, scraping, and chopping. Some archaeologists believe that, in addition to stone tools, Oldowan populations made tools from animal bones, teeth, and horns. This view is losing ground as archaeologists have shown that hyenas, porcupines, and other animals can leave similar deposits of broken bones in caves and elsewhere (Chapter 6).

Although there is no direct evidence of plant use, the wide variety of animal bones found in association with stone tools indicates that our Oldowan forebears were probably *omnivorous*, eating anything they could find. As far as meat is concerned, most archaeologists suggest that they were scavengers who fought hyenas and vultures for carrion. To test this idea, Louis Leakey (Chapter 6) and his two sons foraged on a savannah for a week with nothing but pebble tools and animal bones. The Leakeys were very successful, though probably a sight, prancing naked across the plain, frightening off scavengers, and butchering dead animals. Artifact debris indicates that ancient camps were probably occupied no longer than a few days by social units of only a few individuals. There is no evidence of social differentiation, either within or between communities.

FIGURE **11-4**   *Homo erectus,* here conceived in the process of shaping an Acheulian handaxe.

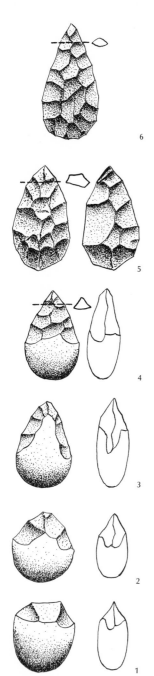

The Acheulian period is marked by the presence of tool kits, which include the first standardized artifacts. In fact, it derives its name from the most distinctive of these, the *Acheulian handaxe*. Manufacture of this tool involved bifacial flaking of a core into a rough pear shape. Grasped at the base, it could be used for controlled cutting, scraping, or chopping. Handaxes did not appear suddenly; in fact, the gradual technological change from pebble tools to handaxes (FIGURE 11-5) can be seen in places like Morocco and Olduvai Gorge. This transition, however, did not occur everywhere. In Asia, pebble tools persisted hundreds of thousands of years longer in a somewhat more standardized form known as the Chopper-chopping tool tradition.

The expansion of populations out of the tropics into colder temperate zones was partly the result of the harnessing of the first energy source beyond human muscles. Several sites from this later part of the Lower Paleolithic, including Choukoutien Cave in China and the open beach site of Terra Amata on the French Riviera, show clear evidence that fire had been brought under control for cooking and probably for warmth and protection. Despite the antiquity of these locations, seeds and bones and other clues to subsistence have been found at some Acheulian and Chopper-chopping tool sites. The people who left these remains were clearly omnivorous; but in addition to scavenging, hunting was an important activity. At Choukoutien, moderate-size quarry such as deer were taken; while at Torralba and Ambrona, in Spain, hunters mired, killed, and butchered mammoths.

The later period of the Lower Paleolithic provides the first clear evidence for structures and for functional differences in settlements. Post molds and stone foundations for perishable shelters were found at Terra Amata, which was probably a base camp. No structures were found at Torralba and Ambrona, which were kill sites, or Tazazmount, a lithic workshop in the Sahara Desert. All evidence, slim though it is, suggests that Acheulian populations were organized at a band level in small communities. As far as we can tell, these were still highly mobile groups; but they did return repeatedly to favored locations, such as Choukoutien, where over 100 feet of deposits accumulated.

A few hints of social differentiation appear in the second period of the Lower Paleolithic. Hunting, especially of large game, probably required task groups. Some archaeologists believe that social boundaries divided the people who made handaxes from those who made choppers. Karl Hutterer, on the other hand, has suggested that the difference is simply utilitarian. He argues that in eastern Asia, a combination of chopping tools and tools made from perishable materials, such as bamboo, would have been equivalent to handaxes. These contrasting views are the basis of another debate over the causes of variability in the archaeological record.

FIGURE **11-5**   Early chipped-stone tools from the Paleolithic period: *1–4* are the relatively simple Oldowan pebble tools; next, a more complex chopping tool; and, at top, the more fully evolved Acheulian handaxe.

In the Middle Paleolithic, known as the *Mousterian* in Europe, a large number of new artifacts appeared; François Bordes recognized more than sixty basic types of chipped-stone implements from this period. Some, such as the *burin*, which is assumed to be a bone-working implement, indicate increased specialization of tools. Sophisticated techniques, such as Levallois flaking (Chapter 8), were extensively used. Certainly, by this period, clothing was being made of animal skins.

Artifacts provide little other evidence of change in subsistence or settlement patterns from the Acheulian, except to document the further expansion of populations through the Old World. As for earlier periods, the impression is of small and highly mobile groups, in this case *Homo sapiens,* our modern genus and species. An important new element was the first use of artifacts symbolically. Archaeologists have found large caches of bear skulls buried in stone-lined pits in caves. The first human burials indicate the existence of some form of funeral, which probably served to recognize and symbolize differences in social standing. Tool kits in Mousterian sites are highly variable from level to level, which has given rise to the Bordes/Binford debates over whether the differences are stylistic or utilitarian (Chapter 4)—a disagreement far from resolved.

The *Upper Paleolithic* signals more and more rapid change. During this period, human groups first entered the New World and Australia. Although there is some debate about the actual date at which people crossed the Bering Straits (Chapter 6), it is agreed that they reached the southern tip of South America by 10,000 B.C. The major technological innovation was the production of blades, a process that originated in the Old World. During this period, the variety of stone tools proliferated greatly and the technical skill involved in their production increased. At this time also bone artifacts, such as harpoons, awls, and needles, were produced in greater quantities. Faunal remains from Upper Paleolithic sites indicate that populations in Europe and the Near East hunted migratory herd animals, such as reindeer and horses, that could be killed in large numbers at one time. Some investigators have suggested that communities grew because of the increased amount of food made available by such kills. In the most favorable areas communities probably ranged somewhere between twenty-five and one hundred people.

One place where communities were heavily concentrated was the Dordogne, in southern France, an area made famous by a new and intriguing artifact—the cave painting (FIGURE 11-6). For generations, modern Europeans were aware of paintings located deep within caves. The composition, draftsmanship, and pigments of these paintings were believed to be too sophisticated to have been made by barbarians who hunted with stone tools. Once authenticated as prehistoric, these paintings of animals and abstract signs became more than an oddity; they were recognized as ancient symbols of human creativity. More recently they have been scrutinized for clues to the beliefs of Paleolithic peoples. Leroi-Gourhan studied the distribution of

FIGURE **11-6** A conception of the artist at work creating the famous Upper Paleolithic cave paintings of the Hall of the Bulls at Lascaux in the Dordogne, France (ca. 15,000-13,000 B.C.). The artist is a member of our species, *Homo sapiens,* and so is anatomically indistinguishable from modern man.

paintings within seventy-three caves to identify patterns in their locations. He found, for example, that animals and other elements often occur in sets. While still enigmatic, these patterns indicate an underlying set of beliefs that, Leroi-Gourhan suggests, is largely concerned with sex.

Alexander Marshack, also interested in studying symbolic designs, focused on sets of parallel lines scratched onto bone artifacts. Such markings were usually interpreted as counts of animals killed in single hunts. On the basis of his studies using electron microscopes and X-ray photography, Marshack argues that the marks in each set were not made all at once and that every seventh and twenty-eighth (and in some cases one hundred fortieth) line is longer or deeper. Combined, these two patterns may be evidence that Upper Paleolithic people were marking off days in relation to short and long cycles of the moon. With such a device it would have been possible to predict the seasonal migration of herd animals and the ripening of wild plants.

Other art forms made their appearance during the Upper Paleolithic. "Venus" figurines of carved stone are probably some of the best-known examples. These small, amply endowed female figures, with their exaggeration of particular sexual features (FIGURE 11-7), make Leroi-Gourhan's hypothesis more plausible.

Cave paintings, "Venus" figurines, other artwork, and even some tools —such as large, finely chipped Solutrean knives and spearpoints and Magdalenian harpoons (FIGURE 11-8)—all indicate the presence of at least some part-time specialists. The ideo-functional works of these specialists, because they were symbolic, served to integrate the larger Upper Paleolithic communities through rituals. It is probably no coincidence that the areas in western Europe where cave paintings are found are also areas that had large populations. Burials show little social differentiation, and the general impression is of larger, but still fairly homogeneous, communities.

Aside from blade technology and dependence on large game animals, the New World *Paleo-Indian* period did not share many characteristics with western Europe. It was, however, a more typical Upper Paleolithic phenomenon: there were only a few kinds of tools, and the main implements were distinctive varieties of spearpoints and knives (FIGURE 11-9). Paleo-Indian populations are known mainly from isolated finds and kill sites such as

FIGURE **11-7**

Upper Paleolithic "Venus" figurine
from Willendorf, Germany
(ca. 20,000 B.C.).

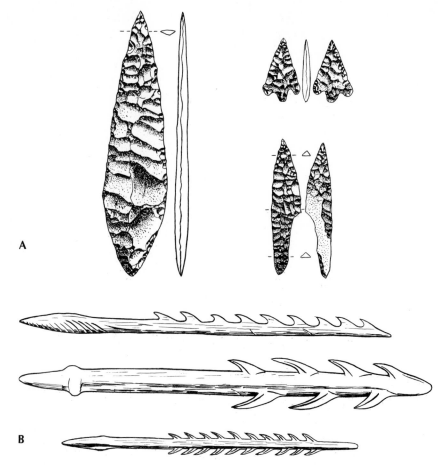

FIGURE **11-8**   Upper Paleolithic artifacts: above, Solutrean knives and spearpoints, and below, Magdalenian harpoons of carved bone.

Naco and Lehner in southern Arizona. A few base camps, such as Linden-meier in northern Colorado, have also been found. The groups that left these remains are thought to have been highly nomadic hunters, but we have almost no data on which to estimate their dependence on plant foods. Mac-Neish has said that a group lucky enough to kill a mammoth probably never stopped talking about it; in fact, archaeologists never stop talking about how many mammoths these groups did kill (Chapter 6).

Mesolithic/   The *Mesolithic* in Europe, beginning around 10,000 B.C., marks the end of
Archaic   the Upper Paleolithic lifeway. Many of the favorite big-game herd mammals of Upper Paleolithic hunters were dying out, particularly in Europe and the Americas. Whether this was due to overexploitation, climate change, or

FIGURE **11-9**

Clovis points associated with mammoth remains at the Lehner Paleo-Indian kill and butchering site in southeastern Arizona (ca. 9,000 B.C.). Shown in the inset are Clovis points from the nearby and contemporaneous Naco site. Note the variations in length among points.

FIGURE **11-10**   Mesolithic tools (facing page) and an artist's reconstruction of a typical Mesolithic community. Most of these tools, or "microliths," were set in wooden holders or handles.

more drastic temperature fluctuations from season to season made little difference to the hunters. Clearly, new subsistence strategies had to be devised. The Mesolithic is viewed as a broadening of the subsistence base, a period of intensive foraging and experimentation with new resources. The floral and faunal remains from Star Carr suggest that people lived by collecting plants and hunting small animals. In regions near lakes, rivers, and the sea, fish and shellfish became an important part of the diet for the first time.

About the same time as the Mesolithic in Europe, a similar *Archaic* lifeway developed from the Paleo-Indian pattern in most areas throughout the New World. One example in western North America is the *Desert Culture,* a generalized hunting and gathering lifeway that used new technologies—baskets, nets, grinding stones, and others—to make use of everything edible that grew or moved.

The most distinctive new tools of the Archaic were grinding stones, probably used for milling seeds; the most distinctive new tools of the Mesolithic were *microliths,* small blades and blade fragments that were set into wooden hafts and used to cut and scrape (FIGURE 11-10). In the Mesolithic/Archaic the number of settlements increased. As might be expected, these small Mesolithic communities had few artifacts with obvious ideo-functions. Also, there were major differences in artifacts from region to region. Some of these differences can be attributed to environmental factors; others, however, may be stylistic and may mark social boundaries.

Mesolithic and Archaic populations expanded into almost every known environment, including some of the world's harshest deserts and frozen tundras. Population, in general, seems to have increased throughout this time; but the days of easy pickings were over. Groups had to "settle in" and learn to exploit a large number of local resources with a minimum of movement. The success of the Mesolithic/Archaic adaptation is indicated by the increased size and length of occupation of some settlements by the end of the period. A few of these communities became the first permanent villages; more soon followed.

**Neolithic/
Formative**

The factors that prompted the development of the sedentary communities of the *Neolithic/Formative* lifeway were apparently widespread, as it seems to have arisen independently many times in the Old and New Worlds. Some permanent villages, such as those in Japan by 9000 B.C., and on the coast of Peru by 6000 B.C., were based on the exploitation of shellfish and other seafoods. Most others, however, depended on domesticated plants and/or animals. Major centers of domestication included southwest Asia and the Zagros Mountains of Iraq (for wheat and related grains, goats, sheep, pigs, cattle, and a variety of fruits and vegetables); Mesoamerica, especially the central Mexican highlands (for maize, pinto beans, chili peppers, avocado, other plants, and turkeys); highland Peru (for potatoes, sweet potatoes, lima beans, and guinea pigs); lowland South America (for manioc); tropical southeast Asia (for breadfruit, taro, rice, coconut, yams, sugar cane, pigs, and chickens); eastern North America (for sunflowers); sub-Saharan Africa (for millet and other grains); and Europe (for barley). Although the reasons for domestication are still poorly understood, once specific plants were cultivated, they were rapidly adopted by surrounding communities. The domestication of new crops continues to this day. Brewers cultivate special varieties of yeast, experimental plantings are being made of kelp, several varieties of pine trees are planted as crops for increased lumber yields, and salmon, shrimp, and lobster are on the verge of domestication.

Domesticated plants were important to settled villagers in both the Old and New Worlds. The case with animals was otherwise; because of a lack of suitable characteristics, few were domesticated in the New World and none was used for pulling cart or plow. In the Old World, domesticated animals were a potential energy source, and early depictions in the Near East of carts pulled by cattle or aurochs show that they did not remain a potential for long. In fact, as the farming lifeway spread, animal power for pulling plows or turning millstones became essential to successful agriculture in some areas.

Subsistence in settled villages has been discussed. It is important only to note that, contrary to popular belief, almost all village farmers still hunted and gathered. Nevertheless, it is also clear that these activities were of secondary importance and that agriculture had now pushed into almost every corner of the earth, either because hunter-gatherers adopted the new lifeway, or because they were rudely displaced by farmers.

When archaeologists began studying domestication they noticed that new tools were associated with new crops. Polished stone axes (presumably for clearing fields), harvesting tools, and ground stone tools for milling grains were the most obvious. From these new stone tools came the name *Neolithic*. It did not take long, however, to realize that ground and polished stone tools were also found in the Mesolithic and Archaic, but in the Old World the term Neolithic remained. The Neolithic and Formative should more properly be called the "Age of Containers" in view of the dramatic increase of artifacts for holding people and things—houses and storehouses, storage pits, and pottery.

In regions where farming was practiced, people began building more substantial houses. These provide clear material evidence for an increase in the number of communities. The remains of houses also indicate that, while most settlements were relatively small, some became quite large. For example, early village sites in the Near East run the gamut from the few houses of Jarmo to the hundreds of houses and other structures of contemporaneous Çatal Hüyük (FIGURE 11-11). Such differences in size suggest a settlement hierarchy, with the few large communities performing political and economic functions for the more numerous small ones surrounding them.

The farming lifeway required a new type of organization—the tribe. To make and use all the artifacts of an agricultural community, we may suppose, required a growth in the number of task groups. Within communities, differences in the goods placed with burials lead us to suspect that there were increased differences in social roles and social standing. Along with this social differentiation, archaeologists have found an explosion of artifacts that seem to be symbols related to beliefs and ideology. Complicated pottery designs and "ceremonial" objects and structures are common to Neolithic villages (FIGURE 10-9).

At the regional level, local styles became distinctive as style zones shrank in size. At the same time as this increase in differentiation, there is evidence for increased integration among regions through the trade of raw

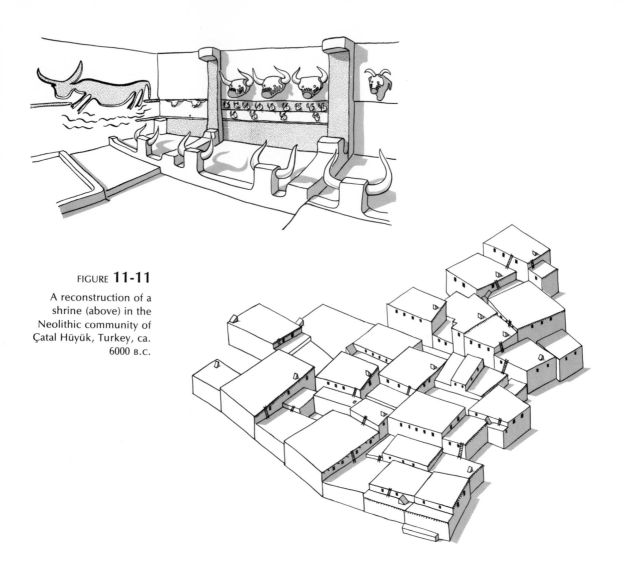

FIGURE **11-11**

A reconstruction of a shrine (above) in the Neolithic community of Çatal Hüyük, Turkey, ca. 6000 B.C.

materials and artifacts. Although long-distance trade did begin earlier, it escalated in the Neolithic. Nevertheless, trade was most likely a down-the-line movement from individual to individual, rather than movement by merchant groups.

As Neolithic villages continued to increase in number, many continued to grow in size. A few of these large villages formed economic and social ties to neighboring communities and became the centers of a new kind of regional system—the chiefdom. Architecture and grave goods support this inference and demonstrate that social inequality had become an important factor in social organization. For example, between 1500 and 500 B.C. several large regional centers developed in Mexico—San Lorenzo, La Venta, and other Olmec settlements on the Gulf Coast; typical of these were multi-ton carved stone heads and large ceremonial pyramids and platforms. At the same time, in highland Oaxaca, San José Mogote was a substantial settlement, with evidence for craft production of trade items such as magnetite mirrors. These and other similar Formative sites were tied together through a trade network that extended over hundreds of kilometers and included basic resources, such as obsidian cutting tools, and socio-functional goods, such as decorated pottery, carved shells, and mirrors.

Bronze Age/ Classic   At some point, these types of precocious Formative systems reached a size where it is convenient to label them as agrarian states (Chapter 3). Such judgments are always arbitrary, for, as we noted, growing societies change gradually. A few decades ago, archaeologists of the Old World believed that changes in social organization were directly related to changes in technology. Focusing on the production of metals, they distinguished Bronze Age societies from Iron Age societies. In the New World the terms used to label similar levels of complexity are *Classic* and *Postclassic*. Whatever terms are used, at this stage we are dealing with state societies of substantially increased complexity founded on a stable agricultural base. The six early complex societies that developed more or less independently are the Sumerian in the Tigris-Euphrates River Valley, the ancient Egyptian, the Harappan civilization in the Indus River Valley, the Shang Dynasty of northeast China, Teotihuacán in the Basin of Mexico, and the Moche of highland Peru (FIGURE 11-12). The areas of fertile lands and dependable water sources where these agrarian states began are, in a real sense, nuclear areas that provided the resource base for large populations.

Major changes in basic types of tools took place only in the Old World, where experiments led quickly from the use of copper to bronze to iron. At first, metallurgy was relevant to warfare and little else. In both the Old and New Worlds the significant changes in technology and social organization occurred in the areas of production and distribution. Innovations, such as the potter's wheel in the Near East and changes in the size and organization of task groups, led to the mass production of pots, textiles, tools, and other commodities long before our industrial age. Traders supplied large volumes of raw materials, sometimes from long distances, and distributed the finished products through regional systems and beyond. Simple examples include the commonplace beveled-rim bowls of major Sumerian cities; the clear sign of Teotihuacán contact—thin orangeware and green obsidian; and the ultimate in standardization seen in the regular size of mud bricks used to build Harappa. Some of these items were transported by the new technology of sailing ships, which seem to have been used mainly in southwest Asia where Near Eastern and Indus civilizations traded by sea. In fact, the Indus site of Lothal, located at the mouth of the Indus River in present-day Pakistan, was a seaport.

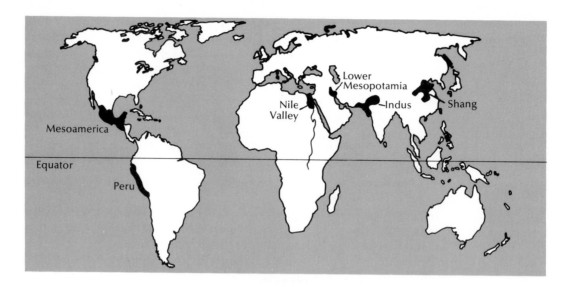

FIGURE **11-12**

Six centers at which complex state societies developed independently. At right, is a reconstruction of a city from one of these—the Sumerian (ca. 2000 B.C.)—that shows the Temple of Ishtar-Kitituon in its setting in the city of Ishchali.

Subsistence was based on specializations. In the Near East, major occupations included farming, fishing, and herding. But societies were more than just basic subsistence specialists. Potters, weavers, builders, and other artisans produced goods to supply the needs of farmers and herders or to exchange for outside resources. This degree of extreme specialization meant that few people were self-sufficient and most depended on a complicated system for exchanging their goods. To keep pace with increasing differentiation, other specialists with expertise in organization and integration were added. We know, for example, that in early Near Eastern cities the exchange of products was managed through temples, palaces, and certain large estates that were also centers from which the beliefs and rules behind many social relations emanated.

With all of this specialization, the size of the minimum group needed to make society work was large. Some Sumerian cities of 2000 B.C. had populations over 30,000; and Teotihuacán, at A.D. 600, had a population that may have exceeded 125,000. The simple settlement hierarchies of the Formative solidified into highly differentiated regional systems. At the center of these systems were large cities, such as Kish in the Near East or Chan Chan in Peru, with satellite towns, villages, and more specialized settlements in the surrounding sustaining regions.

Increased economic specialization was associated with social inequality. This could be seen in the building of tombs and elaborate palaces. Within this environment of social inequality, it was obviously important to promote social integration. Artifacts of a special kind played a prominent role in this promotion. For Americans, the Statue of Liberty, the White House, the Sears Tower in Chicago, and the two Disneylands are such artifacts. For the earliest civilizations, these include the Great Pyramids of Egypt, the ziggurats of the Near East, the Temple of the Sun at Teotihuacán, the Huaca del Sol at Moche, the citadels of Harappan cities, and the walled ceremonial precincts and palaces of Shang China (FIGURE 11-13). These are giant ideo-functional artifacts, created by organizing and collecting people and resources. Roland Fletcher, as we pointed out in Chapter 9, calls them "monstrous visual symbols" (MVSs). These MVSs often represent the major institutions of society. It is interesting that in the United States, churches, factories, and civic buildings are often dwarfed by buildings housing banks, oil and insurance companies, and sports arenas. Members of the upper class of a society can take on the character of MVSs through conspicuous public displays of wealth, such as in elaborate funerals.

Iron Age/ Postclassic

The Iron Age/Postclassic is a variation on Bronze Age/Classic themes. As such, the dividing line between them is extremely blurred. First, mass production becomes a powerful force in social integration. High-quality craft items that were restricted in use to the upper classes during the Classic are copied, mass-produced, and widely distributed. MVSs become less monstrous, but visible in more places. Both of these features of the Postclassic

A

B

C

D

FIGURE **11-13** Some Monstrous Visual Symbols of early civilizations: *A*, the ziggurat at Ur, Iraq
(ca. 2100 B.C.); *B*, the pyramids of Giza, Egypt (ca. 2600 B.C.); *C*, the Royal Shang
tomb at Hou Chuang, Honan, China (ca. 1300 B.C.); *D*, the citadel of
Mohenjo-Daro, Pakistan (ca. 2400 B.C.); *E*, Huaca del Sol of the Moche, Peru (ca.
A.D. 200); and *F*, the Temple of the Sun, Teotihuacán, Mexico (ca. A.D. 100).

can be illustrated in the Maya area, where rare "figural polychromes" were replaced by abundant Yucatecan "dribble wares" and where large temples and palaces gave way to a scattering of small upper-class residences, each complete with a shrine (FIGURE 11-14). The Classic/Postclassic transition involves the substitution of quantity for quality. Archaeologists tend to view this as a general indication of degeneration or social decay. A second difference between Classic and Postclassic is the increased importance of the military and of warfare in the Postclassic, as evidenced in artwork, monuments, weapons, and military and colonial sites involved in empire building.

Just as hunter-gatherer and farming lifeways spread, so too did states. Such complex societies differ from their simpler precursors in that they never seem to achieve stability. The drive for new resources and new markets leads to colonization and empire building. This process does not continue indefinitely. Sooner or later, limits, whether technological, organizational, or environmental, are reached and the processes of growth reverse. A Postclassic society usually ends in the collapse of social integration. Social units, such as communities and regional systems, become smaller and less differentiated and populations become more dispersed. Eventually, new regional systems may begin to expand again, especially in nuclear areas, leading to another Classic/Postclassic cycle.

Colonial expansion and empire building lead to the creation of *secondary states*. As empires expand, their traders and sometimes their missionaries are the first to contact neighboring societies, where they attempt to promote the material lifestyles and ideologies of states. As information filters back to the seat of power, the military soon follows on the heels of traders and missionaries. Thus, either by conscious emulation or by coercion, new regions are brought into state systems. So were France and England brought into the Roman Empire; so, some archaeologists argue, were the Maya of Kaminaljuyu brought into the Teotihuacán Empire.

Until the Industrial Revolution, regions could be divided into three types on the basis of their histories: *marginal areas,* the exclusive domain of hunter-gatherers; *nuclear areas,* which spawned a series of Classic/Postclassic cycles; and between, a large number of *intermediate areas* where agriculture was adopted, but complex societies did not often follow. These last areas supported a variety of tribes and chiefdoms. The builders of the megaliths in Europe, the Pueblo Indians of the Southwest, the Mississippian temple-mound builders of the Southeast, the elaborate Polynesian Island societies, and the tribal agriculturalists of New Guinea—all fit into the mosaic of human societies in intermediate areas.

With the Industrial Revolution and the development of new and powerful energy resources, many of the limits that restrained agrarian states were broken. New means of production, transport, and communication made near-global colonial and commercial empires possible as Postclassic patterns were intensified and expanded to a larger scale. We will discuss these again at the end of the chapter.

Classic/ Postclassic Patterns

If we step back from human history for a longer perspective, many trends in the development of complex societies become evident. This long view is possible only because the major outlines of cultural development are now known. The trends we describe below (and the lessons we draw from them) are not shared by all archaeologists. Nevertheless, they are similar to insights others have derived from the past. Some of the clearest examples can be found in the Classic/Postclassic developments of nuclear areas.

One trend involves decision making in regional systems. Empires are formed by centralization, bringing separate societies under the control of a single political institution. Continued centralization leads to *hypercoherence,* a condition in which decision making is too far removed from individual communities to be timely and to be relevant to local conditions. The outcome is a collapse of centralized control and a return to local autonomy. The deterioration of the farmlands around Lagash is an example. As the crop yields of some communities dropped because of increasing salinity of the soil, overirrigation, and short fallow cycles, the state encouraged cutting fallow time even further. As a result, the salinity problem grew rapidly worse, until crop yields were so low that they would support neither farmers nor bureaucrats. This implies that centralized bureaucracies that control large regional systems are by nature unstable, as follows. When complex societies are growing, their technologies, social organization, and ideologies are geared to growth. But growth cannot go on forever, either because resources are limited or because of the presence of stronger neighbors. All too often, when growth approaches its local limits, the institutions that are geared toward growth resist efforts to stop or even slow it; as a result, societies may persist in a growth mode even when on the edge of growth-related catastrophe. When limits are reached, the final collapse is often devastating.

This pattern is visible in an unexpected way in artifacts. Societies unable to slow growth or change its direction will continue and even intensify their traditional patterns of manufacture. Up to the end, they will produce more and more structures and goods. Such societies may give the impression of great prosperity when, in fact, their economic base has eroded and they are on the brink of failure. This is likely to be the explanation in the case of many of archaeology's seeming mysteries, such as why Classic Maya society collapsed on the heels of a great flourish of building.

While these patterns in behavior are intriguing, perhaps the most interesting to the archaeologist are those that even more directly involve artifacts. Most complex societies follow a trend that moves from the manufacture of relatively few expensive craft items to larger numbers of lower-cost objects that are often mass-produced. Thus, the carefully painted pots of the Maya Classic were inundated in the Postclassic by cheap "dribble wares." The less costly mass-produced items could be afforded by more lower-class people. As a result, the markets for such items are much larger than those for crafts. Usually, new costly crafts aimed at the upper class replace those devalued by mass production. In many societies, craft and mass-produced items do not even compete for the same consumers. In fact, craft items often serve as models for mass-produced copies. The result is a continuous cycle of new craft items and new mass-produced items. Nevertheless, there is an overall trend toward the increased use of mass-production techniques.

This trend is clear in our own Postclassic. At the turn of the century, the first handmade cars were flamboyant symbols of high social standing. During the next decades, while some companies followed the handmade tradition, Henry Ford's assembly lines rolled off cars for the common people. In the 1920s and the 1930s, the wealthy could choose from a number of handmade autos—Duesenbergs, Rolls-Royces, and Cords, among others. One by one, however, most of these companies failed. Today, handmade cars are an ultimate status symbol, available only to the upper class; the rest must muddle through with factory-made Mercedes, Lincolns, and 280Zs. This means that in the Postclassic, they don't make them like they used to.

It means something else as well. Obviously, the trend from craft to mass production affects artifacts with socio-functions and with ideo-functions. As mass production makes socio-functional artifacts available to more people, the material differences between social groups become less pronounced. Thus, while in the early 1900s one major difference between people was in whether they owned a car, today the difference is in what *kind* of car they own. Some ideo-functional artifacts also follow this trend. For example, in the Maya Classic, pottery incensarios used for burning pungent copal were among the most beautiful products of Maya craftsmen. In contrast, Postclassic incensarios were assembled in a great variety of shapes from components mass-produced in molds. While few Classic incensarios have been found, fragments of incensarios are common in the Postclassic. One explanation is provided in the written accounts of a Catholic priest who encountered Postclassic society first-hand. Bishop Diego de Landa reported that, in Maya Postclassic tradition, religious incensarios had to be smashed and replaced after even the simplest of everyday rituals—the ultimate in built-in obsolescence.

MVSs also undergo changes in the Classic/Postclassic pattern (FIGURE 11-14). During Classic periods, a few large MVSs are built at great expense. These usually become the focal points of community integration. Temples I and II at Tikal, and the Great Plaza that the temples face, are Maya examples. In the Postclassic, scaled-down models of MVSs are produced in larger numbers and more locations. Thus, at the Maya Postclassic capital of Mayapán, while the community's biggest temple was dinky at best, each of the grander house compounds had its own small *oratorio*, or shrine, which probably served as the focal point of kin-group ritual.

During the Classic, MVSs serve as potent symbols of community integration. As local craft items are replaced by mass-produced goods, often imported, the obvious economic interdependence reduces the need for MVSs. The increased importance of the military in the Postclassic also reduces the need for MVSs. Thus, in the Maya case, as in others, it seems that integration during the Classic was first achieved through large or expensive MVSs. Eventually, during the Maya Postclassic, such integration was accomplished through economic interdependence, fostered by the widespread distribution of mass-produced artifacts and by military intervention. As the basic institutions changed from religious to more secular organizations, associated beliefs and values, no doubt, changed too; their content, however, is beyond the present reach of archaeology.

GENERAL TRENDS

Although we can see patterns in the histories of complex societies, trends can be perceived on a global scale. The most obvious trend in history is population increase (FIGURE 11-2). As environmental limits have been broken by new adaptive systems, populations have been extremely fruitful and have multiplied. Population probably grew slowly for nearly 2 million years until the farming lifeway changed the environmental limits to growth and set off the world's first population explosion. Growth accelerated again with the development of complex societies, and once more with the Industrial Revolution. It took nearly 2 million years to produce the first billion people, but only seventy-five years for the second. According to present projections, the next billion mark, 5, will be reached by A.D. 2000. While these estimates may be subject to some error, there is no question about the direction of the trend.

If, as we have previously suggested, increases in population lead to increases in the complexity of a society, we might expect to see the same pattern at a global level. Thus, it is no surprise that through time there has been a worldwide increase in the variety of behavioral components, artifacts, and ideologies. Compare the wide range of specialized task groups and specialized artifacts in our society to those in an early base camp such as Terra Amata or even in an early city such as Teotihuacán. Differences in complexity between societies are also evident at any one time; compare Tokyo and an Australian aborigine camp. All of this diversity, to some degree, can be traced to the variability in environmental limits and the continual development and elaboration of new ways in which these limits can be transcended.

In every environment there are limits to the size and complexity of adaptive systems that can be sustained. These limits vary, depending on the kinds of technologies available, the way local resources are used, and the quantities of resources brought in from outside. In some areas, such as the Arctic, the Western Desert of Australia, and the Great Basin of the western United States, local resources will support only simple technologies and extremely small human populations. While every society imports resources to survive, in these "marginal" areas, only hunter-gatherers, whose needs are minimal, have been successful over the long term. Time and again agrarian and industrial states have used imported technologies and resources to found outposts in marginal areas. The last such settlements to be established

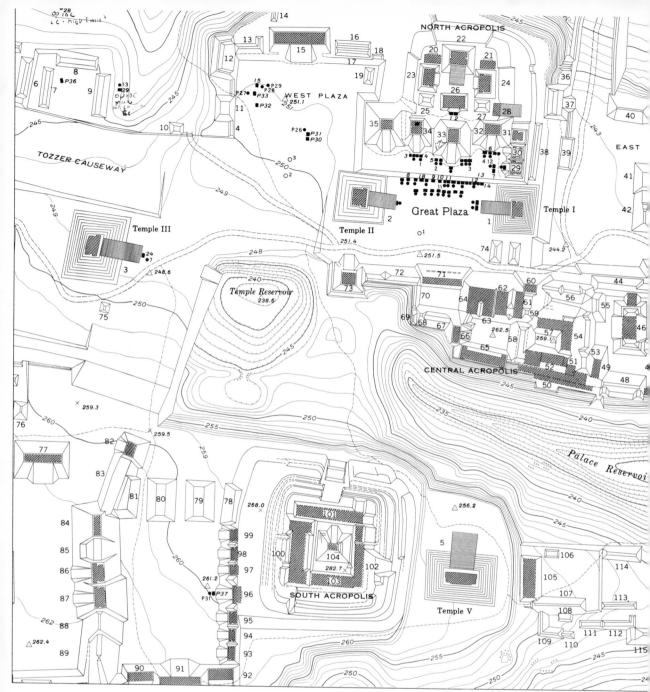

FIGURE **11-14**   Above, a portion of Tikal (ca. A.D. 800), one of the largest Classic Maya sites, and, on facing page, at top, Mayapan (ca. A.D. 1350), the Late Postclassic capital. (One inch equals about 30 meters or 120 feet.) Below on facing page, Classic polychrome pottery and Postclassic "dribble wares."

FIGURE **11-15**

Hadrian's Wall (built across northern Britain 122–128 A.D.), one of the northernmost vestiges of the Roman Empire.

are the first to collapse when their founders encounter difficulties. Marginal landscapes are littered with the remains of these short-lived communities (FIGURE 11-15). Today, small groups of Bushmen hunt and gather across the Kalahari Desert of Africa where the ruins of large communities attest to a brief peak of native African Iron Age expansion. It remains to be seen how long our settlements in peripheral areas will last.

While the existence of limits to growth seems obvious, there is some question as to where these limits are. It is clear that marginal areas present obstacles for the expansion of adaptive systems. But even in nuclear areas, ancient empires seemed unable to exceed certain sizes. We do know from the growth of modern industrial states that these limits can be overcome by production, communication, transport, and other technologies based on the heavy exploitation of nonrenewable energy sources—mainly coal, oil, gas, and uranium. Nevertheless, for this current system there are also clear limits, because nonrenewable energy resources are just that, and can be exhausted. We may, through technological innovations, again be able to transcend these bounds, just as the first city dwellers overcame the limits of their farming villages through irrigation networks and new production technologies. If our industrial state succeeds in transcending its limits with new technologies, we must be prepared to cope with the dramatic changes in our behaviors and beliefs that are sure to follow.

Each time a limit is breached, there is a cost. One clear trend through time seems to be toward greater per capita consumption of energy. This increase in energy use has an environmental price. Even before the Industrial Revolution, the cost was paid in deforestation and soil exhaustion. Although with the development of mass production there has been a decrease in the energy invested per commodity, this is more than compensated for by the trend through time toward more artifacts, with each person in an industrialized society consuming more energy overall. This energy gluttony is being sustained at great environmental cost—hazardous pollution and exhaustion of resources. Thus, material prosperity has been achieved for ever larger populations at the expense of this planet's natural resources.

The Future In viewing the trends of our past, it is possible to offer some scenarios for the future. On the level of organization, the world seems destined to become integrated into even larger and more complex political systems strongly influenced by multinational corporations. We can already see signs of this in the growing sameness of the world's largest cities. In fact, Americans are more likely to experience culture shock visiting the rural hamlet of Egypt, Arkansas, than the Holiday Inn in Cairo, Egypt.

It is clear that we are running out of easily exploited nonrenewable resources. A century ago, oil could be found oozing spontaneously from the soil in Pennsylvania. To obtain oil today, monstrous platforms squat in a thousand feet of water drilling miles into the continental shelf. The oil thus obtained must be moved long distances to refineries through multi-billion-dollar pipelines or in supertankers. This story of oil is typical. Because most of the easily accessible resources have been exploited, the discovery and extraction of new supplies has become almost totally dependent on costly and highly specialized industrial technologies. The process of developing new renewable energy sources, such as solar power, is also dependent on the research and development capability of our industrial base.

The pace of change is rapidly increasing. This suggests that even as we speculate on our future, it is probably already here—changing our lives on a daily basis. Not only at a global level does rapid change prevail, but, in individual societies as well, developmental cycles are becoming shorter. The Roman Empire extended itself from the Near East to Britain and lasted five hundred years. The sun never set on the British Empire, but it lasted less than two hundred and fifty years. This trend of increased rates of change, which is clear from the past, has implications for the future. Lag times, between the point at which the first stresses appear and the point at which these problems can no longer be corrected, are becoming shorter and shorter.

If conversion to renewable-energy technology is not achieved before nonrenewable energy resources are exhausted, the world industrial system will collapse. Without easily exploitable oil, iron, copper, and coal to develop and sustain an industrial technology, we will not have the technological base needed to make the conversion; we will have created an unbreachable limit to growth. Probably within the next century, maybe within our own lifetimes, we will know if industrial societies will persist on this planet.

When faced with such a critical problem, it is especially important to see the past realistically and not just as "happy days." Archaeology provides such an objective view. Because of its access to the lessons of the past and because of its emphasis on the effect of technology and artifacts on behavior, archaeology is coming to play an important role in our changing society. In Chapter 12 we discuss the applications of archaeology.

Hester Davis (b. 1931)   Hester Davis, state archaeologist of Arkansas, oversees the archaeological work carried out in the state. She advises state and federal agencies as well as nongovernmental organizations on their obligations under the law. She reviews conservation archaeology reports to see that both archaeology and Arkansas are served well, and she fosters public awareness of Arkansas' archaeological resources.   □   Above all, Hester Davis is an activist promoting archaeology and the preservation of archaeological resources. In 1972, in an article entitled "The Crisis in American Archaeology," she tried to alert scientists and other concerned citizens to the increasing damage inflicted on archaeological sites by vandals, government building projects, mining, and even the daily activities of farmers. She believed the answer was stronger laws and education of the public. In the 1970s, she has lobbied hard for both state and federal legislation, has coordinated the efforts of others, and has followed her own advice on educating the public (working, for example, on the summer digs of the Arkansas Archeological Society to help train amateurs in proper recovery techniques). She is also a coauthor of *The Indians of Arkansas,* a book that makes prehistory easy reading.   □   Before she has finished, Hester Davis will have infused every aspect of life in Arkansas with archaeological awareness. The preservation of archaeological resources will be thought of—to put it in her own words—"as something necessary to survival."

Hester Davis with her "electric shovel," an archaeologist's dream.

12

ARCHAEOLOGY AND SOCIETY

Anyone who has watched comedian Steve Martin, complete with Pharaonic crown, prance through a rendition of "King Tut" knows that archaeology and the remote past have a role in present-day whimsy (FIGURE 12-1); it also has roles in matters that range from the fantasy image of ancient astronauts bringing civilization to our ancestors to serious problems related to the future of our civilization.

Through all archaeology runs a thread of special human interest—the excitement and mystery of material objects that we can see today, but that were first made and used by people in the distant past. These artifacts are the tangible doorway to our heritage. This was literally true, for example, when Howard Carter broke the seal on the door of Tutankhamen's tomb and entered a vault closed for more than 3,000 years. Carter's discovery in 1922 of the only unlooted Pharaoh's tomb in Egypt was the culmination of a long, systematic search, but only the beginning of the "boy-king's" legacy.

Most obviously, Carter found the chariot, the beds, the thrones of a pharaoh of eighteenth-Dynasty Egypt, but he did much more. The contents of the tomb have directly reached the public in a variety of ways. From 1922 to 1924, the discovery stayed on the front pages of newspapers around the world. Since then, millions of tourists have journeyed to Egypt to see the tomb in the Valley of the Kings and the treasures in the Cairo Museum (FIGURE 12-2). In 1924, 200,000 people crowded through a reproduction of the tomb on the first day of the British Empire Exhibition. At about the

FIGURE **12-1**
Comedian Steve Martin singing his song "King Tut" on television.

same time, the New York legislature passed the "Tut Relic Bill" to save the unwary from reproductions palmed off as original Tut treasures. Objects from the tomb in traveling exhibits have attracted millions of people in lines half a mile long and almost as many ticket scalpers.

SYMBOLS FROM THE PAST

In Fashion and Belief

Tut's popularity and the direct contact with the artifacts of a long dead civilization have proved an inspiration to modern designers and, along with other buried art from the Near East, became a major theme in the Art Deco style. In 1924, the "Isis Collection" premiered in Paris, with many gowns copied from designs in the tomb. Eight years later, Hollywood created "The Mummy," one of the most enduring of the classic monster movies (FIGURE 1-1). Tut styles were incorporated into portable objects, including radio cabinets and slot machines, into murals and mosaics, and even into whole buildings (FIGURE 12-3). The recent tour of Tut's treasures in the United States has led to a resurgence of ancient Egyptian influence in portable art, including commemorative plates, clothing, and jewelry.

Archaeological finds like Tutankhamen's tomb have long been important in setting trends in fashion. We can trace this role as far back as the first

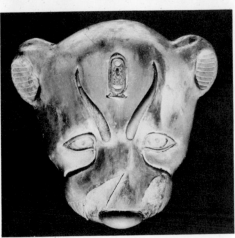

FIGURE **12-2**

From among the thousands of items removed from the tomb of Tutankhamen—a gold life-size funerary head, an alabaster jar, and, directly above, a leopard mask. At right is a more recent treasure—likenesses of Tutankhamen, here being applied to the fingernails of a patron in an exclusive shop in Los Angeles.

FIGURE **12-3**   Art deco facade of a New York City building that incorporates ancient Near Eastern motifs.

FIGURE **12-4**

A tourist of the 1920s looks into the future while Egypt's past provides a background.

excavations at Pompeii, Italy, in the 1700s. It may be even older. In Peru, John Rowe has discovered ancient pots painted to replicate still other pots from centuries earlier. But why do ancient finds so affect fashion? One reason is that they often serve as important symbols in our modern world. In school, we trace our beliefs about democracy back to ancient Greece and the early republics of Rome. The mimicking of "classic" architecture in so many of our public buildings is no accident. It provides a strong material symbol of the historic depth of our political system. In the same way, churches imitate Gothic cathedrals to reinforce religious values, movies use the later periods of the Roman Empire to symbolize decadence, and for decades tourists have been sending home snapshots of themselves in front of the pyramids of Egypt to impress their friends and relatives (FIGURE 12-4).

In Culture and History

The power of materials from the past as symbols of belief is surpassed by their power as symbols of cultural heritage. The legacy of Tutankhamen is obviously a national treasure of Egypt, a symbol of past glories and prestige and Egypt's long endurance as a nation. Most third-world countries, in fact, are making the most of their past (FIGURE 12-5). The Museo Nacional in Mexico City is more than a museum of ancient relics to attract tourists; it is

A

B

C

D

E

F

G

H

I

J

K

L

M

N

FIGURE **12-5** (Facing page) Archaeological sites and artifacts, a source of national pride in many countries, are often depicted on their stamps: From Egypt, pyramids, *A*, the funerary mask of Tutankhamen, *B*, and King Menkaure and two goddesses, *C*; from Mexico, an Olmec head, *D*, and stone carvings from Teotihuacán, *E* and Chiapas, *F*; from Peru, Machu Picchu, *G*, a Nazca pot, *H*, and ancient gold jewelry from Lambayeque, *I*; from Bolivia, Tiahuanaco, *J*; from China, the Great Wall, *K*; from Iran, a cuneiform tablet, *L*; from Greece, the Temple of Apollo, Corinth, *M*; and from the United States, Cliff Palace Pueblo at Mesa Verde, *N*, on the only U.S. stamp to show a prehistoric site or artifact.

a symbol of the cultural achievements of the Mexican people, a reminder to Mexican and tourist alike that Mexico was a thriving center of civilization 2,000 years before Cortes and the Europeans arrived. In Mexico, the museum and archaeological sites are used as classrooms where school children go on field trips to touch their past. The findings of Mexican archaeologists constitute a cornerstone of national pride (see boxed unit, "Eduardo Matos Moctezuma and the Great Temple," p. 376).

Such findings can also be a cornerstone of national politics. In China, ancient remains—such as the beautiful jade burial suits of the Prince Liu Sheng and his wife, dating to the Western Han Dynasty about 2,000 years ago (FIGURE 12-6)—are viewed as illustrating two political messages. The human ingenuity involved in carving the 4,838 wafer-thin jade pieces to fit the curvatures of the bodies, even down to the fingernails, is seen as testimony to the creativity of the Chinese people. In addition, the tremendous human and natural resources consumed by the work are seen as an indictment of the bourgeoisie and upper class of pre-Mao China as exploiters of the downtrodden proletariat, or peasants and workers. In this case, archaeological interpretation and politics go hand in hand.

FIGURE **12-6** Jade burial suit of Prince Liu Sheng of the Western Han Dynasty (ca. 100 B.C.) in China, The wafer-thin pieces making up the suit were contoured to fit the body and sewn together with gold thread.

FIGURE **12-7**   Part of the "great enclosure" at the site of Zimbabwe, Zimbabwe (formerly Rhodesia).

Another such example is offered by the African country formerly called Rhodesia, which was colonized and has been controlled by whites since the eighteenth century. Because blacks native to the region were viewed as inferior, the ruins of the acropolis-like "great enclosure" site of Zimbabwe (FIGURE 12-7)—built of impressive masonry, and obviously old—were attributed to white Phoenicians or to bronzed Ethiopians led by the Queen of Sheba, but never to the local populace. In the 1920s, a British expedition led by Dr. Caton-Thompson carried out the first systematic archaeological research at the site, determining that it apparently had been a major trading center, and cross-dating it to A.D. 1100 by pottery from India and China as well as from Muslim countries to the north. On the basis of the archaeological evidence, Caton-Thompson concluded that Zimbabwe was the result of a long developmental sequence and that it had been built by native blacks. It is no coincidence, then, that when blacks retook their dominant position in Rhodesia recently they renamed their country Zimbabwe.

Although the roots are not deep, white Americans have a cultural heritage that archaeologists have recently begun to explore. The Williamsburg restoration in Virginia is a living museum of America's Colonial past built according to the precepts of its founders' motto—that "the future may learn from the past." The archaeological investigations of Ivor Noël Hume have added significantly to the authenticity of the reconstructions by turning up new information not covered in written documents, including shackles and similar artifacts that indicate the brutal realities of life in an early-American insane asylum. Elsewhere, archaeologists are beginning to uncover the unwritten history of ethnic groups in America whose lifeways are not well documented: pre-Civil War communities of free blacks in New York; Mexican-American settlements near Tucson, Arizona; and temporary camps in northern California of Chinese workers who built the transcontinental railroad in the 1860s. Charles Fairbanks, one of the first archaeologists to excavate slave quarters in the Old South, was surprised to find the bones of wild animals and gun flints in their refuse. This indicated, contrary to both popular belief and historic accounts, that at least some slaves had weapons and that their nutritionally inadequate rations were supplemented by hunting. Findings like these help to provide a more rounded picture of what life was like for different groups of early Americans.

But for all the success stories of archaeology and national pride, there are problems. The heritage and traditions of most Native American groups have been buried under waves of American pioneers and later immigrants and accompanying disease, massacres, and resettlements. The new sense of awareness seen in the American Indian Movement and similar groups is an attempt to regain a lost identity as Native Americans. To reconstruct this identity, most of these groups have turned to their past, either to the works of early cultural anthropologists who observed living tribes or to archaeological research. One would think, therefore, that archaeological work would be welcomed. In fact, many Native Americans, especially those in militant groups, are not pleased with the archaeologist's interest in their ancestors. Some believe that excavations desecrate sacred bones and objects. Some, as a part of establishing their independent identity, adhere to ancient teachings that the findings of archaeologists may contradict and thereby, some feel, undermine the training of the young in native traditions. For example, many native histories teach that tribes lived in their respective territories from the beginning of time. Archaeologists, however, trace Native American populations to immigrants from Asia and believe they have identified major movements of their descendants from territory to territory. These differences are not easily reconciled. Again and again, the results of scientific inquiry conflict with articles of faith. Nevertheless, most archaeologists and Native Americans believe that scientific investigations should continue.

Happily, the relationship between Native Americans and archaeologists is steadily improving as each group finds out more of what the other expects and needs. Archaeologists, in fact, are making major contributions to Indian communities: discovery of ancient sites increases tourism, a major source of revenue on some reservations. Archaeological data have also been used in court cases to establish the validity of Native American land claims.

Native Americans are not the only ones who sometimes reject archaeological evidence. Fort Moultrie, in Charleston, South Carolina, is a national historic site that was a military base from the Revolutionary War until the end of the Second World War. In the 1970s, the National Park Service, aiming to reconstruct the original structure, hired archaeologist Stanley South to locate it exactly and to determine the details of its construction. On the basis of a review of historic documents, South dug exploratory trenches and found the remains of the fort. The only problem was that its location was considered not scenic enough. Rather than disappoint tourists, the Park Service rebuilt the "original" fort some distance from its actual site and banned South's report from its museum.

ARCHAEOLOGICAL PSEUDO-SCIENCE

Archaeologists are faced with another problem area in dealing with the public—that of pseudo-scientists and their whimsical interpretations of the past. Some have proposed a number of theories that claim a single mysterious, and now lost, source for all civilization. In a way, they are like the Heliocentric diffusionists (p. 303), though the assumed source is nothing so commonplace as Egypt.

The mysterious-cradle-of-civilization theory with the longest tradition is that of Atlantis. First mentioned by Plato in a lesson on logic, it was portrayed as a paradise—gold temples, wise rulers, and every kind of earthly delight—that fell victim to a series of natural disasters and in "one terrible day and night sank beneath the sea." Plato claimed that the island of Atlantis lay just outside the Pillars of Hercules—the Straits of Gibraltar—in the Atlantic Ocean that now bears its name. From the beginning, believers in the Atlantis legend elaborated on it. According to later proponents, many inhabitants of the island, seeing their impending doom, left by ship; these "boat people" of Atlantis are taken to be the founders of the world's first civilizations.

One look at a world map and the location and dates of these civilizations shows the basic weakness of the Atlantis theory. The differences in time, in art styles, and in artifact inventories are too great to have had a single origin. The New World, for example, never developed bronze or iron and did not use the wheel, except on small toys. In addition, geologists and oceanographers have found no evidence for a large submerged island in the Atlantic Ocean.

Sociobiology

What is responsible for change in the behaviors of *Homo sapiens?* People on the fringes of science have suggested visits from spacemen, an idea few scholars take seriously. An equally dramatic suggestion, made by well-known scientists called sociobiologists, attributes behavior change to genetic change. This view raises again a question that has perplexed scientists for centuries: nature or nurture? Is behavior coded into our consciousness by genes or is it learned from our families, from the institutions composing our societies, and from our experience of the total environment?

According to sociobiologists, most human behavior is the product of "epigenesis," the interaction of genetic propensity and selective pressures in the environment. In this process, environment has the effect of selecting for survival (in an evolutionary sense) specific gene combinations that act to predispose humans toward specific behavior patterns. In other words, different behaviors are largely the result of different gene frequencies; and heredity, not education, determines what we do. Most anthropologists and archaeologists take the opposing view—that most behavior is learned.

Archaeology, with its long-term perspective, can provide evidence for evaluating the controversial claims of sociobiology. Genetic change is slow and many generations must pass before it manifests itself in the characteristics of a population. Sociobiologists have coined the "thousand-year rule": Under the most favorable conditions, it takes a millennium for epigenesis to significantly change behaviors. What does archaeology say of the thousand-year rule? Take as an example one thousand years of Lowland Maya civilization. During the first two-and-a-half centuries after Christ, simple tribal societies built small clusters of temples in the Petén rain forest. Settlements grew into major ceremonial centers in the Classic period, with spacious public plazas, palace complexes, and carved stone stelae. For the next six hundred years Classic Maya civilization was the most sophisticated in the New World, possessed of a writing system that still defies full translation and an astronomy not rivaled until the time of Galileo. For the first two hundred of those years, the Classic style seemed immutable as it spread from the Petén. At the end of that period there began a fifty-year "hiatus" during which no commemorative stelae were cut in the Classic Maya heartland and during which development seemed stalled. When it resumed, the look of temples, palaces, stelae, glyphs, and pottery differed from region to region, and stylistic change in each proceeded rapidly. Between A.D. 800 and 850, the Maya temples that had breeched the jungle were abandoned to it. Thus, in one millennium (the period of the thousand-year rule) all manner of behaviors and styles came and went —from the farming techniques and plainware pots of everyday life to the priestly paraphernalia and temple facades of sacred ritual—and a whole civilization noisily arose and then fell silent.

The example of the Maya is not the exception; the worldwide archaeological record shows many cases of important kinds of behaviors often changing drastically in less than the thousand-year rule's requisite fifty or so generations. Hence the record of world prehistory and the relatively rapid changes in every archaeological sequence cast doubt on the validity of a central tenet of sociobiology.

FIGURE **12-8**   A mural among the remains of a Minoan trading colony on the island of Thera, which was covered by lava from an eruption around 1200 B.C.

But Atlantis is far from dead. In fact, several Greek archaeologists are very busy resurrecting it. They believe that they have found a factual basis to Plato's original story on Thera, a small volcanic island in the southern Aegean Sea. Once, a Minoan settlement covered much of the island. The palaces were large and decorated with elaborate and beautifully executed murals (FIGURE 12-8). The artifacts were those of a prosperous trade colony. Around 1200 B.C. the volcanic island erupted, and what was not covered by lava sank below sea level. Not only does the nature of the settlement and its demise fit the Atlantis legend, but so do the wanderings of its homeless inhabitants. Egyptian hieroglyphics record the "invasion" of "sea-kings" from the north between 1225 and 1190 B.C. Thus, all the elements of the Atlantis legend are completed in a toned-down but still fascinating story. Nevertheless, there are those who still search in the Atlantic Ocean for the "cradle of civilization."

As fascinating as Atlantis has been to the general public, a new out-of-this-world origin for civilization has stirred an unprecedented level of interest. Eric von Däniken, main advocate of this "ancient astronaut" thesis, claims that civilization was brought to our slow-witted ancestors by space travelers who visited certain areas of the Earth in antiquity. Von Däniken's ancient astronaut story has received imposing publicity, with more than 50 million copies of his books (in thirty-two languages) sold.

Although he has appealed widely to the public, his ideas are not nearly so popular with archaeologists. Most of von Däniken's "facts" are bits of archaeological evidence taken out of context and treated in isolation from other lines of evidence. In *Chariots of the Gods?*, for example, von Däniken considers a carving on the lid of a stone sarcophagus from Palenque, Mexico, dating to A.D. 692, to be the portrayal of a spacesuited astronaut at the controls of a rocket-propelled spaceship. Maya archaeologists, on the other hand, see only a typically dressed Classic Maya figure, naked except for a cloth at the waist, jade anklets, bracelets, and necklace, and a headdress (FIGURE 12-9). To these archaeologists, the "spaceship" looks like a Maya symbol for a corn plant and an earth deity, topped by a quetzal, a parrotlike bird.

FIGURE **12-9**   Carved sarcophagus lid from the Temple of Inscriptions, Palenque (A.D. 692), depicts a very earthly ancient Maya citizen. After J. Eric Thompson, *Ancient Maya relief sculpture*, 1967.

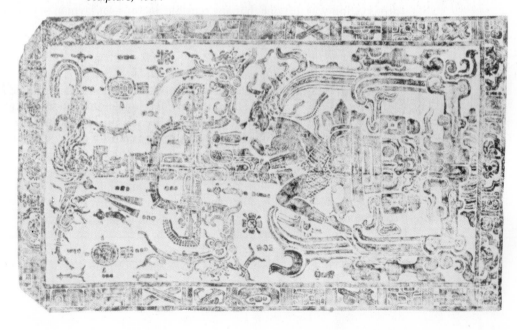

Were von Däniken right, we would expect the coffin to hold the remains of a humanlike creature in a spacesuit made of exotic metals and plastics or totally unfamiliar substances. In fact, the coffin held the bones of a man with jade beads and ornaments at his ankles, wrists, and neck. A jade mosaic mask covered his skull. Using the glyphs in the tomb, Maya scholars have translated his name and the details of his life, including his date of birth in A.D. 603. Von Däniken, however, totally rejects the context of the sarcophagus lid. Perceiving a rough resemblance to present-day rockets, he prefers to theorize on the basis of a vague similarity stretched over twelve centuries.

Mummies are another area where von Däniken provides incomplete context and information. He views Egyptian mummification as an effort to preserve bodies for that time when the gods return from outer space and awaken the sleeping dead. He compares their technique to Robert Ettinger's plan to preserve the bodies (by freezing) of people who had died of a disease that might be curable in the future. This might be a reasonable interpretation were it not for a few aspects of the way Egyptians practiced mummification.

In preparing a corpse for the afterlife, Egyptian priests removed the brain, bit by bit, through the nose. Then its viscera (heart, lungs, stomach, liver, and so on) were extracted and placed in four separate *canopic* jars. Finally, the body was soaked in a glue made of resins, asphalt, and other similar substances. These embalming materials often caused destruction of the body, rather than its preservation. Before the mummy of Tutankhamen could be removed from its coffin, it was necessary to heat the metal shell to over 900° F in order to melt the solidified embalming matter. All in all the preservation was not one that any sensible doctor—or layman—would develop to preserve himself for a return to life. It may explain why movie mummies move so slowly.

Carrying out his theme, von Däniken finds clear signs of the landings of ocean-liner size spaceships, claiming an actual landing site in Yucatán at the great *cenote* near the archaeological ruins of Chichen Itza, built around A.D. 1100. According to von Däniken, this circular hole in the limestone was the result of a rocket blastoff and cannot have been formed by natural forces. It is strange, therefore, that there are literally thousands of cenotes in northern Yucatán and in other areas composed mainly of limestone. Geologists and archaeologists believe that cenotes or "sinkholes" are formed by environmental processes that follow simple geological principles. Water flowing underground dissolves soft limestone and forms caverns, the roofs of which collapse to form cenotes. Thus the two explanations to choose between: thousands of "rocket landings" only where there is limestone, or natural processes that are forming similar holes today (FIGURE 12-10).

Von Däniken cleverly exploits a weakness of American experience— our technology-induced conviction that, before bulldozers and Xerox copiers, nothing monumental could be achieved without supernatural help.

FIGURE **12-10**

A recently formed cenote (sinkhole), this one in contemporary Florida. Such formations are common in limestone topography.

Thus, von Däniken can propose that mere men could not have cut, moved, and set up the stone heads of Easter Island. (Recall from Chapter 8 that Thor Heyerdahl and a few Easter Islanders accomplished all of these tasks with simple tools—FIGURE 8-21.)

In the end, von Däniken's premise explains everything and nothing. It is the ultimate prime cause, but it is unnecessary. The scientific method and the principles of archaeology provide us with the tools to investigate the archaeological record and solve the mysteries of the past. Archaeologists investigate human ingenuity and how it interacted with different environments to produce the panorama of ancient societies that compose the foundations of our world (see boxed unit, "Sociobiology"). Where specific events of the past show patterns and trends, we can learn valuable lessons about our ancestors, ourselves, and perhaps even our future. As pawns of spacemen, on the other hand, we can only helplessly await their return.

On a more positive note, Atlantis and von Däniken heighten public interest in archaeology. After all, von Däniken draws his puzzles—if not his answers—from the archaeological record. Most archaeologists turned to the field originally out of a fascination with the mysteries of the past. A similar fascination by the public is important to archaeologists; it is needed, as we shall see, if we are to conserve and protect dwindling cultural resources from the looters and builders of the present.

FIGURE **12-11**   A prehistoric pueblo in southwestern New Mexico being destroyed by looters using bulldozers.

CULTURAL RESOURCE MANAGEMENT

Like other people, archaeologists have nightmares. A typical one might be called "The Invasion of the Artifact Snatchers." Our heroine has just completed a grueling survey in mountains somewhere in the Southwest. Back at the office, she chooses the one site to unravel a major archaeological mystery. Once the selection is made, weeks are spent securing funds and assembling a crew. Nights are spent sharpening faithful Marshalltown trowels. At last all is ready. But as the crew approaches the site, there is a foreboding in the air. There are new mounds!—and unmistakable tracks of heavy machinery. The crew runs headlong to the site, where our heroine's worst fears pale in comparison to the actual destruction wrought by looters (FIGURE 12-11). Such images have caused many an archaeologist to awake in a cold sweat in the middle of the night.

Looting

Most archaeologists, having had first-hand experience with the havoc wrought by looters, have worked for laws to deter and punish them. Many such laws exist at the federal and state level. As early as 1906, looting on federal lands was made a crime by the Lacey Act (also known as the Antiquities Act). As recently as 1978 a stronger law (the Archaeological Resources Protection Act), with clearer definitions and stiffer penalties, was passed by the Congress. Most states have enacted anti-looting laws patterned after the federal acts, but for several reasons looting continues.

First, federal and state laws protect only sites on public property—a small portion of the land area of the United States. These laws, moreover, are not enforced rigorously; it was not until the 1970s that a looter was successfully prosecuted under the 1906 act. Looting being a profitable business, looters can afford to invest in heavy equipment, including bulldozers and backhoes. They are often armed—especially in third-world countries—and willing to kill. In fact, it is usually the case that the more valuable the loot, the better armed and equipped and the more determined the looters. In the Maya area, looters have been known to descend in helicopters to cut up and remove a stela with special diamond-tipped saws.

Looting is profitable because markets for the loot seem virtually insatiable, with unscrupulous dealers and collectors ready to buy regardless of the source. Representatives of some of our most hallowed museums vie for looters' spoils, so that museums that publicly condemn looting often privately contribute to it.

Some rather bizarre remedies have been suggested, including a proposal that the Society for American Archaeology (SAA) support a task group of skilled technicians who would produce flawless copies with which to flood the ancient artifacts market, devaluing the looters' product.

Looting also presents ethical dilemmas for archaeologists. One noted Maya archaeologist regularly authenticates Maya polychrome pots for art dealers in New York, arguing that by cooperating with dealers he can inspect and photograph the pots before they are sold to private collectors, where they are lost to science.

Acts of Government

A second typical nightmare might have as its hero a county archaeologist who learns on a Friday that the USDA's Soil Conservation Service has just approved a grant to a farmer who will level the last well preserved Mississippian temple mound in the county. Work will begin Monday; the archaeologist has two days. On Saturday morning, he telephones his amateur archaeology friends for help. They've all gone hunting. He realizes that there is only one alternative. After hearing his heart-felt speech, the entire family volunteers.

By noon they have reached the site and, after a chat with the farmer, settle in to work. As darkness approaches, they work by the light of lanterns. Find after find is recorded and removed. At seven Monday morning, deep in a small trench, they begin again. Suddenly, the archaeologist feels a chill. Putting his ear to the ground he screams, "Dozers!" As the bulldozer bears down on them, the archaeologist, flailing vainly against the falling dirt, wakes in a welter of tangled sheets (FIGURE 12-12).

Eduardo Matos Moctezuma and the Great Temple

Recently, Aztec artifacts were found in an excavation for a large sewer behind the main cathedral in Mexico City's Great Plaza. Work was stopped, and archaeologists opened up perhaps the grandest find in the history of Mexican archaeology—the foundation and much of the superstructure of "El Templo Mayor de Tenochtitlán," the Great Temple of the Aztec's capital. Long thought totally razed by the Spanish, the temple was saved by its destruction. Rather than tear it all down, the conquistadors simply cut off the top and filled in around the base to create a high plaza on which to build their churches. And who was more fit to resurrect the temple from its ignominious burial than the archaeologist of the project, Eduardo Matos Moctezuma, a descendant of the last Aztec emperor! Both temple and archaeologist are symbols of the dramatic role archaeology is playing in countries like Mexico, with eminent but long-obliterated pasts.

At the lowest level, Matos uncovered the first temple built—in A.D. 1426, recorded in Aztec histories as the date of the founding of Tenochtitlán on an island in the lake of Texcoco. The temple's many caches—full of carved shells, jade amulets, and other exotic artworks from all over Mesoamerica—attest to the power of the Aztec Empire, while the huge stone carving of *Coyolxauhqui,* the earth monster (which dwarfs the famous calendar stone) and other sculptures, some still brightly painted, add precious details of the ritual life of Mexico at the time of the Conquest. Altogether, the temple represents a spectacular reaffirmation of the rich heritage of the Mexican people.

Matos, himself, represents another tradition in Mexican archaeology, the earnest commitment of scholars to the management of the nation's cultural resources. Archaeologists such as Matos move comfortably from the rigors of the field to contending with bureaucracy. At sites in Puebla, the Basin of Mexico, Chiapas, and Hidalgo—most notably at Tula, a site almost as prominent in Mexican folklore as Tenochtitlán—Matos has conducted extensive surveys and excavations and carried out stabilization and reconstruction. In Mexico he has served as Subchief and Chief of the Department of Prehistoric Monuments, Director of the National School of Anthropology, and President of the Council of Archaeology, which oversees the activities of Mexican and foreign archaeologists.

Here the temple and the excavator—artifact and archaeologist—are woven into the past, present, and future of a nation. It is an exciting time for Mexican archaeologists, one that most American archaeologists can experience only vicariously. Imagine the thrill of opening up a stairway that your ancestor, the emperor, once climbed in glory.

Ironically, another cultural-resource disaster is one in which the chief offender is the guardian of the resources. Prior to 1969, archaeologists were the last to know when sites were to be destroyed by some action of the federal government. In that year, Congress enacted the National Environmental Policy Act (NEPA), according to which all federal projects were to be designed so as to minimize harm to environmental resources, including archaeological sites. This entails having an archaeologist first check a proposed location for a project—say creation of a lake or reservoir by damming a stream. The archaeologist examines records and local museum collections and consults other archaeologists and amateurs to determine whether and what kinds of sites might be endangered by the construction. The result of these research activities is a report called an assessment.

After this the archaeologist surveys the alternate locations for the proposed reservoir. The goal is to rank the possible locations according to their potential to harm the archaeological resources. The survey, which can involve probabilistic sampling, gleaning information from local residents, and consulting aerial photos of the area, becomes the basis for a report known as a preliminary field study. It describes the sites in each possible location, evaluates their importance, and reports not only on the *direct* impacts (of bulldozers and submersion) but also on the *indirect* impacts of pot-hunters and campers who, aided by newly constructed project-related roads, will likely loot and vandalize sites. Ingenious means have been devised to predict

FIGURE **12-12**   Excavating in the path of construction bulldozers in New Zealand.

indirect impacts. Pierre Morenon recorded the distribution of modern trash —pop-tops, cans, candy wrappers—in a New Mexico national forest in order to forecast those areas that would be the most heavily used. Interestingly, Morenon found that modern campers tended to prefer the same locations as prehistoric Indians.

Once the direct and indirect impacts are projected, the archaeologist presents the concerned agency with the preliminary field study. Many other reports may have been commissioned from other specialists and, after consideration of all, a decision is issued—often not the one recommended by the archaeologist.

Once the project location is chosen, archaeological work resumes—usually as a survey that completely covers the area to be affected, identifying resources in great detail, pinpointing site significance, and forecasting impacts with greater precision. In the resulting report, called an intensive field study, the archaeologist proposes ways to mitigate the detrimental impacts of the construction.

Mitigation

Three kinds of mitigation can be proposed—avoidance, preservation, and excavation. In the case of the first, while the archaeologist cannot realistically expect a reservoir to be moved, construction roads can be routed around sites, and details of construction can be altered. In some cases, it is even feasible to propose large-scale modifications—moving the towers of power lines, for example.

Where sites of great significance are found, the archaeologist will be forced to recommend preservation—that the project not be built and that the site or sites be permanently preserved. Where such recommendations are rejected, other options remain. The best of these is to have the site in question listed in the *National Register of Historic Places* (a "Who's Who" of archaeological sites buried in a bureaucratic mound of red tape), which will sometimes protect it from disturbance. This is a routine process that begins with an effort to convince the State Historic Preservation Officer (SHPO) that a site is significant enough for nomination to the National Register. If this effort is successful, the SHPO *and* the President's Advisory Council on Historic Preservation must then be convinced that a thorough "blue-ribbon" excavation will be conducted before a site can be damaged. Either the SHPO or the council can withhold their blessing by contending that the sites are too important to be dismantled by either the agency proposing construction or by archaeologists. The agency, however, can simply ignore the advice of the SHPO or the Advisory Council. At this point, though it is the rare case, archaeologists may seek support from special-interest groups opposed to the construction project for other reasons. The outcome of such action is usually determined in court.

In the third form of mitigation—excavation—the archaeologist identifies the major research problems that could be addressed by thoroughly digging the site about to be lost. Although little more than a trickle at first, funds for excavation became a flood in 1974, when the *Moss-Bennett Act* empowered federal agencies to finance digs of sites slated for destruction. We estimate that, in 1980 alone, over $40 million was spent on archaeological projects under the authority of the Moss-Bennett Act, which indicates that most federal agencies are responsive to recommendations from archaeologists. Such recommendations are complicated, sometimes including a mix of avoidance, preservation, and excavation.

A number of federal agencies, especially the Bureau of Land Management, the U.S. Forest Service, and the National Park Service, control vast amounts of territory, amounting to nearly one-third of the area of the United States. These agencies have ongoing programs of cultural resource management. In addition to responding to immediate threats, project by project, these programs are designed to help the agencies develop long-range plans for managing archaeological resources. For example, in national forests in the American Southwest, areas are surveyed immediately preceding a timber sale. Forests as a whole are being steadily surveyed by probabilistic sampling and the pedestrian tactic. These surveys are the basis for periodic reports that summarize the archaeological potential of each forest as a means of meeting the objectives of a 1971 executive order (EO 11593) that requires federal agencies to identify all cultural resources under their jurisdiction.

ARCHAEOLOGY AND APPROPRIATE TECHNOLOGY

Appropriate technologies are those that are minimal in their effects on the environment and in their consumption of non-renewable resources. Archaeologists have discovered several such technologies that have contemporary practical applications. For example, Don Crabtree (pp. 89–90, FIGURE 4-14), among others, discovered that the obsidian blades used by the Aztecs and Maya for ritual bloodletting and for their version of open-heart surgery are extremely keen, forming edges only ten molecules thick. (In a tacit acknowledgment of this superiority, the Spanish conquerors preferred obsidian over their own metal blades for making fine cuts.) In 1977, when Crabtree underwent surgery, the initial incisions were made with a set of obsidian knives he knapped himself. In 1980, archaeologist Bruce Dahlin, equally convinced of the excellence of obsidian blades, underwent surgery in which obsidian surgical tools were used that were a hundred times sharper than most steel scalpels—as well as cheaper and easier to produce. (In surgery, the sharper the blade, the less the trauma to tissue, and the more rapid the healing.)

In another example, archaeologist Michael Evenari and his colleagues examined the wide variety of ingenious agricultural methods used by the desert societies that existed between 3000 B.C. and A.D. 630 in the Negev, an area with an annual median rainfall of less than 4 inches. They found that the basic method involved exploiting the runoff from small watersheds in a system that made use of local peculiarities of soil and topography rather than elaborate hydraulic apparatus. Evenari and his colleagues applied these ancient techniques on two modern farms in the Negev. The system worked, producing acceptable yields of a variety of crops. The project showed not only the mechanics of how simple agricultural systems operated, but also the possible reasons for their failure at various times in the past. Knowledge of both—the mechanics and the mistakes—is necessary if modern farmers are to succeed again in sustaining agriculture in areas such as the Negev.

MODERN MATERIAL CULTURE STUDIES

Material culture or artifacts are a part of every behavior in which we engage, unless, perhaps, running naked across a desert. Even in this case, to avoid material culture you would have to rid yourself of all jewelry, nail polish, cosmetics, dental fillings, artificial limbs or other manufactured body parts, contact lenses or glasses, and hairspray, while being careful not to trip on beer cans or spent rifle cartridges.

Our immense dependence on technology has important implications for archaeological studies of modern material culture and for our future. We have left a simpler past behind. More than any other generation, we are inundated by artifacts. It is now no joke when Eaton Corporation states that "we're as much a part of the car as the car is a part of your life" or when Dow Chemical Company claims that "life without chemicals is impossible." Over the past few years we have become increasingly conscious of the artifacts in our daily activities. In fact, their symbolic power has become inflated to the point that an artist can attain fame by depicting, on a very large canvas, an ordinary soup can (FIGURE 12-13). This painting can be viewed in several ways: first, as an accurate rendering of a mass-produced artifact familiar to nearly everyone; second, as a symbol of the trends toward less food preparation in the home (and the decreased role of homemaking in family life); third, and perhaps most important, as an indicator of social change, while it is itself a major contributor to that change. Ultimately, the painting draws attention to the ways in which commonplace artifacts both profoundly affect our lives and constitute a record of them.

Most Americans take their technology (and its artifacts) for granted, seeing in it the source of the good life and the solution to most problems. Not enough food? Produce more fertilizer, higher-yielding hybrid plants, bigger farm equipment, and new methods of processing. Thus, according to the traditional American myth, technology quietly and effectively serves our needs; increasingly, however, this image is being contradicted in the real world. Reality has become an accelerating parade of technological backfires, so predictable that a new myth of mistrust—fueled by such events as Three-Mile Island, Love Canal, and Skylab "accidents"—is now competing with the old one of technology as savior. This reaction has given rise to a contrary belief—in the superiority of the "old ways."

This conflict between mythologies is clear on television screens, where heroes with nuclear-powered body parts compete for viewers against the oc-

cupants of little houses on the prairie, happy in their homespun austerity. It is clear in the movies: the classic "2001: A Space Odyssey" (1968) is an enactment of the transition from old to new myths, documenting humanity's struggle with technology gone berserk—in this case in the form of a paranoid computer named Hal. It is clear in the popular press, with *Popular Mechanics* and the *Whole Earth Catalogue* sold side by side on the same newsstand. It is clear in songs, especially those about cars, our multipurpose symbol of social standing. Once the subject of adulation—in such early rock-and-roll classics as "Little Deuce Coupe," "409" (the Beach Boys), and "Hot Rod Lincoln" (Chuck Berry)—these same machines are now faulted for their unsafe design, poor gas mileage, contribution to pollution, and shoddy workmanship; the new songs reverse the old themes of adulation, as in "Oh Lord, Mr. Ford" (Jerry Reed):

It seems your contribution to man
To say the least got a little out of hand
Oh Lord, Mr. Ford, what have you done?

Books such as Packard's *The Wastemakers,* Toffler's *Future Shock,* Schumachers' *Small Is Beautiful,* and Lappé's *Diet for a Small Planet* further document the conflict between myths. The focus of these technological doomsday texts is not technology per se, but its effects on behavior and life styles. Americans, however, are increasingly realizing that the role of artifacts and technology in our society is more complicated than either of the simple myths would have it. Archaeology, with its long-term view of human behavior, allows us to see technology as both problem and solution.

Given the prominence of artifacts in our daily lives, one might think that their effects are being intensively investigated by behavioral scientists. But this is not the case; though more and more behavioral scientists are including artifacts in their studies, material culture is always a minor concern. Environmental psychologists studied Pruitt Igoe (Chapter 10) during its decline. Hundreds of hours were spent interviewing residents to learn their attitudes toward their living quarters and their neighbors. But no effort was made to record the details of the architecture, the location of activity areas, and the nature of artifacts used. In short, only one aspect of the problem—attitudes—was examined; behavior and artifacts were overlooked entirely.

But the Pruitt Igoe problem, like all social problems, involves three elements—beliefs, behaviors, and artifacts—each of which is best studied by a different method: beliefs by interviews and questionnaires; behaviors by direct and indirect observation; and artifacts by measures of the four dimensions of variability. In all of behavioral science, only one discipline—archaeology—is primarily concerned with artifacts and their relationship to behavior. In order to discern specific causes of the less than idyllic Pruitt Igoe lifeway, archaeologists would have approached the problem by concentrating on recording those very artifacts and behaviors that psychologists and others ignored. Of course, archaeologists cannot single-handedly cure all of society's ills. Instead, successful problem solving requires the use of as many perspectives as possible. Each behavioral science has a role to play in fully understanding a problem and finding workable solutions. Archaeologists, who uniquely command the perspective on artifacts, hold a missing piece in the puzzle of our society.

ARCHAEOLOGY AND PUBLIC POLICY

Information gleaned from artifacts can be the basis for many government programs, especially those that regulate commerce and economic development, manage natural resources, or provide food and shelter to the needy. For example, one important question regarding the problem of dwindling supplies of raw materials is: What portion of these materials is lost through waste every year? Although disposal of solid wastes, or garbage, is one of the primary problems facing American cities today, there has been little reliable information on either its composition or its volume. To correct this the Environmental Protection Agency (EPA) launched a program to estimate what was discarded on the basis of industry data on what was manufactured and sold. Some questionable assumptions were made. For example, it was assumed that glass jars not recorded as recycled through official channels had been thrown away. This ignores the frequent reuse of jars in households for storing everything from soup to nuts and bolts. Such assumptions also ignore the frequent reuse of rigid plastic containers (such as butter and margarine tubs or cottage cheese cartons) for storing leftovers and other items. Although overlooking such conservation behaviors may not greatly affect the overall picture of waste, other assumptions, discussed below, are not altogether harmless.

According to final EPA estimates, discarded furniture and durable goods (such as refrigerators, stoves, televisions, and microwave ovens) contribute more than 12,600,000 tons of solid waste yearly to America's landfills. This would mean that the average household throws away about 250 pounds of such items every year—or the equivalent of a couch, two televisions, and a toaster—and businesses throw away even more.

Results in the first decade of the Garbage Project at Tucson (pp. 34–36) do not fit the EPA estimates; only a handful of durables or furniture have been recorded. Observations of landfills also indicate few such items are found in them. Finally, a survey of almost 2,000 illegal dump sites around Tucson failed to find more than an occasional rotting couch or mattress, and a survey of vacant lots within the city produced similar results.

If these items were not being discarded, what was happening to them? This question was answered by an ethnoarchaeological study of Tucson households and of particular reuse behaviors such as yard sales, swap meets, auctions, second-hand goods stores, and others. The average household reported replacing only four of thirteen major items—such as washers, refrigerators, couches, stereos, and dining tables—in the preceding five years, indicating a rather long uselife for most durables and furniture. Tucsonans reported that 30 percent of old durables (the items that were replaced) remained in the household, and nearly all the rest were given away or sold, mainly to friends and relatives; only 6 percent was thrown out.

The EPA investigators pictured households in which everything wears out rapidly and is then discarded; thus their use of production and sales records to estimate what is thrown away. The ethnoarchaeologists found that instead of pumping out artifacts as fast as more were acquired, households displayed pack-rat behavior, with resultant steadily growing inventories. This pattern is not true just of households; the city of Tucson as a whole is similarly accumulating artifacts in its repair shops, junk shops, junk yards, and second-hand goods stores (FIGURE 12-14). Eventually, very old durables are recycled as scrap metal.

FIGURE **12-14** Links in the reuse process: In Tucson, Arizona, at top, a store selling used furniture and appliances; lower left, rear of the store; and lower right, the front yard of another store selling secondhand goods.

The archaeological studies at Tucson show that EPA estimates of waste in the discarding of durables and furniture may be greatly exaggerated. This type of misinformation could become the basis for government policies and programs that would have undesirable side effects. For example, using EPA estimates, regulations were proposed that would make durables more durable—and, thereby, use more resources and energy. This policy was based on the assumption that an increase in durability would decrease the rate of discard and, in the long run, save resources. The ethnoarchaeological data from Tucson challenge this assumption. They suggest that most items are replaced not because they no longer work, but because people want new styles or the "latest" convenience. In fact, items that *are* replaced are usually still functioning and go on functioning in other homes or serve as a source of spare parts to keep similar items working. Contrary to popular belief, this "conspicuous consumption" does not normally lead to waste. Instead, it makes a whole series of "used" durables and furniture available at low cost to poor families and to those just starting out. Tampering with this intricate system for conserving resources could upset it and lead to more waste. Thus, because they may be based on a false assumption—as we have suggested was the case with proposals to increase durability—new regulations can have effects opposite to those intended.

Organizations like the EPA have much information about artifacts, but very little about the behavior associated with them. Information on these behaviors can be obtained by a variety of archaeological and ethnoarchaeological approaches, which range from sorting through garbage to interviewing households.

Obviously, information on current behaviors in Tucson is not sufficient to anticipate the future. Also important is the perspective of time: we need to know the trends in behavior that have brought us to the present (Chapter 11). But past trends and current conditions are poor indicators of the future without general principles for combining our knowledge of the past and present. This can be simply illustrated with a global problem.

An interdisciplinary group of scientists called the Club of Rome recently presented (in the book *Limits to Growth*) a model of "the world system" based on four major variables: population, resources, social services, and pollution. The model included information on very recent trends, current conditions, and a set of rules assumed to describe the interaction of the four variables. In simulation after simulation, each using slightly altered models, computer results were the same—rapid growth of population, resource use, social services, and associated pollution to the year 2000, followed just as rapidly by the exhaustion of resources, the complete befouling of the planet in wastes, the failure of social services, and finally a devastating collapse of population. The authors argued for restraining growth of population and for careful planning of the use of nonrenewable resources. Not everyone accepted these results and their implications. Critics eventually found an error in the mathematics of the simulation model. With the error corrected, and after some additional tinkering, the simulation showed the same rapid growth initially, but followed by equilibrium instead of collapse—and the debate died.

The debate over the Club of Rome model could have benefited from an archaeological perspective founded on general principles derived from past trends in the development of societies. Clearly, one of the most basic general principles to come from the study of archaeology is that all complex societies rise and fall, with only the simplest adaptive systems—bands and tribes

—attaining long-term stability. In fact, the complex societies of the past that have been studied form a string of illustrations of the rise/collapse cycle leading up to the present (Chapter 11). Furthermore, the cycles seem to be getting shorter. Because technology for communication, transportation, and exploitation of resources has become increasingly sophisticated, civilizations rise faster and fall quicker. From the vantage point of the archaeologist, our civilization is the living end of this trend. Archaeology supports the argument for careful planning of growth—slower growth probably means slower decline. Ultimately, computer games that tell us we will be the first complex society to reach stability seem a less realistic basis for anticipating the future than the patterns of prehistory.

GLOSSARY

BIBLIOGRAPHY

INDEX

GLOSSARY

A **A-horizon** The humus-rich, uppermost zone of a soil.

absolute dating Assigning a specific calendrical year to an event or process, usually by use of *tree-ring dating* or historic records.

accumulation model The theory that cultural change occurs gradually as societies accumulate behavioral traits.

act The smallest unit of recurrent behavior involving an artifact.

activity A set of related *acts*.

adaptation The way human societies accommodate their behavior and artifacts to their environment.

aeolian Pertaining to the role of the wind in erosion and in *deposition (environmental)*.

agrarian state The fourth stage in the *stage model*, representing large regional systems or empires based primarily on non-mechanized agriculture and controlled by centralized and specialized bureaucracies.

alluvial deposits Sediments laid down by streams in their channels or on flood plains.

arbitrary level A three-dimensional segment of a deposit whose boundaries are determined by convention or convenience.

archaeological context The state of artifacts in the archaeological record.

archaeological culture Artifacts typical of a specific region at a particular time.

archaeological recovery Removal of artifacts from archaeological context with full recording of their four dimensions of variability.

archaeological sequence Artifacts, behaviors, or phases (periods) ordered in time.

archaeological survey On-ground inspection of a study area for artifacts and sites.

archaeology The study of human societies that emphasizes the interaction between human behavior and artifacts.

artifact Any object affected by human behavior.

artifact type A category of artifacts whose *attributes* are similar; spoons, tables, and bicycles, for example, are artifact types.

assemblage All artifacts excavated at a site or from a specific recovery unit (for example, a burial assemblage).

association Occurrence of two or more artifacts together.

attribute A characteristic of an artifact, such as color, length, weight.

B B-horizon The second zone of a soil, containing materials washed down from the *A-horizon.*

backdirt The *sediments* and soil from an excavation.

band The first stage in the *stage model,* representing hunting-gathering societies.

behavioral component A basic building block of society (for example *households* and *communities*), composed of social units, *activities,* activity areas, and *artifacts.*

bifacially flaked Chipped on both sides or faces (with respect to a stone artifact).

blade Long, thin, parallel-sided flake of stone.

Bronze Age The second age in Thomsen's three-age system, referring to the period when bronze tools were manufactured.

C C-horizon The bottom-most zone of a soil, consisting of unaltered natural sediments.

cache An intentional deposit of artifacts for a social or ideological purpose or for storage.

catastrophism The eighteenth-century theory that earthquakes, volcanic eruptions, and other natural disasters were responsible for the distributions of animal fossils and artifacts.

chiefdom The third stage in the *stage model,* representing regional systems with mixed economies that are integrated through the institution of chief.

chronology building Devising a dated history for a region by combining numerous lines of evidence.

chronometric dating Placing an event or process within a range of dates on a calendrical time scale, usually by means of *radiocarbon* or *potassium/argon* techniques.

collecting The removal of materials in archaeological context from one settlement by the residents of another.

colluvial deposits Deposits formed on slopes near sources of sediment such as mountains.

community The behavioral component comprised of groups of *households* whose members frequently interact.

conceptual scheme The major assumptions or underlying premises of a field of research.

conservation archaeology Archaeology conducted to minimize harm to archaeological sites from land use.

core   A chunk of stone from which *flakes* are removed.

cross-dating   Dating based on association with artifacts whose age is known.

cultural ecology   The study of the ways a society adapts to its environment.

cultural evolution   The study of how and why human adaptive systems have changed over time.

cultural formation processes   Human activities responsible for forming and modifying the archaeological record.

culture   A society's distinctive behaviors, artifacts, and beliefs.

culture-historical school   Those who view the history of archaeological cultures as a product of *migration, diffusion,* and innovation.

cuneiform   The wedge-shaped characters of many ancient Near Eastern languages.

D **datum point**   A fixed point on which all measurements and locations recorded at a site are based.

de facto refuse   Artifacts—often still useable—left behind when an activity area, dwelling, or *settlement* is abandoned.

dendrochronology   See *tree-ring dating.*

deposition (cultural)   The laying down of deposits by human activities that move artifacts from *systemic context* to *archaeological context.*

deposition (environmental)   The laying down of sediments by environmental agents such as wind and water.

depositional environment   The surroundings of artifacts in *archaeological context.*

depositional history   The order in which *strata* were laid down.

depositional stratum or unit   A separable layer of material at a *site.*

developmental cycle   The stages passed through by individuals, behavioral components, artifacts, and artifact types.

diffusion   The spread of ideas from society to society.

disturbance   Movement and damage of artifacts in archaeological context as the by-product of other activities.

domesticated plant   A plant whose genetic characteristics are altered from their natural state by human propagation efforts.

E **earthworks**   Large constructions of or in earth, such as walls, ditches, and mounds.

empire   The behavioral component of regional systems tied together by trade and political and military activities.

environmental formation processes   Biological, chemical, and physical aspects of the environment responsible for forming and modifying the archaeological record.

environmental zone   Regional plant-animal associations that are climatically determined.

ethnic group   The behavioral component of groups of households that recognize a very general common ancestry.

ethnoarchaeology   The study of living societies by archaeologists.

exogamy   The practice of marrying outside of one's community.

experimental archaeology   Archaeology in which the traces left by human behaviors or environmental processes are studied by replication of artifacts, behaviors, and environmental conditions.

externalist model   The view that the causes of change in society are external—for example, environmental stress.

extraction loci   Activity areas where resources are procured.

F   **feature**   Any excavated phenomenon worth recording other than a level or an isolated artifact.

flake   A chip of stone removed from a *core.*

flotation   Separation of plant remains from sediments by floating them to the surface of a liquid.

formal dimension   The physical properties (*attributes, traces*) of artifacts.

frequency dimension   The number of occurrences of an artifact type.

G   **glaciation**   The growth and advance of large ice sheets, which occurred several times over the last four million years.

glyphs   Elements in the complex writing system of the ancient Maya.

grave goods   Artifacts included in a grave.

H   **half-life**   The time elapsed when half the atoms in a sample of a radioactive isotope (such as C^{14} or K^{40}) have decayed, or disintegrated. See *radiocarbon dating* and *potassium/argon dating.*

handaxe   A core tool flaked on both sides, generally fist-size, and commonly manufactured in the later portion of the Lower Paleolithic and the Middle Paleolithic periods.

hard-hammer percussion   See *percussion flaking.*

historical particularism   See *culture historical school.*

historical record   Artifacts, particularly documents and photographs, retained within an adaptive system.

household   The behavioral component consisting of people who regularly eat and sleep together.

housemound   In the Maya area, low earth platforms on which houses were built.

hydration   Formation of a bond between water and some material. See *obsidian hydration dating.*

I   **ideo-function**   The role an artifact has in a society's *ideology.*

ideology   A society's beliefs, attitudes, values, knowledge, and information.

impacts   The changes that archaeological resources undergo as the result of some action.

incensario   A Mesoamerican incense burner.

individual style   The portion of stylistic variability that is the product of the tastes and abilities of the artifact's creator.

industrial state   The fifth stage in the *stage model,* representing large regional systems and empires based primarily on work performed by machines and controlled by centralized and specialized bureaucracies.

institution   A large, formal task group with a portion of its members organized into hierarchies of bureaucrats.

intensity   The spacing between crew members in the *pedestrian tactic.*

internalist model   The view that the causes of change in society are internal—for example, *developmental cycles.*

Iron Age   The third age in Thomsen's three-age system, referring to the period when iron tools were manufactured.

K   **kill site**   The place where hunters killed an animal or animals.

kiva   A ceremonial room, often circular and semi-subterranean, used by Pueblo Indians.

L **law of superposition**   The law according to which later deposits overlie earlier ones.

Levallois technique   The method (common in the Middle Paleolithic) of preparing a tortoise-shaped *core* so that *flakes* struck from it will be of a predictable shape.

lifeway   The day-to-day activities characteristic of a society.

living floor   See *occupation surface*.

looting   The removal of artifacts from archaeological context without documentation of their dimensions of variability.

M **McKellar hypothesis**   The hypothesis that small objects are likely to remain in activity areas as *primary refuse*.

mano   See *metate*.

mass production   The manufacture of an artifact by a task group that uses division of labor, standardization of parts, and simplification of activities.

Maya area   The Yucatan Peninsula of Mexico and the countries of Belize, Guatemala, Honduras, and El Salvador.

megalith   An arrangement or structure of extremely large stones.

Mesoamerica   The area between northern Mexico and Costa Rica.

mesolithic   The period following the *Paleolithic* during which adaptations involved intensive foraging and experimentation with new food resources.

metate   A flat stone on which grain is ground with another stone called a mano.

midden   A trash accumulation.

Middle East   The area (sometimes called the *Near East*) from Afghanistan to Egypt.

migration   The movement of people to establish a new residence.

monstrous visual symbol (MVS)   Large constructions that serve as foci of community integration, such as temples, palaces, and sports arenas.

Mousterian   The Middle Paleolithic period in the Old World from 100,000 to 40,000 B.P.

multistage sampling   The method in which samples are drawn in a series of *stages,* with previous results influencing subsequent *sampling* decisions.

N **natural environment**   Climate, terrain, geological resources, and flora and fauna.

natural level   A three-dimensional segment of a deposit that corresponds to a *depositional stratum*.

Near East   The area (sometimes called the *Middle East*) in the vicinity of the eastern end of the Mediterranean Sea.

neolithic   The first era of village farmers in any region.

neutron activation   A technique of nuclear chemistry by which minute amounts of elements in a material are identified.

nonrenewable resources   Resources, such as oil, that are replenished slowly or not at all.

nuclear areas   Regions where large, complex societies arose again and again.

O **obsidian**   Volcanic glass, a material frequently chipped into razor-sharp tools.

obsidian hydration dating   A technique in which the age of an obsidian artifact is determined from the thickness of the layer of *hydration*.

occupation span   The length of time a settlement is occupied.

occupation surface   A boundary layer between *depositional strata* upon which activities were carried out (also called a living floor).

open sites   Any site not located in a cave or rock shelter.

P   **paleoenvironmental reconstruction**   Inferring of the characteristics of past environments from evidence such as pollen, sediments, floral and faunal remains, and artifacts such as paintings and tools.

paleo-Indians   Hunter-gatherer peoples prevalent in the New World from 12,000 to 10,000 B.P.

paleolithic   The period extending from 2 million to 12,000 B.P.

pedestrian tactic   A method of *archaeological survey* in which surveyors, spaced at regular intervals, systematically walk the area being investigated.

percussion flaking   Removing *flakes* from a *core* by use of a hammer (of stone, bone, antler or wood).

pit   An excavation *recovery unit.*

pithouse   A wooden dwelling in which the lower portion is a pit.

Pleistocene   The geological epoch from 2 million years B.P. to ca. 12,000 B.P.

plow zone   The layer of soil disturbed by plowing, usually the top 10 to 50 centimeters.

population   In *sampling,* all the materials of interest; for example, all the sites in a region or all the artifacts in a site.

population parameter   A characteristic of a population.

potassium/argon (K/A) dating   A chronometric technique for dating in which the proportion of radioactive potassium (K^{40}) to that of its decay product, argon is calculated. See *chronometric dating, half-life,* and *radiocarbon dating.*

potsherd   Any fragment of a ceramic vessel.

precision   In *sampling,* the degree of correspondence among statistics obtained in repeated trials of the same sampling technique.

prehistory   The period before written records in a given area, or the study of that era.

pressure flaking   Producing *flakes* by applying pressure to a *core* with a tool (often an antler).

primary refuse   Trash discarded at the location of use.

prime cause (also **prime mover**)   A factor, such as population growth, used by itself to explain changes in social complexity.

probability sampling   *Sampling* in which *sample units* are selected at random, as by flipping a coin or consulting a table of random numbers.

procurement   Obtaining or extracting resources from the environment.

provenience   The recording by the archaeologist of the location where an artifact was found.

pueblo   A type of village (common to the Southwest United States) composed of clusters of rectangular chambers of stone or adobe blocks roofed with logs.

purposive sampling   *Sampling* in which *sample units* are selected on the basis of specific criteria.

R   **radiocarbon dating**   A chronometric technique for dating once-living matter by calculating the proportions in it of radioactive carbon (C^{14}) and nonradioactive carbon (C^{12}). See *half-life* and *chronometric dating.*

Ramón tree   A nut-bearing tree common in the lowland rain forests of the Yucatan Peninsula.

reclamation   Activities that move objects from archaeological context back into systemic context.

recording unit   A level, feature, or occupation surface used as a reference point to designate the recovery location (*provenience*) of artifacts at a site.

recovery theory   The principles on which are based the choice of techniques to be used in a given archaeological survey and excavation.

recovery units   The two-dimensional (in surface collection) and three-dimensional (in excavation) spaces in which archaeological materials are recovered and recorded at a site.

recycling   The making of an item into a new product.

regional survey   Locating and describing the remains of settlements in a region.

regional system   The behavioral component made up of communities related to each other by trade, political alliances, and other forms of social interaction.

relational dimension   The artifacts that occur in close association with each other.

relative dating   Dating of an event or process according to its chronological position (earlier or later than) relative to another event or process. *Stratigraphy, cross-dating,* and *seriation* are relative-dating techniques.

remote sensing   Observation and recording at a distance, especially by specialized aerial photography of sites and the natural environment.

renewable resources   Resources, such as clay and trees, which are available in virtually inexhaustible quantities or are replenished naturally.

research design   The plan for an archaeological investigation.

research question   A question that a *research design* is intended to answer.

residential mobility   The degree of movement of household social units from dwelling to dwelling, particularly of hunting-gathering communities.

reuse   Change in the user or use of an object.

reverse stratification   Earlier materials overlying later materials.

sample   Any part or subset of a *population.*

sample size   The number of *sample units* chosen for study.

sample statistics   The characteristics of a *sample.*

sample unit   A member of a *population* investigated or examined.

sampling   Selecting from within regions those areas to be surveyed and, within sites, those areas to be excavated.

sampling strata   The subgroups of a *population.*

sampling strategy   The method by which *sample units* are chosen for study.

scavenging   The removal of materials from archaeological context by the residents of a settlement.

scientific method   A method of obtaining information by systematic observation, hypothesis testing, and experimentation.

seasonal round   A yearly cycle of movement (mainly among hunter-gatherers) from settlement to settlement in response to the changing availability of plants, animals, and water.

seasonality   The season or seasons when settlements were occupied.

secondary refuse   Trash deposited at other than the location of use.

secondary state   A society that achieved a state level of organization through contact with another state.

sedentary   Having a fixed or permanent dwelling.

seriation   Ordering a set of *assemblages* in time on the basis of the frequencies of occurrence of *temporal types.*

settlement   A cluster of activity areas used by a community and forming a camp, village, town, or city.

settlement system   The entire set of settlements used by a community; for example, all the base camps and hunting camps used by a band of hunter-gatherers.

shaman   A specialist in magic and curing.

sherd   See *potsherd*.

simple random sampling   *Probability sampling* in which every *sample unit* has an equal chance of being selected.

site   A place that has material remains of human activities.

slip   A thin coat of watery clay applied to the surface of a pot before firing.

social class   A group of people having similar *social standings*.

social differentiation   The number and variety of social roles and classes in a community.

social environment   Human adaptive systems—communities, regional systems, or empires—surrounding a society.

social organization   The way individuals and *social units* interact to form a society.

social role   The activities carried out by an individual in a *social unit*.

social standing   The sum of those individual *social roles* that can be ranked from high to low.

social unit   A group of people organized to carry out particular activities.

society   A human adaptive system.

socio-function   The role of an artifact in a society's social organization.

sociological model of style   A model of the spatial distribution of *styles* in terms of the social interaction between *behavioral components*.

soil   A sediment that has been weathered and altered where it lies.

Southwest   The region composed of Arizona, New Mexico, southern Colorado, and southern Utah, and the Mexican states of Sonora and Chihuahua.

spatial dimension   The exact location of artifacts.

stage   A level of complexity of human adaptive systems such as *band* stage, *chiefdom* stage.

stage model   A model in which the evolution of human societies is represented as a series of *stages*.

stela   In the Maya area, an upright stone monument in the form of a slab or pillar, often carved, and having a rectangular cross-section.

stratified sampling   Division of a *population* into groups (*sampling strata*) that are sampled separately.

stratigraphy   The ordering of *depositional strata* or units into a sequence.

style   Those characteristics of an artifact influenced by a society's *social organization* and/or *ideology*.

systematic sampling   The selection of *sample units* according to some regular interval, such as every tenth one.

systemic context   The state of artifacts as part of an adaptive system.

T   **task groups**   Behavioral components composed of sets of people (not households) that carry out the bulk of a society's activities.

techno-function   The role of an artifact in a society's *technology*.

technological types   Artifact types designated on the basis of techniques and stages of manufacture.

technology   A society's means of procuring resources and producing energy from its environment in order to manufacture and maintain artifacts and, ultimately, life.

tell   In the Near East, a large mound built up from trash and the remains of mud-brick architecture.

temper   The substance, such as crushed shell or sand, mixed with clay for making pottery.

temporal types   *Artifact types* designated on the basis of time of manufacture.

testing   The first stage of excavation, normally undertaken to investigate the way a site formed and sometimes to estimate the *population parameters* of artifacts.

traces   All the physical characteristics of an artifact.

trait   An *artifact type* used to establish relationships among *archaeological cultures*.

transect   A rectangular survey unit.

tree-ring dating (dendrochronology)   Dating of wooden objects by matching their sequence of varying rings (seen in cross section) with known tree-ring sequences.

trench   An excavation *recovery unit*, in the shape of an elongated rectangle, often used to expose the layering of deposits at a site.

tribe   The second stage in the *stage model*, representing village farmers and herders.

type   See *artifact type*.

typology   A set of related *artifact types*.

U **uniformitarianism**   The principle that maintains that processes seen operating today also operated in the past.

unit production   The manufacture of an artifact by a craftsman who performs all the operations in its production.

uselife   The average time that artifacts of a particular *type* remain in use.

use-wear   The gradual attrition or accumulation of materials that occurs on an artifact during use.

utilitarian   Pertaining to the characteristics of an artifact determined by the physical requirements of the job it was made to perform.

W **wattle-and-daub**   A construction technique using mud plastered over a framework of cut branches.

weathering   The alteration of materials by environmental processes.

Worsaae's Law   The law that artifacts deposited together in a grave were in use at the same time.

BIBLIOGRAPHY

1 INTRODUCTION

General

Carter, Howard and A. C. Mace, 1923, *The tomb of Tut-ankh-Amen, discovered by the late Earl of Carnarvon and Howard Carter.* George H. Doran, New York.

Deetz, James, 1967, *Invitation to archaeology.* Natural History Press, Garden City, New York.

Fagan, Brian M., 1981, *In the beginning: an introduction to archaeology,* (4th ed.). Little, Brown and Company, New York.

Hoving, Thomas, 1979, King Tut's tomb: The untold story. *Reader's Digest* 144:176–228.

Sharer, Robert J. and Wendy Ashmore, 1979, *Fundamentals of archaeology.* Cummings, Menlo Park, California.

Thomas, David Hurst, 1979, *Archaeology.* Holt, Rinehart & Winston, New York.

Woodall, J. Ned, 1972, *An introduction to modern archeology.* Shenkman Publishing Company, Cambridge, Massachusetts.

Special Interest

Heizer, Robert F., 1959, *The archaeologist at work: a sourcebook in archaeological method and interpretation.* Harper & Brothers, New York.

Wormington, H. M., 1947, Prehistoric Indians of the Southwest. *The Denver Museum of Natural History, Popular Series 7.*

Technical

Higgs, Eric and Don Brothwell (Eds.), 1969, *Science in archaeology: a survey of progress and research,* (2nd ed.). Thames and Hudson, London.

Kidder, Alfred V. and Samuel J. Guernsey, 1919, Archaeological explorations in northeastern Arizona. *Bureau of American Ethnology, Bulletin 65.*

2 TRADITIONAL AND APPLIED ARCHAEOLOGY

General

Coles, John, 1979, *Experimental archaeology.* Academic Press, New York.

Gould, Richard A., 1980, *Living archaeology.* Cambridge University Press, Cambridge, England.

Gould, Richard A., 1979, Exotic stones and battered bones: ethnoarchaeology in the Australian desert. *Archaeology* 32:29–37.

Griffin, P. Bion and Agnes Estioko-Griffin, 1978, Ethnoarchaeology in the Philippines. *Archaeology* 31:34–43.

MacNeish, Richard S., 1978, *The science of archaeology?* Duxbury Press, North Scituate, Massachusetts.

Martin, Colin, 1978, La Trinidad Valencera: a Spanish Armada wreck. *Archaeology* 31:38–47.

Trinder, Barrie, 1981, Industrial archaeology in Britain. *Archaeology* 34:8–16.

Watson, Patty Jo, Steven A. LeBlanc, and Charles L. Redman, 1971, *Explanation in archeology.* Columbia University Press, New York.

Special Interest

Callender, Donald W., 1976, Reliving the past: experimental archaeology in Pennsylvania. *Archaeology* 29:173–177.

Deetz, J., 1973, Ceramics from Plymouth, 1635–1835: the archaeological evidence. In *Ceramics in America*, I.M.G. Quimby (Ed.), pp. 15–40. The University of Virginia Press, Virginia.

Divale, William T., 1972, Systemic population control in the Middle and Upper Palaeolithic: inferences based on contemporary hunter-gatherers. *World Archaeology* 4:222–243.

Flannery, Kent V., 1973, The origins of agriculture. *Annual Review of Anthropology* 2:271–310.

Giere, Ronald N., 1979, *Understanding scientific reasoning.* Holt, Rinehart & Winston, New York.

Gould, Richard A. and Michael B. Schiffer (Eds.), 1981, *Modern material culture studies: the archaeology of us.* Academic Press, New York.

Grabar, Oleg, 1971, Islamic archaeology: an introduction. *Archaeology* 24:196–199.

Harpending, Henry and Herbert Davis, 1977, Some implications for hunter-gatherer ecology derived from the spatial structure of resources. *World Archaeology* 8:275–286.

Ingersoll, Daniel, John E. Yellen, and William MacDonald (Eds.), 1977, *Experimental archaeology.* Columbia University Press, New York.

Jewell, P. A. and G. W. Dimbleby, 1968, The experimental earthwork on Overton Down, Wiltshire, England: the first four years. *Proceedings of the Prehistoric Society* 32:313–342.

Jones, Peter R., 1980, Experimental butchery with modern stone tools and its relevance for Palaeolithic archaeology. *World Archaeology* 12:153–165.

King, T. F., P. P. Hickman, and G. Berg, 1977, *Anthropology and historic preservation: caring for culture's clutter.* Academic Press, New York.

Newcomer, M. H., 1971, Some quantitative experiments in handaxe manufacture. *World Archaeology* 3:85–94.

Rathje, William L., 1974, The garbage project: a new way of looking at the problems of archaeology. *Archaeology* 27:236–241.

Struever, Stuart (Ed.), 1971, *Prehistoric agriculture.* The Natural History Press, Garden City, New York.

Watson, Patty Jo, 1966, Prehistoric miners of Salt Cave, Kentucky. *Archaeology* 19:237–243.

Watson, Patty Jo, Steven A. LeBlanc, and Charles L. Redman, 1980, Aspects of Zuni prehistory: preliminary report on excavations and survey in the El Morro Valley of New Mexico. *Journal of Field Archaeology* 7:201–218.

Willey, Gordon R. (Ed.), 1974, *Archaeological researches in retrospect.* Winthrop Publishers, Cambridge, Massachusetts.

Yellen, John E., 1977, *Archaeological approaches to the present: models for reconstructing the past.* Academic Press, New York.

Yellen, John E. and Henry Harpending, 1972, Hunter-gatherer populations and archaeological inference. *World Archaeology* 4:244–253.

Technical

Byers, D. S. (Ed.), 1967, *The prehistory of the Tehuacan Valley: environment and subsistence, Vol. 1.* University of Texas Press, Austin.

Fehon, J. R. and A. D. Viscito, 1974, Archeological and historical inventory and preliminary field reconnaissance of Village Creek, Jackson and Lawrence counties, Arkansas. *Arkansas Archeological Survey, Research Report 2.*

Flannery, Kent, 1968, Archeological systems theory and early Mesoamerica. In *Anthropological archeology in the Americas*, Betty J. Meggers (Ed.), pp. 67–87. Anthropological Society of Washington, Washington, D.C.

Gould, Richard A. (Ed.), 1978, *Explorations in ethnoarchaeology.* University of New Mexico Press, Albuquerque.

O'Connell, James F., 1979, Room to move: contemporary Alyawara settlement patterns and their implications for Aboriginal housing policy. In *A Black reality: aboriginal camps and housing in remote Australia.* M. Heppell (Ed.), pp. 97–120, Australian Institute of Aboriginal Studies, Canberra.

Rathje, William L., 1975, Le Projet du Garbage

1975: historic trade-offs. In *Social archeology: beyond subsistence and dating,* Charles L. Redman, Mary Jane Berman, Edward V. Curtin, William T. Langhorne Jr., Nina M. Versaggi, Jeffery C. Wanser (Eds.), pp. 373–379. Academic Press, New York.

Reed, Charles A. (Ed.), 1977, *Origins of agriculture.* Mouton, The Hague.

Schiffer, Michael B. and George J. Gumerman (Eds.), 1977, *Conservation archaeology: a guide for cultural resource management studies.* Academic Press, New York.

Watson, Patty Jo, 1979, Archaeological ethnography in western Iran. *Viking Fund Publications in Anthropology 57.*

Watson, Patty Jo, Steven A. LeBlanc, and Charles L. Redman, 1971, *Explanation in archeology: an explicitly scientific approach.* Columbia University Press, New York.

Ucko, Peter J. and G. W. Dimbleby (Eds.), 1969, *The domestication and exploitation of plants and animals.* Aldine, Chicago.

3 BASIC CONCEPTS OF HUMAN BEHAVIOR

General

Farb, Peter, 1968, Rise and fall of the Indian of the Wild West. *Natural History* 77:32–41.

Harris, Marvin, 1980, *Culture, people, nature: an introduction to general anthropology,* 3rd ed. Harper & Row, New York.

Netting, Robert McC., 1977, *Cultural ecology.* Cummings, Menlo Park, California.

Service, Elman R., 1971, *Primitive social organization,* (2nd ed.). Random House, New York.

White, Leslie A., 1949, *The science of culture.* Farrar, Strauss, New York.

Special Interest

Bennett, John W., 1976, *The ecological transition: cultural anthropology and human adaptation.* Pergamon, New York.

Butzer, Karl W., 1977, Environment, culture, and human evolution. *American Scientist* 65:572–584.

Butzer, Karl W., 1980, Civilizations: organisms or systems? *American Scientist* 68:517–523.

Chang, K. C., 1972, Settlement patterns in archaeology. *Addison-Wesley Modular Publications* 24.

Flannery, Kent, 1972, The cultural evolution of civilizations. *Annual Review of ecology and systematics* 3:399–426.

Sanders, William T. and Joseph Marino, 1970, *New World prehistory: archaeology of the American Indian.* Prentice-Hall, Englewood Cliffs, New Jersey.

Service, Elman R., 1963, *Profiles in ethnology.* Harper & Row, New York.

Steward, Julian H., 1955, *Theory of culture change: the methodology of multilinear evolution.* University of Illinois Press, Urbana.

Technical

Carneiro, Robert L., 1967, On the relationship between size of population and complexity of social organization. *Southwestern Journal of Anthropology* 23:234–243.

Carneiro, Robert L. and S. F. Tobias, 1963, Scale analysis in the study of cultural evolution. *Transactions of the New York Academy of Sciences* 26:196–207.

Casteel, Richard W., 1972, Two static maximum population-density models for hunter-gatherers: a first approximation. *World Archaeology* 4:19–40.

Chang, K. C. (Ed.), 1968, *Settlement archaeology.* National Press Books, Palo Alto, California.

Doran, James, 1970, Systems theory, computer simulations and archaeology. *World Archaeology* 1:289–298.

Fried, Morton H., 1967, *The evolution of political society: an essay in political anthropology.* Random House, New York.

Hardesty, Donald, 1977, *Ecological anthropology.* Wiley, New York.

Harris, David R., 1977, Socio-economic archaeology and the Cambridge connection. *World Archaeology* 9:113–119.

Harris, Marvin, 1980, *Cultural materialism.* Random House, New York.

Miller, James G., 1965, Living systems: basic concepts. *Behavioral Science* 10:193–237.

Miller, James G., 1965, Living systems: structure and process. *Behavioral Science* 10:337–379.

Sahlins, Marshall D. and Elman R. Service, 1960, *Evolution and culture.* University of Michigan Press, Ann Arbor.

Service, Elman R., 1971, *Cultural evolutionism: theory in practice.* Holt, Rinehart & Winston, New York.

Trigger, Bruce, 1971, Archaeology and ecology. *World Archaeology* 2:321–336.

Watson, Patty Jo, Steven A. LeBlanc, and Charles L. Redman, 1974, The Covering Law model in archaeology: practical uses and formal interpretations. *World Archaeology* 6:125–132.

White, Leslie A., 1959, *The evolution of culture.* McGraw-Hill, New York.

4 ARTIFACTS AND BEHAVIOR

General

Andronikos, Manolis, 1978, The royal tomb of Philip II. *Archaeology* 31:33–41.

Deetz, James, 1977, *In small things forgotten: the archeology of early American life.* Doubleday, New York.

Deetz, James, 1967, *Invitation to archaeology.* Natural History Press, Garden City, New York.

Dupree, Nancy Hatch, 1979, T'ang tombs in Chien County, China. *Archaeology* 32:34–44.

Ferguson, Leland (Ed.), 1977, Historical archaeology and the importance of material things. *The Society for Historical Archaeology. Special Publication Series* 2.

Gould, Richard A., 1968, Chipping stones in the Outback. *Natural History* 77:42–49.

Keeley, Lawrence H., 1977, The functions of Paleolithic flint tools. *Scientific American* 237: 108–126.

Özgüç, Tahsin, 1963, An Assyrian trading outpost. *Scientific American* 208:96–106.

Pendergast, David M., 1965, Maya tombs at Altun Ha. *Archaeology* 18:210–217.

Quimby, I. M. G. (Ed.), 1978, *Material culture and the study of American life.* Norton, New York.

Spier, Robert F. G., 1973, *Material culture and technology.* Burgess, Minneapolis, Minnesota.

Special Interest

Binford, Lewis R. and Sally R. Binford, 1969, Stone tools and human behavior. *Scientific American* 220:70–84.

Bordes, François and D. de Sonneville-Bordes, 1970, The significance of variability in Paleolithic assemblages. *World Archaeology* 2:61–73.

Charlesworth, Dorothy, 1972, Tell El-Fara in Egypt: an industrial site in the Nile Delta. *Archaeology* 25:44–47.

Crabtree, Don E., 1968, Mesoamerican polyhedral cores and prismatic blades. *American Antiquity* 33:446–478.

Deagan, Kathleen, 1980, Spanish St. Augustine: America's first "Melting Pot." *Archaeology* 33:22–30.

Deetz, James and Edwin Dethlefsen, 1967, Death's head, cherub, urn and willow. *Natural History* 76:28–37.

Jelinek, Arthur J., 1976, Form, function, and style in lithic analysis. In *Cultural Change and Continuity: Essays in Honor of James Bennett Griffin,* Charles E. Cleland (Ed.), Academic Press, New York, pp. 19–33.

Jovanović, Borislav, 1980, The origins of copper mining in Europe. *Scientific American* 242: 152–167.

Richardson, Miles (Ed.), 1978, *The human mirror.* Louisiana State University Press, Baton Rouge.

Schiffer, Michael B., 1976, *Behavioral archeology.* Academic Press, New York.

Schuyler, Robert (Ed.), 1980, *Archaeological perspectives on ethnicity in America: Afro-American and Asian American culture history.* Baywood, Farmingdale, New York.

Willey, Gordon R. and Philip Phillips, 1958, *Method and theory in American archaeology.* University of Chicago Press, Chicago.

Technical

Ahlstrom, Richard V. N., Jeffrey S. Dean, and William J. Robinson, 1978, Tree-ring studies of Walpi Pueblo. Laboratory of Tree-Ring Research, University of Arizona, Tucson.

Arnold, Dean E. and Bruce F. Bohor, 1975, Attapulgite and Maya Blue: an ancient mine comes to light. *Archaeology* 28:23–29.

Aspinal, A. and S. W. Feather, 1972, Neutron activation analysis of prehistoric flint mines. *Archaeometry* 14:41–53.

Binford, Lewis R., 1962, Archaeology as anthropology. *American Antiquity* 28:217–225.

Binford, Lewis R., 1965, Archaeological systematics and the study of culture process. *American Antiquity* 31:203–210.

Clark, J. Desmond and C. Vance Haynes, Jr., 1970, An elephant butchery site at Mwanganda's Village, Karonga, Malawi, and its relevance for Palaeolithic archaeology. *World Archaeology* 1:390–411.

Dunnell, Robert C., 1978, Style and function: a fundamental dichotomy. *American Antiquity* 43:192–202.

Engelbrecht, William, 1974, The Iroquois: archaeological patterning on the tribal level. *World Archaeology* 6:52–65.

Hill, James N., 1978, Individuals and their artifacts: an experimental study in archaeology. *American Antiquity* 43:245–257.

Hodson, F. R., 1970, Cluster analysis and archaeology: some new developments and applications. *World Archaeology* 1:299–320.

Hodder, Ian (Ed.), 1978, *The spatial organisation of culture*. Duckworth, London.

Hodder, Ian and Clive Orton, 1976, *Spatial analysis in archaeology*. Cambridge University Press, Cambridge.

Longacre, William A., 1981, Kalinga pottery: an ethnoarchaeological study. In *Pattern of the past: studies in honour of David Clarke*, I. Hodder, G. Isaac, and N. Hammond (Eds.), pp. 49–66. Cambridge University Press, Cambridge.

McGuire, Randall H., 1981, A consideration of style in archaeology. *University of Arizona Anthropology Club, Atlatl, Occasional Papers* 2:13–29.

Marshall, Alistair, 1981, Environmental adaptation and structural design in axially-pitched longhouses from Neolithic Europe. *World Archaeology* 13:101–121.

Megaw, J. V. S., 1972, Style and style groupings in continental early La Tène art. *World Archaeology* 3:276–292.

Mellars, Paul, 1970, Some comments on the notion of "functional variability" in stone-tool assemblages. *World Archaeology* 2:74–89.

Mills, Christopher and Robert L. Schuyler, 1976, The Supply Mill on Content Brook in Massachusetts. *Journal of Field Archaeology* 3:61–95.

O'Connor, David, 1974, Political systems and archaeological data in Egypt: 2600–1780 B.C. *World Archaeology* 6:15–38.

Plog, Stephen, 1980, *Stylistic variation in prehistoric ceramics*. Cambridge University Press, New York.

Renfrew, C., J. E. Dixon, and J. R. Cann, 1966, Obsidian and early cultural contact in the Near-East. *Proceedings of the Prehistoric Society* 32:30–72.

Renfrew, C., J. E. Dixon, and J. R. Cann, 1968, Further analyses of Near Eastern obsidian. *Proceedings of the Prehistoric Society* 34:319–331.

Sackett, James R., 1977, The meaning of style in archaeology: a general model. *American Antiquity* 42:369–380.

Spaulding, Albert C., 1960, The dimensions of archaeology. In *Essays in the science of culture in honor of Leslie A. White*, G. E. Dole and R. L. Carneiro (Eds.), pp. 437–456. Crowell, New York.

Stiles, D. N., R. L. Hay, and J. R. O'Neil, 1974, The MNK chert factory site, Olduvai Gorge, Tanzania. *World Archaeology* 5:285–308.

Wobst, H. Martin, 1977, Stylistic behavior and information exchange. In *Papers for the director: research essays in honor of James B. Griffin*, C. E. Cleland (Ed.), pp. 317–334. *University of Michigan, Museum of Anthropology, Anthropological Papers* 61.

5 CULTURAL FORMATION PROCESSES

General

Ascher, Robert, 1968, Time's arrow and the archaeology of a contemporary community. In *Settlement archaeology*, K. C. Chang (Ed.), pp. 43–52. National Press Books, Palo Alto.

Coe, M. D., 1968, America's first civilization: discovering the Olmec. American Heritage, New York.

David, Nicholas, 1971, The Fulani compound and the archaeologist. *World Archaeology* 3:111–131.

Dethlefsen, Edwin and Kenneth Jensen, 1977, Social commentary in the cemetery. *Natural History* 86:32–39.

Jushemski, Wilhelmina, 1975, Vintage Pompeii. *Natural History* 84:52–59.

Maiuri, Amedeo, 1961, Last moments of the Pompeians. *National Geographic* 120:650–669.

Richardson, Lawrence Jr., 1978, Life as it appeared when Vesuvius engulfed Pompeii. *Smithsonian* 9:84–93.

Schiffer, Michael B., 1977, Toward a unified science of the cultural past. In *Research strategies in historical archeology*, Stanley South (Ed.), pp. 13–40. Academic Press, New York.

Sheets, Payson D., 1981, Volcanoes and the Maya. *Natural History* 90:32–41.

Will, Elizabeth Lyding, 1979, Women in Pompeii. *Archaeology* 32:34–43.

Woodbury, Richard B., 1973, *Alfred V. Kidder*. Columbia University Press, New York.

Special Interest

Copeland, Irene, 1977, *The flea market and garage sale handbook*. Popular Library, New York.

DeBoer, Warren R. and Donald W. Lathrap, 1979, The making and breaking of Shipibo-Conibo ceramics. In *Ethnoarchaeology: implications of ethnography for archaeology,* Carol Kramer (Ed.), pp. 102–138. Columbia University Press, New York.

Drucker, Philip, 1972, Stratigraphy in archaeology: an introduction. *Addison-Wesley Modular Publications in Anthropology* 30.

Ferguson, Leland G., 1977, An archeological-historical analysis of Fort Watson: December 1780–April 1781. In *Research strategies in historical archeology,* Stanley South (Ed.), pp. 41–71. Academic Press, New York.

Jones, David E. H., 1971, The great Museum at Alexandria: its ascent to glory. *Smithsonian* 2:52–61.

Lange, Frederick W. and Charles R. Rydberg, 1972, Abandonment and post-abandonment behavior at a rural Central American house-site. *American Antiquity* 37:419–432.

Robbins, L. H., 1973, Turkana material culture viewed from an archaeological perspective. *World Archaeology* 5:209–214.

Rowe, John H., 1962, Worsaae's Law and the use of grave lots for archaeological dating. *American Antiquity* 28:129–137.

Schiffer, Michael B., 1972, Archaeological context and systemic context. *American Antiquity* 37:156–165.

Stanford, Dennis, 1979, Bison kill by ice age hunters. *National Geographic* 155:114–121.

Wilk, Richard and Michael B. Schiffer, 1979, The archaeology of vacant lots in Tucson, Arizona. *American Antiquity* 44:530–536.

Technical

Binford, Lewis R., 1971, Mortuary practices: their study and their potential. In *Approaches to the social dimensions of mortuary practices,* J. A. Brown (Ed.), pp. 6–29. *Society for American Archaeology, Memoirs* 25.

Binford, Lewis R., 1976, Forty-seven trips: a case study in the character of some formation processes of the archaeological record. In *Contributions to anthropology: the interior peoples of Northern Alaska,* Edwin S. Hall, Jr. (Ed.), pp. 299–351. *National Museums of Canada, Museum of Man, Mercury Series* 49.

David, Nicholas, 1972, On the life span of pottery, type frequencies, and archaeological inference. *American Antiquity* 37:141–142.

Fehon, Jacqueline R. and Sandra C. Scholtz, 1978, A conceptual framework for the study of artifact loss. *American Antiquity* 43:271–273.

Haury, Emil W., 1975, *The stratigraphy and archaeology of Ventana Cave,* (2nd ed.). The University of Arizona Press, Tucson.

Keepax, Carole, 1977, Contamination of archaeological deposits by seeds of modern origin with particular reference to the use of flotation machines. *Journal of Archaeological Science* 4:221–229.

Peebles, Christopher S., 1971, Moundville and surrounding sites: some structural considerations of mortuary practices II. In *Approaches to the social dimensions of mortuary practices,* James A. Brown (Ed.), pp. 68–91. *Society for American Archaeology, Memoirs* 25.

Saxe, Arthur A., 1970, Social dimensions of mortuary practices. Ph.D. dissertation, University of Michigan. University Microfilms, Ann Arbor.

Schiffer, Michael B., 1975, The effects of occupation span on site content. In *The Cache River archeological project: an experiment in contract archeology,* assembled by Michael B. Schiffer and John H. House, pp. 265–269. *Arkansas Archeological Survey, Research Series* 8.

Schiffer, Michael B., 1976, *Behavioral Archeology.* Academic Press, New York.

South, Stanley A., 1977, *Method and theory in historical archeology.* Academic Press, New York.

South, Stanley, 1979, Historic site content, structure, and function. *American Antiquity* 44:213–237.

Stanislawski, Michael B., 1969, What good is a broken pot? An experiment in Hopi-Tewa ethnoarchaeology. *Southwestern Lore* 35:11–18.

Stockton, Eugene D., 1973, Shaw's Creek shelter: human displacement of artifacts and its significance. *Mankind* 9:112–117.

Tainter, Joseph A., 1978, Mortuary practices and the study of prehistoric social systems. In *Advances in archaeological method and theory,* Vol. 1, Michael B. Schiffer (Ed.), pp. 105–141. Academic Press, New York.

Tringham, Ruth, Glenn Cooper, George Odell, Barbara Voytek, and Anne Whitman, 1974, Experimentation in the formation of edge damage: a new approach to lithic analysis. *Journal of Field Archaeology* 1:171–196.

White, J. Peter and Nicholas Modjeska, 1978, Where do all the stone tools go? Some examples and problems in their social and spatial distribution in the Papua New Guinea Highlands. In *The spatial organisation of culture,* Ian Hodder (Ed.), pp. 25–38. Duckworth, London.

Wildesen, Leslie, 1982, The study of impacts on archaeological sites. In *Advances in archaeological method and theory, Vol. 5*, Michael B. Schiffer (Ed.), pp. 51–96. Academic Press, New York.

6 ENVIRONMENTAL FORMATION PROCESSES

General

Coe, William R., 1975, Resurrecting the Grandeur of Tikal. *National Geographic* 148:792–798.

Daniel, Glyn E., 1962, *The idea of prehistory.* Watts, London.

Evans, John G., 1978, *An introduction to environmental archaeology.* Cornell University Press, Ithaca, New York.

Haynes, C. Vance Jr., 1966, Elephant hunting in North America. *Scientific American* 214:104–112.

Leakey, Mary D., 1979, 3.6 million years old: footprints in the ashes of time. *National Geographic* 155:446–457.

Leakey, Richard E., 1970, In search of man's past at Lake Rudolf. *National Geographic* 137:712–734.

Leakey, Richard and Roger Lewin, 1977, *Origins.* Dutton, New York.

Payne, Melvin M., 1965, Family in search of prehistoric man. *National Geographic* 127:194–231.

Special Interest

Adovasio, J. M., J. D. Gunn, J. L. Donahue, and R. Stuckenrath, 1978, Meadowcroft Rockshelter, 1977: an overview. *American Antiquity* 43:632–651.

Bankoff, H. Arthur and Frederick A. Winter, 1979, A house-burning in Serbia. *Archaeology* 32:8–14.

Butzer, Karl W., 1971, *Environment and Archeology* (2nd ed.). Aldine, Chicago.

Eliot, Alexander, 1976, Rare drawings by Michelangelo found in crypt. *Smithsonian* 7:82–89.

Gasser, Robert E. and E. Charles Adams, 1981, Aspects of deterioration of plant remains in archaeological sites: the Walpi Archaeological Project. *Journal of Ethnobiology* 1:182–192.

Goodyear, Frank H., 1971, *Archaeological site science.* Elsevier, New York.

Hassan, Fekri A., 1978, Sediments in archaeology: methods and implications for palaeoenvironmental and cultural analysis. *Journal of Field Archaeology* 5:197–213.

Jashemski, Wilhemina F., 1972, A vineyard at Pompeii. *Archaeology* 25:48–56.

Krantz, Grover S., 1970, Human activities and megafaunal extinctions. *American Scientist* 58:164–170.

Leakey, Richard E., 1976, Hominids in Africa. *American Scientist* 64:174–178.

McIntosh, Roderick J., 1977, The excavation of mud structures: an experiment from West Africa. *World Archaeology* 9:185–199.

Mosimann, J. E. and P. S. Martin, 1975, Simulating overkill by Paleoindians. *American Scientist* 63:304–313.

Puleston, D. E., 1971, An experimental approach to the function of Classic Maya chultuns, *American Antiquity* 36:322–326.

Turnbaugh, William A., 1978, Floods and archaeology. *American Antiquity* 43:593–607.

Technical

Behrensmeyer, Anna K. and Andrew P. Hill (Eds.), 1980, *Fossils in the making: vertebrate taphonomy and paleoecology.* University of Chicago Press, Chicago.

Davidson, D. A., 1973, Particle size and phosphate analysis evidence for the evolution of a tell. *Archaeometry* 15:143–152.

Fuchs, C., D. Kaufman, and A. Ronen, 1977, Erosion and artifact distribution in open-air epipalaeolithic sites on the coastal plain of Israel. *Journal of Field Archaeology* 4:171–179.

Gifford, Diane P., 1978, Ethnoarchaeological observations of natural processes affecting cultural materials. In *Explorations in ethnoarchaeology,* Richard A. Gould (Ed.), pp. 77–102. University of New Mexico Press, Albuquerque.

Gifford, Diane P., 1981, Taphonomy and paleoecology: a critical review of archaeology's sister disciplines. In *Advances in archaeological method and theory, Vol. 4,* Michael B. Schiffer (Ed.), pp. 365–438. Academic Press, New York.

Gladfelter, Bruce G., 1977, Geoarchaeology: the geomorphologist and archaeology. *American Antiquity* 42:519–538.

Goldberg, Paul, 1979, Micromorphology of Pech-de-l'Azé II Sediments. *Journal of Archaeological Science* 6:17–47.

Grayson, Donald K., 1980, Vicissitudes and overkill: the development of explanations of Pleistocene extinctions. In *Advances in archaeological method and theory, Vol. 3,* Michael B. Schiffer (Ed.), pp. 357–403. Academic Press, New York.

Isaac, Glynn L. and Elizabeth R. McCown, 1976, *Human origins: Louis Leakey and the east African evidence.* Staples Press, Menlo Park, California.

Leakey, Mary D., 1971, *Olduvai Gorge, Vol. 3: Excavations in Beds I and II.* Cambridge University Press, Cambridge, England.

Limbrey, Susan, 1975, *Soil science and archaeology.* Academic Press, London.

Pyddoke, Edward, 1961, *Stratification for the archaeologist.* Phoenix House, London.

Shackleton, N. J., 1973, Oxygen isotope analysis determining season of occupation of prehistoric midden sites. *Archaeometry* 15:133–141.

Shackley, M. L., 1972, The use of textural parameters in the analysis of cave sediments. *Archaeometry* 14:133–145.

Slager, S. and H. T. J. van de Wetering, 1977, Soil formation in archaeological pits and adjacent loess soils in Southern Germany. *Journal of Archaeological Science* 4:259–267.

Vita-Finzi, Claudio, 1978, *Archaeological sites in their setting.* Thames and Hudson, London.

Wilcox, G. H., 1977, Exotic plants from Roman waterlogged sites in London. *Journal of Archaeological Science* 4:269–282.

Wood, W. Raymond and Donald L. Johnson, 1978, A survey of disturbance processes in archaeological site formation. In *Advances in archaeological method and theory, Vol. 1,* Michael B. Schiffer (Ed.), pp. 315–381. Academic Press, New York.

7 RECOVERY

General

Arens, William, 1979, *The man-eating myth.* Oxford University Press, New York.

Barker, Philip, 1977, *The techniques of archaeological excavation.* Universe Books, New York.

Burrows, Millar, 1955, *The Dead Sea Scrolls.* The Viking Press, New York.

Hester, Thomas R., Robert F. Heizer, and John A. Graham, 1975, *Field methods in archeology.* Mayfield Publishing Co., Palo Alto.

Joukowsky, Martha, 1980, *A complete manual of field archaeology: tools and techniques of field work for archaeologists.* Prentice-Hall, Englewood Cliffs, New Jersey.

Müller-Beck, Hansjürgen, 1961, Prehistoric Swiss lake dwellers. *Scientific American* 205:138–144.

Owen, David I., 1971, Excavating a classical shipwreck. *Archaeology* 24:118–129.

Payne, Robert, 1959, *The gold of Troy.* Funk and Wagnalls, New York.

Struever, Stuart and Felicia Antonelli Holton, 1979, *Koster: Americans in search of their prehistoric past.* Anchor Press/Doubleday, Garden City, New York.

Thompson, M. W., 1977, *General Pitt-Rivers: evolution and archaeology in the nineteenth century.* Moonraker Press, Wiltshire, England.

Watts, Gordon P., Jr., 1981, The Edenton Harbor wrecks: underwater archaeology in America. *Archaeology* 34:14–21.

Wheeler, Mortimer, 1956, *Archaeology from the earth.* Penguin, Baltimore.

Special Interest

Bennett, W. C., 1934, Excavations at Tiahuanaco. *American Museum of Natural History, Anthropological Papers* 34(3):359–494.

Bradley, Richard, 1978, Prehistoric field systems in Britain and north-west Europe—a review of some recent work. *World Archaeology* 9:265–280.

Breiner, Sheldon and Michael D. Coe, 1972, Magnetic exploration of the Olmec Civilization. *American Scientist* 60:566–575.

Browman, David L., 1981, New light on Andean Tiwanaku (Tiahuanaco). *American Scientist* 69:408–419.

Coe, William R., 1962, Maya mystery in Tikal, part 1. *Natural History* 7:10–21.

Coe, William R., 1962, Maya mystery in Tikal, part 2. *Natural History* 71:44–53.

Ebert, James I. and Thomas R. Lyons, 1980, Prehistoric irrigation canals identified from Skylab III and Landsat imagery in Phoenix, Arizona. In *Cultural resources remote sensing,* Thomas R. Lyons and Frances J. Mathien (Eds.), pp. 209–228. Cultural Resources Management Division, National Park Service, Washington, D.C.

Gibson, McGuire, 1977, Nippur: new perspectives. *Archaeology* 30:26–37.

Harris, Edward C., 1979, *Principles of archaeological stratigraphy.* Academic Press, London.

Haury, Emil W., 1967, The Hohokam: first masters

of the American desert. *National Geographic* 131:670–695.

Lyons, Thomas R. and Thomas Eugene Avery, 1977, *Remote sensing: a handbook for archeologists and cultural resource managers.* Cultural Resources Management Division, National Park Service, Washington, D.C.

Millon, R., 1973, *The Teotihuacán map, Vol. 1, Part 1* (text). University of Texas Press, Austin.

Millon, R., B. Drewitt, and G. Cowgill, 1973, *The Teotihuacán map, Vol. 1, Part 2* (maps). University of Texas Press, Austin.

Noël Hume, Ivor, 1969, *Historical archaeology.* Knopf, New York.

Oleson, John Peter, 1977, Underwater survey and excavation in the Port of Pyrgi (Santa Severa), 1974. *Journal of Field Archaeology* 4:297–308.

Pendergast, David M., 1975, The Teotihuacán map: a review article. *Archaeology* 28:164–169.

Pitt-Rivers, A. H. L. Fox, 1906. *The evolution of culture and other essays.* J. L. Myers (Ed.), Clarendon Press, Oxford.

Pritchard, J. B. (Ed.), 1955, *Ancient Near Eastern texts.* Princeton University Press, Princeton.

Redman, Charles L., 1974, Archeological sampling strategies. *Addison-Wesley Modular Publications in Anthropology 55.*

Richardson, L., Jr., 1977, The libraries of Pompeii. *Archaeology* 30:394–407.

Schiffer, Michael B., Theodore E. Downing, and Michael McCarthy, 1981, Waste not, want not: an ethnoarchaeological study of reuse in Tucson, Arizona. In *Modern material culture: the archaeology of Us,* Richard A. Gould and Michael B. Schiffer (Eds.), pp. 67–86. Academic Press, New York.

Willey, Gordon R., Richard M. Leventhal, and William L. Fash, Jr., 1978, Maya Settlement in the Copan Valley. *Archaeology* 31:32–43.

Technical

Aitken, Martin, 1971, Magnetic location. In *Science in archaeology: a survey of progress and research* (2nd ed.), Don Brothwell and Eric Higgs (Eds.), pp. 681–694. Thames and Hudson, London.

Baker, Charles M., 1978, The size effect: an explanation of variability in surface artifact assemblage content. *American Antiquity* 43:288–293.

Clark, Anthony, 1971, Resistivity surveying. In *Science in archaeology: a survey of progress and research* (2nd ed.), Don Brothwell and Eric Higgs (Eds.), pp. 695–707. Thames and Hudson, London.

Dowman, Elizabeth A., 1970, *Conservation in field archaeology.* Methuen and Co., London.

Dyson, Stephen L., 1981, Survey archaeology: reconstructing the Roman countryside. *Archaeology* 34:31–37.

Evans, R. and R. J. A. Jones, 1977, Crop marks and soils at two archaeological sites in Britain. *Journal of Archaeological Science* 4:63–76.

Fewkes, Jesse Walter, 1898, Archeological expedition to Arizona in 1895. Seventeenth Annual Report of the Bureau of American Ethnology, 1895–96, Part 2.

Fladmark, Knut R., 1978, A guide to basic archaeological field procedures. *Simon Fraser University, Department of Archaeology, Publication 4.*

Foard, Glenn, 1978, Systematic fieldwalking and the investigation of Saxon settlement in Northamptonshire. *World Archaeology* 9:357–374.

Glassie, Henry, 1977, Archaeology and folklore: common anxieties, common hopes. In *Historical archaeology and the importance of material things,* Leland Ferguson (Ed.), pp. 23–35. *The Society for Historical Archaeology, Special Publication Series 2.*

Green, J. N., P. E. Baker, B. Richards, and D. M. Squire, 1971, Simple underwater photogrammetric techniques. *Archaeometry* 13:221–232.

Harris, Edward C., 1975, The stratigraphic sequence: a question of time. *World Archaeology* 7:109–121.

Hill, James N., 1970, Broken K Pueblo: prehistoric social organization in the American Southwest. *University of Arizona, Anthropological Paper 18.*

Hirth, Kenneth G., 1978, Problems in data recovery and measurement in settlement archaeology. *Journal of Field Archaeology* 5:125–131.

House, John H. and Ronald W. Wogaman, 1978, Windy Ridge: a prehistoric site in the inter-riverine piedmont in South Carolina. *University of South Carolina, Institute of Archeology, Anthropological Studies 3.*

Jelinek, Arthur J., 1981, The Middle Paleolithic in the Southern Levant from the perspective of the Tabin Care. *Préhistoire du Levant* 598:265–280.

Leakey, M. D., R. L. Hay, D. L. Thurber, R. Protsch, and R. Berger, 1972, Stratigraphy, archaeology, and age of the Ndutu and Naisiusiu Beds, Olduvai Gorge, Tanzania. *World Archaeology* 3:328–341.

LeBlanc, Steven A., 1976, Archaeological recording systems. *Journal of Field Archaeology* 3:159–168.

Lewarch, Dennis E. and Michael J. O'Brien, 1981, The expanding role of surface assemblages in archaeological research. In *Advances in archaeological method and theory*, Michael B. Schiffer (Ed.), pp. 297–342. Academic Press, New York.

Lyons, Thomas R. and Frances J. Mathien (Eds.), 1980, *Cultural resources remote sensing.* Cultural Resources Management Division, National Park Service, Washington, D.C.

Mueller, James W. (Ed.), 1975, *Sampling in archaeology.* University of Arizona Press, Tucson.

Ozawa, K. and M. Matsuda, 1979, Computer assisted techniques for detecting underground remains based on acoustic measurement. *Archaeometry* 21:87–100.

Palmer, Rog, 1977, A computer method transcribing information graphically from oblique aerial photographs to maps. *Journal of Archaeological Science* 4:283–290.

Plenderleith, H. J. and A. E. A. Werner, 1971, *The conservation of antiquities and works of art.* (2nd ed.). Oxford University Press, London.

Plog, Stephen, Fred Plog, and Walter Wait, 1978, Decision making in modern surveys. In *Advances in archaeological method and theory, Vol. 1,* Michael B. Schiffer (Ed.), pp. 383–421. Academic Press, New York.

Schiffer, Michael B., Alan P. Sullivan, and Timothy C. Klinger, 1978, The design of archaeological surveys. *World Archaeology* 10:1–28.

Thomas, David H., 1973, An empirical test for Steward's model of Great Basin settlement patterns. *American Antiquity* 38:155–176.

Watson, Patty Jo, 1976, In pursuit of prehistoric subsistence: a comparative account of some contemporary flotation techniques. *Midcontinental Journal of Archaeology* 1:77–100.

Willey, Gordon R., 1953, Prehistoric settlement patterns in the Virú Valley, Peru. *Bureau of American Ethnology, Bulletin 155.*

8 ANALYSIS

General

Artamonov, M. I., 1965, Frozen tombs of the Scythians. *Scientific American* 212:100–109.

Aveni, Anthony F., 1981, Archaeoastronomy. In *Advances in archaeological method and theory, Vol. 4,* Michael B. Schiffer (Ed.), pp. 1–77. Academic Press, New York.

Brothwell, D. R., 1963, *Digging up bones: the excavation, treatment and study of human skeletal remains.* The British Museum, London.

Coe, M. D., 1973, *The Maya scribe and his world.* Grolier Club, New York.

Erasmus, Charles J., 1965, Monument building: some field experiments. *Southwestern Journal of Anthropology* 21:277–301.

Gray, Jane and Watson Smith, 1962, Fossil pollen and archaeology. *Archaeology* 15:16–26.

Hicks, Ronald, 1979, Archaeoastronomy and the beginnings of a science. *Archaeology* 32:46–52.

Keeley, Lawrence H., 1977, The functions of palaeolithic flint tools. *Scientific American* 237:108–126.

Kennedy, Kenneth A. R., 1981, Skeletal biology: when bones tell tales. *Archaeology* 34:17–24.

Moseley, Michael E. and C. J. Mackey, 1973, Chan Chan, Peru's ancient city of kings. *National Geographic* 143:318–345.

Oakley, Kenneth, 1964, *Man the toolmaker.* University of Chicago Press, Chicago.

Proskouriakoff, Tatiana, 1946, An album of Maya architecture. *Carnegie Institution of Washington, Publication 558.*

Proskouriakoff, Tatiana, 1961, The lords of the Maya realm. *Expedition* 4:14–21.

Rudolph, Richard C., 1965, Newly discovered Chinese painted tombs. *Archaeology* 18:171–180.

Semenov, S. A., 1964, *Prehistoric technology.* Cory, Adams and Mackay, London.

Thomas, David Hurst, 1974, *Predicting the past.* Holt, Rinehart, & Winston, New York.

Wheat, Joe Ben, 1967, A Paleo-Indian bison kill. *Scientific American* 216:44–52.

Williamson, Ray, 1978, Native Americans were the continent's first astronomers. *Smithsonian* 9:78–85.

Special Interest

Afshar, A., W. Dutz, and M. E. Taylor, 1974, Giraffes at Persepolis. *Archaeology* 27:114–117.

Allison, Marvin J., 1979, Pathology in Peru. *Natural History* 88:74–82.

Aveni, Anthony F., 1979, Venus and the Maya. *American Scientist* 67:274–285.

Bartel, Brad, 1979, A discriminant analysis of Harappan Civilization human populations. *Journal of Archaeological Science* 6:49–61.

Bass, George F., 1978, Glass treasure from the Aegean. *National Geographic* 153:768–793.

Beehler, Carolyn Murphy, 1980, Catacomb painting of trees may be an ancient star map. *Smithsonian* 11:158–159.

Benson, Elizabeth P. (Ed.), 1975, *Death and the afterlife in pre-Columbian America.* Dumbarton Oaks Research Library and Collections, Washington.

Brown, James A. (Ed.), 1971, Approaches to the social dimensions of mortuary practices. *Memoirs of the Society for American Archaeology* 25.

Bryant, Vaughn M., Jr., and Glenna Williams-Dean, 1975, The coprolites of man. *Scientific American* 232:100–109.

Brooks, Robert R. R., 1975, Reconstructing Stone Age paintings. *Archaeology* 28:92–97.

Conrad, Geoffrey W., 1978, Models of compromise in settlement pattern studies: an example from coastal Peru. *World Archaeology* 9:281–298.

Dennell, R. W., 1976, The economic importance of plant resources represented on archaeological sites. *Journal of Archaeological Science* 3:229–247.

Dennell, Robin W., 1978, Archaeobotany and early farming in Europe. *Archaeology* 31:8–13.

Donnan, Christopher B., 1972, Moche-Huari murals from Northern Peru. *Archaeology* 25:85–95.

Hamblin, Dora Jane, 1973, Italy's marvelous marble jigsaw puzzle with 20,000 pieces. *Smithsonian* 3:54–61.

Harris, James E. and Kent R. Weeks, 1972, X-raying the Pharaohs. *Natural History* 81:54–63.

Hewett, Cecil, 1977, Understanding standing buildings. *World Archaeology* 9:174–184.

Heyerdahl, Thor, 1958, *Aku-Aku: the secret of Easter Island.* Rand McNally, New York.

Hodges, Henry, 1964, *Artifacts: an introduction to primitive technology.* Praeger, New York.

Hsio-Yen Shih, 1972, The study of ancient Chinese bronzes as art and craft. *World Archaeology* 3:267–275.

Isaac, Glynn, 1971, The diet of early man: aspects of archaeological evidence from lower and middle Pleistocene sites in Africa. *World Archaeology* 2:278–299.

Linton, Ralph, 1944, North American cooking pots. *American Antiquity* 9:369–380.

Moseley, Michael E. 1975, Chan Chan: Andean alternative to the preindustrial city. *Science* 187:219–225.

Moseley, Michael E., 1975, Secrets of Peru's ancient walls. *Natural History* 84:34–41.

Moser, Christopher L., 1974, Ritual decapitation in Moche art. *Archaeology* 27:30–37.

Peacock, D. P. S., 1970, The scientific analysis of ancient ceramics: a review. *World Archaeology* 1:375–389.

Pellicori, Samuel, 1981, The Shroud of Turin through the microscope. *Archaeology* 34:34–43.

Pendergast, David M., 1969, Altunlta, British Honduras (Belize): the Sun God's Tomb. *The Royal Ontario Museum, Art and Archaeology Occasional Papers* 19.

Plazas, Clemencic and Ana Maria Falchetti de Sáerz, 1979, Technology of ancient Colombian gold. *Natural History* 88:37, 40–46.

Rathje, William L., 1970, Socio-political implications of lowland Maya burials: methodology and tentative hypotheses. *World Archaeology* 1:359–374.

Rudolph, Richard C., 1973, Two recently discovered Han tombs. *Archaeology* 26:106–115.

Schmidt, P. and D. H. Avery, 1978, Complex iron smelting and prehistoric culture in Tanzania. *Science* 201:1085–1089.

Sharon, Douglas G. and Christopher Donnan, 1977, The magic cactus: ethnoarchaeological continuity in Peru. *Archaeology* 30:374–381.

Shimada, Izumi, 1978, Economy of a prehistoric urban context: commodity and labor flow at Moche V Pampa Grande, Peru. *American Antiquity* 43:569–592.

Stothert, Karen E., 1979, Unwrapping an Inca mummy bundle. *Archaeology* 32:8–17.

Tainter, Joseph, 1978, Mortuary practices and the study of prehistoric social systems. In *Advances in archaeological method and theory, Vol. 1,* Michael B. Schiffer (Ed.), pp. 105–141. Academic Press, New York.

Turner, C. G. and L. Lofgren, 1966, Household size of prehistoric Western Pueblo Indians. *Southwestern Journal of Anthropology* 22:117–132.

Uerpmann, Hans-Peter, 1973, Animal bone finds and economic archaeology: a critical study of "osteo-archaeological" method. *World Archaeology* 4:307–322.

Vreeland, James, 1977, Ancient Andean textiles: clothes for the dead. *Archaeology* 30:166–178.

Werner, O. and F. Willet, 1975, The composition of brasses from Ife and Benin. *Archaeometry* 17:141–156.

Wheat, Joe Ben, 1967, A Paleo-Indian bison kill. *Scientific American* 216:44–52.

Wilkinson, Richard G., 1975, Techniques of ancient skull surgery. *Natural History* 84:94–101.

Williams, A. R. and K. R. Maxwell-Hyslop, 1976, Ancient steel from Egypt. *Journal of Archaeological Science* 3:283–305.

Williams-Dean, Glenna and Vaughn M. Bryant, Jr., 1975, Pollen analysis of human coprolites from Antelope House. *The Kiva* 41:97–111.

Technical

Adovasio, J. M., 1977, *Basketry technology: a guide to identification and analysis.* Aldine, Chicago.

Anderson, Patricia C., 1980, A testimony of prehistoric tasks: diagnostic residues on stone tool working edges. *World Archaeology* 12:181–194.

Armitage, P. L. and Juliet Clutton-Brock, 1976, A system for classification and description of the horn cores of cattle from archaeological sites. *Journal of Archaeological Science* 3:329–348.

Beck, Curt W., 1970, Amber in archaeology. *Archaeology* 23:7–11.

Bishop, Ronald L., Robert L. Rands, and George R. Holley, 1982, Ceramic compositional analysis in archaeological perspective. In *Advances in archaeological method and theory, Vol. 5*, Michael B. Schiffer (Ed.), pp. 275–330. Academic Press, New York.

Trevor-Deutsch, B. and V. M. Bryant, Jr., 1978, Analysis of suspected human coprolites from Terra Amata, Nice, France. *Journal of Archaeological Science* 5:387–390.

Chaplin, Raymond E., 1971, *The study of animal bones from archaeological sites.* Seminar Press, London and New York.

Chou, Hung-Hsiang, 1973, Computer matching of oracle bone fragments. *Archaeology* 26:176–181.

Clarke, David L. and Bob Chapman, 1978, *Analytical archaeology* (2nd ed.). Columbia University Press, New York.

Collins, Michael B., 1975, Lithic technology as a means of processual inference. In *Lithic technology, making and using Stone tools*, Earl Swanson (Ed.), pp. 15–34. Aldine, Chicago.

Collis, John, 1981, A typology of coin distributions. *World Archaeology* 13:122–128.

Cotter, Maurice J., 1980, Neutron activation analysis of paintings. *American Scientist* 69:17–27.

Fry, Robert E. and Scott C. Cox, 1974, The structure of ceramic exchange at Tikal, Guatemala. *World Archaeology* 6:209–225.

Dean, Jeffrey S., 1969, Chronological analysis of Tsegi Phase sites in northeastern Arizona. *Laboratory of Tree-Ring Research, Papers* 3.

Deetz, James, 1968, The inference of residence and descent rules from archeological data. In *New perspectives in archeology*, Sally R. and Lewis R. Binford (Eds.), pp. 41–48. Aldine, Chicago.

Dimbleby, G., 1967, *Plants and archeology.* Humanities Press, New York.

Dunnell, Robert C., 1971, *Systematics in prehistory.* Free Press, New York.

Ericson, Jonathan E. and E. Gary Stickel, 1973, A proposed classification system for ceramics. *World Archaeology* 4:357–367.

Ford, Richard I., 1979, Paleoethnobotany in American archaeology. In *Advances in archaeological method and theory, Vol. 2*, Michael B. Schiffer (Ed.), pp. 285–336. Academic Press, New York.

Goodyear, Albert C., 1974, The Brand site: a techno-functional study of a Dalton site in northeast Arkansas. *Arkansas Archeological Survey, Research Series* 7.

Grayson, Donald K., 1979, On the quantification of vertebrate archaeofaunas. In *Advances in archaeological method and theory, Vol. 2*, Michael B. Schiffer (Ed.), pp. 199–237. Academic Press, New York.

Grayson, Donald K., 1980, The effects of sample size on some derived measures in vertebrate faunal analysis. *Journal of Archaeological Science* 8:77–88.

Griffiths, Dorothy M., 1978, Use-marks on historic ceramics: a preliminary study. *Historical Archaeology* 12:68–81.

Hammond, N., G. Harbottle, and T. Gazard, 1976, Neutron activation and statistical analysis of Maya ceramics and clays from Lubaantun Belize. *Archaeometry* 18:147–168.

Harrold, Francis, 1980, A comparative analysis of Eurasian palaeolithic burials. *World Archaeology* 12:195–211.

Hayden, Brian (Ed.), 1979, *Lithic use-wear analysis.* Academic Press, New York.

Hedges, R. E. M., 1976, Pre-Islamic glazes in Mesopotamia-Nippur. *Archaeometry* 18:209–213.

Hill, J. N. and R. K. Evans, 1972, A model for classification and typology. In *Models in archaeology*, D. L. Clarke (Ed.), pp. 231–273. Methuen, London.

Huss-Ashmore, Rebecca, Alan H. Goodman, and George J. Armelagos, 1982, Nutritional inference from paleopathology. In *Advances in archaeological method and theory, Vol. 5*, Michael B. Schiffer (Ed.), pp. 395–474. Academic Press, New York.

Keeley, Lawrence H., 1974, Technique and methodology in microwear studies: critical review. *World Archaeology* 5:323–336.

Keeley, Lawrence H., 1980, *Experimental determination of stone tool uses: a microwear analysis.* University of Chicago Press, Chicago.

Keeley, L. H. and M. H. Newcomer, 1977, Microwear analysis of experimental flint tools: a test case. *Journal of Archaeological Science* 4:29–62.

Kidder, A. V., J. D. Jennings, and E. M. Shook, 1946, Excavations at Kaminaljuyú, Guatemala. *Carnegie Institution of Washington, Publication 561.*

Klein, Richard G., Cornelia Wolf, Leslie Freeman, and Kathryn Allwarden, 1981, The use of dental crown heights for constructing age profiles of red deer and similar species in archaeological samples. *Journal of Archaeological Science* 8:1–31.

Körber-Grohne, U., 1981, Distinguishing prehistoric cereal grains of triticum and secale on the basis of their surface patterns using the scanning electron microscope. *Journal of Archaeological Science* 8:197–204.

Longacre, William A., 1970, Archaeology as anthropology: a case study. *University of Arizona, Anthropological Papers* 17.

Proskouriakoff, Tatiana, 1960, Historical implications of a pattern of dates at Piedras Negras, Guatemala. *American Antiquity* 25:454–475.

Proskouriakoff, Tatiana, 1963, Historical data in the inscriptions of Yaxchilan, pt. 1. *Estudios de Cultura Maya* 3:149–167.

Proskouriakoff, Tatiana, 1964, Historical data in the inscriptions of Yaxchilan, pt. 2. *Estudios de Cultura Maya* 4:177–201.

Renfrew, J. M., 1973, *Paleoethnobotany.* Columbia University Press, New York.

Rouse, Irving, 1960, The classification of artifacts in archaeology. *American Antiquity* 25:313–323.

Rowlands, M. J., 1971, The archaeological interpretation of prehistoric metal-working. *World Archaeology* 3:210–224.

Rye, Owen S., 1981, *Pottery technology: principles and reconstruction.* Taraxacum, Washington, D.C.

Saul, Frank P., 1972, Human skeletal remains of Altar de Sacrificios. *Harvard University, Peabody Museum Paper* 63(2).

Sheets, Payson, 1975, Behavioral analysis and the structure of a prehistoric industry. *Current Anthropology* 16:369–391.

Schuler, Frederic, 1962, Ancient glassmaking techniques: the Egyptian core vessel process. *Archaeology* 15:32–37.

Shepard, Anna O., 1965, Ceramics for the archaeologist. *Carnegie Institution of Washington, Publication 609.*

Smith, Ray Winfield, 1970, Computer helps scholars re-create an Egyptian temple. *National Geographic* 138:634–655.

Spaulding, Albert C., 1953, Statistical techniques for the discovery of artifact types. *American Antiquity* 18:305–313.

Spaulding, Albert C., 1973, The concept of artifact type in archaeology. *Plateau* 45(4):149–164.

Tainter, Joseph A., 1975, Social inference and mortuary practices: an experiment in numerical classification. *World Archaeology* 7:1–15.

Tite, M. S., 1972, *Methods of physical examination in archaeology.* Seminar Press, London.

Trell, Bluma L., 1976, Architecture on ancient coins. *Archaeology* 29:6–13.

Tylecote, R. F., 1962, *Metallurgy in archaeology.* Edward Arnold, London.

Ubelaker, Douglas H., 1978, *Human skeletal remains: excavation, analyis, interpretation.* Taraxacum, Washington, D. C.

Watson, Patty Jo, 1977, Design analysis of painted pottery. *American Antiquity* 42:381–393.

Wertime, T. A., 1973, The beginnings of metallurgy: a new look. *Science* 182:875–887.

Whallon, Robert Jr., 1972, A new approach to pottery typology. *American Antiquity* 37:13–33.

White, John R., 1978, Bottle nomenclature: a glossary of landmark terminology for the archaeologist. *Historical Archaeology* 12:58–67.

White, John R., 1978, Archaeological and chemical evidence for the earliest American use of raw coal as a fuel in ironmaking. *Journal of Archaeological Science* 5:391–393.

Wheat, Joe Ben, James C. Gifford, and William Wasley, 1958, Ceramic variety, type cluster, and ceramic system in Southwestern pottery analysis. *American Antiquity* 24:34–47.

Wilcox, David R., 1975, A strategy for perceiving social groups in puebloan sites. In Chapters in the prehistory of eastern Arizona, IV. *Fieldiana: Anthropology* 65:120–159.

Wilcox, David R. and Lynette O. Shenk, 1977, The architecture of the Casa Grande and its interpretation. *Arizona State Museum, Archaeological Series* 115.

Wing, Elizabeth S. and Antoinette B. Brown, 1979,

Paleonutrition: method and theory in prehistoric foodways. Academic Press, New York.

Zier, Christian J., 1980, A classic-period Maya agricultural field in western Belize. *Journal of Field Archaeology* 7:65–74.

9 INFERENCE

General

Casson, Lionel, 1981, Maritime trade in antiquity. *Archaeology* 34:37–43.

Childe, V. Gordon, 1925, *The dawn of European civilization.* Kegan Paul, London.

Crosswhite, Frank S., 1980, The annual Saguaro harvest and crop cycle of the Papago, with reference to ecology and symbolism. *Desert Plants* 2:3–61.

Culbert, T. Patrick, 1974, *The lost civilization: the story of the Classic Maya.* Harper & Row, New York.

Daniel, Glyn, 1972, *Megaliths in history.* Thames and Hudson, London.

Daniel, Glyn, 1980, Megalith monuments. *Scientific American* 243:78–90.

Dixon, J. E., J. R. Cann, and Colin Renfrew, 1968, Obsidian and the origins of trade. *Scientific American* 218:38–46.

Douglass, A. E., 1929, The secret of the Southwest solved by talkative tree rings. *National Geographic* 56:736–770.

Haskins, John F., 1960, The royal Scythians. *Natural History* 69:8–17.

Haury, Emil W., 1962, HH–39: recollections of a dramatic moment in Southwestern archaeology. *Tree-Ring Bulletin* 24:11–14.

Mendelssohn, K., 1971, A scientist looks at the pyramids. *American Scientist* 59:210–220.

Millon, R., 1967, Teotihuacán. *Scientific American* 216:38–49.

Renfrew, Colin, 1971, Carbon 14 and the prehistory of Europe. *Scientific American* 225:63–72.

Stuart, George E., 1975, The Maya riddle of the glyphs. *National Geographic* 148:768–791.

Topping, Audrey, 1978, The first emperor's army: China's incredible find. *National Geographic* 153:440–459.

Special Interest

Adams, Robert McC., 1974, Anthropological perspectives on ancient trade. *Current Anthropology* 15:239–258.

Andrews, Anthony P., 1980, The salt trade of the ancient Maya. *Archaeology* 33:24–33.

Angus, Anne, 1972, The fascinations of discovering engineering's past. *Smithsonian* 2:34–41.

Badawy, Alexander M., 1965, Askut: a Middle Kingdom fortress in Nubia. *Archaeology* 18:124–131.

Bannister, Bryant and William J. Robinson, 1975, Tree-ring dating in archaeology. *World Archaeology* 7:210–225.

Brown, James A., 1976, The Southern Cult reconsidered. *Midcontinental Journal of Archaeology* 1:115–135.

Burl, Aubrey, 1973, Dating the British stone circles. *American Scientist* 61:167–174.

Chang, K. C., 1958, Study of the Neolithic social grouping: examples from the New World. *American Anthropologist* 60:298–334.

Childe, V. Gordon, 1956, *Piecing together the past.* Praeger, New York.

Charlton, Thomas H., 1978, Teotihuacán, Tepeapulco, and obsidian exploitation. *Science* 200:1227–1236.

Clark, J. G. D., 1972, Star Carr: a case study in bioarchaeology. *Addison-Wesley Modular Publications in Anthropology* 10.

Cook, Sherburne F. and Robert F. Heizer, 1968, Relationships among houses, settlement areas, and population in aboriginal California. In *Settlement archaeology,* K. C. Chang (Ed.), pp. 79–116. National Press Books, Palo Alto, California.

Dean, Jeffrey S., 1978, Tree-ring dating in archaeology. *University of Utah, Anthropological Papers 99, Miscellaneous Collection Papers 19–24,* pp. 129–163.

Flannery, Kent V. and Marcus C. Winter, 1976, Analyzing household activities. In *The early Mesoamerican village,* Kent V. Flannery (Ed.), pp. 34–47. Academic Press, New York.

Fox, Aileen, 1976, Prehistoric Maori fortifications in the North Island of New Zealand. *New Zealand Archaeological Association, Monograph* 6.

Frankfort, H., 1956, *The birth of civilization in the Near East.* Doubleday, New York.

Friedman, Irving and Fred W. Trembour, 1978, Obsidian: the dating stone. *American Scientist* 66:44–51.

Greenwood, N. H. and C. W. White, 1970, Mogollon ritual: a spatial configuration of a non-village pattern. *Archaeology* 23:298–302.

Griffin, P. Bion, 1967, A high status burial from Grasshopper Ruin, Arizona. *The Kiva* 33:37–53.

Hellmuth, N., 1978, Teotihuacan art in the Escuintta, Guatemala Region. In *Middle Classic Mesoamerica A.D. 400–700,* E. Paztory (Ed.), pp. 71–85. New York, Columbia University Press.

Libby, Willard F., 1955, *Radiocarbon dating.* (2nd ed.). University of Chicago Press, Chicago.

Longacre, William A. and James E. Ayres, 1968, Archeological lessons from an Apache wickiup. In *New perspectives in archeology,* Sally R. Binford and Lewis R. Binford (Eds.), pp. 151–160. Aldine, Chicago.

Murra, John V. and Craig Morris, 1976, Dynastic oral tradition, administrative records and archaeology in the Andes. *World Archaeology* 7:269–279.

Naroll, Raoul, 1962, Floor area and settlement population. *American Antiquity* 27:587–589.

Parsons, Jefferey, R., 1974, The development of a prehistoric complex society: a regional perspective from the Valley of Mexico. *Journal of Field Archaeology* 1:81–108.

Petrie, W. M. F., 1899, Sequences in prehistoric remains. *Journal of the Royal Anthropological Institute* 29:295–301.

Petrie, W. M. F., 1901, Diospolis Parva. *Egyptian Exploration Fund Memoirs* 20.

Puleston, Dennis E., 1968, *Brosimum Alicastrum* as a subsistence alternative for the Classic Maya of the central southern lowlands. M.A. Thesis, University of Pennsylvania.

Puleston, Dennis E., 1971, An experimental approach to the function of Maya chultuns. *American Antiquity* 36:322–335.

Ralph, E. K. and H. N. Michael, 1974, Twenty-five years of radiocarbon dating. *American Scientist* 62:553–560.

Reid, J. Jefferson (Ed.), 1974, Behavioral archaeology at the Grasshopper Ruin. *The Kiva* 40:1–112.

Renfrew, Colin, 1973, *Before civilization.* Knopf, New York.

Sanders, W. T., 1956, The central Mexican symbiotic region: a study in prehistoric settlement patterns. In *Prehistoric settlement patterns in the New World,* Gordon R. Willey (Ed.), pp. 115–127. *Viking Fund Publications in Anthropology* 23.

Struever, Stuart, 1968, Woodland subsistence-settlement systems in the Lower Illinois Valley. In *New perspectives in archeology,* Sally R. and Lewis R. Binford (Eds.), pp. 285–312. Aldine, Chicago.

Trigger, Bruce, 1978, *Time and traditions: essays in archaeological interpretation.* Columbia University Press, New York.

Wheatley, Paul, 1970, Archaeology and the Chinese city. *World Archaeology* 2:159–185.

Wheeler, M., 1943, *Maiden Castle, Dorset.* Society of Antiquaries, London.

Will, Elizabeth Lyding, 1977, The ancient commercial amphora. *Archaeology* 30:264–270.

Willey, Gordon R. and Philip Phillips, 1958, *Method and theory in American archaeology.* University of Chicago Press, Chicago.

Technical

Aveni, Anthony F., 1981, Archaeoastronomy. In *Advances in archaeological method and theory, Vol. 4,* Michael B. Schiffer (Ed.), pp. 1–77. Academic Press, New York.

Bada, Jeffrey L. and Patricia Masters Helfman, 1975, Amino acid racemization dating of fossil bones. *World Archaeology* 7:160–173.

Blagg, T. F. C., 1980, Roman civil and military architecture in the province of Britain: aspects of patronage, influence and craft organization. *World Archaeology* 12:27–42.

Beale, Thomas, W., 1978, Bevelled rim bowls and their implications for change and economic organization in the later Fourth Millennium B.C., *Journal of Near Eastern Studies* 37:298–313.

Browman, David L., 1981, Isotopic discrimination and correction factors in radiocarbon dating. In *Advances in archaeological method and theory, Vol. 4,* Michael B. Schiffer (Ed.), pp. 241–295. Academic Press, New York.

Chang, K. C., 1972, Settlement patterns in archaeology. *Addison-Wesley Modular Publications in Anthropology* 24.

Curtis, Garniss H., 1975, Improvements in potassium-argon dating: 1962–1975. *World Archaeology* 7:198–209.

Dean, Jeffrey S., 1978, Independent dating in archaeological analysis. In *Advances in archaeological method and theory, Vol. 1,* Michael B. Schiffer (Ed.), pp. 223–255. Academic Press, New York.

Ericson, Jonathon E., 1975, New results in obsidian hydration dating. *World Archaeology* 7:151–159.

Evans, J. G., 1969, Land and freshwater Mollusca in archaeology: chronological aspects. *World Archaeology* 1:170–183.

Evernden, J. F. and G. H. Curtis, 1965, The potassium-argon dating of late Cenozoic rocks in east Africa and Italy. *Current Anthropology* 6:343–385.

Ferguson, C. W., 1968, Bristlecone pine: science and esthetics. *Science* 159:839–846.

Fleischer, Robert L., 1975, Advances in fission track dating. *World Archaeology* 7:136–150.

Fletcher, Roland, 1977, Settlement Studies (micro and semi-micro). In *Spatial Archaeology*, D. L. Clarke. (Ed.), pp. 47–162. Academic Press, New York.

Ford, James A., 1962, A quantitative method for deriving cultural chronology. *Pan American Union, Technical Manual* 1.

Gathercole, P., 1971, "Patterns in Prehistory": an examination of the later thinking of V. Gordon Childe. *World Archaeology* 3:225–232.

Greenleaf, J. Cameron, 1975, The Fortified Hill Site near Gila Bend, Arizona. *The Kiva* 40:213–282.

Griffin, James B. (Ed.), 1952, *Archeology of eastern United States*. University of Chicago Press, Chicago.

Hammond, Norman, 1972, The planning of a Maya ceremonial center. *Scientific American* 226:82–91.

Harrison, Peter D. 1968, Form and function in a Maya "palace" group. *Proceedings of the 38th International Congress of Americanists, Stuttgart* 1:166–172.

Harrison, P. D. and B. L. Turner, 1978, *Prehistoric Maya agriculture*. University of New Mexico Press, Albuquerque.

Hassan, Fekri, 1981, *Demographic archaeology*. Academic Press, New York.

Healan, Dan M., 1977, Architectural implications of daily life in ancient Tollán, Hidalgo, Mexico. *World Archaeology* 9:140–156.

Hodder, Ian, 1974, Regression analysis of some trade and marketing patterns. *World Archaeology* 6:172–189.

Irwin, G. J., 1978, Pots and entrepôts: a study of settlement, trade and development of economic specialization in Papuan prehistory. *World Archaeology* 9:299–319.

Keatinge, Richard W. and Kent C. Day, 1974, Chan Chan: a study of precolumbian urbanism and the management of land and water resources in Peru. *Archaeology* 27:228–235.

McGuire, Randall H. and Christian E. Downum, n.d., A preliminary consideration of desert-mountain trade relations. In *Mogollon archaeology*, P. H. Beckett (Ed.). COAS Publishing and Research, Las Cruces, New Mexico.

McKern, W. C., 1939, The Midwestern Taxonomic Method as an aid to archaeological culture study. *American Antiquity* 4:301–313.

Marcus, Joyce, 1974, The iconography of power among the Classic Maya. *World Archaeology* 6:83–94.

Marquardt, William H., 1978, Advances in archaeological seriation. In *Advances in archaeological method and theory, Vol. 1*, Michael B. Schiffer (Ed.), pp. 257–314. Academic Press, New York.

Michael, H. N. and E. K. Ralph, 1971, *Dating techniques for the archaeologist*. MIT Press, Cambridge.

Michels, Joseph W., 1973, *Dating methods in archaeology*. Seminar Press, New York and London.

Michels, Joseph W. and Ignatius S. T. Tsong, 1980, Obsidian hydration dating: a coming of age. In *Advances in archaeological method and theory, Vol. 3*, Michael B. Schiffer (Ed.), pp. 405–444. Academic Press, New York.

Monks, Gregory G., 1981, Seasonality studies. In *Advances in archaeological method and theory, Vol. 4*, Michael B. Schiffer (Ed.), pp. 177–240. Academic Press, New York.

Newell, H. Perry and Alex D. Krieger, 1949, The George C. Davis Site, Cherokee County, Texas. *Society for American Archaeology, Memoirs* 5.

Nicklin, Keith, 1971, Stability and innovation in pottery manufacture. *World Archaeology* 3:13–48.

Parsons, Jeffrey R., 1972, Archaeological settlement patterns. *Annual Review of Anthropology* 1:127–150.

Plog, Fred T., 1974, *The study of prehistoric change*. Academic Press, New York.

Pozorski, Sheila and Thomas Pozorski, 1979, An early subsistence exchange system in the Moche Valley, Peru. *Journal of Field Archaeology* 6:413–432.

Renfrew, Colin, 1975, Trade as action at a distance: questions of integration and communication. In *Ancient civilization and trade*, Jeremy A. Sabloff and C. C. Lamberg-Karlovsky (Eds.), pp. 3–59. University of New Mexico Press, Albuquerque.

Renfrew, C. and R. M. Clark, 1974, Problems of the radiocarbon calendar and its calibration. *Archaeometry* 16:5–18.

Renfrew, C., J. E. Dixon and J. R. Cann, 1966, Obsidian and early cultural contact in the Near-East. *Proceedings of the Prehistoric Society* 32:30–72.

Renfrew, C., J. E. Dixon, and J. R. Cann, 1968, Further analyses of Near Eastern obsidian.

Proceedings of the Prehistoric Society 34:319–331.

Schiffer, Michael B., 1975, Behavioral chain analysis: activities, organization, and the use of space. In Chapters in the prehistory of eastern Arizona, IV. *Fieldiana: Anthropology* 65:103–119.

Sheets, Payson, 1978, From craftsman to cog: quantitative views of Mesoamerican lithic technology. In Papers on the economy and architecture of the ancient Maya. University of California, *Institute of Archaeology Monograph* VIII.

Tarling, D. H., 1975, Archaeomagnetism: the dating of archaeological materials by their magnetic properties. *World Archaeology* 7:185–197.

Taylor, R. E., 1978, Dating methods in New World archaeology. In *Chronologies in New World archaeology*, R. E. Taylor and Clement W. Meighan (Eds.), pp. 1–27. Academic Press, New York.

Trigger, Bruce, 1980, *Gordon Childe: revolutions in archaeology.* Columbia University Press, New York.

Webster, David, 1978, Three walled sites of the northern Maya lowlands. *Journal of Field Archaeology* 5:375–390.

Winters, Howard, 1969, The Riverton Culture: a second millennium occupation in the central Wabash Valley. *Illinois Archaeological Survey, Monograph* 1.

Wooley, C. L., 1934, *Ur excavations, vol. 2.: the Royal Cemetery,* 2 vols. The British Museum and The University Museum, Philadelphia.

10 EXPLANATION

General

Binford, Lewis R., 1972, *An archaeological perspective.* Seminar Press, New York. (Read Introductions only).

Çambel, Halet and Robert J. Braidwood, 1970, An early farming village in Turkey. *Scientific American* 222:50–56.

Daniel, Glyn, 1975, *One hundred and fifty years of archaeology.* Duckworth, London.

Mellaart, James, 1967, *Çatal Hüyük: a neolithic town in Anatolia.* New Aspects of Archaeology Series. McGraw-Hill Book Company, New York.

Millon, René, 1967, Teotihuacán. *Scientific American* 216:38–48.

Pfeiffer, John E., 1980, The mysterious rise and decline of Monte Albán. *Smithsonian* 10:62–68, 70, 72–75.

Sherwood, John, 1979, Life with Cushing: farewell to desks. *Smithsonian* 10(5):96–113.

Shook, Edwin M., 1960, Tikal: stela 29. *Expedition,* Winter Issue: 29–35.

Smith, Philip E. L., 1972, Changes in population pressure in archaeological explanation. *World Archaeology* 4:5–18.

Willey, Gordon R. and Jeremy A. Sabloff, 1980, *A history of American archaeology* (2nd ed.). W. H. Freeman, San Francisco.

Woodall, J. Ned, 1972, *An introduction to modern archeology.* Schenkman Publishing Company, Cambridge, Massachusetts.

Special Interest

Adams, Richard E. W., 1977, *Prehistoric Mesoamerica.* Little, Brown, Boston.

Boas, Franz (Ed.), 1938, *General anthropology.* D. C. Heath, New York.

Boserup, E., 1965, *The conditions of agricultural growth.* Aldine, Chicago.

Carneiro, Robert, 1970, A theory of the origin of the state. *Science* 169:733–738.

Doyel, David, 1979, The prehistoric Hohokam of the Arizona desert. *American Scientist* 67:544–554.

Flannery, Kent V. and James Schoenwetter, 1970, Climate and man in formative Oaxaca. *Archaeology* 23:144–152.

Gibson, McGuire, 1973, Population shift and the rise of Mesopotamian civilisation. In *The explanation of culture change: models in prehistory,* Colin Renfrew (Ed.), pp. 447–463. Duckworth, London.

Harris, Marvin, 1968, *The rise of anthropological theory.* Crowell, New York.

Hatch, Elvin, 1973, *Theories of man and culture.* Columbia University Press, New York.

Jacobsen, T. and R. M. Adams, 1958, Salt and silt in ancient Mesopotamian agriculture. *Science* 128:1251–1258.

Kirkbride, Diana, 1966, Beidha: an early neolithic village in Jordan. *Archaeology* 19:199–207.

Lamberg-Karlovsky, C. C., 1975, Third millennium modes of exchange and modes of production. In *Ancient civilization and trade,* Jeremy A. Sabloff and C. C. Lamberg-Karlovsky (Eds.), pp. 341–368. University of New Mexico Press, Albuquerque.

Lowie, Robert, 1937, *History of ethnological theory*. Farrar and Rinehart, New York.

Meggers, Betty J., 1954, Environmental limitation on the development of culture. *American Anthropologist* 56:801–824.

MacNeish, Richard Stockton, 1971, Speculation about how and why food production and village life developed in the Tehuacan Valley, Mexico. *Archaeology* 24:307–315.

Mellaart, James, 1963, Deities and shrines of Neolithic Anatolia: excavations at Çatal Hüyük, 1962. *Archaeology* 16:29–38.

Quigley, Caroll, 1961, *The evolution of civilizations: an introduction to historical analysis*. Macmillan Co., New York.

Rathje, William L., 1971, The origin and development of lowland Classic Maya civilization. *American Antiquity* 36:275–285.

Renfrew, Colin, 1973, *Before civilization*. Knopf, New York.

Sanders, William T. and Barbara J. Price, 1968, *Mesoamerica: the evolution of a civilization*. Random House, New York.

Sheets, Payson D., 1979, Maya recovery from volcanic disasters: Ilopango and Cerén. *Archaeology* 32:32–42.

Steward, Julian H., 1955, *Theory of culture change: the methodology of multilinear evolution*. University of Illinois Press, Urbana.

Thomas, Phillip Drennon, 1972, George Catlin: pictorial historian of aboriginal America. *Natural History* 81:30–43.

Weaver, Muriel Porter, 1981, *The Aztecs, Maya, and their predecessors* (2nd ed.). Academic Press, New York.

White, Leslie A., 1949, *The science of culture*. Farrar, Strauss, New York.

White, Leslie A., 1959, *The evolution of culture*. McGraw-Hill, New York.

Yancey, W. L., 1970, Architecture, interaction and social control: the case of a large-scale public housing project. In *Environmental psychology*, H. M. Proshansky, W. H. Ittelsen and R. G. Rivlin (Eds.), pp. 449–459. Holt, Rinehart & Winston, New York.

Yoffee, Norman, 1979, The decline and rise of Mesopotamian civilization: an ethnoarchaeological perspective on the evolution of social complexity. *American Antiquity* 44:5–35.

Technical

Adams, R. E. W. (Ed.), 1977, *The origins of Maya civilization*. University of New Mexico Press, Albuquerque.

Adams, Richard E. W. and Woodruff D. Smith, 1977, Apocalyptic visions: the Maya collapse and Mediaeval Europe. *Archaeology* 30:292–301.

Ball, Joseph W., 1974, A Teotihuacán-style cache from the Maya Lowlands. *Archaeology* 27:2–9.

Binford, Lewis R., 1962, Archaeology as anthropology. *American Antiquity* 28:217–225.

Binford, Lewis R., 1968, Archeological perspectives. In *New perspectives in archeology*, Sally R. and Lewis R. Binford (Eds.), pp. 5–32. Aldine, Chicago.

Binford, Lewis R., 1968, Post-Pleistocene adaptations. In *New perspectives in archeology*, Sally R. and Lewis R. Binford (Eds.), pp. 313–341. Aldine, Chicago.

Binford, Lewis R., 1968, Some comments on historical versus processual archaeology. *Southwestern Journal of Anthropology* 24:267–275.

Binford, Lewis R., 1972, *An archaeological perspective*. Seminar Press, New York.

Binford, Sally R. and Lewis R. Binford (Eds.), 1968, *New perspectives in archeology*. Aldine, Chicago.

Bradley, Richard, 1971, Trade competition and artefact distribution. *World Archaeology* 2:347–352.

Cohen, R. and E. Service (Eds.), 1978, *Origins of the state: the anthropology of political evolution*. ISHI, Philadelphia.

Culbert, T. Patrick (Ed.), 1973, *The Classic Maya collapse*. University of New Mexico Press, Albuquerque.

Downing, Theodore E. and McGuire Gibson (Eds.), 1974, Irrigation's impact on society. *University of Arizona, Anthropological Papers 25.*

Dunnell, Robert C., 1980, Evolutionary theory and archaeology. In *Advances in archaeological method and theory, Vol. 3*, Michael B. Schiffer (Ed.), pp. 35–99. Academic Press, New York.

Farrington, I. S. and C. C. Park, 1978, Hydraulic engineering and irrigation agriculture in the Moche Valley, Peru: c. A.D. 1250–1532. *Journal of Archaeological Science* 5:255–268.

Friedman, J. and M. Rowlands (Eds.), 1979, *The evolution of social systems*. University of Pittsburgh Press, Pittsburgh.

Hill, James N. (Ed.), 1977, *Explanation of prehistoric change*. University of New Mexico Press, Albuquerque.

Hirth, Kenneth and Jorge Angulo Villaseñor, 1981, Early state expansion in central Mexico: Teotihuacán in Morelos. *Journal of Field Archaeology* 8:135–150.

Kappel, Wayne, 1974, Irrigation development and population pressure. In *Irrigation's impact on society*, Theodore E. Downing and McGuire Gibson (Eds.), pp. 159–167. *University of Arizona, Anthropological Papers* 25.

Mackey, James C. and Sally J. Holbrook, 1978, Environmental reconstruction and the abandonment of the Largo-Gallina Area, New Mexico. *Journal of Field Archaeology* 5:29–49.

Meggers, Betty J., 1977, Vegetational fluctuation and prehistoric cultural adaptation in Amazonia: some tentative correlations. *World Archaeology* 8:287–303.

Millon, Rene, 1962, Variations in social responses to the practice of irrigation agriculture. In *Civilizations in desert lands. University of Utah, Anthropological Papers.* 62:56–88.

Moore, Charlotte B. (Ed.), 1974, Reconstructing complex societies: an archaeological colloquium. *American Schools of Oriental Research, Bulletin 20, Supplement.*

Paulsen, Allison C., 1976, Environment and empire: climatic factors in prehistoric Andean culture change. *World Archaeology* 8:121–132.

Price, B. J., 1978, Commerce and cultural process in Mesoamerica. In *Mesoamerican communication routes and cultural combats.* T. A. Lee, Jr., and C. Navarvate (Eds.). *Papers of the New World Archaeological Foundation.* 40:231–245.

Renfrew, Colin (Ed.), 1973, *The explanation of culture change: models in prehistory.* Duckworth, London.

Renfrew, Colin and Kenneth L. Cooke (Eds.), 1979, *Transformations: mathematical approaches to culture change.* Academic Press, New York.

Service, Elman R., 1975, *Origins of the state and civilization.* Norton, New York.

Steward, Julian (Ed.), 1955, Irrigation civilizations: a comparative study. *Pan American Union, Social Science Monograph* 1.

Swanton, J. R., 1946, The Indians of the southeastern United States. *Bureau of American Ethnology, Bulletin* 137.

Vitelli, Giovanna, 1980, Grain storage and urban growth in imperial Ostia: a quantitative study. *World Archaeology* 12:54–68.

Wenke, Robert J., 1981, Explaining the evolution of cultural complexity: a review. In *Advances in archaeological method and theory,* Michael B. Schiffer (Ed.), pp. 79–127. Academic Press, New York.

Wittfogel, Karl A., 1957, *Oriental despotism: a comparative study of total power.* Yale University Press, New Haven.

Wright, Henry T., 1977, Recent research on the origin of the state. *Annual Review of Anthropology* 6:379–397.

11 THE COURSE OF CULTURE

General

Canby, Thomas Y., 1979, The search for the first Americans. *National Geographic* 156:330–363.

Clark, Grahame, 1967, *The stone age hunters.* Thames and Hudson, London.

Culbert, T. Patrick, 1974, *The lost civilization: the story of the Classic Maya.* Harper & Row, New York.

Darlington, C. D., 1970, The origins of agriculture. *Natural History* 79:46–57.

Fagan, Brian M., 1980, *People of the Earth* (3rd Ed.). Little, Brown and Company, New York.

Howell, F. Clark, 1974, *Early man* (2nd Ed.). Time-Life Books, New York.

Leakey, Richard and Roger Lewin, 1977, *Origins.* Dutton, New York.

Marshack, Alexander, 1972, *The roots of civilization.* McGraw-Hill, New York.

Marshack, Alexander, 1975, Exploring the mind of ice age man. *National Geographic* 147:64–89.

Meadows, Donella H., D. L. Meadows, J. Randers, and W. W. Behrens III, 1972, *The limits to growth: a report for the Club of Rome's project on the predicament of mankind.* Universe Books, New York.

Morris, Craig, 1976, Master design of the Inca. *Natural History* 85:58–67.

Moseley, Michael E. and Carol J. MacKey, 1973, Chan Chan: Peru's ancient city of kings. *National Geographic* 143:318–345.

Pfeiffer, John, 1978, *The emergence of man* (3rd Ed.). Harper & Row, New York.

Pfeiffer, John E., 1977, *The emergence of society: a prehistory of the establishment.* McGraw-Hill, New York.

Sabloff, Jeremy A. and William L. Rathje, 1975, The rise of a Maya merchant class. *Scientific American* 233:72–82.

Silverberg, Robert, 1968, *Mound builders of ancient America: the archaeology of a myth.* New York Graphic Society, Greenwich, Connecticut.

Wenke, Robert J., 1980, *Patterns in prehistory: mankind's first three million years*. Oxford University Press, New York.

Special Interest

Adams, Robert McC., 1966, *The evolution of urban society*. Aldine, Chicago.

Anderson, Douglas D., 1968, A stone age campsite at the gateway to America. *Scientific American* 218:24–33.

Bartel, Brad, 1980, Colonialism and cultural responses: problems related to Roman provincial analysis. *World Archaeology* 12:11–26.

Bordes, François, 1968, *The old stone age*. McGraw-Hill, New York.

Bordes, François, 1971, Physical evolution and technological evolution in man: a parallelism. *World Archaeology* 3:1–5.

Brady, Barry J., 1981, Paterson, New Jersey: birthplace of the American Industrial Revolution. *Archaeology* 34:22–29.

Campbell, Bernard, 1979, *Humankind emerging* (2nd Ed.). Little, Brown, Boston.

Chard, Chester S., 1975, *Man in prehistory* (2nd Ed.). McGraw-Hill, New York.

Cohen, Mark N., 1977, *The food crisis in prehistory: overpopulation and the origins of agriculture*. Yale University Press, New Haven.

Dales, George F., 1966, The decline of the Harappans. *Scientific American* 214:92–98, 100.

Jacobsen, T. and R. M. Adams, 1958, Salt and silt in ancient Mesopotamian agriculture. *Science* 128:1251–1258.

Jennings, Jesse D., 1974, *Prehistory of North America* (2nd Ed.). McGraw-Hill, New York.

Jennings, Jesse D. (Ed.), 1978, *Ancient Native Americans*. Freeman, San Francisco.

Harris, David R., 1972, The origins of agriculture in the tropics. *American Scientist* 60:180–193.

Hayden, Brian, 1981, Research and development in the stone age: technological transitions among hunter-gatherers. *Current Anthropology* 22:519–548.

Haynes, C. Vance Jr., 1966, Elephant-hunting in North America. *Scientific American* 214:104–112.

Lamberg-Karlovsky, C. C. and Jeremy A. Sabloff (Eds.), 1973, *The rise and fall of civilizations: a reader*. Cummings, Menlo Park, California.

Leroi-Gourhan, André, 1968, The evolution of Paleolithic art. *Scientific American* 218:58–68, 70.

Livingstone, Daniel A., 1971, Speculations on the climatic history of mankind. *American Scientist* 59:332–337.

Macgowan, Kenneth and Joseph A. Hester, Jr., 1962, *Early man in the New World*. Anchor Books, New York.

MacNeish, Richard S., 1964, The origins of New World civilization. *Scientific American* 211:29–37.

Ortner, Donald J., 1978, Cultural change in the Bronze Age. *Smithsonian* 9:82–87.

Palerm, A. and E. R. Wolf, 1957, Ecological potential and cultural development in Mesoamerica. In *Studies in human ecology, Pan American Union Social Sciences Monograph* 3:1–35.

Redman, Charles L., 1978, *The rise of civilization: from early farmers to urban society in the ancient Near East*. Freeman, San Francisco.

Sears, W. H., 1971, Food production and village life in prehistoric Southeastern United States. *Archaeology* 24:322–329.

Watson, Richard A. and Patty Jo Watson, 1969, *Man and nature: an anthropological essay in human ecology*. Harcourt, Brace & World, New York.

Wells, Peter S., 1980, Contact and change: an example on the fringes of the Classical world. *World Archaeology* 12:1–10.

Wendorf, Fred and Romuald Schild, 1981, The earliest food producers. *Archaeology* 34:30–36.

Wertime, Theodore A., 1973, Pyrotechnology: man's first industrial uses of fire. *American Scientist* 61:670–682.

Willey, Gordon R., 1966, *An introduction to American archaeology, Vol. 1: North and Middle America*. Prentice-Hall, Englewood Cliffs, New Jersey.

Willey, Gordon R., 1971, *An introduction to American archaeology, Vol. 2: South America*. Prentice-Hall, Englewood Cliffs, New Jersey.

Willey, Gordon R. and Philip Phillips, 1958, *Method and theory in American archaeology*. University of Chicago Press, Chicago.

Technical

Allen, Jim, 1973, The archaeology of nineteenth-century British imperialism: an Australian case study. *World Archaeology* 5:44–60.

Bakhteyev, F. Kh. and Zoya V. Yanushevich, 1980, Discoveries of cultivated plants in the early farming settlements of Yarym-Tepe I and Yarym-Tepe II in Northern Iraq. *Journal of Archaeological Science* 7:167–178.

Blanton, Richard E., Jill Appel, Laura Finsten, Steve Kowalewski, Gary Feinman, and Eva Fisch, 1979, Regional evolution in the Valley of Oaxaca, Mexico. *Journal of Field Archaeology* 6:369–390.

Birley, Robin, 1977, A frontier post in Roman Britain. *Scientific American* 236:38–46.

Çambel, Halet and Robert J. Braidwood, 1970, An early farming village in Turkey. *Scientific American* 222:50–56.

Dillehay, Tom D., 1977, Tawantinsuya integration of the Chillon Valley, Peru: a case of Inca geopolitical mastery. *Journal of Field Archaeology* 4:397–405.

Fitting, James E. (Ed.), 1973, *The development of North American archaeology: essays in the history of regional traditions.* Anchor Press, Garden City, New York.

Flannery, Kent V., 1972, The cultural evolution of civilizations. *Annual Review of Ecology and Systematics* 3:399–426.

Gibson, Jon L., 1974, Poverty point: the first North American chiefdom? *Archaeology* 27:96–105.

Grossman, Joel W., 1972, An ancient gold worker's tool kit: the earliest metal technology in Peru. *Archaeology* 25:270–275.

Hassan, Fekri, 1981, *Demographic archaeology.* Academic Press, New York.

Hutterer, Karl L., 1976, An evolutionary approach to the Southeast Asian cultural sequence. *Current Anthropology* 17:221–242.

deLumley, Henry, 1969, A Paleolithic camp at Nice. *Scientific American* 220:42–50.

MacNeish, Richard S., 1976, Early man in the New World. *American Scientist* 64:316–327.

Mellaart, James, 1961, Haçilar: a neolithic village site. *Scientific American* 205:86–97.

Ohel, Milla Y., 1977, Patterned concentrations on living floors at Olduvai, Beds I and II: experimental study. *Journal of Field Archaeology* 4:423–433.

Rathje, William L., 1975, The last tango in Mayapán: a tentative trajectory of production-distribution systems. In *Ancient civilization and trade,* Jeremy A. Sabloff and C. C. Lamberg-Karlovsky (Eds.), pp. 409–448. University of New Mexico Press, Albuquerque.

Singh, P., 1974, *Neolithic cultures of western Asia.* Seminar Press, New York.

Steward, Julian, 1949, Cultural causality and law: a trial formulation of early civilization. *American Anthropologist* 51:1–27.

Taagapera, R., 1968, Growth curves of empires. *General Systems* 8:171–175.

Wilmsen, Edwin N., 1974, *Lindenmeier: a Pleistocene hunting society.* Harper & Row, New York.

Yellen, John E., 1977, Longterm hunter-gatherer adaptation to desert environments: a biogeographical perspective. *World Archaeology* 8:262–274.

12 ARCHAEOLOGY AND SOCIETY

General

Coggins, Clemency, 1970, The Maya scandal: how thieves strip sites of past cultures. *Smithsonian* 1:8–17.

Däniken, Erich von, 1971, *Chariots of the gods?* Bantam Books, New York.

Davis, Hester A., 1971, Is there a future for the past? *Archaeology* 24:300–306.

Davis, Hester A., 1972, The crisis in American archaeology. *Science* 175:267–272.

Deagan, Kathleen, 1980, Spanish St. Augustine: America's first "melting pot." *Archaeology* 33:22–30.

Deetz, James, 1969, The reality of the pilgrim fathers. *Natural History* 78:32–45.

Ekholm, Eric and James Deetz, 1971, Wellfleet Tavern. *Natural History* 80:48–57.

Evenari, Michael, 1974, Desert farmers: ancient and modern. *Natural History* 83:42–49.

Fagan, Brian M., 1975, *The rape of the Nile: tomb robbers, tourists and archaeologists.* Scribner's, New York.

Fairbanks, Charles H., 1976, Spaniards, planters, ships and slaves: historical archaeology in Florida and Georgia. *Archaeology* 29:164–172.

Green, Timothy, 1972, Fifty years later, Tutankhamun's treasures are still a sensation. *Smithsonian* 3:14–25.

Greenwood, Roberta S., 1978, The overseas Chinese at home. *Archaeology* 31:42–49.

Hearn, Maxwell, 1979, An ancient Chinese army rises from underground sentinel duty. *Smithsonian* 10:38–51.

Hoving, Thomas, 1979, King Tut's tomb: the untold story. *Reader's Digest* 114:176–228.

Johnson, William Weber, 1975, To Mexico with pride: a museum of pre-Hispanic art. *Smithsonian* 6:64–71.

Luce, J. V., 1969, *Lost Atlantis: new light on an old legend.* New Aspects of Archaeology Series. McGraw-Hill Book Company, New York.

Lyon, Eugene, 1976, The trouble with treasure. *National Geographic* 149:786–809.

Madden, Robert W., 1974, China unveils her

newest treasures. *National Geographic* 146:848–857.

Martin, Richard A., 1945, Mummies. *Chicago Natural History Museum, Popular Series, Anthropology no. 36.*

Matos Moctezuma, Eduardo, 1980, New finds in the Great Temple. *National Geographic* 158:766–775.

Meadows, Donella H., D. L. Meadows, J. Randers, and W. W. Behrens III, 1972, *The limits to growth: a report for the Club of Rome's project on the predicament of mankind.* Universe Books, New York.

Meyer, Karl E., 1973, *The plundered past: the story of the illegal international traffic in works of art.* Atheneum, New York.

Morse, Robert, 1972, The frescoes of Thera: spectacular finds in ancient Aegean rubble. *Smithsonian* 2:14–23.

Newton, John G., 1975, How we found the Monitor. *National Geographic* 147:48–61.

Noël Hume, Ivor, 1979, First look at a lost Virginia settlement. *National Geographic* 155:734–767.

Otto, John Solomon, 1979, A new look at slave life. *Natural History* 88:8–30.

Prideaux, Tom, 1976, Now it's our turn to be fascinated by Tut's treasure. *Smithsonian* 7:42–51.

Rathje, William L., 1978, The ancient astronaut myth. *Archaeology* 31:4–7.

Story, Ronald, 1976, *The space-gods revealed.* Harper & Row, New York.

Struever, Stuart and John Carlson, 1977, Koster Site: the new archaeology in action. *Archaeology* 30:93–101.

Topping, Audrey, 1977, Clay soldiers: the army of Emperor Chin. *Horizon* 19:4–13.

Wauchope, Robert, 1962, *Lost tribes and sunken continents.* University of Chicago, Chicago.

Special Interest

Bordaz, Jacques, 1962, Rescuing the Nile's treasures. *Natural History* 71:10–23.

Bruhns, Karen O., 1972, The methods of Guaquería: illicit tomb looting in Colombia. *Archaeology* 25:140–143.

Casson, Lionel, 1971, After 2,000 years tours have changed but not tourists. *Smithsonian* 2:52–59.

Clark, J. G. D., 1960, *Archaeology and society: reconstructing the prehistoric past.* Methuen, London.

Cockburn, Eve, 1973, Autopsy team seeks a mummy's medical secrets. *Smithsonian* 4:80–89.

Coles, John R., 1980, Cult archaeology and unscientific method and theory. In *Advances in archaeological method and theory, Vol. 3,* Michael B. Schiffer (Ed.), pp. 1–33. Academic Press, New York.

Cotter, John L., 1979, Archaeologists of the future: high schools discover archaeology. *Archaeology* 32:29–35.

Deagan, Kathleen, 1982, Avenues of inquiry in historical archaeology. In *Advances in archaeological method and theory, Vol. 5,* Michael B. Schiffer (Ed.), pp. 151–177. Academic Press, New York.

Deetz, James, 1977, *In small things forgotten: the archeology of early American life.* Anchor Books, Garden City, New York.

Deloria, Vine Jr., 1978, Largest collection of Indian items is put on display. *Smithsonian* 9:58–65.

Dixon, Keith A., 1977, Applications of archaeological resources: broadening the basis of significance. In *Conservation archaeology,* Michael B. Schiffer and George J. Gumerman (Eds.), pp. 277–290. Academic Press, New York.

Fairbanks, Charles H., 1976, Spaniards, planters, ships and slaves: historical archaeology in Florida and Georgia. *Archaeology* 29:164–172.

Friendly, Alfred, 1976, Philae, "the Pearl of Egypt," is being lifted to a dry and safe setting. *Smithsonian* 6:42–53.

Garlake, Peter, 1973, *Great Zimbabwe.* Thames and Hudson, London.

Hamblin, Dora Jane, 1979, "Carthage must be destroyed!" It was, but now it is reappearing. *Smithsonian* 9:42–55.

King, Thomas F., Patricia Parker Hickman, and Gary Berg, 1977, *Anthropology in historic preservation: caring for culture's clutter.* Academic Press, New York.

Lyon, Patricia J., 1966, Innovation through archaism: the origins of the Ica pottery style *Ñawpa Pacha* 4:31–61.

McGimsey, Charles R., III, 1973, *Archeology and archeological resources.* Society for American Archaeology, Washington, D.C.

McGimsey, Charles R. III and Hester A. Davis, 1969, Indians of Arkansas. *Arkansas Archeological Survey, Popular Series* 1.

Martin, Geoffrey T., 1978, The tomb of Horemheb Commander-in-Chief of Tutankhamun. *Archaeology* 31:14–23.

Mumford, Louis, 1934, *Technics and civilization.* Harcourt, Brace & World, New York.

Pendergast, David M. and Elizabeth Graham, 1981, Fighting a looting battle: Xunantunich, Belize. *Archaeology* 34:12–19.

Noël Hume, Ivor, 1963, *Here lies Virginia.* Knopf, New York.

Rathje, William L., 1979, Modern material culture studies. In *Advances in archaeological method and theory, Vol. 2,* Michael B. Schiffer (Ed.), pp. 1–37. Academic Press, New York.

Schuyler, Robert L. (Ed.), 1978, *Historical archaeology: a guide to substantive and theoretical contributions.* Baywood, Farmingdale, New York.

Schuyler, Robert (Ed.), 1980, *Archaeological perspectives on ethnicity in America.* Baywood, Farmingdale, New York.

Shenker, Israel, 1980, Treasures of the age of Alexander and Philip of Macedon go on U.S. tour. *Smithsonian* 11:126–138.

Smith, F. A., 1976, Quantity and composition of post-consumer solid waste: material flow estimates for 1973 and baseline future projections. *Waste Age.* 9:23–28.

Wotschitzky, Alfons, 1961, Ephesus: past, present and future of an ancient metropolis. *Archaeology* 14:205–212.

Technical

Ascher, Robert and Charles H. Fairbanks, 1971, Excavation of a slave cabin: Georgia, U.S.A. *Historical Archaeology* 5:3–17.

Aveleyra Arroyo de Anda, Luis, 1961, Protecting Mexico's heritage. *Archaeology* 14:261–267.

Coggins, Clemency, 1976, New legislation to control the international traffic in antiquities. *Archaeology* 29:14–15.

Ford, Richard I., 1973, Archeology serving humanity. In *Research and theory in current archeology,* Charles L. Redman (Ed.), pp. 83–93. Wiley-Interscience, New York.

Fowler, Don D., 1982, Cultural resources management. In *Advances in archaeological method and theory, Vol. 5,* Michael B. Schiffer (Ed.), pp. 1–50. Academic Press, New York.

Fritz, John M., 1973, Relevance, archeology and subsistence theory. In *Research and theory in current archeology,* Charles L. Redman (Ed.), pp. 59–82. Wiley-Interscience, New York.

Gould, Richard A. and Michael B. Schiffer (Eds.), 1981, *Modern material culture: the archaeology of US.* Academic Press, New York.

Keller, Gordon N., 1970, Site stabilization and applied archaeology. *Archaeology* 23:107–113.

Kelso, William M., 1979, Rescue archaeology on the James: early Virginia country life. *Archaeology* 32:15–25.

King, Thomas F. and Margaret M. Lyneis, 1978, Preservation: a developing focus of American archaeology. *American Anthropologist* 80:873–893.

Lumsden, Charles J. and Edward O. Wilson, 1981, *Genes, mind and culture: the coevolutionary process.* Harvard University Press, Cambridge.

McGimsey, Charles R., III, 1972, *Public archeology.* Seminar Press, New York.

McGimsey, Charles R., III and Hester A. Davis (Eds.), 1977, *The management of archeological resources, the Airlie House report.* The Society for American Archaeology, Washington D.C.

Morenon, E. P., M. Henderson, and J. Nielsen, 1976, The development of conservation techniques and a land use study conducted near Ranchos de Taos, New Mexico. Southern Methodist University, Fort Burgwin Research Center, Taos, New Mexico.

Noël Hume, Ivor, 1961, Preservation of English and Colonial American sites. *Archaeology* 14:250–256.

Noël Hume, Ivor, 1969, *Historical archaeology.* Knopf, New York.

Pickman, David, 1970, Museum of Fine Arts, Boston: the first one hundred years. *Archaeology* 23:114–119.

Pletsch, T. Daniel, 1974, Antiquities legislation and the role of the amateur archaeologist. *Archaeology* 27:260–261.

Quimby, I. M. G. (Ed.), 1978, *Material culture and the study of American life.* Norton, New York.

Rathje, William L., 1979, Trace measures. In Unobtrusive measurement today, Lee Sechrest (Ed.). *New Directions for Methodology of Behavioral Science* 1:75–91.

Schiffer, Michael B., Theodore E. Downing, and Michael McCarthy, 1981, Waste not, want not: an ethnoarchaeological study of reuse in Tucson, Arizona. In *Modern material culture: the archaeology of US,* Richard A. Gould and Michael B. Schiffer (Eds.), pp. 67–86. Academic Press, New York.

Schiffer, Michael B. and George J. Gumerman (Eds.), 1977, *Conservation archaeology: a guide for cultural resource management studies.* Academic Press, New York.

South, Stanley, 1974, Palmetto parapets. *University of South Carolina, Institute of Archeology and Anthropology, Anthropological Studies 1.*

South, Stanley (Ed.), 1977, *Research strategies in*

historical archeology. Academic Press, New York.

Staski, Edward, 1982, Advances in urban archaeology. In *Advances in archaeological method and theory, Vol. 5,* Michael B. Schiffer (Ed.), pp. 97–149. Academic Press, New York.

Teague, George A. and Lynette O. Shenk, 1977, Excavations at Harmony Borax Works. *National Park Service, Western Archeological Center, Publications in Anthropology 6.*

Thompson, Donald E., 1980, The Precolumbian and Colonial heritage of Rapayán. *Archaeology* 33:44–51.

Trigger, Bruce, 1974, The archaeology of government. *World Archaeology* 6:95–106.

Weitzman, David, 1980, *Traces of the past: a field guide to industrial archaeology.* Scribner's, New York.

Wildesen, Leslie E., 1982, The study of impacts on archaeological sites. In *Advances in archaeological method and theory, Vol. 5,* Michael B. Schiffer (Ed.), pp. 51–96. Academic Press, New York.

Wilk, Richard and Michael B. Schiffer, 1979, The archaeology of vacant lots in Tucson, Arizona. *American Antiquity* 44:530–536.

INDEX

Note: Page numbers in italics refer to the first use of a term in a specific context. Figures and tables are indicated only when they occur on a page different from the text reference, or when they contain additional information not given in the text.

Bordes, François, 67, 89, 335
Boserup, Ester, 307
Boucher de Perthes, Jacques, 299–300
Breakage, 90
Bride price, 79
Brieur, Frederick, 217
British Empire, 318
Broken K Pueblo, 178, 241–42, 273
Bronze Age, 345–49
Bryant, Vaughn, 227
Bulk proveniences, 189
Bundle burial, *112*
Bureaucracies, 314, 351
Burials, 79, 112–14
    analysis of, 231–36
    primary (inhumation), 112
    secondary (bundle), 112
    seriation of, 250–51
    social inequality and, 235
Burrowing, 140–42

C
Caches, 114–15
Cans, tin, 223–24
Capitals of Empires, 84
Carbon-14 dating. *See* Radiocarbon dating
Carneiro, Robert, 59, 61, 307–09
Carrying capacity, *319*, 321
Carter, Howard, 2, 359
Casa Grande, 237
Cataloging, 196
Catastrophism, 133
Caton-Thompson, Gertrude, 366–367
Causality. *See* Explanations
Cave paintings, 335–37
Cenotes, 372
Centralization, 351
Ceramic artifacts, analysis of, 218–21
    See also Sherds
Chairs, functions of, 65–67
Chan Chan, 243, 245 (fig.)
Chang, K. C., 273
Chemical agents, 130
Chichen Itza, 372
Chiefdoms, 54–56
Childe, V. Gordon, 248, 253, 255, 261
China, 365

Chinese artifacts in Tucson, Arizona, 75
Chipped stone, analysis of, 214–17
Chopper-chopping tool tradition, 334
C Horizon, 139
Chronology building. *See* Dating techniques
Chronometric dating techniques, 262
Chultuns, 278
Ciolek-Torrello, Richard, 242
Circumscription hypothesis, 308–09
Clark, J. G. D., 275
Clarke, Grahame, 227
Clarke effect, 119
Classic Age, 345–53
    transition to Postclassic, 351–53
Classification. *See* Typologies
Clasts, 140
Clonts, John, 75
Club of Rome, 385
Coe, Joffre, 138
Coe, Michael, 175–76, 220
Coiling, 218
Cold hammering, 222–23
Collecting processes, 122
Colluvial deposits, 137
Colonial model of trade, 318
Colonies, 80, 82
Communities, 46
    developmental cycles of, 80, 82
Complexity of societies, 52
Computers, 62
Conceptual schemes, 40, 49–61, 304–06
    in accumulation model, 59–61
    new version, 304–06
    stage model of societies, 52–59
Conservation archaeologists, *38*
Conservatory processes, *108*
Cook, Sherburne, 272
Coprolites, *227*
Core construction units, *240*
Cores, 89
Corn
    domestication of, 19–26, 155–56

slash-and-burn method of growing, 277
Cortex, 214
Coxcatlán, 20, 22
Crabtree, Don, 89, 380
Crop marks, 170–71
Cross-dating, 252–53
Cryoturbation, 142
Cuicuilco, 311
Culbert, T. Patrick, 269, 314–15
Cultural anthropology, 301
Cultural ecology, 52, 305
Cultural evolution, theory of, 42, 52, 300–02
Cultural formation processes, *103*, 106–25
    depositional processes, 110–19
        abandonment, 119
        burial, 112–14
        caches, 114–15
        discard, 116–19
        loss, 115–16
    disturbance processes, 123–24
    reclamation processes, 121–23
    reuse processes, 108–10
Cultural heritage, materials from the past as symbols of, 363–68
Cultural norms of a society, *262*
Cultural resource management, 374–80
Culture historical school (historical particularism), 263, 302–04
Cuneiform texts, *200*
Curate items, *119*
Cushing, Frank, 301
Cut and fill cycles, 137, 138 (fig.)

D
Darwin, Sir Charles, 141, 300
Data
    analysis of, 41
    historical. *See* Historical data
    recovery of, 41
    relevant, 40
Dating techniques, 250–65
    absolute, 262
    archaeological-culture classification and, 262–65
    archaeomagnetic dating, 260

Plato, 368
Pleistocene period, 133
Plog, Fred, 275
Plowing, effects of, 123
Plow zone, *123*
Plumb bob, 193
Point proveniences, 189
Polish, 216
Politics, national, 365
Pollen
    analysis of, 227, 228–29
        (figs.)
    recovery of, 193
Polyethylene glycol wax method,
    195
Polythetic types, 213
Population, *156*
    estimates of, 272–75
    !Kung Bushmen camps,
        29–32
    precision and characteristics
        of, 161–62
Population growth (or decline)
    internalist view of change and,
        314–15
    as prime cause, 307–09
    scenarios of change, 319–23
    trends in, 353–56
Population parameters, *156*
Postclassic Age, 349–53
Post molds, *191*
Pot-hunters, 122
Potsherds, *70*
Pottery, 218–21
Precision of sampling techniques,
    160–62
Predictive models for determining
    surface-subsurface rela-
    tions, 174, 176
Preservation, 378
President's Advisory Council on
    Historic Preservation, 378
Pressure flaking, *89*, 214, 215
    (fig.)
Price, Barbara, 309
Prime causes, 307–11
    environmental stress, 310–11
    population pressure/agricul-
        tural intensification,
        307–08
    population pressure/warfare,
        308–09
    trade, 309
Probability sampling, 158
Procurement, 84–87

Profiles (sections), 189
Proskouriakoff, Tatiana, 204
Prospection techniques, 174–76
Proveniences, 189
    labeling of, 196
Pruitt Igoe project, 325–26, 382
Public policy, archaeology and,
    382–86
Pueblo Bonito, 14 (ill.), 15
Pueblo structures (pueblo archi-
    tecture), 11–16, 178,
    241–42
    archaeological sequence of, 11,
        12 (fig.), 13
    techniques of construction, 15,
        16 (fig.)
    See also specific sites
Puleston, Dennis, 278

Q
Quadrats, 165
Quigley, Carroll, 315–16

R
Radiocarbon dating, 255–56,
    258
Radiocarbon years, *255*
Rain forests, 139, 142
Rainwater, 144
Ramón trees, 139
    nuts of, 278
Random numbers, table of, 158,
    159 (table)
Rank-size rule, 83 (fig.), 84
Rathje, William, 34
Reclamation processes, 121–23
Recording procedures, excava-
    tions and, 180–81,
    188–89
Recording units, 188
Recovery, 122–23, 155–203
    ethnoarchaeological fieldwork,
        194–97
    historical research, 200–203
    regional surveys, 163–73
        locating settlements, 163–72
        recording sites, 172–73
    research designs, 155, 156
        (fig.)
    sampling principles and tech-
        niques, 156–63
Recovery units, *173*
    excavation, 186–87
Recycling, 108
Redistribution in chiefdoms, 54

Reese River Valley Project, 165,
    166–67 (figs.), 167
Refuse
    de facto, *119*
    primary, *116*
    secondary, *116*, 269, 270
    See also Discard; Garbage
Refuse disposal, principles of,
    116
Regional environmental pro-
    cesses, 132–39
    environmental zones, 139
    flowing water, 137–38
    glaciation, 133–36
Regional surveys, 163–73
    locating settlements, 163–72
        exposures, 168
        historical sources, 172
        pedestrian tactic, 163,
            165–68
        remote sensing, 168–72
    population estimates, 275
    recording sites, 172–73
Regional systems, 47
    of band societies, 52
    decision making in, 351
    Postclassic, 350
Reid, J. Jefferson, 242, 289
Rejects, *89*
Relational dimension of artifacts,
    64–65
Relative dating techniques,
    261–62
Relevant data, 40
Remote-sensing techniques,
    168–72
Renfrew, Colin, 76, 261, 279,
    309
Replacement cost of grave goods,
    235
Research designs, *155*, 156 (fig.)
Research problem (or question),
    40
Resharpening of tools, 217
Residential mobility, *13*
Retouching of tools, 217
Reuse, 108, 110
Reuse Project, 197
Reverse stratification, *123*
Ridged fields near Maya sites,
    278
Rimsherds, 219–20
Rites of passage, 79
Ritualistic warfare, 281
Riverton Culture, 272

Roman Empire, 56, 57, 281, 284, 316
Root growth, 142
Rowe, John, 363

S

Sample, *156*
Sample size, 156, 158
  precision and, 161
Sample unit, *156*
Sampling, 156–63
  in-site, 176–80
  multistage, 162
  paradox of, 162–63
  precision of techniques of, 160–62
  probability, 158
  simple random, 158, 160
  subjective techniques of, 158
  systematic, 160
Sampling strata, *161*
Sampling strategy, *36*
Sanders, William, 307
Saul, Frank, 233
Scavenging processes, 121–22
Schaefer, Jerome, 277
Schiffer, Michael, 197
Schlepp effect, 117–18
Schliemann, Heinrich, 115, 172
Schmidt, Peter, 223
Scientific method, 40–41
Screening, 191
Seasonality, inferences of, 270–71
Seasonal round, *52*
Secondary use, *108*
Sections (profiles), 189
Sediments, 139–40
  color of, 139
  pedoturbations of, 140–45
    cryoturbation, 142
    faunalturbation, 140–42
    floralturbation, 142
    graviturbation, 142
  submersion in water, 144–45
  texture of, 140
Seeds, 227
  recovery of, *195*
Semeonov, Sergei, 214, 217
Seriation, *163,* 251–52
Settlements (settlement systems), 46
  inferences about, 270, 272
  Mesolithic, 342

Sex, variability in artifacts and, 78
Shadow marks, 170
Shaman, 52
Sharpe, F. H., 168
Shell middens, *147*
Shepard, Anna, 218
Sherds, 147, 219–20
Shoshone, 53
Shovels, 191
Sickle sheen, *216*
Simple random sampling, 158, 160
Sites, 11
  excavation of, *see* Excavation of sites
  future decay and preservation of, 151
Slash-and-burn method, *277*
Slip casting, 218
Slit trenches, 186
Smelting, 223
Smith, Grafton Elliot, 303
Snaketown, 187
Social classes in agrarian states, 57
Social complexity, 306–07
Social differentiation, 284–85, 306–07
  in Acheulian period, 334
  in agrarian states, 57
  investment of resources in artifacts and, 289, 294
  social interaction and, 295
  specialization and, 285
Social environment, 49–50
Social inequality
  in agrarian states, 57
  in Bronze (Classic) Age, 349
  socio-functions and, 93
  in tribal societies, 54
Social integration, 284–85, 306–07
  resource investments and, 294–95
  social interaction and, 295
  specialization and, 285, 287–89
Social interaction, 47
Social mobility in industrial states, 59
Social organization, definition of, 49
Social units, *45*
Sociobiology, 369

Socio-functional typologies, 210
Socio-functions, 65–67
  as stage in life cycle of artifacts, 91, 93–96
Sociological model of style, 72, 74, 211
Soft-hammer percussion technique, 214, 215 (fig.)
Soil marks, 170
Soils, 139–40
  See also Sediments
Solifluction, 142
Sorting artifacts, 196
Soto, Hernando, 323
South, Stanley, 115, 117, 118
Southern Cult, 288, 290–91 (figs.)
Spatial dimension of artifacts, 64
Spatial distributions of styles, disturbances in, 74–78
Spatial variability, 10
Spaulding, Albert, 212
Specialists
  full-time, *55*
  part-time, *54*
Specialization
  in Bronze (Classic) Age, 349
  social differentiation and integration and, 285–89
Spence, Michael, 287
Spengler, Oswald, 315
Spindle whorls, *234*
Split-cobble technique, 214
Stage model of societies, 52–59
  agrarian-states, *56–58*
  band societies, *52–53*
  chiefdoms, *54–56*
  tribes, *53–54*
Star Carr, 275, 340
State Historic Preservation Officer (SHPO), 378
States
  agrarian, *56–58*
  industrial, *58–59*
  Postclassic, 350
Statistical law, *119*
Statistics, *158*
Stela, Maya, *114*
Step trenches, 186, 187 (fig.)
Steward, Julian, 165, 305–06
Stockman, E. D., 124
Stonehenge, 246–47, 261
Stones
  chipped, analysis of, 214–17

PICTURE CREDITS

page
ii   Frontispiece, Monte Alban, © George W. Gardner
2   Griffith Institute, Ashmolean Museum, Oxford
4   Universal Pictures, Inc.
6   Reproduced by permission of Nippon Television Network Corp.
14   © George W. Gardner
16   Arizona State Museum, photos by Helga Teiwes
19   Cave Research Foundation, photo by Roger Brucker
21–22, 25   The Robert S. Peabody Foundation for Archaeology, Phillips Academy, Andover, Massachusetts
27   by permission of The British Association for the Advancement of Science
29   John E. Yellen
30–31   adapted from *Archaeological approaches to the present* by John E. Yellen, Academic Press, 1977, reproduced by permission.
32   James F. O'Connell
34–35   The Garbage Project
38–39   Ted Avery/Plimoth Plantation
42   Michigan Historical Collection, Bently Historical Library, University of Michigan
44–45   © George W. Gardner
48   © Rene Millon, 1973
50   © 1981, by The New York Times Company, Reprinted by permission
51   © George W. Gardner
53   John Wesley Powell Collection, Smithsonian Institution
55   Arizona State Museum, photo by Forman Hanna
57   Courtesy of P. C. Films Company
58   © George W. Gardner
62   Carlen Luke
69   Arizona State Museum, photo by Helga Teiwes
71   Courtesy of James N. Hill. Reproduced by permission of The Society for American Archaeology from American Antiquity, 43(2):248, 1978
76   adapted from "In the Beginning," *An introduction to archaeology*, 4th ed., reproduced by permission of Lindbriar Corp. and Little, Brown & Company.
82   Philadelphia Museum of Art: Given by Mrs. Widener Dixon and George D. Widener
86   University of Colorado Museum
88   top right, Thomas R. Hester, Colha Project; left and bottom, © Craig Aurness/Woodfin Camp & Associates
90   photo by Lloyd Furness, Idaho State University, Idaho Museum of Natural History
92   left, HBJ Photo Studio; right, Bill Kerrigan
94   adapted from Longacre, William A., 1970, Archaeology as anthropology. *Anthropological Papers of The University of Arizona*, No. 17, University of Arizona Press, reproduced by permission.
96   Jericho Excavation Fund
98   © George W. Gardner
100   after Deetz
101   M. B. Schiffer
102   left, Courtesy of The American Museum of Natural

page
      History; right, Instituto Nacional de Cultura, Peru
104   The Peabody Museum of Archaeology and Ethnology, Harvard University
106   © The New York Times
107   © Hazel Hankin
111   top, Randall H. McGuire; bottom, adapted from Fig. 8 of *The Stratigraphy and Archaeology of Ventana Cave*, University of Arizona Press.
113   The Hermitage, reproduced by permission.
117   M. B. Schiffer
120   Arizona State Museum, photo by R. G. Vivian
121   The Bettmann Archive, Inc.
126   R. F. Sison, © National Geographic Society
131   Courtesy of The American Museum of Natural History
132   Payson D. Sheets
134   adapted from Wenke, *Patterns of Prehistory*, Oxford University Press
135   J. M. Adovasio
136   U.S. Geological Survey
141   Arizona State Museum, photo by Helga Teiwes
143   photos by Ruth and Louis Kirk
144   Aerofilms, Ltd.
146   Bernisches Historisches Museum
148   © Jonathan Blair/Woodfin Camp & Associates
149   Peabody Museum of Archaeology and Ethnology, Harvard University
150   Arizona State Museum
155   Reproduced by kind permission of Anthony Pitt-Rivers
159   The Rand Corporation
166   adapted from American Antiquity, Journal of the Society for American Archaeology, Vol. 38, No. 2, April 1973.
167   Courtesy of David Hurst Thomas
169   Remote Sensing Division, Southwest Cultural Resources Center, National Park Service
170   by permission of Robert McC. Adams
171   Royal Commission on Historical Monuments
175   Drs. Elizabeth K. Ralph and Sheldon Breiner
177   David L. Browman
180   The Trustees of The British Museum
182–82   Art Jelinek
184   J. J. Reid, University of Arizona
187   Photo by Arkansas Archaeological Survey
188   by permission, from *The Hohokam* by Emil Haury, Tucson: University of Arizona Press, 1976
198–99   William A. Longacre
200   both, Courtesy of The American Museum of Natural History
202   left, Photograph by Jacob A. Riis, Jacob A. Riis Collection, Museum of the City of New York; right, M. B. Schiffer Collection; bottom, The Bettmann Archive, Inc.
203   International Museum of Photography at George Eastman House
204   Peabody Museum of Archaeology and Ethnology, Harvard University
209   Courtesy of General Electric Company

Illustrators

Fred Haynes: 9, 12, 21, 23, 27, 29, 30, 31, 37, 66, 73, 76, 77,
81, 83, 94, 97, 98 bottom, 100, 101, 111, 129, 134, 138, 157,
164, 166, 175, 179, 190, 192, 193, 194, 228, 254 map, 280,
315, 320, 346 map

Rob Mullen: 68–69, 85, 152, 185, 215, 217, 219, 226, 230,
232, 251, 257, 266, 268, 331 drawings, 332, 333, 334, 336,
338, 340–41

Alan Iselin: 207, 212–13, 234, 252, 264, 286 bottom

Bill Walker: 68 chart, 156, 222, 236 top right, 239, 355

Rino Dussi: 257, 258, 331 chart

Marlene Fein/Ruth Soffer: 292–93

A
B 2
C 3
D 4
E 5
F 6
G 7
H 8
I 9
J 0